Programming Microsoft® Windows® Forms

Charles Petzold

PUBLISHED BY
Microsoft Press
A Division of Microsoft Corporation
One Microsoft Way
Redmond, Washington 98052-6399

Library of Congress Control Number 2005933932

Printed and bound in the United States of America.

1 2 3 4 5 6 7 8 9   QWT   0 9 8 7 6 5

Distributed in Canada by H.B. Fenn and Company Ltd.

A CIP catalogue record for this book is available from the British Library.

Microsoft Press books are available through booksellers and distributors worldwide. For further information about international editions, contact your local Microsoft Corporation office or contact Microsoft Press International directly at fax (425) 936-7329. Visit our Web site at www.microsoft.com/mspress. Send comments to *mspinput@microsoft.com*.

Microsoft, ActiveX, IntelliSense, JScript, Microsoft Press, MSDN, MS-DOS, Visual Basic, Visual C#, Visual Studio, Win32, Windows, and Windows Media are either registered trademarks or trademarks of Microsoft Corporation in the United States and/or other countries.

The example companies, organizations, products, domain names, e-mail addresses, logos, people, places, and events depicted herein are fictitious. No association with any real company, organization, product, domain name, e-mail address, logo, person, place, or event is intended or should be inferred.

Acquisitions Editor: Ben Ryan
Project Editor: Valerie Woolley
Technical Editor: Robert Lyon
Copy Editor: Roger LeBlanc
Indexer: Julie Hatley

Body Part No. X11-50068

Also by Charles Petzold

Programming in the Key of C#:
A Primer for Aspiring Programmers (2003)

Programming Microsoft Windows with Microsoft Visual Basic .NET (2002)

Programming Microsoft Windows with C# (2001)

Code:
The Hidden Language of Computer Hardware and Software (1999)

Programming Windows, 5th Edition (1998)

Programming Windows 95 (1996)

OS/2 Presentation Manager Programming (1994)

Programming Windows:
The Microsoft Guide to Writing Applications for Windows 3.1 (1992)

Programming Windows:
The Microsoft Guide to Writing Applications for Windows 3 (1990)

Programming the OS/2 Presentation Manager (1989)

Programming Windows (1988)

Table of Contents

Introduction

This book shows you how to write programs that run under Microsoft Windows. These can be either regular stand-alone Windows applications (which are now sometimes called *client* applications) or front ends for distributed applications. There are several ways to write such programs. The approach shown in this book uses the C# programming language and the Windows Forms class library, which is part of the Microsoft .NET Framework. Much of this book focuses on the enhancements to Windows Forms in the .NET Framework 2.0, introduced in the fall of 2005.

This book supplements (rather than replaces) my earlier book on Windows Forms programming, *Programming Microsoft Windows with C#* (Microsoft Press, 2002). That book is three times the length of this one and comprehensively covers Windows Forms programming using versions 1.0 and 1.1 of the .NET Framework. The information in that earlier book remains completely valid for the .NET Framework 2.0.

Your Background and Needs

I envision two main classes of readers of this book:

If you're already familiar with Windows Forms programming—perhaps by reading my earlier book—you can view this book as a simple supplement. You can probably skip Chapters 1 and 2 and dive right into the exciting new world of dynamic layout in Chapter 3. Everything from Chapter 3 through the end of the book is new and explores the .NET Framework 2.0 enhancements to Windows Forms.

If you have prior experience with programming for Windows—perhaps using the Microsoft Foundation Classes (MFC) or the native application programming interface (API)—and you want to get up to speed with Windows Forms with minimum fuss, this book can help you get started by introducing you to the core concepts.

I think of this book as a "streamlined" approach to Windows Forms programming, not only because it's relatively short and concise, but also because the .NET Framework 2.0 enhancements to Windows Forms have made it easier than ever to design and deploy Windows applications that are powerful and sharp looking.

Of course, a book as short as this one cannot possibly tell you everything that you might want to know about Windows Forms programming. This book has virtually no coverage of graphics programming, for example. If you'd like to know more about displaying formatted text, vector graphics, and bitmaps, you'll want to consult my earlier book. (One common complaint about *Programming Microsoft Windows with C#* is that it has too *many* graphics!) If you're new to Windows Forms programming and find that this book doesn't deliver enough in-depth coverage of the basics, then, again, *Programming Microsoft Windows with C#* might be a solution.

This book contains just a little introductory information on the C# programming language. Programmers already familiar with C++ and Java should be able to pick up C# fairly quickly. Otherwise, there are books available for learning C#. My book *Programming in the Key of C#* (Microsoft Press, 2003) is targeted at readers learning C# as a first programming language, but the book might also be of interest to experienced programmers.

Organization of This Book

The first two chapters of this book provide a whirlwind introduction to the concepts and tools of Windows Forms programming. Readers with prior experience in Windows Forms programming can skip these two chapters.

Chapter 3 discusses the new support of dynamic layout introduced in the .NET Framework 2.0. Using the new *FlowLayoutPanel* and *TableLayoutPanel* controls, you can now design your forms and dialog boxes without using explicit coordinates and sizes.

Some readers of *Programming Microsoft Windows with C#* thought that the book was a little light on custom controls. Consequently, Chapter 4 focuses entirely on custom controls.

Although the menu, toolbar, and status bar from the .NET Framework 1.0 continue to function just fine under the .NET Framework 2.0, Chapter 5 covers the exciting features of the new *MenuStrip*, *ToolStrip*, and *StatusStrip* controls.

Programming Microsoft Windows with C# doesn't have any information on binding controls to data. I have corrected that deficiency in Chapter 6 and have also provided introductions to the new *DataGridView* and *BindingNavigator* controls.

Chapter 7 applies everything covered earlier in the book to show two complete real-world applications: a Web browser and a tool for exploring Windows Forms controls.

I was recently startled to see the following note in the Introduction to another Microsoft Press book[1]:

> **Note**   To keep the samples in this book as concise as possible, they were written "Petzold style," that is to say, without the use of the designers in Microsoft Visual Studio .NET.

This book is also written "Petzold style." I believe that programmers should learn how to write their own code rather than relying on the code generated by Visual Studio. Windows Forms has made creating applications from scratch easier than ever. Moreover, one of the primary jobs of Visual Studio—giving the programmer a means of designing a form or dialog box with-

---

1.   Rob Jarrett and Philip Su, *Building Tablet PC Applications*, Microsoft Press, 2002.

out specifying explicit coordinates and sizes—has been rendered virtually unnecessary by the new dynamic layout features in the .NET Framework 2.0.

System Requirements

You'll need the following hardware and software to build and run the code samples for this book:

- Microsoft Windows XP with Service Pack 2, Microsoft Windows Server 2003 with Service Pack 1, or Windows 2000 with Service Pack 4

- Visual Studio 2005 Standard Edition or Visual Studio 2005 Professional Edition[2]

- 600 megahertz (MHz) Pentium or compatible processor (1 gigahertz Pentium recommended)

- 192 megabytes (MB) RAM (256 MB or more recommended)

- Video (800 x 600 or higher resolution) monitor with at least 256 colors (1024 x 768 High Color 16-bit recommended)

- CD-ROM or DVD-ROM drive

- Microsoft Mouse or compatible pointing device

Prerelease Software

This book was reviewed and tested against the August 2005 Community Technical Preview (CTP) of Visual Studio 2005. The August CTP was the last preview before the final release of Visual Studio 2005. This book is expected to be fully compatible with the final release of Visual Studio 2005. If there are any changes or corrections for this book, they will be collected and added to a Microsoft Knowledge Base article. See the "Support for this Book" section in this Introduction for more information.

Technology Updates

As technologies related to this book are updated, links to additional information will be added to the Microsoft Press Technology Updates Web page. Visit this page periodically for updates on Visual Studio 2005 and other technologies.

http://www.microsoft.com/mspress/updates/

---

2.   It is also possible to use Microsoft Visual C# 2005 Express Edition for much of this book, although that package is missing a few features (such as a collection of bitmaps and icons) that some programs in this book require. If you download and install the .NET Framework 2.0 Software Development Kit, you can even compile Windows Forms programs on the MS-DOS command line, or you can use alternative development environments such as my Key of C# program, available for download from my Web site. See Chapter 1 for details.

Code Samples

All the code samples discussed in this book can be downloaded from the book's companion content page at the following address:

http://www.microsoft.com/mspress/companion/0-7356-2153-5/

Support for This Book

Every effort has been made to ensure the accuracy of this book and the companion content. As corrections or changes are collected, they will be added to a Microsoft Knowledge Base article. To view the list of known corrections for this book, visit the following article:

http://support.microsoft.com/kb/905047/

Microsoft Press provides support for books and companion content at the following Web site:

http://www.microsoft.com/learning/support/books/

Questions and Comments

If you have comments, questions, or ideas regarding the book or the companion content, or questions that are not answered by visiting the sites above, please send them to Microsoft Press via e-mail to

mspinput@microsoft.com

Or via postal mail to

Microsoft Press

Attn: Programming Microsoft Windows Forms Editor

One Microsoft Way

Redmond, WA 98052-6399

Please note that Microsoft software product support is not offered through the above addresses.

The Author's Web Site

Information about this book (and my other books) can also be found on my Web site:

http://www.charlespetzold.com/

My Web site is also a repository for miscellaneous programming, mathematical, and historical projects that I indulge in during those few hours of the day when I'm not writing books.

Special Thanks

Whenever people talk about the upcoming "revolution" in publishing, in which the author bypasses traditional publishers by depositing writings directly on a Web site, I shudder a bit. Do these "visionaries" not understand the crucial job performed by *editors*? Helping ensure that my prose and code were fit for public consumption were Valerie Woolley, Robert Lyon, and Roger LeBlanc. Of course, any errors that remain in the book are no one's responsibility but my own.

I also extend a deep-felt thanks to the three most important women in my life. In ascending order they are my agent Claudette Moore of the Moore Literary Agency, my mother, and my fiancée Deirdre.

Charles Petzold
New York City
September, 2005

Chapter 1
Creating Applications

Microsoft .NET is a collection of software technologies intended to facilitate development of modern Web-based and Microsoft Windows–based applications. This book focuses on the part of .NET called *Windows Forms*, which you use for writing programs that are variously called "desktop application software" or "client-based Windows applications" or "regular type Windows apps." These programs are in the form of familiar executable (.EXE) files, possibly accompanied by some dynamic-link library (.DLL) files and whatever else the application might need (such as "help" files). Windows Forms should be seen as a modern alternative to older methods of writing Windows applications, such as using the C programming language and the native Windows 32-bit application programming interface (the Win32 API), or programming in C++ with the Microsoft Foundation Classes (MFC).

Orientation

Windows Forms itself is implemented in several of the DLLs that comprise the *.NET Framework*. The .NET Framework must be installed on both the machine you use to develop Windows Forms programs and the machine that runs them. You can obtain various versions of the .NET Framework from the Microsoft Web site *http://msdn.microsoft.com/netframework/downloads/updates*. The programs in this book are based on the .NET Framework 2.0, released in 2005.

Although Windows Forms applications offer the user a familiar visual experience of Windows, they differ from Win32 and MFC programs in a very important way: Windows Forms executables do not contain microprocessor machine code. Instead, they contain binary instructions of Microsoft Intermediate Language (MSIL), which functions as a sort of generic assembly language. (Adventurous programmers can write applications directly in MSIL.) At runtime, the component of the .NET Framework known as the Common Language Runtime (CLR) converts the intermediate language to machine code for the microprocessor, and links the machine code to the required .NET dynamic-link libraries.

Compiling programs at runtime makes .NET applications potentially platform independent. The operating system is also protected against errant or rogue code that might inadvertently or deliberately wreck havoc on the user's machine. The .NET runtime can determine, for example, whether a particular Windows Forms application accesses local files and can then alert the user to that fact. Consequently, a user can run a Windows Forms executable from the Internet with much less worry than in the past. The use of intermediate language is a big part of what is referred to as *managed code*. Strong typing and severe restrictions in the use of pointers also play an important role. Programs written for .NET are sufficiently structured to allow the CLR to implement garbage collection: when memory is low, the CLR can delete all unreferenced objects. Programmers are largely freed from worrying about memory leaks.

If necessary, Windows Forms programs can make use of the native Win32 API, but for the most part they rely on the .NET Windows Forms libraries for all their needs. These libraries are mostly a collection of object-oriented classes that include the traditional fields and methods, and also class members called *properties* and *events*. (You'll see what these are shortly.) Obviously, a programming language that accesses these classes must also implement properties and events. The language must also support all the basic types (integer, floating point, strings, and so forth) used in these classes. The language must store strings and arrays in the same way as the classes. That means that strings are *not* zero-terminated, that they include a string length, and that the size of arrays is also fixed.

For all these reasons, the programming language that you use to write Windows Forms application must comply with the .NET Common Language Specification (CLS). C++, for example, is acceptable only with the *managed extensions* that Microsoft has added to it, which unfortunately doesn't help a language that wasn't very pretty to begin with. More closely integrated with .NET are the languages C# and Microsoft Visual Basic .NET.

C# (pronounced "C Sharp") is based roughly on C and C++ syntax but was designed in conjunction with the CLS. It is, in some sense, the default or generic .NET programming language, and it is the language that I'll use in this book. A number of books exist that help the experienced C or C++ programmer get up to speed with C#. My book *Programming in the Key of C#* (Microsoft Press, 2003) is written for novice programmers, but it might appeal to experienced programmers as well.

Every C# programmer should learn how to consult the *C# Language Specification*, which is the official formal description of the language. This document is available online from Microsoft's C# Web page (at *http://msdn.microsoft.com/library/en-us/cscon/html/vcoriCStartPage.asp*) and is also available in a convenient printed form in the book *The C# Programming Language* by Anders Hejlsberg, Scott Wiltamuth, and Peter Golde (Addison-Wesley, 2003). The *C# Programmer's Reference* (also available online from that same C# Web page) is more informal and sometimes preferable for quick information.

My language choice for this book should not be interpreted as a denigration of other .NET programming languages. With .NET, language choice has become a matter of individual taste. With a little basic knowledge of C#, for example, a Visual Basic .NET programmer can easily translate all the example code in this book. Microsoft also provides two additional CLS-compliant languages, J# and JScript, that are based on other popular (but non-Microsoft) programming languages that begin with the letter J.

Programming Tools

Most programmers who write Windows Forms applications will probably do so using Microsoft Visual Studio, a sophisticated integrated development environment (IDE) with a long history. The first version of Visual Studio to support .NET 2.0 is Visual Studio 2005. Microsoft also makes available stripped-down "express" editions that support individual languages, such as Visual C# and Visual Basic .NET.

You are not required to use Visual Studio, and in the long run, the less you rely on Visual Studio, the better a .NET programmer you'll likely become. Visual Studio doesn't necessarily soften the mind, but its insistence on generating code actually makes Windows Forms seem more complicated and magical than it actually is. There's also a danger that the programmer will be unable to perform very basic chores—such as adding a menu item at runtime—because he or she has never written code to create a menu in the first place.

You can write Windows Forms programs entirely in a simple text editor (such as Windows Notepad) and compile them on the MS-DOS command line. Whether out of poverty, principles, or perversion you decide to explore this option, the only preliminary step is to download and install the .NET Framework Software Development Kit (SDK) from the Web page cited earlier. The SDK is free and comes with documentation and programming tools, including the command-line compilers *csc* (for C#) and *vbc* (for Visual Basic .NET).

Middle roads are also available. Microsoft has implemented the C# compiler engine in a .NET dynamic-link library, making it possible for programmers to create their own C# development environments that are much smaller and simpler than Visual Studio. One such no-frills IDE is called *Key of C#*, which is available for free download from my Web site (*http://www.charles-petzold.com/keycs*). Running *Key of C#* requires the .NET Framework to be installed, of course, but not necessarily the .NET Framework SDK. This means that you can sit down at any machine that has the .NET Framework installed, download *Key of C#*, and do some .NET programming without installing the .NET Framework SDK or Visual Studio. (*Key of C#* has a blazingly fast installation program, and the uninstall is just as quick.)

You can also inhibit Visual Studio's code generation. This allows you to continue to take advantage of some popular features of Visual Studio—such as Microsoft IntelliSense, which helps you remember method, property, and event names—and still write all your own code. I'll discuss how this is done shortly.

The Docs

When you install Visual Studio or the .NET Framework SDK, you also get a program that provides technical documentation of the .NET Framework. This documentation is also available from the online Microsoft Development Network (MSDN) library (*http://msdn.microsoft.com/library*). The most important part of this documentation is the description of all the classes that you can use in your .NET applications. Unfortunately, the location of this vital collection within the hierarchical structure of the documentation is often different in various products and releases. To find it in your particular release, look in the Contents section for labels that say ".NET Framework" and "Class Library." When you find it, you'll unfurl a long list of *namespaces* in alphabetical order, some of which begin with the word "Microsoft" but most of which begin with the word "System."

The namespaces serve to divide all the classes in the .NET Framework into functional groups, making it somewhat easier to find what you're looking for. But that's not the real purpose of namespaces. All classes within a particular namespace have unique names, but these names can duplicate those in other namespaces. For example, there are three classes in the .NET Framework named *Timer*, but they're in three different namespaces, so ultimately there's no ambiguity. Nor would there be a name clash if you purchased a DLL from a third party that also contained a class named *Timer*.

For any type of .NET programming, the most important namespace is *System*, which defines all the basic data types used in .NET programming. You'll probably also make use of *System.Collections* and *System.Collections.Generic* which implement standard ways to store data—such as stacks, queues, and hash tables—and *System.IO*, which includes classes to work with disk files. The *System.Data* and *System.Xml* namespaces provide valuable classes for working with databases and XML. For Windows Forms programming, the essential classes are *System.Windows.Forms*, which has classes for all the controls (buttons, menus, edit fields, and so forth) you can use in your programs, and *System.Drawing*, which has the graphics-related classes.

There is no such thing as becoming "too familiar" with the .NET class documentation. You'll want to devote all your leisure time to browsing and exploring the class documentation, and perhaps cut back on your sleep time as well.

Arranged hierarchically within each namespace are five types of entities, listed here with their corresponding C# keywords:

- *class.*   As in most object-oriented languages, the class is the basic structural element that encapsulates code and data.
- *struct.*   The .NET structure is similar to a class except that it's a value type rather than a reference type. Structures are stored on the stack rather than in the heap, and they are most suitable for small items and those that are often stored in arrays. Structures cannot be inherited.
- *interface.*   The interface looks something like a class. It has methods, but no code is defined in the methods. A class can inherit from multiple interfaces and then include the code for the methods defined in the interfaces. Interfaces turn out to be useful for casting.
- *delegate.*   The delegate is basically a method prototype. You'll see an example later in this chapter.
- *enum.*   The enumeration defines values of constants.

Within classes and structures, you'll find constructors, fields, and methods (as in traditional object-oriented languages), but you'll also find properties and events. Interfaces, delegates, and enumerations can also be defined within classes and structures, and classes and structures can nest other classes and structures, but this is less common.

Development

Many of the concepts of .NET and Windows Forms programming become more apparent through actual programming examples. As the ancient maxim goes, "One line of code is worth a thousand words."

The Littlest Programs

It is possible to write character-mode command-line programs in .NET. They are called *console* programs, and they provide a convenient place to begin .NET programming.

The *System* namespace includes a *Console* class that has methods named *Write* and *WriteLine* for displaying text. (*Writeline* is the same as *Write*, but it inserts a carriage return after the displayed text.) For reading keyboard input from the user, the *Console* class has *Read*, *ReadLine*, and (new with .NET 2.0) *ReadKey*. These are all *static* methods, which means that you reference them by preceding them with the class name itself (*Console*) rather than an object of type *Console*.

The first program is a version of the traditional "hello, world" program.

FirstConsoleProgram.cs

```
//-----------------------------------------------------
// FirstConsoleProgram.cs (c) 2005 by Charles Petzold
//-----------------------------------------------------
class FirstConsoleProgram
{
    public static void Main()
    {
        System.Console.WriteLine("Hello .NET Console");
    }
}
```

As the comment indicates, the name of the file is FirstConsoleProgram.cs; the filename extension stands for *C Sharp*. The program consists of a single class named *FirstConsoleProgram*. C# does not require the filename to be the same as the class name, but some programmers (including me) prefer organizing their code in this way. C# allows multiple classes in a single source code file (which is sometimes convenient, of course) and, beginning with C# 2.0, you can split a class between two or more source code files using the keyword *partial*.

The entry point to a C# program is a method named *Main*, which is similar to its C and C++ counterpart. C# is a case-sensitive language, and *Main* must begin with an uppercase M. *Main* can optionally have a return value and a parameter, which is an array of strings that store the command-line arguments that the user might have typed when running the program:

```
public static int Main(string[] args)
```

The *Main* method must be defined as *static* because it must exist when the program starts execution; that is, the existence of *Main* must not depend on the creation of an object of type *FirstConsoleProgram*. Because *Main* is static, another class in the same program could refer to this method as:

```
FirstConsoleProgram.Main()
```

The *Main* method contains a single call to *System.Console.WriteLine*, which is a fully qualified name consisting of a namespace, a class, and the method. If you had a number of calls to *System.Console.WriteLine* or you made use of other classes and methods in the *System* namespace, you can lessen your typing a bit by including a *using* directive near the top of your program.

```
SecondConsoleProgram.cs
//----------------------------------------------------------
// SecondConsoleProgram.cs (c) 2005 by Charles Petzold
//----------------------------------------------------------
using System;

class SecondConsoleProgram
{
    public static void Main()
    {
        Console.WriteLine("Hello again, .NET Console");
    }
}
```

The *using* directives help the compiler determine the fully qualified names of any classes you use in the program. If there's a possible ambiguity (for example, you have a *using* directive for both *System.Threading* and *System.Timers* and you're using a *Timer* class from one of those two namespaces), you must use a fully qualified name for the class.

You could compile this program on the command line using the C# compiler csc.exe, or you could use my Key of C# program, but it's more likely you'll use Visual Studio, so I'll focus on that.

Visual Studio Projects

In Visual Studio, you work with "projects." When doing Windows Forms programming, a project is a collection of files that contribute to a single executable or dynamic-link library. The project could consist of a single source code file or multiple source code files. If it consists of more than one, they must all be written in the same language. Thus, we can speak of "C# Projects" and "Visual Basic .NET Projects." Visual Studio stores project information in an XML-format file with extensions such as .csproj (for C# projects) or .vbproj (for Visual Basic .NET projects).

Visual Studio also allows you to group multiple projects (perhaps involving different languages) into "solutions." You can work on the various projects in a solution at the same time and compile them all in a process called "building the solution." Because these projects are probably related to each other in some way, Visual Studio lets you specify dependencies when you're building the solution. For example, a solution might contain three projects: a dynamic-link library written in C#, and two programs that use the DLL written in Visual Basic .NET and C++ .NET. (If you're using Visual C# rather than Visual Studio, all the projects in a solution must be written in C#.) You'll want Visual Studio to compile the DLL before the two programs. Visual Studio stores information about solutions in text files with the extension .sln.

You have a few options in Visual Studio to create a simple console program. They all start by selecting New Project from the File menu. When Visual Studio's New Project dialog box comes up, you'll want to select C# and Windows on the left. (This step isn't necessary with the simpler New Project dialog box in Visual C#.) To avoid having Visual Studio generate code for you—always a good idea when you're learning how to write the code yourself—select a project type of Empty Project. Also choose a name for the project and a directory location. Visual Studio uses the project name to create a subdirectory at that location for the project. Visual Studio always creates a .solution (.sln) file as well. If this project will be the only project in the solution, you'll want to clear the Create Directory For Solution check box. If you do not, Visual Studio will also create a solution subdirectory to hold the project subdirectory, and that's probably more subdirectories than you need. (In Visual C#, you select a location for the project the first time you save the project.)

The Empty Project is *so* empty it doesn't even contain a source code file. Select Add New Item from the Project menu or right-click the project name at the right. You get a dialog box with lots of options. Select Code File, which is an empty C# source code file. You can now type in the program.

Frequently when you're typing in Visual Studio, you'll see a list of possible classes and C# keywords. When you type a period after *Console*, for example, you'll get a list of members of the *Console* class. You can select *WriteLine* from the list, for example. The dynamic assistance that Visual Studio provides while you type is called *IntelliSense*, and it has become perhaps the most beloved feature ever of any Microsoft application. (You can control IntelliSense by choosing Options from the Tools menu, and selecting Text Editor, C#, and IntelliSense at the left of the dialog box.)

When your program is ready to be compiled, you select Build Solution from the Build menu or press F6. Errors will appear in the window below the source code. To run the program, select Start Debugging or Start Without Debugging from the Debug menu, or press F5 or Ctrl+F5. If the program has not been compiled since the last change, Visual Studio will compile it first.

Let's close this solution (by choosing Close Solution from the File menu) and try a different approach in which Visual Studio generates some code for you. From the File menu, select New Project. When the New Project dialog box appears, select Console Application. If you let Visual Studio use its own name for the Console Application project, it will create a project named ConsoleApplication1 and a file such as the one in the following code sample.

```
Program.cs
using System;
using System.Collections.Generic;
using System.Text;

namespace ConsoleApplication1
{
    class Program
    {
        static void Main(string[] args)
        {

        }
    }
}
```

Visual Studio has included what it believes to be the most likely *using* directives you'll need, and it has also given the class its own namespace. Unless you plan to create a humongous program in which you might need to reuse certain names for classes, namespaces in programs are pretty much superfluous. (Namespaces play a much more important role in DLLs.)

Once a solution is created and loaded in Visual Studio, you can add additional new or existing projects to this solution by selecting New and then Project from the File menu or by clicking the solution name (located on the far right at the top of the Solution Explorer) with the right mouse button and selecting New Project or Existing Project from the Add menu. You can add more files to the project by selecting Add New Item or Add Existing Item from the Project menu or by right-clicking the project name and selecting New Item or Existing Item from the New menu.

And, of course, you can add your own C# code to Program.cs file, and compile and run it as before.

References

As you might have noted, .NET programs require no header files to tell the C# compiler about library functions, nor does the compiler need library files to insert code into the executable or to provide links to DLLs. How does the compiler know that the *System* namespace contains a class named *Console* that has a method named *ReadLine* that accepts a string argument?

The C# compiler obtains this information directly from the dynamic-link library in which the *Console* class is stored. All .NET DLLs contain "metadata" that disclose information about the contents of the DLL. (A .NET program can access this information itself using classes defined in the *System.Reflection* namespace.) Near the top of the first documentation page of the *Console* class, you'll see a line that begins with the word *Assembly* and indicates that the *Console* class is stored in the assembly "mscorlib (in mscorlib.dll)," which once stood for "Microsoft Common Object Runtime Library" and now stands for "Multilanguage Standard Common Object Runtime Library," and which includes all the most common classes.

A Windows Forms program requires classes in other DLLs. All the classes in the *System.Windows.Forms* namespace, for example, are stored in the *System.Windows.Forms* assembly, which is the file named *System.Windows.Forms.dll*. To successfully compile a program that uses these classes, the C# compiler needs to know that it must access this DLL. When accessed by the compiler to obtain metadata, these DLLs are known as *references*.

Visual Studio needs to know about these references for a couple reasons. Most obviously, Visual Studio passes these references to the C# compiler. But Visual Studio wants to be told explicitly what references the program uses because it accesses the metadata in the DLLs long before the compiler runs. That's how Visual Studio implements IntelliSense. IntelliSense even works with DLLs that you create.

From Console to Windows

A simple Windows Forms program is almost as easy as the console program. Let's create an Empty Project in Visual Studio named FirstWinFormsProgram. But before you type in the source code, select Add Reference from the Project menu or right-click the word *References* in the Solution Explorer at the right and select Add Reference. In the Add Reference dialog box, make sure the .NET tab is selected. Any nontrivial Windows Forms application will require *System*, *System.Drawing*, and *System.Windows.Forms*. Some applications (not this one, however) will also often require *System.Data* and *System.Xml*. You can select multiple references by holding down the Ctrl key as you click them.

Now that the references are set, IntelliSense can do its job. If you're ever typing in a program and IntelliSense seems not to be working, double-check your references and *using* directives.

In the FirstWinFormsProgram project, add a new Code File item named FirstWinFormsProgram.cs and type in the following code:

FirstWinFormsProgram.cs
```
//-------------------------------------------------------
// FirstWinFormsProgram.cs (c) 2005 by Charles Petzold
//-------------------------------------------------------
using System.Windows.Forms;

class FirstWinFormsProgram
{
    public static void Main()
    {
        Application.Run(new Form());
    }
}
```

Notice the *using* directive. This program makes use of the *Application* and *Form* classes, both of which are defined in the *System.Windows.Forms* namespace. Don't confuse a project's references and a source code file's *using* directives, although they may use similar names. The references are dynamic-link libraries, and they are always required. The *using* directives refer to namespaces, and they are always optional. But if you leave out the *using* directives, you'll have to fully qualify the class names. In this program you'd need to refer to *System.Windows.Forms.Application* and *System.Windows.Forms.Form*. There are many more namespaces than libraries. For example, *System.Drawing.dll* contains classes from namespaces *System.Drawing*, *System.Drawing.Drawing2D*, *System.Drawing.Imaging*, and *System.Drawing.Printing*, which are also often used in Windows Forms programming.

At any rate, just as with the console program, you can tell Visual Studio to compile and run the program by pressing Ctrl+F5. A little window pops up:

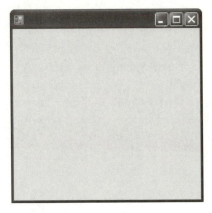

And despite a client area that resembles a desert and the absence of any text in the title bar, it is nevertheless fully functional and capable of being moved, resized, minimized, maximized, and closed. (You'll also notice that the window is accompanied by a command-line window just like the one that appeared when running console programs. More about this shortly.)

The expression

```
new Form()
```

creates an object of type *Form*, which is the Windows Forms class that encapsulates the standard application window. The program passes the *Form* object to the static *Run* method of the *Application* class. This method—innocent as its name might sound—is what turns a console program into a Windows program. In Windows programming jargon, this method *creates a message queue* for receiving messages that Windows sends to applications.

The *Application.Run* method does not return until the *Form* object passed to the method is closed by the user. This is how it must be: if *Application.Run* returned after displaying the form, *Main* would end, the program would terminate, and system cleanup would destroy the window. You can also verify this fact by putting a *Console.WriteLine* statement in the program after *Application.Run*. (You'll need to fully qualify the *Console* class name or insert another *using* directive for *System*.) And, yes, you can write to the console in a Windows program. Any console output from the program appears on the command-line window that accompanies the application window.

In exploring Windows Forms, and in developing and debugging Windows Forms applications, *Console.WriteLine* is one of the best tools around. That's why I like having that command-line window accompany my Windows Forms programs. It's also a great escape hatch: Sometimes you'll do something that causes your program to go into an infinite loop or otherwise "hang." If so, just click the command-line window to give it the input focus, press Ctrl+C, and the program is instantly terminated.

Of course, you would never give a Windows Forms program with a command-line window to end users, and that's why you can get rid of it if you want. It's controlled by a compiler switch (named *target* if you're using the command-line compiler) that you can set in Visual Studio in the Project Properties window. Select Properties from the Project menu or right-click the project name in the Solution Explorer and then click Properties. Change Output Type from Console Application to Windows Application and recompile, and the command-line window will be gone.

It may seem reasonable that we would need to set the Project Type to Windows Application to create a Windows Forms application in the first place. But no. This option really only affects the ability of the program to display console output. What separates a Windows program from a non-Windows program is the *Application.Run* call in the program code.

Fixing the Flaws

The FirstWinFormsProgram shown earlier has a serious flaw. The program creates an object of type *Form* that it passes directly to the *Application.Run* method. Because this method does not return until the form is closed, the program has no access to the form and can't do anything with it.

One simple solution is for the program to create the *Form* object first, and then to set some properties of it. The program then passes that object to *Application.Run*.

FormProperties.cs

```
//-------------------------------------------------
// FormProperties.cs (c) 2005 by Charles Petzold
//-------------------------------------------------
using System;
using System.Drawing;
using System.Windows.Forms;

class FormProperties
{
    public static void Main()
    {
        Form frm = new Form();
```

```
        frm.Text = "My WinForms Program";
        frm.Width *= 2;

        Application.Run(frm);
    }
}
```

Text and *Width* are members of the *Form* class. They are obviously not methods because methods have parentheses for arguments. They might look like fields, but they're not fields either, because both *Text* and *Width* are implemented by code. *Text* and *Width* are actually *properties*, and they exemplify an important feature of the .NET Framework. Most classes define many properties that serve to define characteristics of the object. Because properties look like fields but are implemented with code, properties are sometimes called "smart fields."

The *Text* property refers to the text that appears in the program's title bar. The *Width* property is the width of the program's window in units of pixels. The program effectively obtains the width of the *Form* object, doubles it, and then sets the *Width* property to that value. The window is expanded to twice the width of its default:

In a system without properties, the *Form* object would have to implement "get" and "set" methods (named *get_Width* and *set_Width*, for example), and you would double the window's width like this:

```
frm.set_Width(2 * frm.get_Width());
```

Actually, this is how properties are implemented in Intermediate Language and how you reference them if you're coding in J#. Certainly the property syntax makes for cleaner code. Visual Studio takes further advantage of a class's properties by displaying them in a table, letting you (the programmer) change them, and then generating the appropriate code. (You'll see this shortly.)

In the .NET Framework documentation, you won't actually see the *Text* and *Width* properties listed in the hierarchy under *Form*. These properties are defined in the *Control* class, from which *Form* descends. If you look at the page titled "Form Members," you'll see, among other things, the entire list of *Form*'s methods and properties, including those it inherits and those it implements itself.

Events and Event Handlers

Programs do more than set various properties. Programs must also respond to user input, and for this task they make use of another important element of .NET languages, which is the *event*. An event is a general-purpose mechanism for one class or object to signal another class or object through a method call. The event is a formalized, structured, and safer version of the old callback function. The method that gets called is known as the *event handler*. Event handlers are safer than callbacks because the method must have exactly the correct arguments and return value, and no amount of casting can override that.

The events implemented by a particular class are listed in the class documentation along with the constructors, fields, properties, and methods. A class also inherits events. The *Control* class defines many events that *Form* inherits.

For example, the *Control* class implements (and the *Form* class inherits) an event named *Click*, which occurs whenever the user clicks the control (or the client area of the form) with the mouse. Somewhere in the source code of the *Control* class, the *Click* event is probably defined like this:

```
public event EventHandler Click;
```

The C# keyword *event* defines this member as an event. The definition of the *Click* event makes reference to *EventHandler*. *EventHandler* is called a *delegate* (also a C# keyword), defined in the *System* namespace as:

```
public delegate void EventHandler(object sender, EventArgs e);
```

The delegate is basically a function prototype and mandates how an event handler for *Click* must be defined in your program. You can name the event handler whatever you choose, but it must have the same return value as the delegate and the same two arguments, which you can also rename:

```
void MyClicker(object objSrc, EventArgs args)
{
    ...
}
```

You attach the event handler to the event by specifying 1) the object implementing the event, 2) the event in which you're interested, 3) the delegate associated with the event, and 4) your event handler. These are all wrapped up in a very special syntax:

```
frm.Click += new EventHandler(MyClicker);
```

Notice the compound assignment operator (+=). You use the same syntax with -= rather than += to *detach* an event handler (which is not often required). Beginning with C# 2.0, you can use an abbreviated syntax that I'll take advantage of in this book:

```
frm.Click += MyClicker;
```

The *MyClicker* method must still be defined like the *EventHandler* delegate, of course.

Now, whenever the user uses the mouse to click the client area of the form, the *Form* object raises the *Click* event, which causes a call to the *MyClicker* method in your program. The first argument to *MyClicker* is *objSrc*, which is the object raising the event, in this case, the *Form* object that the program created. Within the event handler, you can cast it to an object of type *Form*:

```
Form frm = (Form) objSrc;
```

or

```
Form frm = objSrc as Form;
```

The event handler can then access properties and methods of the *Form* object. The *EventArgs* argument, on the other hand, contains nothing of interest. A *Click* event is not accompanied with any additional information. (Other mouse-related events, such as *MouseDown* and *MouseHover,* come with additional information in the second argument of the event handler.)

Another important event is called *Paint*, which indicates when the visual surface of the control or form requires a paint job. The first *Paint* event occurs when the form is created. Subsequent *Paint* events occur when the form is minimized and then restored, when it's resized, or when it's obscured by another form and then brought to the foreground again. Although programs are not restricted to drawing on the surface of a form during a *Paint* event, they must be structured so that they can use the *Paint* event to re-create any text or graphics that appear on the form.

The *Paint* event handler is defined in the *Control* class like so:

```
public event PaintEventHandler Paint;
```

The *PaintEventHandler* delegate is defined in the *System.Windows.Forms* namespace:

```
public delegate void PaintEventHandler(object sender, PaintEventArgs e);
```

Thus, you must define a *Paint* event handler with a second argument of *PaintEventArgs* rather than *EventArgs*:

```
void MyPainter(object objSrc, PaintEventArgs args)
{
    ...
}
```

The program installs the event handler using the *PaintEventHandler* delegate:

```
frm.Paint += new PaintEventHandler(MyPainter);
```

or:

```
frm.Paint += MyPainter;
```

The *PaintEventArgs* class is defined in *System.Windows.Forms*. It inherits from *EventArgs* but includes two properties: *Graphics* and *ClipRectangle*. The event handler uses the *Graphics* object in connection with the graphics drawing methods defined in the *Graphics* class. The *ClipRectangle* indicates the rectangle containing the invalid region to which the *Graphics* object is restricted.

The following program implements event handlers for both *Click* and *Paint*. The program responds to *Click* by displaying a message box, and to *Paint* by displaying some text in the client area.

```
FormEvents.cs
//-------------------------------------------
// FormEvents.cs (c) 2005 by Charles Petzold
//-------------------------------------------
using System;
using System.Drawing;
using System.Windows.Forms;

class FormEvents
{
    public static void Main()
    {
        Form frm = new Form();

        frm.Text = "My Events Program";
        frm.Width *= 2;
        frm.Click += MyClicker;
        frm.Paint += MyPainter;

        Application.Run(frm);
    }
    static void MyClicker(object objSrc, EventArgs args)
    {
        MessageBox.Show("The form has been clicked!", "Click");
    }
    static void MyPainter(object objSrc, PaintEventArgs args)
    {
        Form frm = (Form)objSrc;
        Graphics grfx = args.Graphics;
        grfx.DrawString("Hello, Windows Forms", frm.Font,
                    SystemBrushes.ControlText, 0, 0);
    }
}
```

In this program, the event handlers must be defined as *static*. The program doesn't create an object of type *FormEvents*, so any nonstatic methods in the class would be useless. Although the event handlers are effectively called from outside the *FormEvents* class, they need not be defined as *public*.

In response to a mouse click of the client area, the program displays a message box. The code in *MyPainter* displays some text in the client area using the *DrawString* method of the *Graphics* class. The arguments of this method are the text to be displayed, the font, the color of the text (in the form of a graphics brush), and the *x* and *y* coordinates where the upper-left corner of the text string is to be displayed relative to the upper-left corner of the client area.

MyPainter could have created its own font of any available typeface and size, but it chooses to use the form's default font, which is stored in a property of the *Form* class named *Font*. To access this property, the method casts *objSrc* to an object of type *Form* and obtains its *Font* property. The *Form* object passed to the event handler is the same object that was created in *Main*. The program could have stored the *Form* object it creates as a static field so that any method in the program has access to it.

Inheriting from Form

Although the previous program shows a plausible approach to creating and using a *Form* object, that's not the way it's usually done. You'll have more flexibility and a more satisfying programming experience if you instead define a class that inherits from *Form*:

```
class MyForm: Form
{
    ...
}
```

You can then create an object of that class as the argument to *Application.Run* in *Main*. Perhaps you'll want to define another class in your program solely for the static *Main* method:

```
class MyProgram
{
    public static void Main()
    {
        Application.Run(new MyForm());
    }
}
```

Because *MyForm* is a class that inherits from *Form*, it has access to all the public and protected methods, properties, and events of *Form*. Consequently, it can set properties of the form in its constructor:

```
class MyForm: Form
{
    public MyForm()
    {
        Text = "My Inherited Form";
        Width *= 2;
    }
}
```

In C#, a constructor has the same name as the class, but no return value. This is the first method in this chapter that isn't defined as *static*. The constructor applies to an object of type *MyForm*. The properties don't need to be prefaced with the object name. In fact, there is no *MyForm* object until an object has been created by the code in *Main*. You can use the C# keyword *this* in a constructor, method, or property to refer to the current object:

```
this.Text = "My Inherited Form";
```

Typing *this* and a period in Visual Studio is a good way to invoke IntelliSense, which will then list all nonstatic members of the class.

You can also install event handlers. Notice that the event handlers are no longer static because they apply to an object of type *MyForm*:

```
class MyForm: Form
{
    public MyForm()
    {
        Text = "My Inherited Form";
        Width *= 2;
        Click += MyClicker;
        Paint += MyPainter;
    }
    void MyClicker(object objSrc, EventArgs args)
    {
        MessageBox.Show("The button has been clicked!", "Click");
    }
    void MyPainter(object objSrc, PaintEventArgs args)
    {
        Graphics grfx = args.Graphics;
        grfx.DrawString("Hello, Windows Forms", Font,
```

```
                          SystemBrushes.ControlText, 0, 0);
        }
}
```

However, there's an easier way to work with events when you inherit from *Form*. For every event that the *Control* class (and hence the *Form* class) implements, there exists a corresponding method. This method has the same name as the event but preceded by the word *On*—for example, *OnPaint* and *OnClick*. These methods have a single argument, which is the same as the second argument to the event handler. (The first argument is not needed because any properties or methods of the object can be referred to directly or by using the keyword *this*.) These methods are defined as *virtual*, which means that a program that descends from *Control* or *Form* can override the methods using the *override* keyword. Because these virtual methods in *Control* are defined as *protected*, the overrides must also be defined as *protected*:

```
class MyForm: Form
{
    public MyForm()
    {
        Text = "";
        Width *= 2;
    }
    protected override void OnClick(EventArgs args)
    {
        MessageBox.Show("The button has been clicked!", "Click");
    }
    protected override void OnPaint(PaintEventArgs args)
    {
        Graphics grfx = args.Graphics;
        grfx.DrawString("Hello, Windows Forms", Font,
                        SystemBrushes.ControlText, 0, 0);
    }
}
```

Earlier, I showed a separate class named *MyProgram* that has a static *Main* method that creates an object of type *MyForm*. It is also possible (and often convenient) to put the *Main* method right in the class that inherits from *Form*, eliminating the need for a separate class just for *Main*:

```
class MyForm: Form
{
    public static void Main()
    {
        Application.Run(new MyForm());
    }
    ...
}
```

This code might look a bit weird because *Main* is a member of the *MyForm* class, and yet it's responsible for creating an instance of *MyForm*. The only reason this code works is because *Main* is defined as *static* and hence is independent of any potential objects of type *MyForm*.

Here's the complete program.

```
InheritFromForm.cs
//-------------------------------------------------
// InheritFromForm.cs (c) 2005 by Charles Petzold
//-------------------------------------------------
using System;
using System.Drawing;
using System.Windows.Forms;

class InheritFromForm: Form
{
    public static void Main()
    {
        Application.Run(new InheritFromForm());
    }
    public InheritFromForm()
    {
        Text = "Inherit from Form";
        Width *= 2;
    }
    protected override void OnClick(EventArgs args)
    {
        MessageBox.Show("The form has been clicked!", "Click");
    }
    protected override void OnPaint(PaintEventArgs args)
    {
        Graphics grfx = args.Graphics;
        grfx.DrawString("Hello, Windows Forms", Font,
                        SystemBrushes.ControlText, 0, 0);
    }
}
```

One warning: The *OnClick* and *OnPaint* methods in *Control* are responsible for raising the *Click* and *Paint* events. Because *InheritFromForm* overrides these methods, the *Click* and *Paint* events for *InheritFromForm* are effectively disabled. If *InheritFromForm* (or any class that inherited from *InheritFromForm*) attempted to attach event handlers for the *Click* and *Paint* events, the event handlers wouldn't work. If this is a problem, the *OnClick* and *OnPaint* methods that you're overriding should begin with code that invokes the overridden methods, for example:

```
base.OnPaint(args)
```

Properties and Events in Visual Studio

You now have sufficient background to understand much of what Visual Studio does when you create a project of type Windows Application. Visual Studio generates sufficient code ready for compilation spread out over several files. It also shows you a Design View of the form that you can interactively modify and dress up with controls.

The Program.cs file that Visual Studio creates contains the *Main* method in a class named *Program* in a superfluous namespace with the same name as the project (*WindowsApplication1* by default):

```
Program.cs
using System;
using System.Collections.Generic;
using System.Windows.Forms;

namespace WindowsApplication1
{
    static class Program
    {
        /// <summary>
        /// The main entry point for the application.
        /// </summary>
        [STAThread]
        static void Main()
        {
            Application.EnableVisualStyles();
            Application.SetCompatibleTextRenderingDefault(false);
            Application.Run(new Form1());
        }
    }
}
```

The comments above the *Main* method show an example of XML documentation of your code. A compilation option allows you to specify a file that consists of all the program documentation formatted in this way. This is a great way to document your code. The only reason I don't use it in this book is that it would take up precious real estate on the page.

Main is preceded directly by a method *attribute* that consists of the word *STAThread* in square brackets. This informs the .NET runtime to begin the program in "single-threaded apartment" (STA) so that it can properly interact with Component Object Module (COM) components. (See the documentation on *STAThreadAttribute* in the *System* namespace for a tiny bit more information.) It shouldn't be so, but Windows Forms programs without this attribute that use the clipboard will likely crash. I'll use *STAThread* in all future programs in this book.

The *EnableVisualStyles* method of *Application* involves the appearance of some controls. See the documentation of the *FlatStyle* enumeration for details. The call results in somewhat more "modern" looking controls, so I'll call this method in all future programs in this book.

The Form1 class is defined in the Form1.cs file.

Form1.cs

```csharp
using System;
using System.Collections.Generic;
using System.ComponentModel;
using System.Data;
using System.Drawing;
using System.Windows.Forms;

namespace WindowsApplication1
{
    partial class Form1 : Form
    {
        public Form1()
        {
            InitializeComponent();
        }
    }
}
```

Form1 is derived from *Form*. Notice the use of the *partial* keyword in the class definition; this is the keyword that lets you scatter a class all over the place. The *InitializeComponent* method is also in the *Form1* class but in another source code file named Form1.Designer.cs.

Form1.Designer.cs

```csharp
namespace WindowsApplication1
{
    partial class Form1
    {
        /// <summary>
        /// Required designer variable.
        /// </summary>
        private System.ComponentModel.IContainer components = null;

        /// <summary>
        /// Clean up any resources being used.
        /// </summary>
        /// <param name="disposing">true if managed resources should be disposed;
        /// otherwise, false.</param>
        protected override void Dispose(bool disposing)
        {
            if (disposing && (components != null))
            {
                components.Dispose();
            }
            base.Dispose(disposing);
        }

        #region Windows Form Designer generated code

        /// <summary>
        /// Required method for Designer support - do not modify
        /// the contents of this method with the code editor.
```

```
        /// </summary>
        private void InitializeComponent()
        {
            this.components = new System.ComponentModel.Container();
            this.AutoScaleMode = System.Windows.Forms.AutoScaleMode.Font;
            this.Text = "Form1";
        }

        #endregion
    }
}
```

The code involving the *components* object is some Visual Studio boilerplate. The *Container* class is a collection of *Component* objects. The *Control* class derives from the *Component* class, as do several other classes in Windows Forms that encapsulate Windows resources referenced by handles. The documentation for *Component* recommends that such objects be disposed explicitly rather than disposed automatically during garbage collection or at program termination. Assembling these objects in a *Container* facilitates that process.

When Visual Studio displays the design view of the form, it also displays a property window in the lower-right corner. You can change any properties of the form and also (by clicking the lightning-bolt icon) view the form's events. To change the size of the form, for example, find the *Size* property, which has two properties, *Width* and *Height*. You can also change the size of the form in Design View directly by dragging one of the little boxes on the sizing border. Whatever approach you use, Visual Studio inserts code in Form1.Designer.cs like this (for example):

```
this.ClientSize = new System.Drawing.Size(565, 266);
```

Children of the Form

The client area of the form is the surface the application uses to display visual information to the user. A Windows Forms program can cover the client area with text and graphics, it can populate the client area with controls (both predefined and customized), or it can combine graphics output with controls. Controls available to Windows Forms programs include the familiar buttons, edit fields, list boxes, scroll bars, and also more sophisticated controls. (The next chapter discusses most of the Windows Forms controls in .NET 2.0.) These days, application client areas are often divided into logical areas; this approach, too, makes use of controls such as panels and splitters, which are discussed in Chapter 3.

All controls are descended from the *Control* class, and it is there that you'll find those properties, methods, and events that apply to all controls. One of these important properties is *Parent*, which is also an object of type *Control*. A control always appears on the visual surface of its parent. The location of the control is specified relative to the upper-left corner of the parent (or, when the parent is a *Form* object, relative to the upper-left corner of the form's client area).

Unless the control is also a form, a control without a parent is invisible. A program can explicitly make a control invisible by setting the *Visible* property to *false*. Used more frequently is the *Enabled* property. A control with this property set to *false* is displayed in a dull color and does not accept any input from the user.

The *Button* class implements the familiar push button that often appears in dialog boxes containing the word OK or Cancel. The following program shows how to create a *Button* object, position it on the surface of the form, and attach a handler for the button's *Click* event.

Like the rest of the programs in this book, I put this program together by first creating an Empty Project in Visual Studio, and then adding an empty C# Code File.

```
FormWithButton.cs
//------------------------------------------------------
// FormWithButton.cs (c) 2005 by Charles Petzold
//------------------------------------------------------
using System;
using System.Drawing;
using System.Windows.Forms;

class FormWithButton: Form
{
    [STAThread]
    public static void Main()
    {
        Application.EnableVisualStyles();
        Application.Run(new FormWithButton());
    }
    public FormWithButton()
    {
        Text = "Form with Button";

        Button btn = new Button();
        btn.Parent = this;
        btn.Text = "Click me!";
        btn.Location = new Point(50, 25);
        btn.AutoSize = true;
        btn.Click += ButtonOnClick;
    }
    void ButtonOnClick(object objSrc, EventArgs args)
    {
        MessageBox.Show("The button was clicked!", "Button");
    }
}
```

The form's constructor creates an object of type *Button* and assigns the *Parent* property to *this*, which is the *Form* object. The *Text* property is the text that appears on the button. The *Location* property indicates that the upper-left corner of the button appears 50 pixels to the right and 25 pixels down from the upper-left corner of the form's client area. The button's *AutoSize* property is set to *true*, which means that the button will set its own size to accommodate the text that it must display. Finally, the program makes its *ButtonOnClick* method the event handler for the button's *Click* event. The event and all these properties are defined in *Control* and inherited by the *Button* class and all other control classes.

The *AutoSize* property seems to work well in creating a good size for the button:

If the event handler needs to obtain the *Button* object raising the event, it can cast the first argument to an object of type *Button*:

```
Button btn = (Button) objSrc;
```

or

```
Button btn = objSrc as Button;
```

A single event handler can handle *Click* events from multiple buttons. The event handler can determine which button is which by a variety of methods. Using the *Text* property is one approach but certainly not the best way. You don't want to change your event handler every time you change the button text. Using the *Name* property is better. That's another string you are free to set to whatever you want. The *Tag* property is also available. You have complete control over this property; it's not used for anything else, and it can be set to any object.

You'll find that you won't need to install event handlers for every control you create. The *CheckBox* control, for example, generates a *Click* event whenever the user clicks the control. But by default the control itself toggles its check mark on and off. Generally, you'll only need to determine its current state, which you can do by looking at its Boolean *Checked* property.

When you have a form with a multitude of controls, the controls might need to refer to each other. For example, clicking one control might have the effect of disabling or enabling other controls. The most straightforward way for one control's event handler to refer to other controls is to store each *Control* object as a field, for example:

```
Button btnCancel;
```

In the constructor, you create the object and set its properties:

```
btnCancel = new Button();
...
```

Or you can define and create the object in the field:

```
Button btnCancel = new Button();
```

The C# compiler sets up a special method that executes all code in fields before executing the code in the class's constructor.

In the spirit of object-oriented philosophy—which holds that data and objects should be mostly hidden and made accessible to outside code only when necessary—I prefer storing an object as a field only when there's no other way to make it visible to multiple methods.

I may be stingy with fields, but Visual Studio certainly isn't. Visual Studio stores *all* control objects as fields. In Visual Studio, if you've created a Windows Application project, you can create a button on your form by selecting Button from the Toolbox on the far left, and then dropping it into the form. Visual Studio adds a private field to the *Form1* class containing the instance of the *Button* class:

```
private System.Windows.Forms.Button button1;
```

Visual Studio also generates the following code (or something like it) concerning the *Button* object:

```
this.button1 = new System.Windows.Forms.Button();
this.button1.Location = new System.Drawing.Point(92, 55);
this.button1.Name = "button1";
this.button1.Size = new System.Drawing.Size(104, 47);
this.button1.TabIndex = 0;
this.button1.Text = "button1";
this.Controls.Add(this.button1);
```

You can move or size the button directly, or you can change the button properties in the table in the lower-right corner of Visual Studio. Notice that Visual Studio does not assign the *Parent* property of the button to the *Form* object. Instead, it does something equivalent in the last of those six button-related statements:

```
this.Controls.Add(this.button1);
```

Controls is a property of the *Form* class. (*Form* actually inherits the property from *Control*.) The *Controls* property is of type *Control.ControlCollection*, which means that *ControlCollection* is a class defined within the *Control* class. Still, however, the class is public so that it can be referenced outside the *Control* class. The *ControlCollection* class implements the *ICollection*, *IEnumerable*, and *IList* interfaces, which are all involved in maintaining a collection of objects that allows adding objects to the collection, removing them, and searching,

The *Controls* property of *Control* is basically a collection of child controls. Adding a control to the *Controls* property of the *Form* object is equivalent to setting the *Parent* property of the control to the *Form* object. Removing a control from the collection is equivalent to setting the control's *Parent* property to *null*, and vice versa. A program can index the *Controls* property like an array to obtain all the child controls of a form (or other control). You can also use the *Find* method of *Control.ControlCollection* to obtain a *Control* object using the control's *Name* property.

Suppose two children of the same form are positioned so as to visually overlap. Which one appears on top of the other? This depends on the control's *z-order*. (The term comes from three-dimensional graphics. It's the additional coordinate after the normal *x* and *y* coordinates.) The z-order is equivalent to the control's index in the *Controls* collection, which is the order that the controls are assigned to the collection or have their *Parent* property set. Controls created early have a lower index, but they are considered to be at the top of the z-order because they appear visually on top of controls created later. A program can change z-ordering of controls at run time with the *BringToTop* and *SendToBack* methods.

As you create controls in Visual Studio, it generates code to assign the *TabIndex* property with consecutive numbers beginning with 0. The *TabIndex* property indicates the order in which child controls will receive the keyboard input focus when you use the Tab key to cycle among the controls. Visual Studio explicitly sets this property so that you (the programmer) can change the tab ordering in Visual Studio by using the Tab Order item from the View menu.

If all the *TabIndex* properties of multiple controls are zero (which is the case if there's no code that sets the properties), the tab order is determined by the z-order—that is, the order that the controls are added to the control collection. If you're designing a form haphazardly and chaotically in Visual Studio, it's likely you'll need to reorder the tab indexes. If you're designing a form in code and actually giving the process some thought, the order of the controls in code will determine the tab order.

Visual Studio also inserts calls to *SuspendLayout* and *ResumeLayout*. These calls are not required but are suggested to prevent the form from doing too much work while properties are set in the controls.

Subclassing Controls

It is customary for Windows Forms programs to define a class that inherits from *Form*. It is also customary for programs simply to create instances of controls rather than to define new classes that inherit from the existing control classes. However, deriving new control classes is useful when you need to extend a control in some way or when you want a control to store a bit more information than is available through the *Tag* property.

Suppose you want a button that displays a message box whenever the user clicks the button. Let's call this class *MessageButton*. You want the caption of the message box to be the same text as the button. The class can obtain that text string from the *Text* property of the button. But you want the text within the message box to be something else unique to each button. You might consider storing this text as a public field in your new class:

```
class MessageButton: Button
{
    public string MessageBoxText = "";
    ...
}
```

The *OnClick* method has access to this field, of course, and because it's *public* a program that creates an instance of *MessageButton* can also set this field:

```
MessageButton mbbtn = new MessageButton();
mbbtn.MessageBoxText = "Text in the message box.";
...
```

There's nothing wrong with making *MessageBoxText* a field of the class. But if you look through the .NET Framework class documentation, you won't find very many fields, and many of those you do find will be *const* fields for a collection of constant values.

What you will find instead are properties. Very often a property provides a public access to a private field. The property is often useful because it can also include some code, perhaps for validity checking or for taking some action when something about the object is changed. For example, when the *Control* class has its *Text* or color properties changed, it immediately repaints to control to reflect that change. That type of response is not possible with fields.

Suppose that you want the button to be disabled unless *MessageBoxText* has a text string at least one character long. If *MessageBoxText* is simply a field, the class cannot detect when the field is changed. But a *MessageBoxText* property can easily set the *Enabled* property of the button whenever the property is changed.

The code for *MessageButton* has a private field, a constructor that initializes the *Enabled* property to *false*, and a *MessageBoxText* property that enables the button only when the text is more than one character in length.

```
MessageButton.cs
//-----------------------------------------------
// MessageButton.cs (c) 2005 by Charles Petzold
//-----------------------------------------------
using System;
using System.Drawing;
using System.Windows.Forms;

class MessageButton: Button
{
    string strMessageBoxText;

    public MessageButton()
    {
        Enabled = false;
```

```
        }
        public string MessageBoxText
        {
            set
            {
                strMessageBoxText = value;
                Enabled = value != null && value.Length > 0;
            }
            get
            {
                return strMessageBoxText;
            }
        }
        protected override void OnClick(EventArgs args)
        {
            MessageBox.Show(MessageBoxText, Text);
        }
    }
```

Notice the definition of the *MessageBoxText* property. You can tell that it's a property definition by the lack of parentheses after *MessageBoxText* and by the presence of the *set* and *get* accessors. Within the *set* accessor, the special word *value* refers to the value being set to the property. Because the *MessageBoxText* property is defined as a *string*, *value* is also a *string* and you can determine its length with the *Length* property.

In Visual Studio, I created an Empty Project named MessageButtonDemo and then included an empty C# Code File for MessageButton.cs. After creating the *MessageButton* class, I added a second empty C# Code File for MessageButtonDemo.cs, which is the program that demonstrates how the button is used.

MessageButtonDemo.cs

```
//-------------------------------------------------
// MessageButtonDemo.cs (c) 2005 by Charles Petzold
//-------------------------------------------------
using System;
using System.Drawing;
using System.Windows.Forms;

class MessageButtonDemo: Form
{
    [STAThread]
    public static void Main()
    {
        Application.EnableVisualStyles();
        Application.Run(new MessageButtonDemo());
    }
    public MessageButtonDemo()
    {
        Text = "MessageButton Demo";
```

```
        MessageButton msgbtn = new MessageButton();
        msgbtn.Parent = this;
        msgbtn.Text = "Calculate 10,000,000 digits of PI";
        msgbtn.MessageBoxText = "This button is not yet implemented!";
        msgbtn.Location = new Point(50, 50);
        msgbtn.AutoSize = true;
    }
}
```

You might want to try commenting out the statement that sets *MessageBoxText*, or try setting the property to *null* or an empty string, to ensure that the button-enabling code works correctly.

As you were typing the MessageButtonDemo.cs code into Visual Studio, you undoubtedly noticed that IntelliSense worked with the *msgbtn* variable just as if it were an instance of an "official" .NET class. That's why I created the *MessageButton* class first. Otherwise IntelliSense wouldn't have known what to make of *MessageButton* and might have started barking in distress. For centuries, it seems, programmers have debated whether it's better to program in a top-down manner (create the overall structure first and then code all the subroutines) or a bottom-up approach (create the subroutines first and then build up to the *Main* method). Visual Studio has now settled that argument. To get IntelliSense to work, bottom-up is best.

Now that you have the *MessageButton* class, you can use it in any program. You need only to include MessageButton.cs in a project and compile the files together. Whenever you need to add an existing source code file into a Visual Studio project, pick the Existing Item menu item from the Add options and specify that you want a *link* to the file. (In the Add Existing Item dialog box, click the little tiny arrow on the Add button and select Add As Link.) That link ensures that the file won't be copied and that multiple copies of the file won't be hanging around to confuse you when you need to change it.

Device-Independent Coding

The *Control* class defines two properties, named *Location* and *Size*, that you use to explicitly position and size controls. (I'll discuss alternatives to explicit positioning and sizing in Chapter 3.) The *Location* property is a *Point* structure, which contains two integer fields, named *X* and *Y*. These indicate the position of the upper-left corner of the control relative to the upper-left corner of its parent. Units are pixels. The *Size* property is the size of the control in pixels, expressed as a *Size* structure, which contains two fields, named *Width* and *Height*. (The *Point* and *Size* structures can be found in the *System.Drawing* namespace.)

We have all seen Windows programs that contain only partially visible controls or controls insufficiently large for the text they display. These problems result from programmers failing to code in a device-independent manner.

Just as printers have a device resolution of 300, 600, or 1200 dots per inch (dpi), the video display also has a particular device resolution. By default, this resolution is 96 dpi, but the user can change it by invoking the Display Properties dialog box through the Windows Control Panel or by right-clicking the screen. From the Settings tab, click the Advanced button, and you can choose any resolution between 19 dpi and 480 dpi. (Not even this dialog box is coded to accept this wide range of resolutions!) One alternative to 96 dpi is 120 dpi, which generally makes most text on the screen 25 percent larger and is popular among users born before the moon landing. The 96 and 120 dpi resolutions are sometimes called Small Fonts and Large Fonts, although the Display Properties dialog box calls them Normal Size and Large Size. A Windows Forms program can obtain the resolution of any graphics output device, including the video display, using the *DpiX* and *DpiY* properties of the *Graphics* class.

The default Windows Forms font is about 8 points, which you can obtain with the *SizeInPoints* property of the *Font* class. (Points are 1/72 inch; the point size is the height of the font including descenders but excluding diacritics.) The *Height* property of the *Font* class is a pixel dimension that includes a little extra space for spacing consecutive lines of text. You'll find the *Height* value to be 13 for Small Fonts and 16 for Large Fonts. A rough approximation of the average width of font characters is 1/2 the height.

Armed with these concepts, you can position and size controls in a device-independent manner. A good rule of thumb for buttons is to make them 1 3/4 times the font height. The width should be based on the number of characters displayed by the button, plus two (or four to be safe), times an average character width or half the font height. Here's a small program that sizes the client area and button based on the font height and positions the button in the center of the client area.

DeviceIndependentButton.cs

```
//----------------------------------------------------------
// DeviceIndependentButton.cs (c) 2005 by Charles Petzold
//----------------------------------------------------------
using System;
using System.Drawing;
using System.Windows.Forms;

class DeviceIndependentButton: Form
{
    [STAThread]
    public static void Main()
    {
        Application.EnableVisualStyles();
        Application.Run(new DeviceIndependentButton());
    }
    public DeviceIndependentButton()
    {
        Text = "Device-Independent Button";
        int fntht = Font.Height;

        ClientSize = new Size(fntht * 30, fntht * 10);
```

```
        Button btn = new Button();
        btn.Parent = this;
        btn.Text = "Lookin' good!";
        btn.Size = new Size(17 * fntht / 2, 7 * fntht / 4);
        btn.Location = new Point((ClientSize.Width - btn.Width) / 2,
                                 (ClientSize.Height - btn.Height) / 2);
    }
}
```

The first argument to the *Size* constructor accounts for the 13 characters of the text, plus four, multiplied by half the font height. The second argument is 1 3/4 times the font height. Here's the program running with a screen resolution of 96 DPI:

And here's the same program with a screen resolution of 120 DPI:

It's larger, of course, but similarly proportioned.

Visual Studio strives for device-independence by using a pair of properties named *AutoScaleDimensions* and *AutoScaleMode*. (These replace the *AutoScaleBaseSize* property in .NET 1.x.) These two properties are defined in the *ContainerControl* class, which is a descendent of *Control* and from which *Form* directly inherits. The *AutoScaleMode* property takes on values from the *AutoScaleMode* enumeration; values can be *AutoScaleMode.Dpi*, *AutoScaleMode.Font*, or *AutoScaleMode.Inherit*.

If you set the *AutoScaleMode* property to *AutoScaleMode.Font*, the *Form* class will scale all the dimensions you've used based on the ratio of the size of the form's *Font* property to the size you specify in the *AutoScaleDimensions* property.

When you work in Visual Studio to design a form, Visual Studio stores all the locations and dimensions in device coordinates and also adds two statements setting the *AutoScaleDimensions* and *AutoScaleMode* properties. If you're working in a Windows session in which Small Fonts are installed, these two statements will be

```
this.AutoScaleDimensions = new System.Drawing.SizeF(6F, 13F);
this.AutoScaleMode = System.Windows.Forms.AutoScaleMode.Font;
```

The *SizeF* structure is similar to *Size* but with floating-point dimensions rather than integer dimensions. The numbers 6 and 13 are the average width and height in pixels of the default Windows Forms font.

When you run this program in a Windows session with Large Fonts, the *Form* class scales its own size and its child controls based on the average size of the *Form*'s default font, which is now 8 pixels wide and 16 pixels tall. Horizontal coordinates and widths are scaled by the ratio 8/6, and vertical coordinates and heights are scaled by 16/13.

Of course, if you design a form in a Windows session using Large Fonts, Visual Studio will insert in your code the lines

```
this.AutoScaleDimensions = new System.Drawing.SizeF(8F, 16F);
this.AutoScaleMode = System.Windows.Forms.AutoScaleMode.Font;
```

If you design part of the form under Small Fonts and continue under Large Fonts, Visual Studio will adjust the locations and sizes of all the existing controls accordingly.

The other option for the *AutoScaleMode* property is the enumeration value *AutoScaleMode.Dpi*, which refers to the resolution of the video display. Visual Studio could just as well insert the lines

```
this.AutoScaleDimensions = new System.Drawing.SizeF(96, 96);
this.AutoScaleMode = System.Windows.Forms.AutoScaleMode.Dpi;
```

if you're designing the form with Small Fonts (equivalent to 96 dots-per-inch resolution), and

```
this.AutoScaleDimensions = new System.Drawing.SizeF(120, 120);
this.AutoScaleMode = System.Windows.Forms.AutoScaleMode.Dpi;
```

for a Large Fonts system.

If you prefer to code the locations and sizes of your controls, you can use the auto-scale feature in more flexible ways. For example, veteran Windows programmers are accustomed to using resource scripts to define the layouts of dialog boxes. Resource scripts have a special coordinate system with horizontal coordinates based on 1/4 the average width of the default font and vertical coordinates based on 1/8 the height of the font. Thus, if the average width is about half the height, horizontal and vertical are equal. To mimic this coordinate system, use

```
AutoScaleDimensions = new Size(4, 8);
AutoScaleMode = AutoScaleMode.Font;
```

If you want to position and size controls in units of 1/10 of an inch, you can use

```
AutoScaleDimensions = new Size(10, 10);
AutoScaleMode = AutoScaleMode.Dpi;
```

To work correctly, *AutoScaleDimensions* and *AutoScaleMode* must be set in that order and must appear towards the end of the constructor after the form's client area has been sized and all controls have been created and made children of the form.

Here's an auto-scale form and button that's visually similar to the DeviceDependentButton program.

```
AutoScaleButton.cs
//-----------------------------------------------
// AutoScaleButton.cs (c) 2005 by Charles Petzold
//-----------------------------------------------
using System;
using System.Drawing;
using System.Windows.Forms;

class AutoScaleButton: Form
{
    [STAThread]
    public static void Main()
    {
        Application.EnableVisualStyles();
        Application.Run(new AutoScaleButton());
    }
    public AutoScaleButton()
    {
        Text = "Auto-Scale Button";

        ClientSize = new Size(240, 80);

        Button btn = new Button();
        btn.Parent = this;
        btn.Text = "Lookin' good!";
        btn.Size = new Size(17 * 4, 14);
        btn.Location = new Point((ClientSize.Width - btn.Width) / 2,
                                 (ClientSize.Height - btn.Height) / 2);

        AutoScaleDimensions = new Size(4, 8);
        AutoScaleMode = AutoScaleMode.Font;
    }
}
```

Assembly Information

Another file that Visual Studio creates as part of a standard Windows Application is called AssemblyInfo.cs. This file contains a series of attributes that the compiler uses to set information in the .EXE or .DLL file relating to the program's copyright and version information. This information is accessible by a user from the properties dialog box in Windows Explorer. This is the type of thing that's important for a program that you're giving or selling to other people but is entirely unnecessary when you're writing code for yourself to learn Windows Forms programming.

You can put any or all of these items anywhere in your source code. Here are the ones I use in my Key of C# program:

```
[assembly: AssemblyTitle("Key of C#")]
[assembly: AssemblyDescription("Small C# IDE for .NET")]
[assembly: AssemblyCompany("www.charlespetzold.com")]
[assembly: AssemblyProduct("Key of C#")]
[assembly: AssemblyCopyright("(c) Charles Petzold, " + Version.Copyright)]
[assembly: AssemblyVersion(Version.Major + "." + Version.Minor + ".*")]
```

These particular attributes make reference to a structure named *Version* that the Key of C# program uses elsewhere—for example, in the About dialog box. When changing a version or copyright data, all I need to do is change the *Version* structure.

The word *assembly* followed by a colon in these attributes is the attribute target. It indicates that the attribute that follows applies to the assembly, which is usually just a .EXE or .DLL file. The source code file in which you put the attributes requires a *using* directive for *System.Reflection* because the attributes correspond to classes in that namespace. For example, *Assembly-Title* refers to the *AssemblyTitleAttribute* class.

Perhaps the most important of these attributes is *AssemblyVersion*. You specify the version as a series of four numbers—called the Major Version, Minor Version, Build Number, and Revision—separated by periods. If you use an asterisk rather than a Build Number and Revision, the C# compiler assigns the Build Number the number of days since January 1, 2000, and it assigns the Revision half the number of seconds since midnight. This ensures that each build gets a higher number without any work on your part. Although it's called *AssemblyVersion*, this version number also becomes the file version and product version of the file unless you also include the *AssemblyFileVersion* attribute, in which case that becomes the file version and product version.

Dialog Boxes

An application uses dialog boxes to obtain information from the user beyond what is convenient through controls, menus, and toolbars on the application window. Dialog boxes are most often invoked through menu or toolbar items. Often a menu item indicates that it displays a dialog box using an ellipsis (...).

There are two general types of dialog boxes: *modal* and *modeless*.

Modal Dialog Boxes

The modal dialog box is by far the more common. When the dialog box is displayed, the user cannot switch back to the application window without first dismissing the dialog. The user had been working with the application but is now in a different *mode*. The user must switch from dialog mode back to application mode by closing the dialog box.

Modal dialog boxes generally contain a collection of controls, including two buttons, labeled "OK" and "Cancel." (There is nothing to prevent a dialog box from having menus and toolbars, but they are very rare.) The OK and Cancel buttons both close the dialog box, removing it from the screen and returning the user to the application. If the user clicks Cancel, the application ignores anything the user set in the dialog box.

In Windows Forms, a dialog box is simply another descendent of the *Form* class:

```
class MyDialogBox: Form
{
    ...
}
```

A program invokes the dialog box by creating an instance of that class and calling the *ShowDialog* method, usually in response to a click of a menu item:

```
MyDialogBox dlg = new MyDialogBox();
dlg.ShowDialog();
```

The *ShowDialog* method doesn't return until the user closes the dialog box.

A dialog box often has a slightly different appearance than an application window. Traditionally, the dialog has no sizing border (although sizing borders on dialogs are sighted more and more these days), no minimize box, and no maximize box. (You'll see how this is done shortly.) It was once common to not include caption bars with modal dialog boxes, but that's no longer the rule. The caption bar gives the user the opportunity to move the dialog box to another location on the screen, perhaps to see something underneath it.

The dialog box must signal to the application whether the user closed the dialog box by pressing OK or Cancel. The dialog box closes itself in a special way by setting the *DialogResult* property of the dialog box form to a member of the *DialogResult* enumeration, specifically either *DialogResult.OK* or *DialogResult.Cancel*. The *ShowDialog* method originally called by the application form to invoke the dialog box then returns, and it returns the value that the dialog box set to its *DialogResult* property.

So, the most basic approach is for the dialog box to implement *Click* event handlers for the OK and Cancel buttons that set the *DialogResult* property appropriately. Here's the *Click* event handler for the OK button:

```
void OkButtonOnClick(object objSrc, EventArgs args)
{
    DialogResult = DialogResult.OK;
}
```

The application form displays the dialog box and processes the results in code that looks like this:

```
if (dlg.ShowDialog() == DialogResult.OK)
{
    ...
}
```

Windows Forms has simplified this process a bit by implementing *DialogResult* properties in the *Button* class. (Although this property is certainly related to the *DialogResult* property of the *Form* class, the two properties are not the same. Both *Form* and *Button* implement their own *DialogResult* properties; they do not both inherit this property from *Control*.) If the *Dialog-Result* property of the button is set to one of the members of the *DialogResult* enumeration, the button will automatically respond to a click by setting the *DialogResult* property of the form, effectively closing the form.

Let's see how all this works in the context of a simple application. The program will consist of two classes, one for the main application form and the other for the dialog box. Here's the dialog box class.

ModalDialogBox.cs

```
//-----------------------------------------------
// ModalDialogBox.cs (c) 2005 by Charles Petzold
//-----------------------------------------------
using System;
using System.Drawing;
using System.Windows.Forms;

class ModalDialogBox: Form
{
    CheckBox cbGrayShades;

    public ModalDialogBox()
    {
        Text = "Change Color";

        FormBorderStyle = FormBorderStyle.FixedDialog;
        ControlBox = false;
        MinimizeBox = false;
        MaximizeBox = false;
        ShowInTaskbar = false;
        StartPosition = FormStartPosition.Manual;
        Location = ActiveForm.Location +
                   SystemInformation.CaptionButtonSize +
                   SystemInformation.FrameBorderSize;
```

```
        ClientSize = new Size(144, 56);

        cbGrayShades = new CheckBox();
        cbGrayShades.Parent = this;
        cbGrayShades.Text = "Gray Shades Only";
        cbGrayShades.Location = new Point(16, 8);
        cbGrayShades.Size = new Size(80, 12);

        Button btn = new Button();
        btn.Parent = this;
        btn.Text = "OK";
        btn.Location = new Point(16, 32);
        btn.Size = new Size(48, 14);
        btn.DialogResult = DialogResult.OK;
        AcceptButton = btn;

        btn = new Button();
        btn.Parent = this;
        btn.Text = "Cancel";
        btn.Location = new Point(80, 32);
        btn.Size = new Size(48, 14);
        btn.DialogResult = DialogResult.Cancel;
        CancelButton = btn;

        AutoScaleDimensions = new Size(4, 8);
        AutoScaleMode = AutoScaleMode.Font;
    }
    public bool GrayShades
    {
        set
        {
            cbGrayShades.Checked = value;
        }
        get
        {
            return cbGrayShades.Checked;
        }
    }
}
```

The constructor begins by setting the caption bar text for the dialog box; this caption should bear some relationship to the menu item that invoked the dialog box. The properties that follow give the dialog box a non-sizing border (standard for dialog boxes) and hide the control box, minimize box, and maximize box. Setting the *ShowInTaskBar* property to *false* prevents the dialog box from showing up in the user's taskbar.

Without setting the next two properties, the dialog box would be displayed at the next default position on the screen established by Windows. I prefer that the dialog box come up in a location that is somewhat to the right and below the upper-left corner of the application window. The constructor references the *ActiveForm* property to obtain the currently active form, which will be the form that invokes the dialog box. (You can experiment with the *StartPosition* and *Location* properties for other possibilities.)

The program next creates a check box with the text "Gray Shades Only" and two buttons, labeled "OK" and "Cancel." The constructor code assigns the *DialogResult* property of these two buttons to *DialogResult.OK* and *DialogResult.Cancel*, respectively.

The constructor code also assigns the *AcceptButton* and *CancelButton* properties of the dialog box form to the OK and Cancel button objects. These two properties also play an important role in proper dialog box design. The *AcceptButton* property makes the OK button the form's *default* button. It has a thick border and responds to a press of the Enter key even if another control has the input focus. This allows the user to close a dialog box and signal OK to the application just by pressing the Enter key. (If another *button* in the dialog box has the input focus, however, that button becomes the default button and responds to the Enter key.) The *CancelButton* property allows the user to cancel the dialog box at any time just by pressing the Escape key.

Finally, the dialog box class includes a public property that allows code external to the class access to the current checked state of the *CheckBox* control. The property, called *GrayShades*, is defined as a *bool*. The dialog box is essentially treated as an object for obtaining a Boolean value from the user.

No event handlers are installed; this particular dialog box doesn't need them.

The class that makes use of this dialog box is called *ModalDialogDemo*. The ModalDialog-Box.cs and ModalDialogDemo.cs files make up the ModalDialogDemo project.

```
ModalDialogDemo.cs
//-----------------------------------------------
// ModalDialogDemo.cs (c) 2005 by Charles Petzold
//-----------------------------------------------
using System;
using System.Drawing;
using System.Windows.Forms;

class ModalDialogDemo: Form
{
    [STAThread]
    public static void Main()
    {
        Application.EnableVisualStyles();
        Application.Run(new ModalDialogDemo());
    }
    public ModalDialogDemo()
    {
        Text = "Modal Dialog Demo";

        Button btn = new Button();
        btn.Parent = this;
        btn.Text = "Change Color";
        btn.Location = new Point(16, 16);
        btn.AutoSize = true;
        btn.Click += ButtonOnClick;
```

```
    }
    void ButtonOnClick(object objSrc, EventArgs args)
    {
        ModalDialogBox dlg = new ModalDialogBox();

        if (dlg.ShowDialog() == DialogResult.OK)
        {
            Random rnd = new Random();
            int iShade = rnd.Next(255);

            if (dlg.GrayShades)
                BackColor = Color.FromArgb(iShade, iShade, iShade);
            else
                BackColor = Color.FromArgb(iShade, rnd.Next(255), rnd.Next(255));
        }
    }
}
```

The constructor mostly just creates a button and installs a handler for the *Click* event. Although normally a menu item or toolbar item invokes the dialog box, in this program the button does the job. The *Click* handler begins by creating an object of type *ModalDialogBox* and then calling that object's *ShowDialog* method to display the dialog box. When the dialog box is closed, *ShowDialog* returns. If it returns the result *DialogResult.OK*, the program changes the background of the form to a random color. If the user selected the Gray Shades Only check box, the color is restricted to a random gray shade. (Most programs that use dialog boxes are more deterministic than this one.)

When the application form references the property *dlg.GrayShades*, it is actually referencing the check state of the check box. Even though the dialog box is closed and gone from the screen at this point, the form and all its controls still exist in memory. These controls continue to exist until *dlg* goes out of scope, in which case it becomes eligible for disposal and garbage collection. Likewise, the application could have initialized the check box control after creating the dialog box object but before calling *ShowDialog*. An application could initialize the dialog box consistent with current application settings or consistent with the last time the dialog box was invoked.

Modeless Dialog Boxes

The modeless dialog box is much less common. This type of dialog box is considered to be *modeless* because it allows the user to switch focus between the dialog box and the main application window. (The dialog box continues to be visually in front of the application, however.) One common use of the modeless dialog box is search and replace operations. You want to give the user the option to fix something in the document without completely dismissing the dialog box.

The modeless dialog box doesn't contain OK or Cancel buttons, but it does have the standard Close box to the right of the caption bar. The dialog box achieves this appearance by setting the *FormBorderStyle* property to *FixedDialog,* and *MinimizeBox* and *MaximizeBox* to *false,* just as with the modal dialog box, but leaving *ControlBox* set to *true.* Although the *ControlBox* property really refers to the menu icon at the left of the caption bar, the combination of these properties causes the close box to be displayed but the menu icon to be suppressed.

To keep the modeless dialog box in front of the application window, set the *Owner* property of the dialog box to the main application form. The main window can do this after creating the dialog box:

```
dlg.Owner = this;
```

A program invokes a modeless dialog box by calling the *Show* method of *Form* rather than *ShowDialog.* As you'll recall, the *ShowDialog* method doesn't return until the dialog box is closed. *Show,* however, returns immediately so that the main window can continue interacting with the user.

Once *Show* returns, the modeless dialog box is left somewhat stranded with a peculiar problem. The dialog box must usually inform the main window when one of its buttons has been clicked. It can solve this problem using an event. The dialog box defines an event that's raised whenever it wants the main window to be informed of some change, and the main window installs a handler for that event.

Let's call the event *Change,* and assume that any event handler installed for *Change* must be in accordance with the *EventHandler* delegate. The following code would appear in the dialog box class:

```
public event EventHandler Change;
```

You can, if you want, also define your own delegates and base your events on those delegates.

Whenever the class wants to raise this event, it calls the event *Change* as if it were a method, passing arguments defined by the delegate:

```
if (Change != null)
    Change(this, new EventArgs());
```

Change will be equal to *null* if no event handlers have been installed for that event, and *Change* mustn't be called in that case. The first argument is the object raising the event.

The *ModelessDialogBox* class creates a check box like *ModalDialogBox* but with only one button labeled "Change."

ModelessDialogBox.cs

```
//-------------------------------------------------
// ModelessDialogBox.cs (c) 2005 by Charles Petzold
//-------------------------------------------------
using System;
using System.Drawing;
using System.Windows.Forms;

class ModelessDialogBox: Form
{
    CheckBox cbGrayShades;

    public event EventHandler Change;

    public ModelessDialogBox()
    {
        Text = "Change Color";

        FormBorderStyle = FormBorderStyle.FixedDialog;
        MinimizeBox = false;
        MaximizeBox = false;
        ShowInTaskbar = false;
        StartPosition = FormStartPosition.Manual;
        Location = ActiveForm.Location +
                    SystemInformation.CaptionButtonSize +
                    SystemInformation.FrameBorderSize;

        ClientSize = new Size(144, 56);

        cbGrayShades = new CheckBox();
        cbGrayShades.Parent = this;
        cbGrayShades.Text = "Gray Shades Only";
        cbGrayShades.Location = new Point(32, 8);
        cbGrayShades.Size = new Size(80, 12);

        Button btn = new Button();
        btn.Parent = this;
        btn.Text = "Change";
        btn.Location = new Point(48, 32);
        btn.Size = new Size(48, 14);
        btn.Click += ButtonOnClick;
        AcceptButton = btn;

        AutoScaleDimensions = new Size(4, 8);
        AutoScaleMode = AutoScaleMode.Font;
    }
    public bool GrayShades
    {
        set
        {
            cbGrayShades.Checked = value;
        }
        get
        {
```

```
                    return cbGrayShades.Checked;
        }
    }
    void ButtonOnClick(object objSrc, EventArgs args)
    {
        if (Change != null)
            Change(this, new EventArgs());
    }
}
```

Notice how the dialog box raises the *Change* event whenever the user clicks the Change button.

The *ModelessDialogDemo* class displays this modeless dialog box. Both files are part of the ModelessDialogDemo project.

ModelessDialogDemo.cs
```
//---------------------------------------------------
// ModelessDialogDemo.cs (c) 2005 by Charles Petzold
//---------------------------------------------------
using System;
using System.Drawing;
using System.Windows.Forms;

class ModelessDialogDemo: Form
{
    [STAThread]
    public static void Main()
    {
        Application.EnableVisualStyles();
        Application.Run(new ModelessDialogDemo());
    }
    public ModelessDialogDemo()
    {
        Text = "Modeless Dialog Demo";

        Button btn = new Button();
        btn.Parent = this;
        btn.Text = "Change Color";
        btn.Location = new Point(16, 16);
        btn.AutoSize = true;
        btn.Click += ButtonOnClick;
    }
    void ButtonOnClick(object objSrc, EventArgs args)
    {
        ModelessDialogBox dlg = new ModelessDialogBox();

        dlg.Owner = this;
        dlg.Change += DialogOnChange;
        dlg.Show();
    }
    void DialogOnChange(object objSrc, EventArgs args)
    {
```

```
      ModelessDialogBox dlg = (ModelessDialogBox) objSrc;
      Random rnd = new Random();
      int iShade = rnd.Next(255);

      if (dlg.GrayShades)
          BackColor = Color.FromArgb(iShade, iShade, iShade);
      else
          BackColor = Color.FromArgb(iShade, rnd.Next(255), rnd.Next(255));
   }
}
```

During the *ButtonOnClick* event handler, the program creates the dialog box, sets the owner to the main application form, installs a handler for the dialog box's *Change* event, and displays the dialog box with *Show*. *Show* returns after the dialog box is displayed; the main application window can now respond to user input as before.

When the user clicks the Change button in the dialog box, the dialog box raises the *Change* event. The main form responds to that event in its *DialogOnChange* handler. The event handler can obtain the dialog box object by casting the first argument to object of type *ModelessDialogBox*.

If you experiment with DialogBoxDemo, you'll find that you can click the Change Color button several times and actually create multiple copies of the dialog box. This is probably undesirable in a real application. There are a couple ways to avoid that problem. One approach is to store the *dlg* object as a field and simply skip the dialog box creation logic if *dlg* is not equal to *null*. Or, better yet, you can disable the Change Color button in *ButtonOnClick* when you create the dialog box:

```
((Button) objSrc).Enabled = false;
```

The problem now is that the button must be re-enabled when the dialog box is closed. For that, the form can install a handler for the dialog box's *Closed* event:

```
dlg.Closed += DialogOnClosed;
```

The event handler enables the button when the dialog box is closed:

```
void DialogOnClosed(object objSrc, EventArgs args)
{
    Controls[0].Enabled = true;
}
```

In a real program, the button object would probably be saved as a field. Here I've simply accessed the first item in the form's *Controls* collection.

The .NET Framework 2.0 defines seven standard dialog boxes all descended from *CommonDialog*: *ColorDialog*, *FolderBrowserDialog*, *FontDialog*, *OpenFileDialog* and *SaveFileDialog* (both descended from *FileDialog*), *PageSetupDialog*, and *PrintDialog*.

DLLs

Dynamic-link libraries contain code and data that programs and other DLLs can use. Source code for dynamic-link libraries looks much the same as program source code except for three major differences:

- DLLs have no *Main* method.

- Classes must be defined as *public* to be visible outside the DLL.

- It is courteous to include a *namespace* definition.

The namespace is good idea in case you (or somebody else using your DLL) wants to use another DLL that has the same class name in your DLL. The namespace avoids name clashes. A recommended format for the namespace is a company name, a period, and a product name. Here's source code that implements the *MessageButton* class in a DLL.

```
MessageButtonLib.cs
//------------------------------------------------
// MessageButtonLib.cs (c) 2005 by Charles Petzold
//------------------------------------------------
using System;
using System.Drawing;
using System.Windows.Forms;

namespace Petzold.ProgrammingWindowsForms
{
    public class MessageButton: Button
    {
        string strMessageBoxText;

        public MessageButton()
        {
            Enabled = false;
        }
        public string MessageBoxText
        {
            set
            {
                strMessageBoxText = value;
                Enabled = value != null && value.Length > 0;
            }
            get
            {
                return strMessageBoxText;
            }
        }
        protected override void OnClick(EventArgs args)
        {
            base.OnClick(args);
            MessageBox.Show(MessageBoxText, Text);
        }
    }
}
```

It's quite similar to the MessageButton.cs file except that now there's a *namespace* definition and the class is defined as *public*. I've also added a statement to the *OnClick* method to call the same method in the base class (which is *Button*). Without this statement, a program couldn't attach a *Click* event handler for *MessageButton*.

To compile MessageButtonLib.cs on the command line, you use the */target:library* flag and the compiler creates a MessageButtonLib.dll file. In Visual Studio, you can begin by creating a Class Library project, or, in the properties dialog box for the project, specify the Output Type to be Windows Class Library.

I created the MessageButtonLib project in a Visual Studio solution named MessageButton-LibraryDemo. In that same solution, I created another project named ProgramUsingLibrary that has a single source code file resembling the earlier MessageButtonDemo program.

ProgramUsingLibrary.cs

```
//---------------------------------------------------
// ProgramUsingLibrary.cs (c) 2005 by Charles Petzold
//---------------------------------------------------
using System;
using System.Drawing;
using System.Windows.Forms;
using Petzold.ProgrammingWindowsForms;

class ProgramUsingLibrary: Form
{
    [STAThread]
    public static void Main()
    {
        Application.EnableVisualStyles();
        Application.Run(new ProgramUsingLibrary());
    }
    public ProgramUsingLibrary()
    {
        Text = "Program Using Library";

        MessageButton msgbtn = new MessageButton();
        msgbtn.Parent = this;
        msgbtn.Text = "Calculate 10,000,000 digits of PI";
        msgbtn.MessageBoxText = "This button is not yet implemented!";
        msgbtn.Location = new Point(50, 50);
        msgbtn.AutoSize = true;
    }
}
```

Notice the new *using* directive referring to the namespace in the DLL. As with any *using* directive, it's optional. If I didn't use it, I'd have to refer to the fully qualified class name *Petzold.ProgrammingWindowsForms.MessageButton*.

What's not optional, however, is a new reference. We've been compiling our Windows Forms programs with references to the *System*, *System.Drawing*, and *System.Windows.Forms* assemblies, all of which are DLLs. We now need a reference to MessageButtonLib.dll so that the compiler can obtain the necessary metadata needed to compile this program.

On the command line, you can include a */reference* flag indicating the location of the Message-ButtonLib.dll file. In Visual Studio, you can bring up the Add Reference dialog box and choose the Projects tab. There you will see the MessageButtonLib assembly conveniently listed.

When Visual Studio builds the solution, you want it to compile the DLL before compiling the program that uses the DLL. After you've indicated that the DLL is a reference to the program, Visual Studio should realize that the program relies on the DLL, so when you look at the Build Order tab of the Project Dependencies dialog box (obtainable from the Project menu or by right-clicking the solution name) you should see everything in order.

When you have multiple projects in a solution, Visual Studio compiles everything but runs only one project. It indicates this startup project in boldface type in the Solution Explorer. If that's not ProgramUsingLibrary, right-click the project name and select Set As Startup Project.

Now you're ready to build the solution. Visual Studio compiles the DLL and then compiles the program. Because the ProgramUsingLibrary.exe files requires MessageButtonLib.dll to run, Visual Studio copies the DLL file into the directory with the EXE file.

It's hard to believe that creating a DLL was once regarded as an advanced Windows programming topic.

Chapter 2
The Control Cornucopia

Without a doubt, the most important class in Windows Forms is *Control*. From this single class spills a cornucopia of tools for building Windows Forms applications. Not only is *Control* the base class for such familiar controls as buttons, tree views, toolbars, and menus, it is also the base class for *Form*—the class that encapsulates the main window of a Windows Forms application and performs additional duty as dialog boxes.

As you've seen, the default *Form* object features a title bar with a system menu at the left and minimize, maximize, and close buttons at the right. Around the circumference is a sizing border. Within the window is the form's client area—the canvas on which the program presents information and tools to the user. Programs can display text and graphics directly on this client area, and receive keyboard and mouse input through methods such as *OnKeyPress* and *OnMouseDown*. But most modern programs instead populate the client area with child controls—essentially delegating the jobs of user input and graphical output. Programs can also create their own custom controls, either from scratch, by enhancing existing controls, or by combining multiple controls.

This chapter is a guide to the controls defined in the *System.Windows.Forms* namespace, with descriptions of the most important properties and events (and, occasionally, methods) you need to use these controls. Of course, a single chapter (nor an entire book) can ever replace the .NET Framework documentation.

Some descendents of the *Control* class are *not* discussed in this chapter because they get more extensive treatment in later chapters.

Chapter 3 covers the *SplitContainer* control, as well as controls derived from *Panel*, including *FlowLayoutPanel*, *SplitterPanel*, and *TableLayoutPanel*. I don't discuss the *Splitter* control in this book because it's been superseded by *SplitContainer* and *SplitterPanel*. (*Splitter* is the subject of the beginning of Chapter 22 in my earlier book *Programming Microsoft Windows with C#* [Microsoft Press, 2002].)

Chapter 5 focuses on *ToolStrip*, *MenuStrip*, *ContextMenuStrip*, *StatusStrip*, and all other controls that begin with the prefix *ToolStrip*. I don't discuss the .NET Framework 1.x menu or the *ToolBar* and *StatusBar* controls because they have been superseded by *MenuStrip*, *ToolStrip*, and *StatusStrip*. (The .NET Framework 1.x menu is discussed in Chapter 14 of *Programming Microsoft Windows with C#*. *ToolBar* and *StatusBar* are covered in Chapter 20.)

Chapter 6 explores the *BindingNavigator* and *DataGridView* controls, and all controls that begin with the prefix *DataGridView*. I don't discuss *DataGrid* or *DataGridTextBox* in this book because they have been superseded by *DataGridView* and *DataGridViewTextBoxEditingControl*.

Chapter 7 presents programs that make use of *MdiClient*, *PropertyGrid*, and *WebBrowser*.

Controls in General

Almost everything you see on the screen in Microsoft Windows is a control of some sort. Indeed, a control can be roughly defined as a visual object. Controls generally occupy a rectangular area on the screen—although they can be nonrectangular in appearance or hidden from view—and are capable of receiving user input from the keyboard and mouse. You'll find many events (and corresponding *On* methods) defined in the *Control* class that signal user input. Keyboard events are *KeyDown*, *KeyUp*, and *KeyPress*, and mouse events include *MouseDown*, *MouseUp*, and *MouseMove*, among others. Controls also need to "paint" themselves on the screen; that job is commonly performed in the control's *OnPaint* method.

By consolidating user input into simpler events, controls provide a layer of abstraction between the application and the user. For example, to use a *Button* control, a program need do little more than specify the text displayed by the button and install an event handler for the *Click* event. The *Button* control itself handles everything else.

It is often useful to experiment with controls to see how they work. You can do this in Microsoft Visual Studio, of course, or you can use a program called ControlExplorer that I've written solely for this purpose. Because ControlExplorer uses some programming techniques discussed in later chapters, it can be found among the programs in Chapter 7.

ControlExplorer has a menu that lists every public class in the *System.Windows.Forms* assembly that derives from *Control*. The menu's hierarchy parallels the inheritance hierarchy. When you select a control from the menu, the program creates that control in the upper-left corner of the client area. The program also displays a dialog box that lets you change many properties of the control, examine read-only properties, and observe events generated by the control.

As I discuss each control in the following sections, you might want to explore that control using ControlExplorer.

Parents and Children

One of the most important properties defined by the *Control* class is *Parent*, which you set to another object of type *Control*. A control must have a valid *Parent* if it is to be visible on the screen. A control is always positioned relative to its parent and always appears on the surface of its parent. If the control is sized and positioned so that part of the control is hanging off the side of its parent, that part of the control will not be visible.

The big exception to this rule is the *Form* class. An object of type *Form* generally has its *Parent* property set to *null*, which really means that the form's parent is the desktop. However, if the *TopLevel* property of *Form* is set to *false* (meaning that the form's parent is *not* the desktop), a *Form* object can be a child to another control. This technique is used in Multiple Document Interface (MDI) applications. (The *Form* class defines a property named *Owner* that you can set to another object of type *Form*. A form will always appear in front of its owner on the screen and will be minimized or closed if the owner is minimized or closed. This facility is useful for modeless dialog boxes. The owner of a modeless dialog box should be set to the application that created it.)

In the simplest case, an object of type *Form* creates a bunch of controls and sets the controls' *Parent* property to itself. You might see this code in a form's constructor:

```
Button btn = new Button();
btn.Parent = this;
```

The statement that assigns the *Parent* property of the button is functionally equivalent to the statement

```
this.Controls.Add(btn);
```

or

```
Controls.Add(btn);
```

Controls is a property defined by the *Control* class and inherited by *Form*. It is an object of type *Control.ControlCollection*—that is, an instance of the *ControlCollection* class that is defined within the *Control* class. The *Controls* property essentially stores all the children of the *Control*. The *Add* method adds a control to the collection, and *Remove* removes it:

```
Controls.Remove(btn);
```

That statement is functionally equivalent to

```
btn.Parent = null;
```

The *Controls* property can be indexed like an array. Indices begin at zero. For example, a form can obtain the fourth control added to its collection with the expression

```
Controls[3]
```

This expression returns an object of type *Control*. If the form knows that this object is a *Button*, for example, it can be cast to an object of type *Button* using

```
Controls[3] as Button
```

or

```
(Button) Controls[3]
```

There is a difference between these two casts: The *as* expression returns *null* if *Controls[3]* is not a *Button* object. The C-style casts throws an exception if *Controls[3]* is not a *Button*. A program can test whether a particular *Control* object is a *Button* using an *is* expression, as shown in the following code:

```
if (Controls[3] is Button)
{
    Button btn = Controls[3] as Button;
    ...
}
```

A form can step through all the controls in its control collection using a *for* loop:

```
for (int i = 0; i < Controls.Count; i++)
{
    Control ctrl = Controls[i];
    ...
}
```

It's also common to use a *foreach* loop for this job:

```
foreach (Control ctrl in Controls)
{
    ...
}
```

Although any control can be a parent to other controls, in actual practice, only a few descendents of *Control* are commonly used as parents. These are *Form*, *Panel* and its descendents, and *GroupBox*. In the simplest case, controls are children of the form, but the parent-child hierarchy can go much deeper: A *Form* can populate its client area with several *Panel* controls, for example, and these panels can be parent to their own child controls.

Controls descended from *Panel* and *ContainerControl* (including *Form*) provide focus management among their children. Generally, the user can navigate among controls using the Tab key. Only controls whose *TabStop* property is set can receive input focus. The order in which controls receive input focus is governed by the *TabIndex* property of sibling controls, or the z-order, which is the order that controls are added to the control collection.

Controls that share the same parent (and are hence members of the same control collection) are known as *sibling* controls.

Visibility and Response

By default, controls are both visible and enabled. If you set the *Visible* property to *false*, the control will disappear from the surface of its parent. The control still exists and is still a member of the parent's control collection, but otherwise it's as if it's gone. All children of the invisible control will also become invisible.

Much more common than changing a control's *Visible* property is changing the *Enabled* property. A control with its *Enabled* property set to *false* is still visible on the screen, but it's given a somewhat washed-out appearance. A disabled control cannot receive input focus, and it does not respond to keyboard or mouse input.

It is common to enable and disable controls based on the settings of other controls. For example, in a File Open dialog box, the Open button is disabled if the user has not yet specified a file name.

Location and Size

Traditionally, each control is assigned a specific size and a location relative to the upper-left corner of its parent. The location of a control is set by the *Location* property, which is a *Point* object, which has two properties, *X* and *Y*. The coordinates are in units of pixels and indicates the location of the upper-left corner of the control relative to the upper-left corner of its parent. The size of the control is governed by the control's *Size* property, an object of type *Size*, which has two properties, *Width* and *Height*.

The following code sets the location of a button at the point (50, 100) and gives it a size of 75 pixels wide and 25 pixels high:

```
btn.Location = new Point(50, 100);
btn.Size = new Size(75, 25);
```

The problem, of course, is that your program can run on different systems with different screen resolutions. You might also need to translate the program to another language. Some languages are more succinct or verbose than others, and that can affect the size of a control that needs to display text.

As controls get more complex, it becomes difficult to anticipate and set a proper size for the control. In fact, it makes more sense for the control itself to determine its proper size, and for controls to be arranged dynamically at runtime based on the sizes they want to be. Dynamic layout has become such an important design concept that the entire next chapter is devoted to it.

Some new properties in the .NET Framework 2.0 help out. *Control* defines a new read-only property named *PreferredSize* that returns the size the control wants to be based on its contents and the current font. A read/write property named *AutoSize* is very powerful. Normally this property is *false* for most controls, but if you set it to *true*, the *Size* property of the control will be set to *PreferredSize*.

Some (but not all) controls have an *AutoSizeMode* property that you set to a member of the *AutoSizeMode* enumeration. The values *GrowOnly* and *GrowAndShrink* affect how the control reacts at runtime when its contents change.

Also new in the .NET Framework 2.0 are properties named *Padding* and *Margin*. These properties are used in dynamic layout and are discussed in the next chapter.

Two other properties important in layout are *Dock* and *Anchor*. The *Dock* property causes a control to be positioned flush against a particular side of its parent and extend the full width of that side. To use docking, you set this property to a member of the *DockStyle* enumeration: *Left*, *Right*, *Top*, *Bottom*, or *Fill*. For example, it is common for a toolbar to have a *Dock* property of *DockStyle.Top* and a status bar to have *DockStyle.Bottom*. A *Dock* property of *DockStyle.Fill* causes the control to fill up the parent's client area.

The *Anchor* property causes a control to remain a constant distance from a particular side or sides of its parent when the size of the parent changes. The property can be set to any combination of members of the *AnchorStyles* enumeration. The default setting is *AnchorStyles.Left | AnchorStyles.Right*, which means that when a parent is changed in size, the control remains in the same position relative to the left and right sides.

I'll have much more to say about *Dock* and *Anchor* in the next chapter.

Fonts and Color

Every control has a *Text* property, although some controls (such as scroll bars) don't display any text. For a *Form* object, the *Text* property is the text displayed in the form's title bar.

A control inherits its initial *Font*, *BackColor*, and *ForeColor* properties from its parent. If these properties in the parent are later changed, the control changes its own properties accordingly. However, if you explicitly set different properties for the control, the control will retain those properties and not be affected by the parent.

You set a *Font* property to an object of type *Font*. For example, the statement

```
btn.Font = new Font("Times New Roman", 24, FontStyle.Italic);
```

sets the button font to 24-point italic Times New Roman.

The *BackColor* and *ForeColor* properties denote the background color and foreground color of the control. The foreground color is often the color of the control's text. Some controls ignore these properties or use them in different ways. You can set these properties to any *Color* object you create (commonly by using the static *Color.FromArgb* method) or one of the static members of the *Color* structure:

```
btn.ForeColor = Color.HotPink;
```

By default, the *BackColor* and *ForeColor* properties of controls are set to *SystemColors.Control* and *SystemColors.ControlText*, respectively. The default *Form* object has these default colors, as well. Because *SystemColors.Control* is commonly gray, the background of a form's client area is gray, which is more common for dialog boxes than main application windows. If you prefer having your form display black text on a white background, include these statements in the form's constructor:

```
BackColor = SystemColors.Window;
ForeColor = SystemColors.WindowText;
```

It's better to refer to system colors rather than white and black so as not to override the preferences of users who see the screen better with white text on a black background. For these users, *SystemColors.Window* will be black and *SystemColors.WindowText* will be white.

The *BackgroundImage* property lets you specify an image (either a bitmap or a metafile) in the background of the control. A new property in the .NET Framework 2.0 named *Background-ImageLayout* gives you control over situations where the image is not exactly the same size as the control.

Keeping Track of Controls

Your form might have a number of child controls. As an example, consider a dialog box with a collection of controls and an OK button. It could be that the dialog box can entirely ignore what the user is doing until the OK button is pressed. At that point, the dialog box would interrogate all the controls to obtain text, check marks, and so forth. A program structured in this way wouldn't need to set event handlers for all the other controls. Instead, it would need a way to access each control.

One approach is to store each control object as a field. Every control is then accessible throughout the class. There are other techniques, however. Throughout the form class, you have access to all the child controls through the *Controls* collection. You can identify a particular control in that collection through its type, its *Text* property, or the *Name* property, which is provided specifically for this purpose.

In fact, beginning in the .NET Framework 2.0, you can even index the *Controls* collection using the *Name* property. Suppose you gave one of your buttons this name:

```
btn.Name = "ok";
```

In some other method in your form, you could obtain this button object with the following code:

```
Button btn = Controls["ok"] as Button;
```

The *Controls* collection returns an object of type *Control* and the *as* expression casts it to an object of type *Button*. The *Controls* property is an instance of the *Control.ControlCollection* class, and this class provides a number of methods, such as *Contains* and *Find*, that help you manage a collection of child controls.

You can also attach arbitrary objects to a control using the *Tag* property. The *Tag* property is useful for identifying a bunch of similar controls. For example, if you used check-box controls for applying italics and boldfacing to text, you could identify the check-box control by setting the *Tag* property equal to *FontStyle.Italic* and the other using *FontStyle.Bold*.

Image Lists

As you've seen, the *Controls* property defined by the *Control* class stores a collection of child controls. The .NET Framework is full of collections like this, and some classes—such as *Image-List*—exist mostly to serve as a collection of objects. *ImageList* is a collection of *Image* objects (a category that includes bitmaps and metafiles) of the same size and color depth. *ImageList* is not a control, but it is used extensively with controls.

The primary property of *ImageList* is named *Images*, which is an object of type *ImageList.Image-Collection*. You first need to create an object of type *ImageList*:

```
ImageList imglst = new ImageList();
```

You can then add images to the list using the *Add* method of *ImageList.ImageCollection*. If *img* is an *Image* object of some sort, the code is

```
imglst.Images.Add(img);
```

Beginning in the .NET Framework 2.0, you can also associate a text "key" with the image:

```
imglst.Images.Add("arrow", img);
```

You can then obtain that image by indexing the *Images* property using the key

```
imglst.Images["arrow"]
```

This is a good way to organize a bunch of icons or other images used in a program.

Where do these images come from? You can make them yourself, or you can take advantage of a collection of bitmaps and icons included in Visual Studio 2005 (but not, unfortunately, in Visual C# 2005 Express Edition). These can be found in a ZIP file located in the directory *\Program Files\Microsoft Visual Studio 8\Common7\VS2005ImageLibrary*. I'll have an example using icons from this collection toward the end of the chapter.

ToolTips

Like *ImageList*, the *ToolTip* class is not a control, but it works closely in conjunction with controls. A ToolTip is some helpful text in a little balloon that generally appears when the mouse pointer hovers over a control. The *ToolTip* class lets you organize all the ToolTips for controls on a particular form.

You first create an object of type *ToolTip*, probably in the constructor of the form:

```
ToolTip tips = new ToolTip();
```

Then, for each control in the form that you want to assign a ToolTip, you call *SetToolTip*. Here's an example for a *Button* control named *btn*:

```
tips.SetToolTip(btn, "Displays the Help window");
```

The *ToolTip* class contains several properties—named *AutomaticDelay*, *InitialDelay*, *ReshowDelay*, and *AutoPopDelay*—that control the time required for a ToolTip to be displayed and how long it is displayed, but generally the defaults work well.

Static (and Not Quite so Static) Controls

The Microsoft Win32 API had a couple of static box–like controls. These are so trivial to implement that Windows Forms doesn't even bother to provide them. Instead, what I think of as "static" controls are those that generally have a minimum amount of interactivity with the user. (Nevertheless, they can still respond to mouse clicks if you want.) In this section, I discuss the following controls shown in the partial class hierarchy from *Control*:

Control

> *GroupBox*
>
> *Label*
>
> > *LinkLabel*
>
> *PictureBox*
>
> *ProgressBar*

GroupBox

The group box displays a line around its perimeter with some optional text at the top indicated by its *Text* property. The line around the control is a darker variation of the group box's background color.

Traditionally, you use a group box as a parent to radio buttons. All the radio buttons within a particular group box are mutually exclusive. Pressing the keyboard arrow keys moves the input focus and check mark from one radio button to another. The *GroupBox* is not a descendent of *ContainerControl* because *ContainerControl* implements navigation using the Tab key.

It's not necessary for radio buttons to be children of a *GroupBox*. Any control can serve as a common parent to a group of mutually exclusive radio buttons. It's not the group box that handles the checking and unchecking logic but the radio buttons themselves. In the next chapter, I show a replacement to the *GroupBox* that doesn't require the radio buttons to be explicitly positioned.

Label

A label is a control for displaying noneditable text to the user. Specify the text as the control's *Text* property. Although a label can wrap text into multiple lines, it does not display scroll bars if the text is too large to fit the control. If you have lots of text to display but still don't want the user to edit it, you can use a *TextBox* control with the *ReadOnly* property set to *true*.

Besides text, a label can display an *Image* object, which can be either a *Bitmap* object or a *Metafile* object. (These classes are defined in the *System.Drawing* and *System.Drawing.Imaging* namespaces.) One approach is to set the *Image* property to a loaded file:

```
lbl.Image = Image.Load("SillyCat.jpg");
```

You can also use images that are defined as resources and are bound into the program's executable file. I demonstrate how to do this toward the end of this chapter.

LinkLabel

The *LinkLabel* is surely not a *static* control—it's closer to a *Button* in functionality—but I'm including it in this section because it derives from *Label*. The control displays a text string that is wholly or partly differentiated to indicate that clicking it triggers some action, such as launching an application or bringing up a Web page. In addition to defining the normal *BackColor* and *ForeColor* properties, the *LinkLabel* defines four other color properties:

- *LinkColor* (default is blue)
- *DisabledLinkColor* (grayish)
- *ActiveLinkColor* (red when the link is triggered)
- *VisitedLinkColor* (a dark magenta)

The *LinkArea* property of *LinkLabel* is an object of type *LinkArea*, which is a structure with two integer properties named *Start* and *Length*. For example, suppose you've defined the *Text* property of a *LinkLabel* control like this:

```
lnklbl.Text = "Click here to display the page."
```

Perhaps you want the word "here" to be the link. Define *LinkArea* to indicate that the link starts at the sixth character position and is four characters in length:

```
lnklbl.LinkArea = new LinkArea(6, 4);
```

The appearance of this part of the character string is governed by the *LinkBehavior* property, which you set to a member of the *LinkBehavior* enumeration. There are four members:

- *AlwaysUnderline*
- *HoverUnderline*

- *NeverUnderline*

- *SystemDefault*

The default is *SystemDefault*, which obtains the behavior from the user's Microsoft Internet Explorer options.

You can also have multiple links on a single label. In that case, you use a property of *LinkLabel* called *Links*. *Links* is a *LinkLabel.LinkCollection* object, which is a collection of *LinkLabel.Links* objects.

When the user clicks the link, the *LinkLabel* triggers a *LinkClicked* event. An event handler for *LinkClicked* must be defined in accordance with the *LinkLabelLinkClickedEventHandler* delegate. The *LinkLabelLinkClickedEventArgs* object that accompanies the event includes an object of type *LinkLabel.Links* to identify the link that was clicked.

A Windows Forms program can respond to a clicked link by starting another process, using the *Process.Start* method of the *System.Diagnostics* namespace. You don't need the name of the executable associated with the link—you can pass a filename or a URL.

Here's a small program that creates a single *LinkLabel* control with three different links associated with three different Web pages:

LinkLabelDemo.cs

```
//---------------------------------------------
// LinkLabelDemo.cs (c) 2005 by Charles Petzold
//---------------------------------------------
using System;
using System.Diagnostics;
using System.Drawing;
using System.Windows.Forms;

class LinkLabelDemo : Form
{
    [STAThread]
    public static void Main()
    {
        Application.EnableVisualStyles();
        Application.Run(new LinkLabelDemo());
    }
    public LinkLabelDemo()
    {
        Text = "LinkLabel Demo";
        Font = new Font("Times New Roman", 14);

        LinkLabel lnklbl = new LinkLabel();
        lnklbl.Parent = this;
        lnklbl.Dock = DockStyle.Fill;
        lnklbl.LinkClicked += LinkLabelOnLinkClicked;

        lnklbl.Text = "Jane Austen Societies exist in North America, the " +
```

```
                           "United Kingdom, and Australia, among other places.";

        string str = "North America";
        lnklbl.Links.Add(lnklbl.Text.IndexOf(str), str.Length,
                         "http://www.jasna.org");

        str = "United Kingdom";
        lnklbl.Links.Add(lnklbl.Text.IndexOf(str), str.Length,
                         "http://www.janeaustensoci.freeuk.com");

        str = "Australia";
        lnklbl.Links.Add(lnklbl.Text.IndexOf(str), str.Length,
                         "http://www.jasa.net.au");
    }
    void LinkLabelOnLinkClicked(object objSrc, LinkLabelLinkClickedEventArgs args)
    {
        LinkLabel.Link lnk = args.Link;
        string strLink = lnk.LinkData as string;

        Process.Start(strLink);
    }
}
```

To make the text a bit more visible, the constructor defines a new *Font* property for the form. This font will be inherited by all child controls of the form.

The only child of this form is a *LinkLabel* control, which is given a *Dock* property of *DockStyle.Fill* so that it's the same size as the form's client area. The text displayed by the control will automatically wrap if the width of the control is not large enough.

After setting the *Text* property, the program sets three links using a three-argument *Add* method of the *Links* property. Rather than manually counting characters, I decided to define a short text string corresponding to the link and then use the *IndexOf* method of the *String* class to determine where that short string was located in the label's *Text* property. The *Length* property defined by the *String* class provides the string's length. A URL is passed as the third argument to *Add*. This URL becomes the *LinkData* property of a *LinkLabel.Link* object created by the *Add* method. The *LinkLabel* shows those links in the customary way:

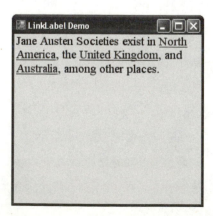

Clicking one of the links triggers a *LinkClick* event and a call to the *LinkLabelOnLinkClicked* method defined in the program. The first argument is the control generating the link. If the event handler needed to know where the event came from, it could cast that argument to an object of type *LinkLabel*:

```
LinkLabel lnklbl = objSrc as LinkLabel;
```

But it doesn't need that information. The event handler instead obtains the *LinkLabel.Link* object from the second argument to the event handler, and then casts the *LinkData* property to an object of type *string*. That's the URL associated with the link. Passing that string to *Process.Start* launches your default Web browser.

PictureBox

The *PictureBox* control displays an image, which is either a bitmap or a metafile. You specify this image by the *Image* property. Or you can create an *ImageList* collection of various images and set the *PictureBox* property *ImageList* to that object. You denote the image you want to display by using either *ImageIndex* (a numeric index within the image list) or *ImageKey* (which lets you reference the image with a text string).

The *SizeMode* property of *PictureBox* gives you control over the way the image is stretched to fit the control. Set *SizeMode* to a member of the *PictureBoxSizeMode* enumeration. For the first three options in the following list, the image is displayed in its pixel size with no stretching:

- *Normal*: The image is oriented at upper-left corner of the control.
- *CenterImage*: The image is positioned in the center of the control.
- *AutoSize*: The control is sized to the image.
- *StretchImage*: The image is stretched to the control's size.
- *Zoom*: The image is stretched without distortion.

The *PictureBox* control is demonstrated in the ImageDirectory program in Chapter 4 and the ImageFiler program in Chapter 5.

With the .NET Framework 2.0, the *PictureBox* control has several new properties that let you specify a URL or a local file name by using the *Load* or *LoadAsync* methods. The *LoadAsync* method loads the file in a secondary thread of execution and signals completion with the *LoadCompleted* event. You can even specify an *InitialImage* to be displayed while the image is loading and an *ErrorImage* if an error occurs during loading.

Another event named *LoadProgressChanged* optionally delivers a progress percentage to your application. You can use this to display a *ProgressBar* control.

ProgressBar

The primary properties of the *ProgressBar* are *Minimum*, *Maximum*, and *Value*, all of which are integers. As a job is progressing, you set *Value* to a number ranging from *Minimum* to *Maximum*.

Alternatively, you can increase *Value* by passing an integer argument to the *Increment* method. Or you can call the *PerformStep* method, which increases *Value* by the amount you specified in the *Step* property.

New in the .NET Framework 2.0 is the *Style* property, which you set to a member of the *ProgressBarStyle* enumeration:

- *Blocks* (the default)
- *Continuous*
- *Marquee*

However, the *Marquee* option just shows some animation and not progress, and it's available only when your program is running under Windows XP.

Of course, if you really want to endear yourself to the hearts of users, you will focus less on making the progress bar unusual and more on making it accurately reflect the progress of the job. A progress bar that moves from 0 to 95 percent in 30 seconds and then hangs at the 95 percent mark for several minutes does not qualify.

Push Buttons and Toggles

A control qualifies as a button not just because it can be clicked—every control can be clicked to generate a *Click* event—but mostly because it gives visual feedback to the user when it's been clicked. The three types of buttons all derive from the abstract *ButtonBase* class:

Control

    ButtonBase (abstract)

        Button

        CheckBox

        RadioButton

The regular *Button* is for triggering actions, the *CheckBox* is for indicating on/off options, and the *RadioButton* usually indicates one of several mutually exclusive options.

It is common for buttons to display text, of course, but some buttons—particularly instances of the *Button* class—display images, either alone or with text. The *ButtonBase* class defines an *Image* property that is inherited by all three types of buttons and lets you specify a bitmap or metafile to be displayed. Alternatively, you can set the *ImageList* property of *ButtonBase* and specify the particular image by using the *ImageIndex* or *ImageKey* properties. (Using the *Image-List* makes sense only if you're working with a lot of buttons that have images. You'd specify the same *ImageList* object for all these buttons but different *ImageIndex* or *ImageKey* properties for each button.)

If you want the button to display both text and an image, you'll want to set the *TextImage-Relation* property defined by *ButtonBase*. You set this property to a member of the *TextImage-Relation* enumeration, which has members *ImageAboveText*, *ImageBeforeText*, *TextAboveImage*, *TextBeforeImage*, and *Overlay*.

The *TextAlign* and *ImageAlign* properties indicate how the text or image is positioned within the control. Both are members of the *ContentAlignment* enumeration, which has nine members—all the combinations of *Top*, *Middle*, and *Bottom* with *Left*, *Center*, and *Right*. The default for both *TextAlign* and *ImageAlign* is *ContentAlignment.MiddleCenter*.

Button

The *Button* class adds little to *ButtonBase*. Almost always, you'll want to install a handler for the *Click* event. The only exception is when you set the *DialogResult* property to a member of the *DialogResult* enumeration (generally, *DialogResult.OK* or *DialogResult.Cancel*) as demonstrated in Chapter 1.

CheckBox

CheckBox controls commonly display a little square to the left of the text. However, if you set the *Appearance* property to *Appearance.Button* (the default is *Appearance.Normal*), the control will resemble a push button, except that the state will toggle. You can also alter the appearance of the *CheckBox* control by setting the *CheckAlign* property to a member of the *ContentAlignment* enumeration. The default is *ContentAlignment.MiddleLeft*, which means that the check box appears vertically aligned with the middle of the text and to the left of the text.

The Boolean *Checked* property indicates whether the button currently displays a checkmark. The *CheckedChanged* event signals when the check mark state changes.

By default, the *AutoCheck* property is *true*, meaning that the button automatically toggles its check mark and fires a *CheckedChanged* event based on keyboard or mouse input. If you need to respond whenever the check mark changes (for example, to enable or disable other controls), you'll want to install a handler for the *CheckedChanged* event. If you don't need to respond to each change, it might be possible to just take note of the *Checked* property when the user finishes the form and presses the OK button.

If you set the *AutoCheck* property to *false*, you'll probably want to trap the *Click* event and control the checking and unchecking yourself by setting the *Checked* property programmatically. Setting the *Checked* property in this way will also generate a *CheckedChanged* event.

Sometimes checked boxes need to display an indeterminate state besides being simply check or unchecked. For example, suppose a *CheckBox* exists for controlling italic text. If the currently selected text has both italic and nonitalic text, the *CheckBox* should be set to an indeterminate state. (On the other hand, if the currently selected text uses a font that doesn't support italic, the *CheckBox* should be disabled.)

To use this third state, first set the Boolean *ThreeState* property to *true*. Rather than using the *Checked* property for the checked state, use the *CheckState* property. This is a value from the *CheckState* enumeration, whose members are *Unchecked*, *Checked*, and *Indeterminate*. Rather than installing a handler for *CheckedChange*, install a handler for *CheckStateChanged*. If you've called the *EnableVisualStyles* method of the *Application* class, the indeterminate state will appear as a little square box. If you haven't called it, a gray check mark will be displayed.

If *AutoCheck* is set to *true*, repeatedly clicking a three-state check box will make it change in a cycle from unchecked to checked to indeterminate and back to unchecked. If this is not what you want, set *AutoCheck* to *false* and install a *Click* event handler to manually set the *CheckState*.

RadioButton

The *RadioButton* control normally displays a circle to the left of its text. Like the *CheckBox* control, the *RadioButton* class has an *Appearance* property that you can set to *Appearance.Button* to make the control look like a push button, and it has a *CheckAlign* property that lets you move the check circle someplace else in relation to the text.

Just like *CheckBox* also, the *RadioButton* has a Boolean *Checked* property, and whenever this *Checked* property changes, a *CheckedChanged* event is fired.

By default, the *AutoCheck* property is *true*, but here's where the *RadioButton* is quite unlike the *CheckBox*: If *AutoCheck* is *true* and a *RadioButton* is currently checked, clicking the mouse on the button has no effect. If *AutoCheck* is *true* and the *RadioButton* is currently unchecked, clicking the mouse on the button causes it to become checked. In addition, all *sibling* radio buttons become unchecked. This is how only one sibling *RadioButton* is checked at any time. By convention, a collection of mutually exclusive radio buttons are made children of a *GroupBox*, but they can really have any common parent.

Here's a program that assembles seven *RadioButton* controls on the form's client area:

```
ColorRadioButtons.cs
//-------------------------------------------------
// ColorRadioButtons.cs (c) 2005 by Charles Petzold
//-------------------------------------------------
using System;
using System.Drawing;
using System.Windows.Forms;
```

```
class ColorRadioButtons : Form
{
    public static void Main()
    {
        Application.EnableVisualStyles();
        Application.Run(new ColorRadioButtons());
    }
    public ColorRadioButtons()
    {
        Text = "Color Radio Buttons";

        Color[] aclr = { Color.Red, Color.Orange, Color.Yellow, Color.Green,
                        Color.Blue, Color.Indigo, Color.Violet };

        int y = Font.Height;

        foreach (Color clr in aclr)
        {
            RadioButton radio = new RadioButton();
            radio.Parent = this;
            radio.Location = new Point(Font.Height, y);
            radio.Text = clr.Name;
            radio.AutoSize = true;
            radio.Tag = clr;
            radio.CheckedChanged += RadioButtonOnCheckedChanged;

            y += radio.Height;
        }
    }
    void RadioButtonOnCheckedChanged(object objSrc, EventArgs args)
    {
        RadioButton radio = objSrc as RadioButton;
        BackColor = (Color)radio.Tag;
    }
}
```

An array of *Color* objects store the colors of the rainbow. In the *foreach* loop, the text of each button is assigned the name of the color. The *Tag* property—used for storing arbitrary data—gets assigned the *Color* object itself. All the radio buttons have the same event handler for the *CheckedChanged* event.

The first argument to this event handler is the object raising the event. This is cast to a *RadioButton*, and then the *Tag* property of the control is cast to a *Color* object, which is then used to set the *BackColor* property of the form. This color also becomes the background color of the radio buttons themselves:

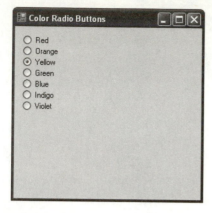

Notice also the keyboard interface provided for sibling radio buttons: You can move the checked button using the cursor arrow keys.

Just as with *CheckBox*, you don't need to install a handler for the *CheckedChanged* event if you don't need to respond immediately to the changes. However, at some point you'll need to determine which radio button is checked, and for this job you'll have to loop through the sibling radio buttons and examine their *Checked* properties.

If you set *AutoCheck* to *false*, you'll want to handle the *Click* event and do all the checking and unchecking yourself. You can, if you want, have more than one radio button checked at a time and make users quite confused.

Scroll Bars

Scroll bars are most commonly found on the right side and at the bottom of controls such as *ListBox*, *ComboBox*, and *TextBox* (when used in a multiline mode as in Windows Notepad). These controls display scroll bars automatically. Controls that derive from *ScrollableControl*—including *Form* and *Panel*—also display scroll bars when their *AutoScroll* property is set to *true* and child controls are arranged so that the layout exceeds the parent's size.

In addition to those automatic scroll bars, you can also create scroll-bar controls yourself. Viewed abstractly, a scroll bar allows the user to pick a particular integer from a continuous range of integers. The scroll-bar thumb indicates a position within this range. Similar in functionality but different in appearance is the track bar. The class hierarchy is:

Control

    ScrollBar (abstract)

        HScrollBar

        VScrollBar

    TrackBar

The *TrackBar* control has an *Orientation* property that governs whether it's horizontal or vertical. Both the scroll-bar and track-bar controls change the thumb position automatically in response to the user without program participation.

Horizontal and Vertical Scrolls

The most important properties implemented by *ScrollBar* are *Minimum*, *Maximum*, *SmallChange*, *LargeChange*, and *Value*. These are all integers. The program sets all these properties to initial values; the user can then change the *Value* property by clicking or manipulating the scroll bar.

Clicking the arrows at each end of the scroll bar increase or decrease *Value* by *SmallChange*, which is almost always set to 1; clicking anywhere between the arrows and the thumb changes the *Value* by *LargeChange*. The user can also move the thumb directly with the mouse. If the scroll bar has the input focus, it responds to the cursor arrow keys, Page Up, Page Down, Home, and End.

Value does *not* range from *Minimum* to *Maximum*. *Value* ranges from *Minimum* to (*Maximum* - *LargeChange* + 1). To understand the rationale behind this, consider a word-processing document. Let's assume that the document has 1000 lines (numbered 0 through 999), and the document window in the program is currently large enough to display 20 lines. Use these values directly in setting the scroll-bar properties: set the scroll bar *Mininum* to 0, the *Maximum* to 999, and *LargeChange* to 20. Use the scroll bar *Value* to determine the line of the document to display at the top of the program's window. When the user scrolls down to the bottom of the document, *Value* equals (*Maximum* - *LargeChange* + 1) or 980. Display line 980 at the top of the window, and line 999 will be at the bottom of the window.

The advantage of this scheme is that the scroll bar can base the size of the thumb on the ratio between *LargeChange* and *Maximum* because that's the proportion of the document that is currently in view.

ScrollBar implements two crucial events: *ValueChanged* and *Scroll*. *ValueChanged* is the much easier event to handle, and it occurs (as its name suggests) whenever the *Value* property changes. Within the event handler, you can obtain the new value just by using the following code:

```
void ScrollOnValueChanged(object objSrc, EventArgs args)
{
    int ivalue = ((ScrollBar) objSrc).Value;
    ...
}
```

However, there are cases when you're not getting quite enough information from *ValueChanged*. If the user grabs the scroll-bar thumb with the mouse and quickly moves it back and forth, your program might have a hard time keeping up. If that's the case, you might want to process the *Scroll* event. Event handlers for the *Scroll* event must be defined in accordance with the *ScrollEventHandler* delegate. The event handler is delivered an object of type *Scroll-EventArgs*, which has four properties, named *OldValue*, *NewValue*, *ScrollOrientation*, and *Type*. (*OldValue* and *ScrollOrientation* are new with the .NET Framework 2.0.)

A program handling the *Scroll* event can actually prevent the scroll-bar thumb from responding to the user by setting the *NewValue* to *OldValue* (which is also the existing *Value* property). The *ScrollOrientation* property is a member of the *ScrollOrientation* enumeration, which has two values *HorizontalScroll* and *VerticalScroll*. This property lets you use the same event handler for both a horizontal and vertical scroll and easily differentiate between them.

The *Type* property is an object of type *ScrollEventType*, an enumeration that indicates precisely how the user is manipulating the scroll bar. The nine members of *ScrollEventType* are defined in the following table:

Member	Description
SmallDecrement	Mouse: Left or top arrow button
	Keyboard: Left or Up arrow key
SmallIncrement	Mouse: Right or bottom arrow button
	Keyboard: Right or Down arrow key
LargeDecrement	Mouse: Left or top area
	Keyboard: Page Up key
LargeIncrement	Mouse: Right or bottom area
	Keyboard: Page Down key
ThumbPosition	Mouse button released from scroll-bar thumb
ThumbTrack	Mouse button pressed on scroll-bar thumb, or mouse moving scroll-bar thumb
First	Keyboard: Home key
Last	Keyboard: End key
EndScroll	Scrolling operation completed

A program with sluggish scroll-bar response can ignore everything except when the *Type* property is *ScrollEventType.EndScroll*.

For example, if the user clicks the right or bottom scroll-bar arrow key and holds it, the scroll bar generates two alternating events for every movement of the thumb: First a *Scroll* event with a *Type* property of *ScrollEventType.SmallIncrement* and a *NewValue* one greater than the *Value* property. If the program doesn't alter *NewValue* (the normal case), a *ValueChanged* event follows. When the thumb finally reaches *MaxValue*, *ValueChanged* events cease, but *Scroll* events continue. Finally, when the user releases the mouse button, a final *Scroll* event is generated with a *Type* property of *ScrollEventType.EndScroll* and a *NewValue* the same as *Value*.

When the user grabs and moves the scroll-bar thumb with the mouse, the scroll bar generates alternating *Scroll* events and *ValueChanged* events. The release of the user's finger from the mouse button is signaled by two final *Scroll* events with *Type* properties of *ScrollEvent-Type.ThumbPosition* and *ScrollEventType.EndScroll*.

Track Bars

The *TrackBar* control is conceptually similar to the two scroll-bar controls, but it looks quite different and functions a bit differently. Like the *ScrollBar* class, the *TrackBar* class contains the integer properties *Minimum*, *Maximum*, *SmallChange*, *LargeChange*, and *Value*. *Value* ranges from *Minimum* to *Maximum*.

The same *TrackBar* class supports both horizontal and vertical track bars, settable through the *Orientation* property. The corresponding *Orientation* enumeration contains two fields, *Horizontal* and *Vertical*.

The track bar displays little lines known as *ticks*. The *TickStyle* property and enumeration lets you specify *None*, *TopLeft*, *BottomRight*, or *Both*. The default is *TickStyle.BottomRight*, which means that the ticks appear on the bottom of horizontal track bars and at the right of vertical track bars.

The *TickFrequency* property is an integer that specifies the number of discrete *Value* settings between tick marks. The total number of ticks equals (*Maximum - Minimum + 1*) / *TickFrequency*. The default is 1, so watch out: If you change the default *Maximum* value from 10 to 100, for example, the ticks will probably compound into a single black bar.

Like the scroll bar, the track bar implements *Scroll* and *ValueChanged* events. However, when handling user input, there seems to be no difference between these two events: The two events occur in tandem, and both are delivered with simple *EventArgs* objects. Programmatic changes of the track bar Value property trigger *ValueChanged* events but not *Scroll* events.

Scroll bars are familiar to users and should probably be used for scrolling items on the screen. Track bars are probably best restricted to letting the user choose a discrete value from a range. It's probably helpful to include a label that indicates the selected value. For an example, look at the track bar in the Settings tab of the Display Properties dialog box (which can be invoked through Control Panel or by right-clicking the screen).

The up/down control (sometimes called a *spin control*) is an alternative to the track bar for picking discrete values from a range.

Text-Editing Controls

Windows Forms has several controls for entering and editing text, as shown in the following class hierarchy:

Control

> *TextBoxBase* (abstract)
>
>> *MaskedTextBox*
>>
>> *TextBox*
>>
>>> *DataGridTextBox*
>>>
>>> *DataGridViewTextBoxEditingControl*
>>
>> *RichTextBox*

I discuss the *DataGridViewTextBoxEditingControl* (which essentially replaces the older *DataGridTextBox* control) in Chapter 6.

The most important property of a text-editing control is, of course, *Text*, which is the text appearing in the control. A program can initialize the text in the control just by setting the *Text* property, and a program can retrieve the text entered or edited by a user by accessing the *Text* property. If *txtbox* is an object of type *TextBox*, the control can be cleared of text with the statement

```
txtbox.Text = "";
```

Text can be appended to the text already in the control with code like this:

```
txtbox.Text += " and that's the truth";
```

Many important properties of these controls are defined in the abstract *TextBoxBase* class. The *Multiline* property—which indicates whether the control can accept and display multiple lines of text—is *false* by default for *TextBox* and *MaskedTextBox* but *true* by default for *RichTextBox*. The *WordWrap* property is familiar to users of Windows Notepad. It applies only to multiline controls and is *true* by default. You can make a control display uneditable text by setting the *ReadOnly* property to *true*.

The user can select text using the keyboard or mouse. The *SelectedStart* and *SelectedLength* properties are integers indicating the character index where the selection begins and the length in characters. *SelectedText* is the selected text itself. *TextBoxBase* implements its own clipboard cut, copy, paste, and undo operations based on the standard keyboard combinations (Ctrl+X, Ctrl+C, Ctrl+V, and Ctrl+Z, respectively). In addition, methods named *Cut*, *Copy*, *Paste*, and *Undo* are provided for performing these clipboard operations programmatically, perhaps in response to menu commands.

The most important event for using these controls is *TextChanged*, which occurs whenever the *Text* property changes.

MaskedTextBox

The *MaskedTextBox* is new with the .NET Framework 2.0. It is designed for single-line text entry where certain configurations of numbers or letters are required, such as the entry of telephone numbers, currency amounts, dates, or e-mail addresses. Much of the documentation for using this control can be found in the description of the *Mask* property, which is the character string that governs the proper input.

If the user tries to type something prohibited by the mask, a *MaskInputRejected* event is fired. It is accompanied by a *MaskInputRejectedEventArgs* object that has two properties: *Position* is an integer index of the character in question, and *RejectionHint* is a text string intended to be displayed directly to the user, perhaps in a *Label* control nearby.

TextBox

The *TextBox* control is the simplest form of text-editing control, but it's sophisticated enough to be the basis of Windows Notepad.

TextBox adds just a few properties to *TextBoxBase*. Perhaps the most important is *ScrollBars*, which you can set to the enumeration value *ScrollBars.Vertical*, *ScrollBars.Horizontal*, or *ScrollBars.Both*. The default is *ScrollBars.None*, which means that scroll bars will not be displayed even if the text in the control warrants them. (If the *WordWrap* property is *true*, horizontal scroll bars won't be displayed, regardless of the *ScrollBars* setting.)

If you're using a *TextBox* control for password entry, you can set *PasswordChar* to a character that will appear when the user types. Also useful in this respect is the *CharacterCasing* property. Set the property to the enumeration value *CharacterCasing.Lower* or *CharacterCasing.Upper* to convert all typed characters to lowercase or uppercase.

RichTextBox

The *RichTextBox* control stores text in the Microsoft Rich Text Format (RTF), which goes back many years[1] and supports paragraph and character formatting. The URL *http://support.microsoft.com/kb/q86999* has a link to the RTF 1.7 specification. In its Win32 form, the *RichTextBox* control is the basis of the Windows WordPad program.

The *RichTextBox* is multiline by default. Like *TextBox*, *RichTextBox* has a *ScrollBars* property, but for *RichTextBox*, the property must be set to a member of the *RichTextScrollBars* enumeration. The default is *RichTextScrollBars.Both*, which displays both horizontal and vertical scroll bars, but only when they're required. Other options are *None*, *Horizontal*, *Vertical*, *ForcedHorizontal*, *ForcedVertical*, and *ForcedBoth*. The *Forced* values display the scroll bars even if they're not required.

---

1. For an early discussion, see the article by Nancy Andrews, "Rich Text Format Standard Makes Transferring Text Easier," *Microsoft Systems Journal*, Vol. 2, No. 1, March 1987.

The *RichTextBox* control allows a program to specify formatting only on the currently selected text. You get or set formatting on the current selection by using properties that begin with the word *Selection*. In some cases—when the user selects some text and then selects Font from the Format menu, for example—this scheme is ideal. The program can create a new *Font* object named *fnt* (for example) and set it to the *SelectionFont* property of the *RichTextBox* control:

```
rtb.SelectionFont = fnt;
```

However, if a program needs to set the color for some text that's not currently selected—perhaps to indicate the source of an error in a text editor as part of a rudimentary integrated development environment—the process is messier. The program needs to save the values of the *SelectionStart* and *SelectLength* properties indicating the user's current selection. Then the *Select* method needs to be called with a character index and length to select the text to be colored. This selection can be colored by setting the *SelectionColor* property to the desired *Color* object. The program concludes by using *Select* to restore the value of the user's selection.

SelectionBackColor and *SelectionColor* are *Color* properties for the background and text colors, respectively, of the selection. *SelectionFont* is of type *Font*. The only other character formatting is *SelectionCharOffset*, which is the horizontal offset expressed in pixels. Use a positive value for superscripting and a negative value for subscripting.

Everything else is paragraph formatting. *SelectionAlignment* is a member of the enumeration *HorizontalAlignment*, which has three members: *Left*, *Right*, and *Center*. There is no "justified" setting. *SelectionBullet* is a Boolean to force bullet marks to appear before each paragraph. *SelectionIndent*, *SelectionRightIndent*, and *SelectionHangingIndent* are all integer values specified in units of pixels. *SelectionRightIndent* is measured from the right side of the control. The indentation of the first line of the paragraph is indicated by *SelectionIndent* and is measured from the left side of the control. *SelectionHangingIndent* is the indentation of the remainder of the paragraph relative to *SelectionIndent*. (This is not quite how normal word-processing programs let you specify indentation.) *SelectionTabs* is an array of integers indicating tab positions.

Chapter 4 shows how to write a WordPad-like ruler that works with the *RichTextBox* to specify indentation and tabs. Chapter 5 has a WordPad-like toolbar that lets you set character formatting and alignment.

The *Text* property of the *RichTextBox* sets and retrieves only naked text without any RTF tags. Use the *Rtf* property to obtain the rich text in all its glory. *RichTextBox* has built-in file I/O methods named *LoadFile* and *SaveFile*.

List and Combo Boxes

In the most general and abstract sense, the *ListBox* control allows a user to pick one or more items from a list of items. The *ComboBox* optionally allows the user to enter a text item that is not in the list. These controls derive from the abstract *ListControl* class:

Control

    ListControl (abstract)

        ComboBox

            DataGridViewComboBoxEditingControl

        ListBox

            CheckedListBox

I'll discuss the *DataGridViewComboBoxEditingControl* in Chapter 6.

In recent years, the *ListBox* control has fallen out of fashion in favor of the *ComboBox*, which takes up less screen real estate. The only feature of value that *ListBox* has that *ComboBox* doesn't is its ability to allow the selection of multiple items. However, *CheckedListBox* is visually preferable for that particular feature.

Nevertheless, I discuss *ListBox* in the greatest detail because it historically predates the other controls and many of its concepts are carried over into those controls.

ListBox

A list box displays a scrollable collection of objects. By default, the user can choose one (or possibly several) with the keyboard or the mouse. The selected object or objects are highlighted.

You set the items to be displayed in the *ListBox* through the *Items* property, which is an object of type *ListBox.ObjectCollection*. The *ListBox.ObjectCollection* class defines an *Add* method that you use to add any object to the collection. The items are displayed using the text representation available from each object's *ToString* method. The *Sorted* property of *ListBox* automatically sorts the items. You can then index the *Items* property of the *ListBox* object like an array.

You can also fill the list box by attaching a data source, which is an object that implements the *IList* interface (for example, an array) or a *DataSet* object. If *astrStateNames* is an array of state names, you can fill the list box with the statement

```
lstbox.DataSource = astrStateNames;
```

I'll have more to say about this and related techniques in Chapter 6.

The *SelectedIndex* property is the index of the currently selected item. It could be -1 if no item is selected. The *SelectedItem* property is the actual item (of type *object*). It could be *null*. If an item is selected, the expression

```
lstbox.SelectedItem
```

is equivalent to

`lstbox.Items[lstbox.SelectedIndex]`

and

`lstbox.Text`

is the same as

`lstbox.SelectedItem.ToString()`

By default, the user can select only one item from the list box. However, you can allow multiple selections by setting the *SelectionMode* property to a member of the *SelectionMode* enumeration: *None*, *One*, *MultiSimple*, and *MultiExtended*. The *MultiSimple* option changes the appearance of the *ListBox* somewhat by separating the selection (indicated by highlighting) and input focus (indicated by a dotted line). The cursor keys move the input focus; pressing the spacebar or clicking with the mouse selects or deselects an item. The *MultiExtended* option allows only consecutive items to be selected by holding down the Shift key while pressing the arrow keys.

For multiselection list boxes, you retrieve the selected items by using the read-only properties *SelectedIndices* (an object of type *ListBox.SelectedIndexCollection*, which you can index like an array of integers) or *SelectedItems* (an object of type *ListBox.SelectedObjectCollection*, which you can index like an array of objects).

To be informed whenever the selected item or items change, you can install an event handler for either *OnSelectedIndexChanged* or *OnSelectedValueChanged*.

If you would prefer that the items in the list box be displayed by something other than *ToString*, you can use a feature of the *ListBox* control called "owner draw." In this case, your program is notified through events when it's time to draw the item.

To use owner-draw, first set the *DrawMode* property to either *DrawMode.OwnerDrawFixed* (which means all the items in the list box have the same height) or *DrawMode.OwnerDraw-Variable* (which means that items can have different heights). By default, the *DrawMode* property is set to *DrawMode.Normal*, which means that the control does the drawing.

If all the items have the same height, set the *ItemHeight* property to that height. Otherwise, you'll need to handle the *MeasureItem* event. Define the event handler in accordance with the *MeasureItemEventHandler* delegate. The *MeasureItemEventArgs* object delivered with the message has the read-only properties *Graphics* and *Index*, which is the integer index of the item. The *Graphics* property is an object of type *Graphics*, which can be helpful for calculating the height of the item. Your responsibility is to set the *ItemHeight* and *ItemWidth* properties to the height and width of the item.

If you're implementing owner draw, you'll also need to install an event handler for *DrawItem*. The handler is called for each item to be displayed, accompanied by an object of type *DrawItemEventArgs* with several read-only properties: the *BackColor*, *ForeColor*, and *Font* properties are those of the *ListBox*. The *Bounds* property is a *Rectangle* object in which you'll do your drawing. You're supplied with a *Graphics* object and an *Index* of the item. The *State* property is a member of the *DrawItemState* enumeration, which indicates whether the item is selected, has input focus, and so forth. The *DrawItemEventArgs* class also includes two methods, *DrawBackground* and *DrawFocusRectangle*, that can help in drawing the item.

CheckedListBox

If you're implementing a multiple-selection *ListBox*, you might want to consider using a *CheckedListBox* instead. This style of list box displays check boxes to the left of each item. The keyboard and mouse interfaces are conceptually a bit easier than in multiple-selection list boxes, and the check marks make clear which items have been chosen by the user. (The ControlExplorer program in Chapter 7 uses a checked list box for the user to indicate which events to display.)

With checked list boxes, the *SelectionMode* can be only *SelectionMode.One* or *SelectionMode.None*. (The latter seems to produce odd behavior and should be avoided.) At any time, only one item is selected and appears highlighted. Multiple items can be checked, however, and are indicated by check marks in the check boxes. You can make the check boxes appear sunken by setting the *ThreeDCheckBoxes* property to *true*.

The keyboard arrow keys change the selected (highlighted) item. The spacebar toggles the check mark, that is, changes it from unchecked to checked or vice versa.

When you click an item with the mouse, the item is selected and appears highlighted. When you click it again, the check mark is toggled. The check mark remains in that state when the selection changes. You'll probably want to avoid forcing the user to click an item twice to check it, and you can do so by setting the *CheckOnClick* property to *true*. That change causes the check mark to be toggled whenever the item is clicked.

Two additional *Add* methods to the item collection let you initialize the check marks as you're adding items. You can set the second argument to *true* or *false* to set the check state:

```
ckdlstbox.Add("New Jersey", true);
```

Or you can use the *CheckState* enumeration (discussed earlier in connection with *CheckBox* controls) to set the state to the members *Checked, Unchecked,* or *Indeterminate*:

```
ckdlstbox.Add("New York", CheckState.Indeterminate);
```

You can change the check state later by specifying the index of the item

```
SetItemChecked(5, true)
```

An overload of the method works with the CheckState enumeration:

```
SetItemCheckState(7, CheckState.Unchecked)
```

The read-only properties *CheckedIndices* and *CheckedItems* provide collections of integer indices or objects that are currently checked. You can also be informed whenever a check mark changes by installing a handler for the *ItemCheck* event. The handler must be defined in accordance with the *ItemCheckEventHandler* delegate. The *ItemCheckEventArgs* object delivered with the event has properties for the item *Index* and its *CurrentValue* and *NewValue*, both expressed as members of the *CheckState* enumeration.

ComboBox

The "combo" of the *ComboBox* control refers to the combination of a list box and a text box at the top. Normally, only the text box is visible with a down-arrow at the right. Clicking the arrow makes the list box appear underneath. By default, the user can type in the text box to select an item in the list box or edit the text that appears there, or to type entirely new text. Any text the user types is *not* automatically added to the list-box collection; the program must do that on its own. Many programs will want to prohibit the user from editing the text. That behavior is governed by the *DropDownStyle* property, which is a member of the *ComboBoxStyle* enumeration:

- *Simple*: Editable text, the list is always present
- *DropDown*: Editable text, the list drops down (default)
- *DropDownList*: Noneditable text, the list drops down

A program can cause the list box to drop down (or determine whether it's currently dropped) using the *DroppedDown* property.

As with *ListBox*, a program can use the *SelectedIndex* and *SelectedItem* properties to set or obtain the currently selected item. Combo boxes do not provide a multiple-selection option. The currently selected item also appears in the text box part of the control and is available through the *Text* property. If the user is currently typing something into the text box field, *SelectedIndex* equals -1 and *SelectedItem* is *null*.

As with *ListBox*, you can determine when the selection has changed by installing event handlers for *SelectedIndexChanged* or *SelectedValueChanged*. The *TextChanged* event signals when the text changes in the top part of the *ComboBox*, either by a change in selection or by the user typing into the control.

The *ComboBox* supports owner draw just like *ListBox*. I demonstrate an owner-draw *ComboBox* control in the FontDialogMimic program of Chapter 3.

Up/Down Controls

Up/down controls are also called *spin controls*. Because the up/down controls include both an edit box and buttons, they are considered container controls with a long progeny:

Control

    ScrollableControl

        ContainerControl

            UpDownBase (abstract)

                NumericUpDown

                DomainUpDown

The *NumericUpDown* control allows a number to be selected from a range. *DomainUpDown* is similar to *ListBox* in that it allows selecting one object out of a collection. Both use buttons labeled with arrows, and both respond to the cursor arrow keys.

NumericUpDown

The most important properties of the *NumericUpdown* control are *Minimum*, *Maximum*, *Increment*, and *Value*, which are all *decimal* values. (The C# *decimal* type corresponds to the *Decimal* structure in the *System* namespace. Unlike *float* and *double*, the *decimal* data type allows storage of exact values with up to 28 decimal places.) *DecimalPlaces* is another important property of *NumericUpDown*. You might initialize such a control like so:

```
updn.DecimalPlaces = 2;
updn.Minimum = 5.25m;
updn.Maximum = 5.50m;
updn.Interval = 0.05m;
```

Then by using the arrow keys or clicking the arrows, *Value* can take on the values 5.25, 5.30, 5.35, 5.40, 5.45, and 5.50. However, the user can type something else between *Minimum* and *Maximum*—for example, 5.33. Then, after pressing the up-arrow key, the next value is 5.38.

Two Boolean properties are *false* by default. *ThousandsSeparator* causes a comma (or whatever is culturally appropriate) to be displayed in large numbers, and *Hexadecimal* displays the results in base 16.

The control beeps if the user attempts to enter something outside the range, and it sets the *Value* to either *Minimum* or *Maximum*. Setting the *ReadOnly* property to *false* prohibits the user from typing a value.

The crucial event is *ValueChanged*.

DomainUpDown

The *DomainUpDown* control looks like the *NumericUpDown* control, but it stores objects and displays text strings. The *Items* property is a collection of objects stored in an instance of the *DomainUpDown.DomainUpDownItemCollection* class. You can add items just like in a *ListBox*:

```
domain.Items.Add("New Jersey");
domain.Items.Add("New York");
domain.Items.Add("New Hampshire");
domain.Items.Add("New Mexico");
domain.Items.Add("New Rochelle");
```

A change in the selected item is indicated by the *SelectedItemChanged* event. You can then access the item by the *SelectedItem* property or indexing the *Items* collection with *SelectedIndex*.

Dates and Times

The .NET Framework defines a *DateTime* structure in the *System* namespace that's used extensively throughout .NET for storing and rendering dates and times. A new *DateTime* object is generally obtained in one of two ways: through use of the static *Now* property, which creates a *DateTime* object with the current date and time, or by using one of the many constructors that allow specifying a date, with or without a time. For example, here's the creation of a *DateTime* object representing August 29, 2006:

```
DateTime dt = new DateTime(2006, 8, 29);
```

The *DateTime* structure provides read-only properties named *Year*, *Month*, *Day*, *Hour*, *Minute*, *Second*, and *Millisecond* for obtaining information about the date and time, and it also provides several methods for formatting the date and time in accordance with cultural conventions.

Windows Forms has two standard date-related controls. The *MonthCalendar* control is intended to obtain a date from the user; the *DateTimePicker* control can obtain both a date and a time from the user, but it is often used to obtain just a date.

MonthCalendar

The *MonthCalendar* control displays a calendar month with the current date circled in red and displayed at the bottom. The user can select up to seven consecutive days using the mouse or the keyboard. With the keyboard, use the arrow keys to move to the first date of the range, hold down the Shift key, and use the arrow keys to move to the last date. To flip the page to other months, click the arrows at the top or press Page Up or Page Down.

A program obtains the currently selected range from the two properties *SelectionStart* and *SelectionEnd*, both of which are of type *DateTime*. (Alternatively, the *SelectionRange* property is an object of type *SelectionRange*, which has *Start* and *End* properties.)

A program can be notified of a change in the selected dates by installing a handler for the *Date-Changed* event based on the *DateRangeEventHandler*. The event delivers an object of type *Data-RangeEventArgs*, which has two *DateTime* properties named *Start* and *End*. (The other event implemented by the *MonthCalendar* class is called *DateSelected*, but it doesn't really provide anything useful.)

To extend or limit the number of consecutive days the user can select, use the *MaxSelection-Count* property. You can set the property to 1 to restrict the user to a single date. Normally, the user can go back in time several centuries or travel several millennia into the future. To restrict time travel, you set the *MinDate* and *MaxDate* properties to *DateTime* values.

You can suppress the display of the current date at the bottom of the control by setting *Show-Today* to *false*. Suppress the circling of the current date by setting *ShowTodayCircle* to *false*. Set a different date for "today" with the *TodayDate* property. The *ShowWeekNumbers* property causes the weeks to be numbered at the left of the calendar, starting with the first full week of the year.

If you want the calendar to be displayed differently based on local customs, don't change the *FirstDayOfWeek* property from the enumeration value *Day.Default*. Leaving the property alone allows the control to correctly begin with *lundi* (Monday) when your program is run in France.

The *BoldedDates*, *MonthlyBoldedDates*, and *AnnuallyBoldedDates* properties are all arrays of *DateTime* objects. The *MonthCalendar* class includes *Add* and *Remove* methods for creating and maintaining these arrays.

The *MonthCalendar* control will size itself appropriately. With default settings, the control requires approximately 13 font heights in width and 11 font heights in height. A program can try to set the *Size* property, but the control will reject anything too small to fit a single month. If the *Size* property is made large enough for multiple months to be displayed (horizontally or vertically or both), the control will display multiple months and reduce the *Size* property to the exact value required to display those months.

To deliberately display multiple months, examine the read-only *SingleMonthSize* property at runtime. This property takes account of the current font and the *ShowToday* and *Show-WeekNumbers* properties. The total width needs to be a little more than an integral multiple of *SingleMonthSize.Width* because the control adds a little internal horizontal spacing between the months. (Probably the approach that combines safety and simplicity is to add another half of *SingleMonthSize.Width*.) The height can be a little less than *SingleMonthSize.Height* because the single month size includes the current date, and that appears only on the bottom of the control.

For example, to display six months with three months across and two months down, use

```
moncal.Size = new Size(7 * moncal.SingleMonthSize.Width / 2,
                       2 * moncal.SingleMonthSize.Height);
```

If you then need to know the exact size of the control, check the *Size* property.

DateTimePicker

Although the *DateTimePicker* control goes beyond the *MonthCalendar* control in allowing the user to select both a date and time, it's often used just for dates. (In fact, that's its default mode.) Unlike *MonthCalendar*, the *DateTimePicker* doesn't allow the user to choose a range of dates.

When first created, the *DateTimePicker* looks something like a combo box, with a text field and an arrow at the right. To initialize the control, a program can set the *Value* property to an object of type *DateTime*; otherwise, the control will initialize itself with the value *DateTime.Now*.

After *Value*, the most crucial property of *DateTimePicker* is *Format*, which you set to a member of the *DateTimePickerFormat* enumeration. The default is *Long*, which displays a date such as "Tuesday, August 02, 2005" (with standard U.S. English regional settings). The *DateTime-PickerFormat.Short* option displays "8/1/2005" and *DateTimePickerFormat.Time* displays just the time. For custom formats and combinations of date and time, set the *Format* property to *DateTimePickerFormat.Custom* and use *CustomFormat* to specify the components of the date and time you want to display.

Whatever format you choose, the user can directly edit the various fields (month, day, year, and so forth). Clicking the right arrow causes a calendar month to drop down, which you can navigate just as in *MonthCalendar*.

The *ValueChanged* event indicates when the *Value* property changes.

The following program displays two *DateTimePicker* controls on a small window and calculates the number of years, months, and days between the two dates. The LifeYears program is based on a similar Win32 API program I wrote for a friend who needed it for putting together some genealogical information. In that version, I labeled the two controls "Birth Date" and "Death Date." Because I figured that most readers of this book would experiment with the program by calculating how long they've lived, I decided to denote the controls with less ominous labels.

```
LifeYears.cs
//-----------------------------------------
// LifeYears.cs (c) 2005 by Charles Petzold
//-----------------------------------------
using System;
using System.Drawing;
using System.Windows.Forms;

class LifeYears : Form
{
    DateTimePicker dtpBeg, dtpEnd;
    Label lblResult;
```

```
    [STAThread]
    public static void Main()
    {
        Application.EnableVisualStyles();
        Application.Run(new LifeYears());
    }
    public LifeYears()
    {
        Text = "LifeYears";

        Label lbl = new Label();
        lbl.Parent = this;
        lbl.Text = "Begin Date: ";
        lbl.AutoSize = true;
        lbl.Location = new Point(Font.Height, Font.Height);

        int xDateTimePicker = lbl.Right;

        lbl = new Label();
        lbl.Parent = this;
        lbl.Text = "End Date: ";
        lbl.AutoSize = true;
        lbl.Location = new Point(Font.Height, 3 * Font.Height);

        xDateTimePicker = Math.Max(xDateTimePicker, lbl.Right);

        lbl = new Label();
        lbl.Parent = this;
        lbl.Text = "Life Years:";
        lbl.AutoSize = true;
        lbl.Location = new Point(Font.Height, 5 * Font.Height);

        xDateTimePicker = Math.Max(xDateTimePicker, lbl.Right);

        dtpBeg = new DateTimePicker();
        dtpBeg.Parent = this;
        dtpBeg.AutoSize = true;
        dtpBeg.Location = new Point(xDateTimePicker, Font.Height);
        dtpBeg.ValueChanged += DateTimePickerValueChanged;

        dtpEnd = new DateTimePicker();
        dtpEnd.Parent = this;
        dtpEnd.AutoSize = true;
        dtpEnd.Location = new Point(xDateTimePicker, 3 * Font.Height);
        dtpEnd.ValueChanged += DateTimePickerValueChanged;

        lblResult = new Label();
        lblResult.Parent = this;
        lblResult.AutoSize = true;
        lblResult.Location = new Point(xDateTimePicker, 5 * Font.Height);

        ClientSize = new Size(dtpEnd.Right + Font.Height, 7 * Font.Height);
    }
    void DateTimePickerValueChanged(object objSrc, EventArgs args)
    {
```

```
        if (dtpBeg.Value >= dtpEnd.Value)
        {
            lblResult.Text = "";
        }
        else
        {
            DateTime dtBeg = dtpBeg.Value;
            DateTime dtEnd = dtpEnd.Value;

            int iYears = dtEnd.Year - dtBeg.Year;
            int iMonths = dtEnd.Month - dtBeg.Month;
            int iDays = dtEnd.Day - dtBeg.Day;

            if (iDays < 0)
            {
                iDays += DateTime.DaysInMonth(dtEnd.Year,
                                    1 + (dtEnd.Month + 10) % 12);

                iMonths -= 1;
            }
            if (iMonths < 0)
            {
                iMonths += 12;
                iYears -= 1;
            }
            lblResult.Text = String.Format("{0} year{1}, {2} month{3}, {4} day{5}",
                                iYears, iYears == 1 ? "" : "s",
                                iMonths, iMonths == 1 ? "" : "s",
                                iDays, iDays == 1 ? "" : "s");
        }
    }
}
```

The controls are positioned—and the application window is sized—based on the height of the default font and the sizes of the controls when *AutoSize* is set to *true*:

Whenever one of the dates changes, a *ValueChanged* event is triggered, and LifeYears is notified by a single event handler installed for both controls. The handler determines the difference between the two dates and sets the label named *lblResult* accordingly.

DateTime objects can be subtracted to obtain an elapsed time. The difference between two *DateTime* objects is a *TimeSpan* object, which represents an elapsed time in units of tenths of microseconds. Properties in the *TimeSpan* structure named *Microseconds*, *Seconds*, *Minutes*, *Hours*, and *Days* let you convert that into something less miniscule, but there are no similar properties in *TimeSpan* named *Months* and *Years*, and for good reason. Months and years don't have a uniform number of days. I wanted the LifeYears program to calculate a result in years, months, and days that would be similar to the approach a person would take. If the begin date is the 10th of the month and the end date is the 15th of the month, I wanted the label to display "5 days" regardless of the years or months involved.

The tricky part in that calculation involved a begin day of a month that was greater than an end day—for example, a begin date of May 20 and an end date of October 10. I wanted the calculation to result in 4 months (that is, from May 20 to September 20) and 20 days (September 20 to October 10). This goal required taking account of the number of days in the month preceding the end date. The static *DaysInMonth* method of *DateTime* and some modulo arithmetic did the trick. (The only reason *DaysInMonth* has an argument for the year is to return the proper value for February. Otherwise, the year argument is irrelevant.)

Tree View and List View

The *TreeView* and *ListView* controls are familiar to users of Microsoft Windows as the two major components of the Windows Explorer program. A *TreeView* control displays a hierarchical list and is often used to display a directory tree or something patterned after a directory tree. A *ListView* control displays a list of items in several formats, including a table that contains other information about each item. In Windows Explorer, the *ListView* control displays files and subdirectories located in the directory selected in the *TreeView* control. Both controls derive directly from *Control*:

Control

    TreeView

    ListView

TreeView

Each item in the hierarchical list displayed by a *TreeView* control is called a "node" and is an object of type *TreeNode*. Each node is potentially a parent to other nodes. A node's children are stored in the property of the *TreeNode* class called *Nodes*, which is an object of type *TreeNodeCollection*—a collection of other *TreeNode* objects. *TreeView* itself also has a property named *Nodes* that contains the top-level nodes of the hierarchy.

You can create a *TreeNode* object by using a parameterless constructor and setting the *Text* property:

```
TreeNode nodeCats = new TreeNode();
nodeCats.Text = "Cats";
```

Or you can pass the text of the node directly to a one-argument constructor:

```
TreeNode nodeSiamese = new TreeNode("Siamese");
```

You can then make one of these nodes a child of the other using the *Add* method of the node's *TreeNodeCollection* accessible through the *Nodes* property:

```
nodeCats.Nodes.Add(nodeSiamese);
```

Or you can implicitly create a node by passing the text of the node to another version of the *Add* method:

```
nodeCats.Nodes.Add("Calico");
```

Of course, you'll need a *TreeView* object to display all these nodes:

```
TreeView tree = new TreeView();
```

You can add the top-level nodes to the *TreeView* control by using the same *Add* methods:

```
tree.Nodes.Add(nodeCats);
tree.Nodes.Add("Dogs");
```

You can later access these nodes by indexing the *Nodes* property. For example, the statement

```
TreeNode node = tree.Nodes[0].Nodes[1];
```

retrieves the node for the Calico cat.

TreeNode has a bunch of properties to facilitate navigating through the nodes. These include *Parent*, which is the parent node, and the properties *FirstNode*, *LastNode*, *NextNode*, and *PrevNode*, all of which return sibling nodes. Another interesting property of *TreeNode* is named *FullPath*, and it returns a text string consisting of the concatenation of the *Text* properties of all the parent nodes going back to the beginning, separated by the backslash. For example, the expression

```
nodeCalico.FullPath
```

returns the string Cats\Calico. If you'd prefer that the backslash not be used, you can change it to some other string by setting the *PathSeparator* property of *TreeView*.

Of course, the *FullPath* property with the default backslash separator is ideal for using the *TreeView* control in its common role of displaying directories. However, it's very easy to write inefficient code for such a control. The following program creates a *TreeView* control listing all the directories on your drive C, but depending on the size and complexity of the directory organization on your system, it could take quite a bit of time to finish the job:

NaiveDirectoryTreeView.cs

```
//------------------------------------------------------
// NaiveDirectoryTreeView.cs (c) 2005 by Charles Petzold
//------------------------------------------------------
using System;
using System.Drawing;
using System.IO;
using System.Windows.Forms;

class NaiveDirectoryTreeView : Form
{
    [STAThread]
    public static void Main()
    {
        Application.EnableVisualStyles();
        Application.Run(new NaiveDirectoryTreeView());
    }
    public NaiveDirectoryTreeView()
    {
        Text = "Naive Directory TreeView";

        TreeView tree = new TreeView();
        tree.Parent = this;
        tree.Dock = DockStyle.Fill;

        TreeNode nodeDriveC = new TreeNode("C:\\");
        tree.Nodes.Add(nodeDriveC);

        AddDirectories(nodeDriveC);
    }
    void AddDirectories(TreeNode node)
    {
        string strPath = node.FullPath;
        DirectoryInfo dirinfo = new DirectoryInfo(strPath);
        DirectoryInfo[] adirinfo;

        try
        {
            adirinfo = dirinfo.GetDirectories();
        }
        catch
        {
            return;
        }

        foreach (DirectoryInfo di in adirinfo)
        {
            TreeNode nodeDir = new TreeNode(di.Name);
            node.Nodes.Add(nodeDir);
            AddDirectories(nodeDir);
        }
    }
}
```

Just offhand, the program looks very cleanly structured. The constructor creates a *TreeView* control and an object of type *TreeNode* representing drive C. It then passes this *TreeNode* to the recursive *AddDirectories* method.

AddDirectories uses the *FullPath* property of the node passed to the method to create an object of type *DirectoryInfo* (a class defined in the *System.IO* namespace). The *GetDirectories* method of this class returns an array of *DirectoryInfo* objects for all the subdirectories of that path. (Some directories might prohibit access to themselves. That's why *GetDirectories* is called in a *try* block.) For each subdirectory, a new node is created, it is added to the node passed to the method, and *AddDirectories* is called recursively with that new node.

The problem is that the NaiveDirectoryTreeView program must traverse the entire drive before it can display the results. Because the program is performing this job in the constructor of the form, the program's main window is not displayed until the job is completed.

Still, however, once it displays itself on the screen, NaiveDirectoryTreeView has no further work to do and provides a good means for you to experiment with the default operation of a *TreeView* control. At any time, one node is selected, indicated by highlighting. Nodes can be either "expanded" (to show their child nodes) or "collapsed." Each node that contains child nodes displays a plus sign (+) when the node is collapsed and a minus sign (-) when it's expanded. (You can control the display of these symbols and lines connecting the nodes with the *ShowPlusMinus*, *ShowLines*, and *ShowRootLines* properties of *TreeView*.)

Expanding and collapsing nodes can be controlled programmatically through the *Expand*, *ExpandAll*, *Collapse*, and *Toggle* methods of *TreeView*. *TreeNode* also has the Boolean properties *IsExpanded* and *IsSelected*. The *SelectedNode* property of *TreeView* lets you obtain and set the selected node.

There are also a whole collection of events that let you know what's going on. Each expansion, each collapse, and each change of selection is accompanied by a pair of events: *BeforeExpand* and *AfterExpand*, *BeforeCollapse* and *AfterCollapse*, and *BeforeSelect* and *AfterSelect*. The *Before* events are accompanied by an object of type *TreeViewCancelEventArgs*. The event handler lets you stop the operation by setting the *Cancel* property to *true*. If *Cancel* remains *false*, the *After* event will occur accompanied by an object of type *TreeViewEventArgs*. Both *TreeViewCancel-EventArgs* and *TreeViewEventArgs* have a *Node* property that indicates the node involved in the operation and an *Action* property that is a member of the *TreeViewAction* enumeration. The *Action* property lets you know whether the node is expanding or collapsing, and whether the mouse or keyboard is involved.

So, rather than walking the entire directory tree when the *TreeView* control is first created, you can wait until a *BeforeExpand* event takes place for a particular directory before obtaining all the subdirectories of that node. Well, not quite. You actually need to be one step ahead: If you haven't obtained all the subdirectories for a particular node, the plus sign won't be displayed and the node won't be expandable anyway. (The code to handle this correctly is coming up shortly.)

It is common for nodes in a *TreeView* control to be accompanied with little icons. Indeed, the folder icons in Windows Explorer change from "closed" to "open" when the directory is selected.

The images displayed by the *TreeView* control are stored in the *ImageList* property. The *Image-Index* and *SelectedImageIndex* properties of *TreeView* indicate the default images for nonselected and selected nodes. (Alternatively, you can refer to the images in the *ImageList* collection by name using *ImageKey* and *SelectedImageKey*.) The *TreeNode* class as well includes *ImageIndex*, *SelectedImageIndex*, *ImageKey*, and *SelectedImageKey* properties for specifying images for each individual node. These properties always reference the *ImageList* of the *TreeView* to which the node belongs.

Here's more efficient code for displaying a directory tree. The *DirectoryTreeView* class is implemented as a custom control that inherits from *TreeView*.

```
DirectoryTreeView.cs
//-------------------------------------------------------
// DirectoryTreeView.cs (c) 2005 by Charles Petzold
//-------------------------------------------------------
using System;
using System.Drawing;
using System.IO;
using System.Windows.Forms;

class DirectoryTreeView : TreeView
{
    public DirectoryTreeView()
    {
        // Get the images used in the tree.
        ImageList = new ImageList();
        ImageList.Images.Add(new Icon(GetType(), "Resource.CLSDFOLD.ICO"));
        ImageList.Images.Add(new Icon(GetType(), "Resource.OPENFOLD.ICO"));
        ImageList.Images.Add(new Icon(GetType(), "Resource.35FLOPPY.ICO"));
        ImageList.Images.Add(new Icon(GetType(), "Resource.CDDRIVE.ICO"));
        ImageList.Images.Add(new Icon(GetType(), "Resource.DRIVENET.ICO"));
        ImageIndex = 0;
        SelectedImageIndex = 1;

        DriveInfo[] drives = DriveInfo.GetDrives();

        foreach (DriveInfo drive in drives)
        {
            // Create the drive node.
            TreeNode nodeDrive = new TreeNode(drive.RootDirectory.Name);

            // Set the image index depending on the drive type.
            if (drive.DriveType == DriveType.Removable)
                nodeDrive.ImageIndex = nodeDrive.SelectedImageIndex = 2;
```

```
            else if (drive.DriveType == DriveType.CDRom)
                nodeDrive.ImageIndex = nodeDrive.SelectedImageIndex = 3;

            else
                nodeDrive.ImageIndex = nodeDrive.SelectedImageIndex = 4;

            // Add the node to the tree and add the subdirectories.
            Nodes.Add(nodeDrive);
            AddDirectories(nodeDrive);

            // Make drive C the selected node.
            if (drive.RootDirectory.Name[0] == 'C')
                SelectedNode = nodeDrive;
        }
    }

    void AddDirectories(TreeNode node)
    {
        node.Nodes.Clear();

        DirectoryInfo dirinfo = new DirectoryInfo(node.FullPath);
        DirectoryInfo[] adirinfo;

        try
        {
            adirinfo = dirinfo.GetDirectories();
        }
        catch
        {
            return;
        }
        // Add node for each subdirectory.
        foreach (DirectoryInfo dir in adirinfo)
        {
            TreeNode nodeDir = new TreeNode(dir.Name);
            node.Nodes.Add(nodeDir);
        }
    }
    protected override void OnBeforeExpand(TreeViewCancelEventArgs args)
    {
        base.OnBeforeExpand(args);

        BeginUpdate();

        // Add the subdirectories of each subnode about to be displayed.
        foreach (TreeNode node in args.Node.Nodes)
            AddDirectories(node);

        EndUpdate();
    }
}
```

DirectoryTreeView.cs is part of the DirectoryTreeViewDemo project. (DirectoryTreeView-Demo.cs is coming up shortly.) Also included in this project are five icon (.ICO) files. I found these files in the collection shipped with Visual Studio 2005. I used the Add Existing Item option to make them a part of this project.

Each of the icon files must be flagged as an Embedded Resource. You do this by first selecting the file in Solution Explorer. In the Properties window, set the Build Action property to Embedded Resource. This causes the icon file to become part of the .EXE file as a resource. The program can then load the resource at runtime. You'll note that at the beginning of the *DirectoryTreeView* constructor the icons are loaded using a constructor for the *Icon* class:

```
new Icon(GetType(), "Resource.CLSDFOLD.ICO")
```

The first argument must be an object of type *Type* referring to any class defined by the program. The *GetType()* call works just fine. The expression *typeof(DirectoryTreeView)* would also work. The second argument to the constructor is the file name of the icon preceded by the word "Resource." This part of the name can actually be anything you want, but you must specify it as part of the properties for the project. Display the project properties, and take note of the Default Namespace string. By default, Visual Studio assigns this name to be the same name as the project—in this case, "DirectoryTreeViewDemo." You must change that name to "Resource" or the program will not be able to load in the icons. If I had left the Default Namespace as "DirectoryTreeViewDemo," the icons would be loaded with code like this:

```
new Icon(GetType(), "DirectoryTreeViewDemo.CLSDFOLD.ICO")
```

There's nothing wrong with that, but I plan to use the DirectoryTreeView.cs file in another project before the end of this chapter, and that project would have a different Default Namespace string. Don't confuse this Default Namespace name with any other namespace in your .NET programs. This name is used solely in connection with resources.

After the constructor has loaded the icons, it sets the *ImageIndex* and *SelectedImageIndex* properties to 0 and 1, respectively, to indicate that the folder image and the open-folder image are the default images for the control.

A new class in the .NET Framework 2.0 called *DriveInfo* is used to obtain information about the machine's disk drives. The *DriveType* property then allows associating a reasonable image with each drive. For each drive, the *AddDirectories* method adds nodes for all the top-level sub-directories. This allows the *TreeView* to display a plus sign if the drive has directories.

Thereafter, whenever the user opens another directory, nodes for the subdirectories of that directory are already present, but *AddDirectories* adds nodes for the subdirectories of the newly visible directories.

The DirectoryTreeViewDemo project is rounded out with the tiny DirectoryTreeViewDemo.cs file.

DirectoryTreeViewDemo.cs

```
//------------------------------------------------------
// DirectoryTreeViewDemo.cs (c) 2005 by Charles Petzold
//------------------------------------------------------
using System;
using System.Drawing;
using System.Windows.Forms;

class DirectoryTreeViewDemo : Form
{
    [STAThread]
    public static void Main()
    {
        Application.EnableVisualStyles();
        Application.Run(new DirectoryTreeViewDemo());
    }
    public DirectoryTreeViewDemo()
    {
        Text = "DirectoryTreeView Demo";

        DirectoryTreeView tree = new DirectoryTreeView();
        tree.Parent = this;
        tree.Dock = DockStyle.Fill;
    }
}
```

The program just creates an object of *DirectoryTreeView* and fills its client area with the control. You'll note that the program displays itself much faster than NaiveDirectoryTreeView.

The *TreeView* control has a couple other interesting features beyond what I've demonstrated. Set the *CheckBoxes* property to *true* to display check boxes with each node. It's similar to the *CheckedListBox* control but with hierarchical data rather than a simple list. The Boolean *Checked* property of *TreeNode* indicates whether a particular node is checked. Associated with this feature and new in the .NET Framework 2.0 are the properties *StateImageList* in *TreeView* and the properties *StateImageIndex* and *StateImageKey* in *TreeNode*.

If you'd like to allow the users to edit the labels, first set the *LabelEdit* property of the *TreeView* property to *true*. You must decide how the user will enter editing mode. It's generally with a right-click, so you can install a handler for the *NodeMouseClick* event, check whether the *Button* property of the argument is *MouseButtons.Right*, and then call *BeginEdit* for the node.

The *TreeView* then generates a *BeforeLabelEdit* event. The *NodeLabelEditEventArgs* object with this event has three properties: *Node*, *Label*, and *CancelEdit*. The read-only *Node* property is the *TreeNode* object being edited. The *Label* property is *null*. You can cancel editing by setting the *CancelEdit* property to *true*. Otherwise, you'll get an *AfterLabelEdit* message with another *NodeLabelEventArgs* object. You will probably want to handle this event. The *Node* property still reflects the node before editing; the *Text* property of that object is the *pre-edit* text. The *Label* property has the new text. (The *Label* property will be *null* if the user cancels the editing, perhaps by pressing the Escape key or clicking somewhere else.) Here is where you can determine whether the editing was legitimate. For example, Windows Explorer doesn't let you rename a directory to a zero-character string, and it displays a cautionary text box if you change a filename extension. If you want to prohibit the change, set *CancelEdit* to *true*. Otherwise, the *Text* of the node will be set to the *Label* property.

ListView

In Windows Explorer, you can change the display of files in several ways—to show (for example) just filenames with icons or a detailed list of files showing their sizes, file types, modified dates, and possibly other information. These different displays correspond to an important property of *ListView* named *View*. You set this property to a member of the *View* enumeration: *Details*, *List*, *LargeIcon*, *SmallIcon*, and *Tile*.

ListView is a complex control, and this discussion will just scratch the surface.

One of the first steps in setting up a *ListView* control is defining the columns that appear when *View.Details* is selected. The *Columns* property of *ListView* is an object of type *ColumnHeaderCollection*, which is a collection of *ColumnHeader* objects. You can create the *ColumnHeader* objects individually and add them to the *Columns* property, or you can use one of several *Add* methods provided by *ColumnHeaderCollection*, for example:

```
lstview.Columns.Add("File Name", 100, HorizontalAlignment.Left);
```

The first argument specifies the text that appears in the column, the second argument is the column width, and the last argument indicates whether the column header text and the contents of the column will be aligned left, right, or center.

In the *Details* view, each row of the display is an object of type *ListViewItem*. At the very least, you specify the *Text* property that appears in the first column of the display. *ListViewItem* contains a property named *SubItems* for the second and subsequent columns of the display. *SubItems* is an object of type *ListViewItem.ListViewSubItemCollection* and is a collection of *ListViewSubItem* objects. All the *ListViewItem* objects associated with a *ListView* are collected in the *Items* property of *ListView*.

In summary, a *ListView* control is a collection of *ListViewItem* objects, and each *ListViewItem* object contains a collection of *ListViewSubItem* objects.

The *ListView* has two properties, named *SmallImageList* and *LargeImageList*, each of type *ImageList*, for storing the small and large icons used in displaying items.

Here's a class that derives from *ListView* to display a list of files somewhat like Windows Explorer:

DirectoryListView.cs

```
//----------------------------------------------------
// DirectoryListView.cs (c) 2005 by Charles Petzold
//----------------------------------------------------
using System;
using System.Diagnostics;
using System.Drawing;
using System.IO;
using System.Windows.Forms;

class DirectoryListView : ListView
{
    string strDirectory;

    public DirectoryListView()
    {
        // Create the ListView columns.
        Columns.Add("Name", 150, HorizontalAlignment.Left);
        Columns.Add("Size", 100, HorizontalAlignment.Right);
        Columns.Add("Type", 100, HorizontalAlignment.Left);
        Columns.Add("Date Modified", 150, HorizontalAlignment.Left);

        // Create the ListView image lists.
        SmallImageList = new ImageList();
        LargeImageList = new ImageList();
        LargeImageList.ImageSize = new Size(32, 32);
    }

    public string Directory
    {
        get { return strDirectory; }
        set
        {
            // Clear all items and the image lists.
            Items.Clear();
            SmallImageList.Images.Clear();
            LargeImageList.Images.Clear();

            // Load the Folder icon.
            Icon icn = new Icon(GetType(), "Resource.Folder.ico");
            SmallImageList.Images.Add(icn);
            LargeImageList.Images.Add(icn);

            // Create DirectoryInfo object based on requested directory.
            DirectoryInfo dirinfo = new DirectoryInfo(strDirectory = value);

            // Obtain all the subdirectories and add them to the ListView.
            foreach (DirectoryInfo dir in dirinfo.GetDirectories())
            {
                ListViewItem item = new ListViewItem(dir.Name);
                item.ImageIndex = 0;
                item.Tag = "dir";
                item.SubItems.Add("");
```

```
                    item.SubItems.Add("File Folder");
                    item.SubItems.Add(dir.LastAccessTime.ToString());

                    Items.Add(item);
                }

            int iImage = 1;

            // Obtain all the files and add them to the ListView.
            foreach (FileInfo file in dirinfo.GetFiles())
            {
                ListViewItem item = new ListViewItem(file.Name);

                icn = Icon.ExtractAssociatedIcon(
                            Path.Combine(file.DirectoryName, file.Name));

                SmallImageList.Images.Add(icn);
                LargeImageList.Images.Add(icn);
                item.ImageIndex = iImage++;

                item.SubItems.Add(file.Length.ToString("N0"));
                item.SubItems.Add(
                    Path.GetExtension(file.Name).ToUpper() == ".EXE" ?
                        "Executable" : "Document");
                item.SubItems.Add(file.LastWriteTime.ToString());

                Items.Add(item);
            }
        }
    }
protected override void OnMouseDown(MouseEventArgs args)
{
    base.OnMouseDown(args);

    // Change the view on a right button click.
    if (args.Button == MouseButtons.Right)
        View = (View)(((int)View + 1) % 5);
}
protected override void OnItemActivate(EventArgs args)
{
    base.OnItemActivate(args);

    // If a directory being clicked, change to that directory.
    if ((string)SelectedItems[0].Tag == "dir")
    {
        Directory = Path.Combine(Directory, SelectedItems[0].Text);
    }
    else
    {
        // Otherwise, launch the programs associated with the file(s).
        foreach (ListViewItem item in SelectedItems)
        {
            try
```

```
          {
                Process.Start(Path.Combine(Directory, item.Text));
          }
          catch
          {
          }
        }
      }
    }
  }
```

This file is part of a project named DirectoryListViewDemo that also includes an icon file named Folder.ico. As with the previous project, the icon must be flagged as an Embedded Resource, and the Default Namespace property of the project must be set to "Resource."

The constructor creates four columns to be displayed in the *Details* view. It then creates two *ImageList* objects and assigns these to the *SmallImageList* and *LargeImageList* properties. Hereafter, the list view can refer to these *ImageList* objects by these properties. By default, the *ImageSize* property of an *ImageList* object is a *Size* object with a width of 16 and a height of 16. If the *ImageSize* property is not changed, any image added to the *ImageList* is sized to that dimension. A size of 16-pixels square (which is about the height of a default text character) is fine for small icons, but the large icons should be larger, so the *ImageSize* property of the *ImageList* stored by the *LargeImageList* property of *DirectoryListView* is made 32-pixels square.

DirectoryListView defines a new public property named *Directory* that indicates the directory it displays. Most of the real action in this class occurs during the *set* accessor of this property. The list view control must be filled with all the files and subdirectories in that directory.

The *set* accessor begins by clearing all the existing items from the control itself and from the two image lists. It then loads the Folder.ico file, which is the icon to display with directories. Because it is the first image in each image list, it is referenced with an index of 0.

The *set* accessor next creates an object of type *DirectoryInfo* and obtains all the subdirectories in the directory. For each one, a new *ListViewItem* is created. The *ImageIndex* is set to 0 (indicating the folder icon), and the *Tag* property is set to "dir" to distinguish the item as a directory. Each item has three subitems. The first is the size, which for a directory is 0, the second is the type ("File Folder"), and the third is the last access time.

Next, the *set* accessor obtains all the files in the directory. For each file, the static *Icon.ExtractAssociatedIcon* method obtains the icon associated with the file. For document files, information concerning the associated executable and its location on the user's system ultimately comes from the Windows registry. The icon is added to both image lists, and the index of the image becomes the *ImageIndex* property of the item.

Unfortunately, there's no .NET Framework method I can find like *Icon.ExtractAssociatedIcon* that reveals the file type (like "Visual Studio Project file" that Windows Explorer displays for .csproj files). A program would have to dig in the Windows registry for this information. This class simply chooses between the strings "Executable" or "Document," depending on the file-name extension.

Because we haven't learned enough to create a toolbar or menu item to change the list view *View* property, I decided to change the view based on a right mouse click. That's the role of the *OnMouseDown* method that comes next in the program.

Finally, the *OnItemActivate* method signals when the user has double-clicked an item or pressed Enter. Only then does this class take some action. If the *Tag* property indicates a directory, *OnItemActivate* sets the *Directory* property of the class to this directory. For a file (and there could be more than one selected file), the method calls the *Process.Start* method to launch the application.

The DirectoryListViewDemo project also includes the following simple program:

```
DirectoryListViewDemo.cs
//-----------------------------------------------------------
// DirectoryListViewDemo.cs (c) 2005 by Charles Petzold
//-----------------------------------------------------------
using System;
using System.Drawing;
using System.Windows.Forms;

class DirectoryListViewDemo : Form
{
    [STAThread]
    public static void Main()
    {
        Application.EnableVisualStyles();
        Application.Run(new DirectoryListViewDemo());
    }
    public DirectoryListViewDemo()
    {
        Text = "DirectoryListView Demo";
        Width *= 2;

        DirectoryListView dirlv = new DirectoryListView();
        dirlv.Parent = this;
        dirlv.Dock = DockStyle.Fill;
        dirlv.View = View.Details;
        dirlv.Directory = "C:";
    }
}
```

The last statement sets the *Directory* property of the *DirectoryListView* control to the root directory of the *C* drive. You can switch to another directory by clicking the directory name in the *ListView*, but you can't go back to a parent directory.

Let's fix that by linking the *DirectoryTreeView* and *DirectoryListView* controls together into a rudimentary Windows Explorer–type program. The PrimevalFileExplorer includes DirectoryTreeView.cs, DirectoryListView.cs, and all the icons used by both classes. The icons must be flagged as Embedded Resource, and the Default Namespace property of the project must be set to "Resource." The project also includes this file:

PrimevalFileExplorer.cs

```
//-------------------------------------------------
// PrimevalFileExplorer.cs (c) 2005 by Charles Petzold
//-------------------------------------------------
using System;
using System.Drawing;
using System.Windows.Forms;

class PrimevalFileExplorer : Form
{
    DirectoryTreeView tree;
    DirectoryListView list;

    public static void Main()
    {
        Application.EnableVisualStyles();
        Application.Run(new PrimevalFileExplorer());
    }
    public PrimevalFileExplorer()
    {
        Text = "Primeval File Explorer";

        tree = new DirectoryTreeView();
        tree.Parent = this;
        tree.Dock = DockStyle.Left;
        tree.AfterSelect += TreeViewOnSelect;

        list = new DirectoryListView();
        list.Parent = this;
        list.Dock = DockStyle.Right;

        Width *= 2;
    }
    protected override void OnResize(EventArgs args)
    {
        base.OnResize(args);
        tree.Width = list.Width = Width / 2;
    }
    void TreeViewOnSelect(object objSrc, TreeViewEventArgs args)
    {
        list.Directory = args.Node.FullPath;
    }
}
```

The two controls divide the client area of the program in half. By overriding the *OnResize* method, the program can adjust the controls' widths appropriately. In the next chapter, you'll see how to install a splitter to divide the client area in such a way.

The *PrimevalFileExplorer* class installs a handler for the *Select* event of *DirectoryTreeView* and then just sets the *Directory* property of the *DirectoryListView* with the *FullPath* property of the selected node. What the PrimevalFileExplorer program does *not* do, however, is change the *DirectoryTreeView* selection in accordance with a change of directory in the *DirectoryListView*. That job would require breaking the new directory path apart into separate directories, and then matching up the pieces with nodes.

Chapter 3
Panels and Dynamic Layout

Few programming experiences are more discouraging than seeing your carefully designed form or dialog box collapse into chaos on somebody else's computer. Whether it's due to an unusual screen resolution or an odd default font choice, there's just no denying that controls aren't supposed to overlap, and truncated text in a button is just plain wrong.

One of the most important improvements to Windows Forms in the .NET Framework 2.0 is a commitment to *dynamic layout*. The basic idea is simple: Wait until run time to complete the sizing and positioning of controls, and perhaps perform additional adjustments as the user changes the size of the form. Dynamic layout is a valuable tool in designing Microsoft Windows programs and is also a important part of future Windows user-interface design philosophy.

Approaches to Layout

Traditionally, Windows programmers have positioned controls on forms and dialog boxes with hard-coded coordinates and sizes. To avoid disasters when the program is run on different systems with different screen resolutions or font sizes, various techniques have been used.

Programmers using Microsoft Win32 or Microsoft Foundation Class (MFC) library specify locations and dimensions in a special device-independent coordinate system based on one-eighth of the height and one-quarter the width of the Windows system font. Generally, this coordinate system is restricted to dialog box templates in the program's resource script. When the dialog box is loaded and displayed, Windows converts these units to pixels based on the current system font.

Even with device-independent coordinates, layout was always such an unpleasant chore that one of the first "luxury" programming tools Microsoft developed for Windows was a visual dialog box editor.[1] Programmers were then able to design dialog boxes interactively by moving and sizing controls, and the editor would generate the appropriate resource script. Such editors later became primary features of integrated development environments such as Microsoft Visual Basic and Microsoft Visual Studio.

Windows Forms introduced a new model for achieving device-independent layout. Like its Visual Studio ancestors, Visual Studio 2005 continues to let programmers design forms and dialog boxes interactively while adding a couple of twists. First, as you position and size a

---

1. Charles Petzold, "Latest Dialog Editor Speeds Windows Application Development," *Microsoft Systems Journal*, Vol. 1, No. 1 (October 1986).

control, Visual Studio inserts coordinates and sizes right into your C# code as part of the control-creation logic. Here's some typical code generated by Visual Studio:

```
this.button1 = new System.Windows.Forms.Button();
this.button1.Location = new System.Drawing.Point(69, 52);
this.button1.Size = new System.Drawing.Size(77, 27);
```

This code occurs in the constructor of a class derived from *Form*, and *button1* is a field of this class. The code's a little bulky, of course: The *this* keyword isn't needed, and most programmers would avoid fully qualified class and structure names with a couple of *using* statements.

What's shocking about this code—particularly to anyone familiar with the dangers involved—is that these locations and dimensions are in units of *pixels*.

Obviously, these raw pixel coordinates can't be used at run time without a little massaging. Along with the hard-coded pixel dimensions and sizes, Visual Studio also generates the following statements that set two properties of the form:

```
this.AutoScaleDimensions = new System.Drawing.SizeF(6F, 13F);
this.AutoScaleMode = System.Windows.Forms.AutoScaleMode.Font;
```

These are new properties in the .NET Framework 2.0, and they replace the similar *AutoScale-BaseSize* property in the .NET Framework 1.x. These two statements indicate that the programmer designed and positioned the button based on a default font size of 6 pixels wide and 13 pixels high. That font size is associated with the default screen resolution of 96 dots per inch (dpi). When the program is run on a system with a different resolution and a different font size, all the sizes and coordinates of the form's controls are adjusted based on the ratio between the font size of the machine running the program and the font size passed to *AutoScaleDimensions*.

Layout Headaches

Although these techniques for achieving device independence all work to a certain degree, they don't solve all the problems with layout. Specifying explicit sizes and positions—even in a device-independent manner—has become much less desirable in recent years for several reasons.

First, as applications are translated into different languages, it is often discovered that a control sized for one language is not adequate to fit the text of another language. Rather than force a redesign of the form and dialog boxes, it would be better if the control "automagically" compensated for the language, and the dialog box adjusted its size in response.

Secondly, high-definition monitors—monitors capable of 200 or 300 dpi—will undoubtedly become much more common in the years ahead. Programs today should be made fully receptive to running on high-resolution monitors in the future. Programmers might *think* they're programming devices independently, but it's hard to be really sure.

The third problem—and the problem perhaps with the most radical implications—involves controls themselves. As controls have become more complex, it has become more difficult for the programmer to anticipate the footprint that the control will require. The optimum size of a control is probably best left to the control itself and might be successfully determined only at run time. The form or dialog box that hosts that control should accommodate itself to the size the control wants to be.

In the past, forms have imposed sizes on controls. In the future—which can start right now—controls choose their own dimensions and forms graciously accommodate those dimensions.

The new paradigm of dynamic layout can alleviate many problems of traditional layout. The program essentially waits until run time to position controls based on the sizes the controls want to be, which might be based on the resolution of the machine, the default font, the size of the program's window, and perhaps other factors known only to the controls themselves.

This concept is not as odd as it might have seemed 10 or 20 years ago because we now have everyday experience with one kind of dynamic layout. It's called HTML. HTML has shown us that it's possible to have a loose layout model that accommodates itself, more or less successfully, to different default font sizes and different browser window sizes. There is much to despise in HTML, of course, but we have to admit one thing: the layout facility implemented in every Web browser is much more sophisticated than anything typically implemented in regular old Windows programs.

The *AutoSize* Property

One feature that makes dynamic layout possible in Windows Forms is the Boolean *AutoSize* property implemented in *Control* and inherited by every class that derives from *Control*. Windows Forms in the .NET Framework 1.x had a few controls that implemented *AutoSize*, but now it's ubiquitous. The property is generally *false* by default, but if you set it to *true*, the control will automatically resize itself based on its contents. A button, for example, will always display all the text you put in it.

Some controls also implement the *AutoSizeMode* property. You set this property to one of the two members of the *AutoSizeMode* enumeration: *GrowAndShrink* or *GrowOnly* (the default).

The following programs demonstrates *AutoSize* with both a button and the form hosting that button. The autosized button adjusts itself to the size required to display its text, and the autosized form adjusts itself to the size of the button.

```
AutoSizeDemo.cs
//------------------------------------------
// AutoSizeDemo (c) 2005 by Charles Petzold
//------------------------------------------
using System;
using System.Drawing;
using System.Windows.Forms;
```

```
class AutoSizeDemo : Form
{
    [STAThread]
    public static void Main()
    {
        Application.EnableVisualStyles();
        Application.Run(new AutoSizeDemo());
    }
    public AutoSizeDemo()
    {
        Text = "AutoSize Demo";
        AutoSize = true;
        AutoSizeMode = AutoSizeMode.GrowAndShrink;

        Button btn = new Button();
        btn.Parent = this;
        btn.AutoSize = true;
        btn.Text = "Look back on time with kindly eyes,\n" +
                   "He doubtless did his best;\n" +
                   "How softly sinks his trembling sun\n" +
                   "In human nature's west!";
    }
}
```

The form contains a single *Button* control that displays a short poem by Emily Dickinson. The *AutoSize* property is set to *true* for both the form and button. In addition, the program sets the *AutoSizeMode* property of the form to *AutoSizeMode.GrowAndShrink*. Otherwise, the form would keep its default size, which is larger than the size required to display the button.

Although this form has a regular sizing border, it will not allow you to change the size of the form. When you set the *AutoSizeMode* of a form to grow-and-shrink, you should probably also give the form a nonsizeable border.

Although this little program gives you a small taste of the power of *AutoSize*, it's not exactly exhibiting dynamic layout. The button happens to be positioned at the upper-left corner of the form's client area because by default its *Location* property is the point (0, 0).

If the program ventured to display a second button, it would have to do something a little different. Here's a program that displays a second button that's positioned immediately to the right of the first button.

ManualLayoutDemo.cs

```
//-------------------------------------------------
// ManualLayoutDemo.cs (c) 2005 by Charles Petzold
//-------------------------------------------------
using System;
using System.Drawing;
using System.Windows.Forms;

class ManualLayoutDemo : Form
{
    [STAThread]
    public static void Main()
    {
        Application.EnableVisualStyles();
        Application.Run(new ManualLayoutDemo());
    }
    public ManualLayoutDemo()
    {
        Text = "Manual Layout Demo";
        AutoSize = true;
        AutoSizeMode = AutoSizeMode.GrowAndShrink;

        Button btn = new Button();
        btn.Parent = this;
        btn.AutoSize = true;
        btn.Text = "Look back on time with kindly eyes,\n" +
                    "He doubtless did his best;\n" +
                    "How softly sinks his trembling sun\n" +
                    "In human nature's west!";

        Button btn2 = new Button();
        btn2.Parent = this;
        btn2.AutoSize = true;
        btn2.Location = new Point(btn.Right, 0);
        btn2.Text = "He ate and drank the precious words,\n" +
                    "His spirit grew robust;\n" +
                    "He knew no more that he was poor,\n" +
                    "Nor that his frame was dust.\n" +
                    "He danced along the dingy days,\n" +
                    "And this bequest of wings\n" +
                    "Was but a book. What liberty\n" +
                    "A loosened spirit brings!";
    }
}
```

By the time the form's constructor creates the second button, the first button already knows its position and size. The constructor can use that information to position the second button:

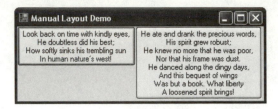

Although this program shows a little bit of what's involved in dynamic layout, it doesn't go nearly far enough. If the text or the font of the first button ever changed, the second button would have to be moved to accommodate the new size.

In general, a *layout manager* (as such things are called) would have to be invoked whenever a control's size changed, and then it would shift around the other controls accordingly. If you're interested in exploring this stuff, start with the *Layout* event implemented by *Control* and the *LayoutEngine* class defined in the *System.Windows.Forms.Layout* namespace. If you're not interested in writing your own dynamic-layout logic, you can take advantage of two new panels named *FlowLayoutPanel* and *TableLayoutPanel* that handle dynamic layout for you. One is based on a flow model and the other on a table model. Our experience with HTML suggests that these two models are suitable for a wide range of layout challenges.

The ultimate goal in this chapter (and one of my personal goals) is to design forms that are both attractive and geometrically flexible without using explicit coordinates or sizes. I don't care if Visual Studio embeds those coordinates in my code or I put them there myself: I just don't want them anymore.

Panels and Containers

Every control has a property named *Controls* that can store a collection of other controls, known as children. For most controls, however, this *Controls* property is pretty much left dormant; only for controls such as forms and panels does the facility to have child controls become essential.

Let's take a selective look at the class hierarchy, listing mostly those controls I'll focus on in this chapter:

Control

    ScrollableControl

        ContainerControl

            Form

            SplitContainer

        Panel

            FlowLayoutPanel

SplitterPanel

TableLayoutPanel

The ability to host a collection of child controls adequately is the primary characteristic of *ScrollableControl*. This control is so named because it can automatically display scroll bars if the control is not large enough to display all its children. Often a control that hosts children is called a *container*, even though *ContainerControl* is derived from *ScrollableControl*.

A *ContainerControl* is a control that consists of two or more other controls. *Form* comes under this category because (conceptually, at least) it combines a client area and nonclient areas. Although *Panel* is derived from *ScrollableControl* rather than *ContainerControl*, it, too, is considered to be a container because its primary duty is to be a parent to other controls.

This chapter discusses *Panel*, *SplitContainer* (and the related *SplitterPanel*), *FlowLayoutPanel*, and *TableLayoutPanel*. But I'll discuss some of the more standard (.NET Framework 1.x) techniques for quasi-dynamic layout first, and then get into the newer stuff.

Dock and Anchor

Two handy layout-related properties introduced in the .NET Framework 1.0 are *Dock* and *Anchor*. At first, these two properties might seem similar, and they might even seem similar after much experience. The *Dock* property is undoubtedly the more common in traditional layout, but the *Anchor* property has gained new prominence, as we'll see later in this chapter.

Docking Techniques

The *Dock* property is implemented by *Control* and inherited by all its descendents. You set the *Dock* property to any member of the *DockStyle* enumeration: *None*, *Top*, *Bottom*, *Left*, *Right*, and *Fill*. For most controls, the default setting is *DockStyle.None*.

If you set the *Dock* property of a control to *DockStyle.Top* (for example), the control is positioned flush against the top of its container (for example, the client area of a form) and extends to the left and right sides. *DockStyle.Top* might be appropriate for a toolbar, for example, while *DockStyle.Bottom* is good for a status bar. (In fact, the default *Dock* properties for the *ToolBar* and *StatusBar* controls—as well as their .NET Framework 2.0 replacements, *ToolStrip* and *StatusStrip*—are exactly what we might expect.)

Generally, you'll have some controls docked along the edges of the form, and then another control in the middle of it all. To that central control you give a *Dock* property of *DockStyle.Fill*.

The basic rules are: If you set a *Dock* property for one control, you should also give each of its sibling controls a *Dock* property other than *DockStyle.None*. One sibling and one sibling only should have *DockStyle.Fill*. Following these basic rules will help ensure that sibling controls do not overlap. (Docked controls *will* overlap anyway if the container becomes too small.)

Of course, once you start assigning multiple sibling controls different (or the same) *Dock* properties, you'll need to know how they interact.

As controls are assigned a *Parent* property (or as they are added to the parent through the *Add* method of the *Controls* property), the controls are given a *z-order*. (The term refers to the third axis in three-dimensional graphics.) The z-order is the order of the controls in the parent's control collection. A control at the *top* of the z-order is the first control to be added to the collection. It is referenced by an index of 0 in its parent's *Controls* property, and it is visually on top of other controls if the controls overlap. A control at the *bottom* of the z-order is the last control to be added to the control collection and is visually underneath other controls. The z-order can be rearranged with the *BringToFront* and *SendToBack* methods.

If multiple sibling controls are docked on the same edge of the parent, the control closest to the bottom of the z-order is actually against that edge. The control nearest the top of the z-order is closest to the center of the parent.

This all implies another simple rule: *Work from the center out*. That is, start by creating the central control with a *Dock* property of *DockStyle.Fill*. Then work outward. The last controls you create should be those along the edge.

Here's an example that demonstrates these techniques. It's a primitive Notepad clone that also includes a *TreeView* control at the left of the *EditBox*. Like most of the programs in this chapter, the controls don't do much and have only enough content to identify them:

PrimevalNotepad.cs

```csharp
//-----------------------------------------------
// PrimevalNotepad.cs (c) 2005 by Charles Petzold
//-----------------------------------------------
using System;
using System.Drawing;
using System.Windows.Forms;

class PrimevalNotepad : Form
{
    [STAThread]
    public static void Main()
    {
        Application.EnableVisualStyles();
        Application.Run(new PrimevalNotepad());
    }
    public PrimevalNotepad()
    {
        Text = "Primeval Notepad";

        TextBox txtbox = new TextBox();
        txtbox.Parent = this;
        txtbox.Dock = DockStyle.Fill;
        txtbox.Multiline = true;

        TreeView tree = new TreeView();
```

```
        tree.Parent = this;
        tree.Dock = DockStyle.Left;
        tree.Nodes.Add("tree");

        StatusStrip stat = new StatusStrip();
        stat.Parent = this;
        stat.Items.Add("status");

        ToolStrip tool = new ToolStrip();
        tool.Parent = this;
        tool.Items.Add("tool");

        MenuStrip menu = new MenuStrip();
        menu.Parent = this;
        menu.Items.Add("menu");
    }
}
```

The program doesn't explicitly assign the *Dock* property of the *StatusStrip*, *ToolStrip*, and *MenuStrip* controls; those controls themselves set the appropriate default. But notice that the program assigns the *Parent* property of the *ToolStrip* before *MenuStrip*. That ensures that the *ToolStrip* is under the *MenuStrip*:

Also notice that the program creates the *TreeView* before the three controls that appear above it and below it. If *TreeView* were created last, it would extend the full height of the client area. The menu, toolbar, and status bar would then be shortened, and it would all look very peculiar.

If you think that the *TreeView* and *TextBox* controls in PrimevalNotepad should be separated by a splitter under user control, I agree with you. That's coming up soon.

Plain Panels

You might want a form that has a menu, toolbar, and status bar, but you don't want a big *TextBox* (or some other control) in the middle. You want the interior area to be populated by a *bunch* of controls: labels, list boxes, spin buttons, and so forth.

It is certainly possible to have some controls (such as *MenuStrip* and *ToolStrip*) docked inside a form and have other controls be nondocked children of the form. These nondocked children can be explicitly positioned so that they are visible between the toolbar and the status bar. But keep in mind that you'll be positioning the controls relative to the upper-left corner of the client area. Part of that client area is already covered by the *MenuStrip* and *ToolStrip* controls. You'll need to make sure that you aren't positioning your controls behind those other controls. What's worse is when the form is made so narrow that the menu or toolbar wraps to a second line! Then you'll have to move all your controls down a bit.

A much better solution is to have just a plain do-nothing control in the center of the client area with a *Dock* property of *DockStyle.Fill*, and have that be the parent to all the other little controls (labels, list boxes, spin buttons, and so forth). This do-nothing control is called a *Panel*. Children of the panel are positioned relative to the upper-left corner of the panel rather than to the upper-left corner of the form.

Here's a program that demonstrates having a central *Panel* instead of a *TextBox*:

```
SimplePanel.cs
//-----------------------------------------
// SimplePanel.cs (c) 2005 by Charles Petzold
//-----------------------------------------
using System;
using System.Drawing;
using System.Windows.Forms;

class SimplePanel : Form
{
    [STAThread]
    public static void Main()
    {
        Application.EnableVisualStyles();
        Application.Run(new SimplePanel());
    }
    public SimplePanel()
    {
        Text = "Simple Panel";

        Panel pnl = new Panel();
        pnl.Parent = this;
        pnl.Dock = DockStyle.Fill;
        pnl.AutoScroll = true;

        TreeView tree = new TreeView();
        tree.Parent = this;
        tree.Dock = DockStyle.Left;
        tree.Nodes.Add("tree");

        StatusStrip stat = new StatusStrip();
        stat.Parent = this;
        stat.Items.Add("status");
```

```
        ToolStrip tool = new ToolStrip();
        tool.Parent = this;
        tool.Items.Add("tool");

        MenuStrip menu = new MenuStrip();
        menu.Parent = this;
        menu.Items.Add("menu");

        Label lbl = new Label();
        lbl.Parent = pnl;
        lbl.AutoSize = true;
        lbl.Text = "Label control at top of panel";

        lbl = new Label();
        lbl.Parent = pnl;
        lbl.AutoSize = true;
        lbl.Text = "Label control at bottom of panel";
        lbl.Location = new Point(300, 300);
    }
}
```

The central *Panel* control is given two children: a *Label* control at the top of the *Panel*, and another *Label* control 300 pixels to the right and below that one. Unless the panel is large enough, that bottom one won't be visible. The program sets the *AutoScroll* property of the panel to *true* so that the user can scroll it into view:

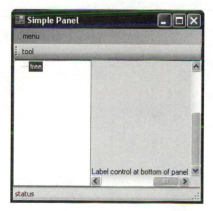

Keep in mind that this *AutoScroll* facility is available in all controls that inherit from *Scrollable-Control*. It's not used much for normal forms, but it can be of great use for a panel that displays many controls of the same sort (for example, picture boxes).

With a regular *Panel*, you'll have to explicitly position all the controls (or use docking). However, you can alternatively use a *FlowLayoutPanel* or *TableLayoutPanel*, which I'll show later in this chapter. Or, you can have a *SplitContainer* and use that as a parent to other panels. When you think of user-interface in Windows Forms, start thinking about *hierarchies* of panels and controls.

Anchors

The *Anchor* property is similar to *Dock* in that it associates a control with one or more edges of the control's container. However, *Anchor* doesn't cause a control to hug the edge of the container. *Anchor* instead keeps the control a uniform distance from the edge.

Another difference: A program's *Dock* property can be assigned only one member of the *DockStyle* enumeration. A program's *Anchor* property can be assigned multiple members of the *AnchorStyles* enumeration combined with the C# bitwise OR operator. Notice that the plural *AnchorStyles* rather than the singular *DockStyle* suggests the use of multiple members.

Each *AnchorStyles* member is a single bit. The members (and their values) are *None* (a value of 0), *Top* (1), *Bottom* (2), *Left* (4), and *Right* (8).

The default *Anchor* property is not *AnchorStyles.None*. It's *AnchorStyles.Top | AnchorStyles.Left*. That's why when you make a form larger, the controls inside that form stay in place relative to the form's top-left corner. Set *Anchor* to *AnchorStyles.Bottom | AnchorStyles.Right*, and the control will keep the same distance from the bottom right corner. Set *Anchor* to *AnchorStyles.None* and the control will hover inside the form as it's made larger. Set *Anchor* to all four sides, and the control will hover and expand and contract in size as the form's size changes.

In traditional layout, the *Anchor* property perhaps has its greatest benefit in allowing the user to resize controls by resizing the form in which the controls appear. Here's an example. The program uses the height of the font to position four labels and accompanying text boxes.

AnchorFields.cs

```
//---------------------------------------------
// AnchorFields.cs (c) 2005 by Charles Petzold
//---------------------------------------------
using System;
using System.Drawing;
using System.Windows.Forms;

class AnchorFields : Form
{
    [STAThread]
    public static void Main()
    {
        Application.EnableVisualStyles();
        Application.Run(new AnchorFields());
    }
    public AnchorFields()
    {
        Text = "Anchor Fields";
        int iSpace = Font.Height;
        int y = iSpace;

        for (int i = 0; i < 4; i++)
        {
            Label lbl = new Label();
```

```
        lbl.Parent = this;
        lbl.AutoSize = true;
        lbl.Text = (new string[] { "Name:", "Address:", "Job:",
                                "Very personal information:" })[i];
        lbl.Location = new Point(iSpace, y);

        TextBox txtbox = new TextBox();
        txtbox.Parent = this;
        txtbox.Location = new Point(lbl.Right + iSpace, y);
        txtbox.Size = new Size(ClientSize.Width - iSpace - txtbox.Left,
                            txtbox.Height);
        txtbox.Anchor |= AnchorStyles.Right;

        y = txtbox.Bottom + iSpace;
    }
  }
}
```

In that penultimate line of code, the *Anchor* property of the *TextBox* controls becomes *AnchorStyles.Left | AnchorStyles.Top | AnchorStyles.Right*. The control keeps the same distance from the left and top edges, as is customary, but it also keeps the same distance from the right edge. Make the form wider, and the *TextBox* controls become wider as well:

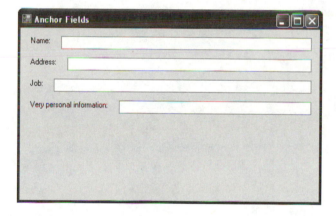

You can't mix *Dock* and *Anchor*. Whenever a program sets the *Dock* property of a control to something other than *DockStyle.None*, the *Anchor* property is reset to its default. Similarly, setting *Anchor* to something other than its default causes *Dock* to be reset to *DockStyle.None*.

As you'll see later in this chapter, with the introduction of the *FlowLayoutPanel* and *TableLayoutPanel*, the *Anchor* property has become almost as essential as *Dock*.

Splitters

A splitter is a thin horizontal or vertical bar used to adjust the relative sizes of two screen areas. Splitters are found in Windows Explorer separating the tree view on the left and the list view on the right; in Visual Studio separating the editor, Solution Explorer, and Error List window; and in Internet Explorer whenever a Web page uses frames.

In the .NET Framework 1.x, the Windows Forms splitter was a control named *Splitter* that you wedged between two other controls (usually panels, list views, or tree views) through a precise docking order. If you got the docking order wrong, the splitter was apt to end up on the edge of the window rather than between the two controls. (See Chapter 22, "Tree View and List View," of my book *Programming Microsoft Windows with C#* [Microsoft Press, 2002] for the gory details.)

The *Splitter* control is still available in the .NET Framework 2.0, but for new programs you'll probably want to use *SplitContainer* instead. The *SplitContainer* control is much easier to use. It creates two panels of type *SplitterPanel* and displays these on its surface separated by a thin (4-pixel) horizontal or vertical splitter. Moving that splitter with the mouse changes the relative size of the two *SplitterPanel* controls.

The three most important properties of *SplitContainer* are *Panel1* and *Panel2* (which give you access to the two *SplitterPanel* controls that *SplitContainer* creates) and *Orientation*, which is a member of the *Orientation* enumeration and specifies that the splitter appear as a *Vertical* bar (the default) or *Horizontal*.

(It's possible to create your own *SplitterPanel* controls, but they would be of limited use. The *SplitterPanel* constructor requires a *SplitContainer* argument, yet the *Panel1* and *Panel2* properties of *SplitContainer* are read-only.)

Let's take a look.

PrimevalExplorer.cs

```
//-------------------------------------------------
// PrimevalExplorer.cs (c) 2005 by Charles Petzold
//-------------------------------------------------
using System;
using System.Drawing;
using System.Windows.Forms;

class PrimevalExplorer : Form
{
    [STAThread]
    public static void Main()
    {
        Application.EnableVisualStyles();
        Application.Run(new PrimevalExplorer());
    }
    public PrimevalExplorer()
    {
        Text = "PrimevalExplorer";

        SplitContainer split = new SplitContainer();
        split.Parent = this;
```

```
        split.Dock = DockStyle.Fill;

        TreeView tree = new TreeView();
        tree.Parent = split.Panel1;
        tree.Dock = DockStyle.Fill;
        tree.Nodes.Add("tree");

        ListView list = new ListView();
        list.Parent = split.Panel2;
        list.Dock = DockStyle.Fill;
        list.Items.Add("list");
    }
}
```

Notice that all *Dock* properties are set to *DockStyle.Fill*. The parent of the *TreeView* control is the left panel (*Panel1*) of the *SplitContainer*, and the parent of the *ListView* is the right panel (*Panel2*).

This program could easily include a menu, toolbar, and status bar. Just be sure to add them to the parent *after* the *SplitContainer*.

When you widen or narrow the window, both panels increase or decrease proportionally. That's a consequence of the *FixedPanel* property being set to the enumeration value *Fixed-Panel.None*. Set *FixedPanel* to *FixedPanel.Panel1* if you want resizing to affect only *Panel2* (probably what the user expects from past experience), or set it to *FixedPanel.Panel2* for an odder effect.

You can create more complex splits by creating additional *SplitContainer* controls and setting their parents equal to *Panel1* or *Panel2* of the previous *SplitContainer*.

Padding and Margin

Two new properties of Windows Forms controls in the .NET Framework 2.0 are *Padding* and *Margin*. Both provide a little extra space, one inside the control and the other outside the control. I've almost mastered which is which by repeating the following mantra about 200 times:

Padding, inside. *Margin*, outside.

The *Padding* property provides extra space *inside* a control. For example, here's a normal button with its *AutoSize* property set to *true*:

Autosized Button

The only difference with this next button is that it has 20 pixels of extra padding on all four sides:

Autosized Button

The autosize facility takes padding into account when determining the control's size.

The *Padding* property is an object of type *Padding*, which is a structure that defines two parametered constructors. The most general is:

```
new Padding(iLeft, iTop, iRight, iBottom)
```

All arguments are in units of pixels. When you want to add the same padding to all four sides, you can use this shortcut:

```
new Padding(iAll);
```

The *Padding* structure has five read/write properties: *Left*, *Top*, *Right*, *Bottom*, and *All* (which will equal -1 if the four sides aren't the same). The *Horizontal* and *Vertical* properties are read-only. *Horizontal* is the sum of *Left* and *Right*, and *Vertical* is the sum of *Top* and *Bottom*.

For a container control, such as a form or a panel, the padding is inserted around the edges of the container's interior. *Docked* controls are thus offset from the edge. Here's the Primeval-Notepad program I showed earlier:

Here's the same program with 20 pixels of padding added to the form:

Now this looks very peculiar, and it's not something you're likely to do, but padding, as you'll see, is a useful tool in layout techniques shown later in this chapter.

You'll recall the *AutoSizeDemo* program at the beginning of this chapter:

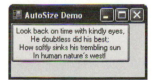

This program cries out for a little padding. However, if we add the 20 pixels of padding to the form, something peculiar occurs:

The padding is there, and the form's size reflects the padding, but all 40 pixels of horizontal and vertical padding are on the right and bottom. That's because the button has a specific location at point (0, 0). Even though the code doesn't say so, that's the default *Location* property.

The *Margin* property—which is also a structure of type *Padding*—affects spacing *between* controls, and to see how this works we're going to have to explore the two new sophisticated layout panels introduced in the .NET Framework 2.0: *FlowLayoutPanel* and *TableLayoutPanel*.

Remember: *Padding* inside; *Margin* outside.

Flow Layout Panel

The *FlowLayoutPanel* implements something resembling the layout model of HTML except that instead of working with text and images, you're working entirely with controls. (If you actually do want text, use a *Label* control. If you want an image to flow with the text, use a *PictureBox* control.) The *FlowLayoutPanel* takes responsibility for arranging its child controls sequentially from left to right (by default) and then from top to bottom.

The direction that *FlowLayoutPanel* arranges the controls is governed by the *FlowDirection* property. The property is a member of the *FlowDirection* enumeration, by default *FlowDirection.LeftToRight*. Other possibilities are *TopDown*, *RightToLeft*, and *BottomUp*.

In the default mode, the *FlowLayoutPanel* arranges its child controls left to right across the panel. If the next control will exceed the space available for it, it will be placed on the next row (or column if you've set *FlowDirection* to *TopDown* or *BottomUp*.) That's a consequence of the default *true* setting of the *WrapContents* property.

If you set *WrapContents* to false, you'll need to handle the row (or column) breaks yourself, and even if you use the default *WrapContents* value, you might want to start a new row (or column) with a particular control. If *flow* is an object of type *FlowLayoutPanel*, and *ctrl* is a child of *flow*, then call

```
flow.SetFlowBreak(ctrl, true);
```

to put this control in a new row or column. The *GetFlowBreak* method returns a Boolean value with a control argument.

Docking and Anchoring in Flow Layout

Dock and *Anchor* might not seem like they make a lot of sense for controls in a *FlowLayoutPanel*, but they play powerful roles. You use the *Dock* and *Anchor* properties on a child control in a flow panel to set the control's vertical alignment (for horizontal flow direction) or horizontal alignment (for vertical flow direction).

If the flow direction is horizontal, the height of any particular horizontal row of controls is governed by the height of the tallest control in that row. All the controls are aligned at the top of that row. For any particular control, you have four choices:

- Aligned with the top of the tallest control (default)
- Aligned with the bottom of the tallest control
- Aligned in the center of the tallest control
- Vertically expanded to be the same height as the tallest control

You can control the vertical alignment of a control with the control's *Anchor* property:

- *AnchorStyles.Top*: Aligned at the top
- *AnchorStyles.Bottom*: Aligned at the bottom
- *AnchorStyles.Top | AnchorStyles.Bottom*: Aligned in the center
- *AnchorStyles.None*: Vertically expanded to the same height.

The *AnchorStyles.Left* and *AnchorStyles.Right* bits are ignored.

You can get some of these same effects using the *Dock* property, in which case it overrides any nondefault *Anchor* property you might have set:

- *DockStyle.Top*: Aligned at the top
- *DockStyle.Bottom*: Aligned at the bottom
- *DockStyle.Fill* or *DockStyle.Left* or *DockStyle.Right*: Vertically expanded

Because the *Anchor* property is more versatile, I'd recommend sticking with that for vertically aligning controls.

When the flow direction is vertical (top to bottom or bottom to top), the width of each column of controls is governed by the widest control. The controls are normally aligned at the left. Use the *Anchor* property to change the alignment relative to the widest control in the column:

- *AnchorStyles.Left*: Aligned at the left (default)
- *AnchorStyles.Right*: Aligned at the right
- *AnchorStyles.Left | AnchorStyles.Right*: Aligned in the center
- *AnchorStyles.None*: Horizontally expanded to the same width

The *AnchorStyles.Top* and *AnchorStyles.Bottom* bits are ignored.

If you'd like to experiment with using the *Anchor* and *Dock* properties to change alignment in a *FlowLayoutPanel*, I've put together a little program.

FlowPanelAlignment.cs

```csharp
//--------------------------------------------------
// FlowPanelAlignment.cs (c) 2005 by Charles Petzold
//--------------------------------------------------
using System;
using System.Drawing;
using System.Windows.Forms;

class FlowPanelAlignment : Form
{
    [STAThread]
    public static void Main()
    {
        Application.EnableVisualStyles();
        Application.Run(new FlowPanelAlignment());
    }
    public FlowPanelAlignment()
    {
        Text = "Flow Panel Alignment";

        FlowLayoutPanel flow = new FlowLayoutPanel();
        flow.Parent = this;
        flow.Dock = DockStyle.Fill;
        flow.Text = "Flow Panel";
        flow.Click += ClickHandler;

        Random rand = new Random(DateTime.Now.Millisecond);

        for (int i = 0; i < 20; i++)
        {
            Button btn = new Button();
            btn.Parent = flow;
            btn.Text = "Button " + (i + 1);
            btn.Click += ClickHandler;

            // Set a random size (but not too random)
            Size sz = btn.PreferredSize;
            sz.Width = (int)(sz.Width * (1 + 2 * rand.NextDouble()));
            sz.Height = (int)(sz.Height * (1 + 2 * rand.NextDouble()));
            btn.Size = sz;
        }
    }
    void ClickHandler(object objSrc, EventArgs args)
    {
        Control ctrl = (Control)objSrc;

        Form frm = new Form();
        frm.Text = ctrl.Text;
        frm.Owner = this;

        PropertyGrid prop = new PropertyGrid();
        prop.SelectedObject = objSrc;
```

```
        prop.Parent = frm;
        prop.Dock = DockStyle.Fill;

        frm.Show();
    }
}
```

The program creates a *FlowLayoutPanel* that fills the form's client area. Next, the program creates 20 buttons on this parent with a width and height that randomly varies from the button's preferred size to three times that size. Here's a typical display:

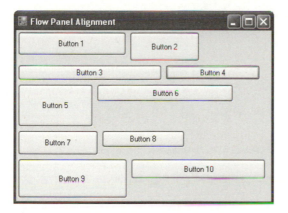

Now here's the best part: if you click a button or the form, you'll invoke a dialog box that contains a *PropertyGrid* control for the button or form. You can change the button's *Dock* or *Anchor* properties and see the effect. What you'll find (when the flow direction is horizontal) is that you can't horizontally align the buttons—you can't make them budge left or right, and you can't center a horizontal line of controls. What you can do is vertically align the buttons (up or down) as you prefer.

While you're experimenting with control properties, try setting the *Margin* property of one of the buttons. By default, the *Margin* property is 3 pixels on all sides. If you make it larger, you'll see that the button is given more space between itself, the adjoining buttons, and the edge of the client area. You can also set the *Padding* property of the form to provide more air between the edge of the client area and the array of buttons within.

If you set the *AutoSize* property of the *FlowLayoutPanel* to *true*, no wrapping will occur except that which you explicitly set with *SetFlowBreak*.

Let's use *FlowLayoutPanel* for a simple About box, using as a model the About box shown in Chapter 16, "Dialog Boxes," of *Programming Microsoft Windows with C#*. That one required a lot of explicit coordinates and arithmetic to calculate them. The only explicit numbers in this version are font point sizes and character offsets.

FlowPanelAboutBox1.cs

```csharp
//-------------------------------------------------
// FlowPanelAboutBox1.cs (c) 2005 by Charles Petzold
//-------------------------------------------------
using System;
using System.Diagnostics;
using System.Drawing;
using System.Windows.Forms;

class FlowPanelAboutBox1 : Form
{
    [STAThread]
    public static void Main()
    {
        Application.EnableVisualStyles();
        Application.Run(new FlowPanelAboutBox1());
    }
    public FlowPanelAboutBox1()
    {
        Text = "Flow Panel About Box #1";
        AutoSize = true;
        AutoSizeMode = AutoSizeMode.GrowAndShrink;
        FormBorderStyle = FormBorderStyle.FixedDialog;

        FlowLayoutPanel flow = new FlowLayoutPanel();
        flow.Parent = this;
        flow.AutoSize = true;
        flow.FlowDirection = FlowDirection.TopDown;

        Label lbl = new Label();
        lbl.Parent = flow;
        lbl.AutoSize = true;
        lbl.Anchor = AnchorStyles.None;
        lbl.Margin = new Padding(Font.Height);
        lbl.Text = "AboutBox Version 1.0";
        lbl.Font = new Font(FontFamily.GenericSerif, 24, FontStyle.Italic);

        LinkLabel lnk = new LinkLabel();
        lnk.Parent = flow;
        lnk.AutoSize = true;
        lnk.Anchor = AnchorStyles.None;
        lnk.Margin = new Padding(Font.Height);
        lnk.Text = "\x00A9 2005 by Charles Petzold";
        lnk.Font = new Font(FontFamily.GenericSerif, 16);
        lnk.LinkArea = new LinkArea(10, 15);
        lnk.LinkClicked +=
            delegate { Process.Start("http://www.charlespetzold.com"); };

        Button btn = new Button();
        btn.Parent = flow;
        btn.AutoSize = true;
        btn.Anchor = AnchorStyles.None;
```

```
        btn.Margin = new Padding(Font.Height);
        btn.Text = "OK";
    }
}
```

Notice that the *AutoSize* property of the form is set to *true*. The form will size itself to its child, the *FlowLayoutPanel*, which also has its *AutoSize* property set to *true* to size itself to its three children. The *FlowDirection* is *TopDown* so that the three controls will be arranged vertically. All three children have their *AutoSize* properties set to *true*, as well as the *Anchor* property set to *AnchorStyles.None,* for centering the controls horizontally. All three controls have also been given a *Margin* equal to the default font height, just so everything isn't jammed together too tightly:

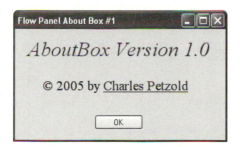

Rather than define a separate method for the *LinkClicked* event handler of the *LinkLabel* control, I used an anonymous method (new in Visual C# 2005) with the keyword *delegate*. Anonymous methods are often handy for event handlers when the handler contains only a line or two of code. For anything much larger, I think they become visually confusing.

Of course, most traditional About boxes have icons as well. If we wanted the icon above or below the first line of text, that would be no problem. But suppose we want the icon to the left of that first line of text. How do we do it?

One simple approach is to use two flow panels. Instead of the first line of text, a second flow panel with a horizontal orientation hosts the icon and the text string. I created the icon in Visual Studio as part of the FlowPanelAboutBox2 project, and I flagged it as an Embedded Resource.

FlowPanelAboutBox2.cs

```
//------------------------------------------------
// FlowPanelAboutBox2.cs (c) 2005 by Charles Petzold
//------------------------------------------------
using System;
using System.Diagnostics;
using System.Drawing;
using System.Windows.Forms;

class FlowPanelAboutBox2 : Form
{
```

```
[STAThread]
public static void Main()
{
    Application.EnableVisualStyles();
    Application.Run(new FlowPanelAboutBox2());
}
public FlowPanelAboutBox2()
{
    Text = "Flow Panel About Box #2";
    AutoSize = true;
    AutoSizeMode = AutoSizeMode.GrowAndShrink;
    FormBorderStyle = FormBorderStyle.FixedDialog;
    Icon = new Icon(GetType(), "FlowPanelAboutBox2.AforAbout.ico");

    FlowLayoutPanel flow = new FlowLayoutPanel();
    flow.Parent = this;
    flow.AutoSize = true;
    flow.FlowDirection = FlowDirection.TopDown;

    FlowLayoutPanel flow2 = new FlowLayoutPanel();
    flow2.Parent = flow;
    flow2.AutoSize = true;
    flow2.Margin = new Padding(Font.Height);

    PictureBox picbox = new PictureBox();
    picbox.Parent = flow2;
    picbox.Image = Icon.ToBitmap();
    picbox.SizeMode = PictureBoxSizeMode.AutoSize;
    picbox.Anchor = AnchorStyles.None;

    Label lbl = new Label();
    lbl.Parent = flow2;
    lbl.AutoSize = true;
    lbl.Anchor = AnchorStyles.None;
    lbl.Text = "AboutBox Version 2.0";
    lbl.Font = new Font(FontFamily.GenericSerif, 24, FontStyle.Italic);

    LinkLabel lnk = new LinkLabel();
    lnk.Parent = flow;
    lnk.AutoSize = true;
    lnk.Anchor = AnchorStyles.None;
    lnk.Margin = new Padding(Font.Height);
    lnk.Text = "\x00A9 2005 by Charles Petzold";
    lnk.Font = new Font(FontFamily.GenericSerif, 16);
    lnk.LinkArea = new LinkArea(10, 15);
    lnk.LinkClicked +=
        delegate { Process.Start("http://www.charlespetzold.com"); };

    Button btn = new Button();
    btn.Parent = flow;
    btn.AutoSize = true;
    btn.Anchor = AnchorStyles.None;
    btn.Margin = new Padding(Font.Height);
    btn.Text = "OK";
}
}
```

Now the icon is positioned as we might expect:

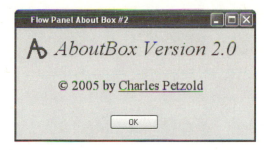

Bye, Bye, *GroupBox*

The *GroupBox* control is recognized by users primarily as a grouping of mutually exclusive radio buttons. Yet, the existing *GroupBox* requires that the radio buttons be explicitly positioned in its interior. Wouldn't it be nice to have a *GroupBox* that arranged its children just like a *FlowLayoutPanel*?

The *GroupBox* is due for an overhaul, and the time is now. The *GroupPanel* control shown below derives from *FlowLayoutPanel* and does its best to imitate the appearance of a *GroupBox*.

GroupPanel.cs
```csharp
//------------------------------------------
// GroupPanel.cs (c) 2005 by Charles Petzold
//------------------------------------------
using System;
using System.Drawing;
using System.Windows.Forms;

class GroupPanel : FlowLayoutPanel
{
    int xDpi, yDpi;

    public GroupPanel()
    {
        FlowDirection = FlowDirection.TopDown;
        WrapContents = false;
        AutoSize = true;
        AutoSizeMode = AutoSizeMode.GrowAndShrink;

        Graphics grfx = CreateGraphics();
        xDpi = (int)grfx.DpiX;
        yDpi = (int)grfx.DpiY;
        grfx.Dispose();

        Padding = new Padding(xDpi / 10, yDpi / 10 + Font.Height,
                              xDpi / 10, yDpi / 10);
    }
    public string Check
    {
```

```
        set
        {
            RadioButton radio = Controls[value] as RadioButton;
            if (radio != null)
                radio.Checked = true;
        }
        get
        {
            foreach (Control ctrl in Controls)
            {
                RadioButton radio = ctrl as RadioButton;
                if (radio != null && radio.Checked)
                    return radio.Name;
            }
            return "";
        }
    }
    protected override void OnFontChanged(EventArgs args)
    {
        base.OnFontChanged(args);
        Padding = new Padding(Padding.Left, yDpi / 10 + Font.Height,
                                Padding.Right, Padding.Bottom);
    }
    protected override void OnPaint(PaintEventArgs args)
    {
        Graphics grfx = args.Graphics;
        int yIndent = yDpi / 25 + Font.Height / 2;
        int xIndent1 = xDpi / 10, xIndent2;

        if (Text != null && Text.Length > 0)
        {
            grfx.DrawString(" " + Text + " ", Font,
                            new SolidBrush(ForeColor), xIndent1, yDpi / 25);
            xIndent2 = xIndent1 + (int) (grfx.MeasureString(" " + Text + " ",
                                                            Font).Width);
        }
        else
        {
            xIndent2 = xIndent1;
        }

        Pen pnLight = new Pen(ControlPaint.Light(BackColor));
        Pen pnDark = new Pen(ControlPaint.Dark(BackColor));

        grfx.DrawLine(pnDark, xIndent1, yIndent, 0, yIndent);
        grfx.DrawLine(pnDark, 0, yIndent, 0, Height - 2);
        grfx.DrawLine(pnDark, 0, Height - 2, Width - 2, Height - 2);
        grfx.DrawLine(pnDark, Width - 2, Height - 2, Width - 2, yIndent);
        grfx.DrawLine(pnDark, Width - 2, yIndent, xIndent2, yIndent);

        grfx.DrawLine(pnLight, xIndent1, yIndent + 1, 1, yIndent + 1);
        grfx.DrawLine(pnLight, 1, yIndent + 1, 1, Height - 3);
        grfx.DrawLine(pnLight, 0, Height - 1, Width - 1, Height - 1);
        grfx.DrawLine(pnLight, Width - 1, Height - 1, Width - 1, yIndent);
```

```
        grfx.DrawLine(pnLight, Width - 3, yIndent + 1, xIndent2, yIndent + 1);
    }
}
```

The constructor obtains the horizontal and vertical resolution (in dots per inch) and uses that as well as the font height to set the *Padding* property. Because the control displays text at the top, the padding at the top must allow for that text, and the *Padding* property must be changed if the font changes. Because this control is primarily for hosting radio buttons, it contains a property to set and get the currently clicked radio button based on the *Name* property. The rest of the code is dedicated to the control drawing logic.

Here's a dialog box that makes use of two *GroupPanel* controls.

ColorFillDialog.cs

```
//-------------------------------------------------
// ColorFillDialog.cs (c) 2005 by Charles Petzold
//-------------------------------------------------
using System;
using System.Drawing;
using System.Reflection;
using System.Windows.Forms;

class ColorFillDialog : Form
{
    protected GroupPanel grppnl1, grppnl2;
    protected CheckBox chkbox;

    public ColorFillDialog()
    {
        Text = "Color/Fill Select";
        FormBorderStyle = FormBorderStyle.FixedDialog;
        ControlBox = MinimizeBox = MaximizeBox = ShowInTaskbar = false;
        AutoSize = true;
        AutoSizeMode = AutoSizeMode.GrowAndShrink;

        FlowLayoutPanel flow = new FlowLayoutPanel();
        flow.Parent = this;
        flow.AutoSize = true;
        flow.FlowDirection = FlowDirection.TopDown;

        FlowLayoutPanel flow2 = new FlowLayoutPanel();
        flow2.Parent = flow;
        flow2.AutoSize = true;
        flow2.Anchor = AnchorStyles.None;

        grppnl1 = new GroupPanel();
        grppnl1.Parent = flow2;
        grppnl1.AutoSize = true;
        grppnl1.Text = "Color";

        grppnl2 = new GroupPanel();
        grppnl2.Parent = flow2;
```

```
        grppnl2.AutoSize = true;
        grppnl2.Text = "Background";

        grppnl1.SuspendLayout();
        grppnl2.SuspendLayout();

        // Get property information for SystemInformation class.
        Type type = typeof(Color);
        PropertyInfo[] apropinfo = type.GetProperties();

        // Loop through the property information.
        foreach (PropertyInfo pi in apropinfo)
        {
            if (pi.CanRead && pi.GetGetMethod().IsStatic)
            {
                // Get the property names and values.
                if (pi.Name[0] == 'S' || pi.Name[0] == 'P')
                {
                    RadioButton radio = new RadioButton();
                    radio.Parent = pi.Name[0] == 'S' ? grppnl1 : grppnl2;
                    radio.AutoSize = true;
                    radio.Text = radio.Name = pi.Name;
                }
            }
        }
        grppnl1.ResumeLayout();
        grppnl2.ResumeLayout();

        chkbox = new CheckBox();
        chkbox.Parent = flow;
        chkbox.AutoSize = true;
        chkbox.Text = "Fill Ellipse";
        chkbox.Anchor = AnchorStyles.None;

        FlowLayoutPanel flow3 = new FlowLayoutPanel();
        flow3.Parent = flow;
        flow3.AutoSize = true;
        flow3.Anchor = AnchorStyles.None;

        Button btn = new Button();
        btn.Parent = flow3;
        btn.AutoSize = true;
        btn.Text = "OK";
        btn.DialogResult = DialogResult.OK;
        AcceptButton = btn;

        btn = new Button();
        btn.Parent = flow3;
        btn.AutoSize = true;
        btn.Text = "Cancel";
        btn.DialogResult = DialogResult.Cancel;
        CancelButton = btn;
    }
    public Color Color
    {
```

```
        set { grppn11.Check = value.Name; }
        get { return Color.FromName(grppn11.Check); }
    }
    public Color Background
    {
        set { grppn12.Check = value.Name; }
        get { return Color.FromName(grppn12.Check); }
    }
    public bool Fill
    {
        set { chkbox.Checked = value; }
        get { return chkbox.Checked; }
    }
}
```

The dialog box uses three flow panels and two group panels. Using reflection, the constructor obtains the members of the *Color* class but ignores all colors that don't begin with the letters S or P. These colors become radio buttons in the two group panels.

These two files as well as the ColorFill.cs file shown next are part of the ColorFill project, and it's similar to a program in *Programming Microsoft Windows with C#* (Chapter 16, "Dialog Boxes").

ColorFill.cs

```
//------------------------------------------
// ColorFill.cs (c) 2005 by Charles Petzold
//------------------------------------------
using System;
using System.Drawing;
using System.Windows.Forms;

class ColorFill : Form
{
    Color clrEllipse = Color.Salmon;
    bool bFillEllipse = false;

    [STAThread]
    public static void Main()
    {
        Application.EnableVisualStyles();
        Application.Run(new ColorFill());
    }
    public ColorFill()
    {
        Text = "Color Fill";
        ResizeRedraw = true;
        BackColor = Color.PowderBlue;

        Menu = new MainMenu();
        Menu.MenuItems.Add("&Options");
        Menu.MenuItems[0].MenuItems.Add("&Color...", MenuColorOnClick);
    }
```

```
    void MenuColorOnClick(object objSrc, EventArgs args)
    {
        ColorFillDialog dlg = new ColorFillDialog();
        dlg.Color = clrEllipse;
        dlg.Fill = bFillEllipse;
        dlg.Background = BackColor;

        if (dlg.ShowDialog() == DialogResult.OK)
        {
            clrEllipse = dlg.Color;
            bFillEllipse = dlg.Fill;
            BackColor = dlg.Background;
            Invalidate();
        }
    }
    protected override void OnPaint(PaintEventArgs args)
    {
        Graphics grfx = args.Graphics;
        Rectangle rect = new Rectangle(0, 0, ClientSize.Width - 1,
                                             ClientSize.Height - 1);
        if (bFillEllipse)
            grfx.FillEllipse(new SolidBrush(clrEllipse), rect);
        else
            grfx.DrawEllipse(new Pen(clrEllipse), rect);
    }
}
```

Here's the dialog box:

Another program in *Programming Microsoft Windows with C#* that cries out for conversion to *FlowLayoutPanel* is the ImageDirectory program shown in Chapter 22, "Tree View and List

View." The *ImagePanel* class has the job of displaying and positioning a bunch of *PictureBox* controls on its surface. That's an ideal job for *FlowLayoutPanel*, and I show such a program in the next chapter.

FlowLayoutPanel is not suitable, however, for a form containing a bunch of controls of various types and sizes, where you want the controls to line up both horizontally and vertically. The *TableLayoutPanel* is a better tool for that job.

Table Layout Panel

TableLayoutPanel displays its children in a grid of rows and columns. Normally, each child control occupies a cell in this grid, but child controls can occupy multiple adjoining grids. Of course, other panels, including other *TableLayoutPanel* controls, can also occupy these cells. Because of the processing required to maintain the tables, however, it's probably best not to go overboard with nested tables. In many cases, a *FlowLayoutPanel* will do just as well as a child of a *TableLayoutPanel*.

You can use *TableLayoutPanel* in one of two basic ways. Most commonly, you'll enable the *AutoSize* property of *TableLayoutPanel* and the panel's container. That way, the table and its container are just as big as they need to be for the controls in the table.

Alternatively, you can give the user the ability to change the size of the table's container, either in a form with a sizeable border or on half of a *SplitContainer*. In this case, you give the *Table-LayoutPanel* a *Dock* property of *DockStyle.Fill*. Documentation warns that this is not the most efficient way to use *TableLayoutPanel*, but it's ideal for some offbeat purposes.

Automatic Table Growth

Let's assume that we're in the constructor of some container, probably either a *Form* or *Panel*. We create a *TableLayoutPanel* like so:

```
TableLayoutPanel table = new TableLayoutPanel();
table.Parent = this;
table.AutoSize = true;
```

The table is usually positioned at the upper-left corner of its parent, but the parent could be a *FlowLayoutPanel* or another *TableLayoutPanel*. If you don't set the *AutoSize* property to *true*, the size of the table won't automatically grow to display all the cells; you'd have to give the table an explicit pixel size.

When you're first experimenting with the *TableLayoutPanel*, you'll probably want to give the cells a border:

```
table.CellBorderStyle = TableLayoutPanelCellBorderStyle.Single;
```

Other cell border styles are available (*Inset*, *InsetDouble*, *Outset*, *OutsetDouble*, and *Outset-Partial*), but for most common layout tasks, you probably won't want a cell border at all.

The next step is to create a control (for example, a *Button*) that you want in this table:

```
Button btn = new Button();
btn.Text = "Button 1";
btn.AutoSize = true;
```

As usual, the *AutoSize* property of the control ensures that the button is made large enough to fit its text.

You can make the button a child of the table in one of two ways:

```
btn.Parent = table;
```

or

```
table.Controls.Add(btn);
```

If you were to keep creating more buttons (each with an incrementing text) and adding them to the table, you'd get a table with a single column like this:

As each control is added, the table adds another cell. By default, the cells are in a single column. This behavior is governed by three properties of *TableLayoutPanel*: *RowCount*, *Column-Count*, and *GrowStyle*.

By default, *RowCount* and *ColumnCount* are 0 and *GrowStyle* is the enumeration member *Table-LayoutPanelGrowStyle.AddRows*. The *RowCount* and *ColumnCount* properties do *not* tell you how many rows and columns the table has. The *TableLayoutPanel* does *not* change these properties from their initial values or the values your program assigns to them.

With the default *GrowStyle* setting of *TableLayoutPanelGrowStyle.AddRows*, the *RowCount* property is ignored. You can set *ColumnCount* to the number of columns you want. A setting of 0 is the same as 1. If you set *ColumnCount* to 2, for example, the table will grow to arrange the controls like this:

For *ColumnCount* equal to 3, the table will grow to a width of three columns:

And so forth. You can change the *ColumnCount* property at any time while controls are being added (or after they've all been added), and the controls will be rearranged to reflect the new setting.

If you set *GrowStyle* to *TableLayoutPanelGrowStyle.AddColumns*, the *ColumnCount* property is ignored. You set *RowCount* equal to the number of rows you want. When *RowCount* is equal to 0, the controls are arranged just like the default setting:

This strikes me as a bit inconsistent. I think the cells should be arranged the same as when *RowCount* equals 1, which is horizontally:

For higher *RowCount* values, the controls are subject to rearrangement as more controls are added. For example, when *RowCount* equals 2, the first two controls are arranged like so:

Button 1

Button 2

But when the third control is added, the second one is moved to a new column:

The fourth control is added where you might expect:

But the fifth control causes another rearrangement:

That's how the *RowCount* property of 2 restricts the number of rows to 2.

The following program is a simple mock-up of the user interface of a dialog box for setting the elements of a matrix transform used in Windows Forms graphics. A functional version of this dialog box (and a program that uses it) is described in Chapter 18, "Edit, List, and Spin," of my book *Programming Microsoft Windows with C#*. That version has statements like these:

```
label.Location = new Point(8, 8 + 16 * i);
label.Size = new Size(64, 8)
```

This new version lets the *TableLayoutPanel* and *AutoSize* do all the positioning and sizing. The *GrowStyle* property is left at its default value (*AddRows*), and the *ColumnCount* property is set to 2.

```
MatrixElements.cs
//------------------------------------------------
// MatrixElements.cs (c) 2005 by Charles Petzold
//------------------------------------------------
using System;
using System.Drawing;
using System.Windows.Forms;

class MatrixElements : Form
{
    [STAThread]
    public static void Main()
    {
        Application.EnableVisualStyles();
        Application.Run(new MatrixElements());
```

```
    }
    public MatrixElements()
    {
        Text = "Matrix Elements";
        FormBorderStyle = FormBorderStyle.FixedDialog;
        AutoSize = true;
        AutoSizeMode = AutoSizeMode.GrowAndShrink;

        TableLayoutPanel table = new TableLayoutPanel();
        table.Parent = this;
        table.Padding = new Padding(Font.Height);
        table.AutoSize = true;
        table.ColumnCount = 2;

        table.SuspendLayout();

        for (int i = 0; i < 6; i++)
        {
            Label lbl = new Label();
            lbl.Parent = table;
            lbl.AutoSize = true;
            lbl.Text = new string[] { "X Scale:", "Y Shear:", "X Shear:",
                                      "Y Scale:", "X Translate",
                                      "Y Translate:" }[i];

            NumericUpDown updn = new NumericUpDown();
            updn.Parent = table;
            updn.AutoSize = true;
            updn.DecimalPlaces = 2;
        }

        Button btn = new Button();
        btn.Parent = table;
        btn.AutoSize = true;
        btn.Text = "Update";

        btn = new Button();
        btn.Parent = table;
        btn.AutoSize = true;
        btn.Text = "Methods...";

        table.ResumeLayout();
    }
}
```

Notice the use of *SuspendLayout* and *ResumeLayout*. Omitting them makes a noticeable difference in the initialization of the form. The only occurrence of explicit numeric sizing is the use of *Font.Height* in setting the *Padding* property of the *TableLayoutPanel*, giving it a little air around the inside of the form:

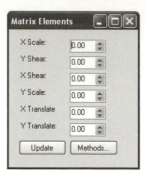

It doesn't exactly have that "hand-crafted" look that we might be fond of, but it comes close.

This dialog box shows precisely the type of layout suitable for *TableLayoutPanel*. A *FlowLayoutPanel* just wouldn't work right. If you set a *FlowDirection* of *LeftToRight* and break after every up/down control, the up/down controls would be vertically uneven because each would be positioned based on the width of the label that precedes it. If you set a *FlowDirection* of *TopDown* and break after the first button, the labels wouldn't match up with the up/down controls because they have different default heights.

So far I've discussed two options for the *GrowStyle* property—*AddRows* and *AddColumns*. The third and final option is *TableLayoutPanelGrowStyle.FixedSize*. Here the number of rows and columns is fixed by *RowCount* and *ColumnCount*. (Set these two properties to non-zero numbers *before* you set *GrowStyle* to *FixedSize*.)

With a fixed-size *GrowStyle*, the cells are populated from left to right, and then top down, much like *TableLayoutPanelGrowStyle.AddRows*. The big difference is when the number of controls exceeds the fixed number of cells (*RowCount* times *ColumnCount*). At that point, *TableLayoutPanel* will raise an exception.

Earlier I showed how you make a control a child of *TableLayoutPanel* by setting the *Parent* property of the control, or by calling the *Add* method of the *Controls* property of *TableLayoutPanel*. The *Controls* property is an object of type *TableLayoutControlCollection*, and an additional *Add* method is defined:

```
table.Controls.Add(ctrl, col, row);
```

The *col* and *row* arguments are the zero-based column and row coordinates that indicate where you want the control in the table. You can use this version of the *Add* method with any *GrowStyle*. If there's another control already in that cell when you call this *Add* method, that control will be pushed out to an adjoining cell, and other cells can be rearranged based on the *GrowStyle*, *RowCount*, and *ColumnCount* properties.

Cell Positions

In certain circumstances—such as when adding controls with a *GrowStyle* of *AddColumns* or when putting a control into a cell in which another control resides—the *TableLayoutPanel* rearranges the controls among the cells of the table. The mechanics behind the dynamic rearranging of controls are revealed somewhat with an exploration of six methods of *TableLayoutPanel* that involve cell positions.

The two *TableLayoutPanel* methods *GetCellPosition* and *SetCellPosition* both involve the use of the *TableLayoutPanelCellPosition* structure, which has two properties named *Column* and *Row*. You can use these two methods with any control that is a child of the *TableLayoutPanel*. In the following example, *lstbox* is a *ListBox* control and *table* is a *TableLayoutPanel*. Suppose that *lstbox* is added to the table's control collection using the *Add* method with column and row coordinates:

```
table.Controls.Add(lstbox, col, row);
```

The program then calls *GetCellPosition*:

```
TableLayoutPanelCellPosition cellpos = table.GetCellPosition(lstbox);
```

As you might hope and expect, the *cellpos* properties *Column* and *Row* will indicate those same column and row values. If *lstbox* had been added to the table's control collection using the simple *Add* method

```
table.Controls.Add(lstbox);
```

or by setting the list box's *Parent* property

```
lstbox.Parent = table;
```

then calling *GetCellPosition* will reveal that *cellpos.Column* and *cellpos.Row* both equal −1, which means that this control has not been given explicit cell coordinates. The table is free to move the control to another cell if necessary. The control, in other words, is free to flow.

The two methods *GetColumn* and *GetRow* are entirely consistent with *GetCellPosition*, but they simply return integers. For that reason, they might be easier to use.

Suppose you put one control into a cell and then put another control into the same cell:

```
table.Controls.Add(lstbox, 3, 2);
table.Controls.Add(btn, 3, 2);
```

The second *Add* pushes the *ListBox* out of its cell into another cell. But if you pass both these controls to *GetCellPosition* (or *GetColumn* or *GetRow*), you'll discover that both controls have a column of 3 and a row of 2 because that's what your program specified. These two controls have greater priority over that cell than controls with row and column positions of −1, but you're not guaranteed that the control is actually in that particular cell.

The *SetCellPosition*, *SetColumn*, and *SetRow* methods of *TableLayoutPanel* are restricted to controls that are already children of the table. You can use these methods to move a control to a different cell. If you set the row and column to −1, the control is moved to the first empty cell.

If you need to know in which cell a particular control *really* resides, use *GetPositionFromControl*, which also returns an object of type *TableLayoutCellPosition*:

```
TableLayoutPanelCellPosition cellpos = table.GetPositionFromControl(lstbox);
```

Now *cellpos.Column* and *cellpos.Row* indicate the actual cell in which the list box is located. Another method of *TableLayoutPanel* is

```
Control ctrl = table.GetControlFromPosition(col, row);
```

If no control is in that cell, the method returns *null*.

Column and Row Styles

By default, the width of a cell is the width of the control in that cell. But because all cells in a particular column have the same width, the width of the cell is really the width of the widest control in that cell's column. Similarly, the height of a cell is the height of the tallest control in that cell's row. There are other options, and these are known as column and row *styles*.

The *ColumnStyles* and *RowStyles* properties of *TableLayoutPanel* are both collections. The collections are of type *TableLayoutColumnStyleCollection* and *TableLayoutRowStylesCollection*, respectively, and they are collections of *ColumnStyle* objects and *RowStyle* objects.

Both *ColumnStyle* and *RowStyle* are descended from *TableLayoutStyle*. *TableLayoutStyle* has one property named *SizeType*. *ColumnStyle* adds a *Width* property and *RowStyle* adds a *Height* property.

The *SizeType* property is a member of the *SizeType* enumeration. *SizeType* has three members: *AutoSize* (the default), *Absolute*, and *Percent*.

This is confusing, I know. But what it all boils down to is fairly straightforward. Keep in mind that you don't need to mess with *RowStyle* or *ColumnStyle* at all if you want your rows and columns to be autosized. Otherwise, in your code, you'll have multiple statements that look something like this:

```
table.RowStyles.Add(new RowStyle(SizeType.Absolute, 75));
```

The first of these statements applies to the first row, the second to the second row, and so forth. You don't need to set a *RowStyle* for *all* the rows in your table—only up to the last row that shouldn't be autosized.

With *SizeType.AutoSize*, the width of the column (or height of the row) is based on the largest control in the column (or row). The actual controls in that column (or row) might or might not have their *AutoSize* properties set. The *Width* property of the *ColumnStyle* property (or the *Height* property of *RowStyle*) is ignored.

A setting of *SizeType.Absolute* means that the column width (or row height) is specified in a pixel dimension given in the *Width* (or *Height*) property.

When the *TableLayoutPanel* sets the widths and heights of the columns and rows, it uses columns and row with styles of *SizeType.Absolute* and *SizeType.AutoSize* first. It then allocates the remaining space among columns and rows that have a style setting of *SizeType.Percent*. The actual *Width* and *Height* numbers associated with *SizeType.Percent* don't matter—just their relative proportions.

I said that the *TableLayoutPanel* "allocates the remaining space" for the *SizeType.Percent* styles. This implies that *SizeType.Percent* makes no sense for tables with the *AutoSize* property set to *true*. It's really suited for tables with an explicit size or with a *Dock* property of *DockStyle.Fill*.

After the *TableLayoutPanel* has determined the size of all the columns and rows, your program can obtain those pixel dimensions as arrays of integers:

```
int[] aiWidths = table.GetColumnWidths();
int[] aiHeights = table.GetRowHeights();
```

These are perhaps also the easiest methods to use if you want to know the actual number of columns and rows in the table:

```
iNumCols = table.GetColumnWidths().Length;
iNumRows = table.GetRowHeights().Length;
```

Dock and *Anchor*

To align a control in a cell, you can set the control's *Dock* or *Anchor* properties. You can ignore *Dock* for this purpose because anything *Dock* can do, *Anchor* can also do, and more.

You set the *Anchor* property of a control to one or more of the members of *AnchorStyles* separated by the C# bitwise OR operator. As you'll recall, the *AnchorStyles* members are *Left*, *Top*, *Right*, *Bottom*, and *None*. This is all you need to remember: The inclusion of any *AnchorStyles* member makes the control touch that side of the cell. Otherwise, the control is centered in its cell. The control's size is not changed unless it needs to touch opposite sides.

For example, to put the control in the upper-right corner of the cell, use *AnchorStyles.Top | AnchorStyles.Right*. To put the control at the bottom of the cell centered horizontally, use *AnchorStyles.Bottom*. To vertically center the control but have it extended to the left and right, use *AnchorStyle.Left | AnchorStyles.Right*. To make the control hover in the middle of the cell, use *AnchorStyles.None*.

Veteran Windows programmers might recognize the next program. The Color Scroll program was originally published in the May 1987 issue of *Microsoft Systems Journal*, and a version has appeared in every Windows programming book I've written since then.

Curiously enough, starting with its earliest incarnation, the primary purpose of the Color Scroll program has always been to demonstrate dynamic layout! (I just didn't know what it was called back then.) As the user changed the size of the program's window, the program resized and repositioned its controls using a bunch of arithmetic. With a *TableLayoutPanel*, the program works much the same but the arithmetic is gone. (Or rather, the arithmetic is gone from *my* code. There's probably quite a bit in *TableLayoutPanel* itself.)

ColorScrollTable.cs

```
//------------------------------------------------
// ColorScrollTable.cs (c) 2005 by Charles Petzold
//------------------------------------------------
using System;
using System.Drawing;
using System.Windows.Forms;

class ColorScrollTable : Form
{
    Panel pnlColor;
    Label[] alblValue = new Label[3];

    [STAThread]
    public static void Main()
    {
        Application.EnableVisualStyles();
        Application.Run(new ColorScrollTable());
    }
    public ColorScrollTable()
    {
        Text = "Color Scroll with TableLayoutPanel";

        // Create a SplitContainer that fills the client area.
        SplitContainer splt = new SplitContainer();
        splt.Parent = this;
        splt.Dock = DockStyle.Fill;
        splt.SplitterDistance = ClientSize.Width / 2;

        // The TableLayoutPanel is on the left of the splitter.
        TableLayoutPanel table = new TableLayoutPanel();
        table.Parent = splt.Panel1;
        table.Dock = DockStyle.Fill;
        table.BackColor = Color.White;
        table.ColumnCount = 3;
        table.RowCount = 3;

        // Save the right SplitterPanel as a field.
        pnlColor = splt.Panel2;
```

```csharp
        // Two arrays for color names and initial values.
        string[] astrColors = { "Red", "Green", "Blue" };
        int[] aiPanelColor = new int[3] { pnlColor.BackColor.R,
                                          pnlColor.BackColor.G,
                                          pnlColor.BackColor.B };

    // Loop through the three columns (red, green, blue).
    for (int col = 0; col < 3; col++)
    {
        // Label at the top identifies red, green, or blue.
        Label lbl = new Label();
        lbl.AutoSize = true;
        lbl.Anchor = AnchorStyles.None;
        lbl.Text = astrColors[col];
        lbl.ForeColor = Color.FromName(astrColors[col]);
        table.Controls.Add(lbl, col, 0);

        // Scrollbar to set new values.
        VScrollBar vscrl = new VScrollBar();
        vscrl.Parent = table;
        vscrl.Anchor = AnchorStyles.Top | AnchorStyles.Bottom;
        vscrl.TabStop = true;
        vscrl.LargeChange = 16;
        vscrl.Maximum = 255 + vscrl.LargeChange - 1;
        vscrl.Value = aiPanelColor[col];
        vscrl.ValueChanged += OnScrollValueChanged;
        table.Controls.Add(vscrl, col, 1);

        // Label showing color value is bound to scrollbar.
        alblValue[col] = new Label();
        alblValue[col].AutoSize = true;
        alblValue[col].Anchor = AnchorStyles.None;
        alblValue[col].ForeColor = Color.FromName(astrColors[col]);
        alblValue[col].DataBindings.Add("Text", vscrl, "Value");
        table.Controls.Add(alblValue[col], col, 2);

        // ColumnStyles allocate three columns equally.
        table.ColumnStyles.Add(new ColumnStyle(SizeType.Percent, 33));
    }

    // RowStyles let the middle row be as large as possible.
    table.RowStyles.Add(new RowStyle(SizeType.AutoSize));
    table.RowStyles.Add(new RowStyle(SizeType.Percent, 100));
    table.RowStyles.Add(new RowStyle(SizeType.AutoSize));
}
// When a scrollbar value changes, change the panel background color.
void OnScrollValueChanged(object objSrc, EventArgs args)
{
    pnlColor.BackColor = Color.FromArgb(int.Parse(alblValue[0].Text),
                                        int.Parse(alblValue[1].Text),
                                        int.Parse(alblValue[2].Text));
}
}
```

Here's the program in action:

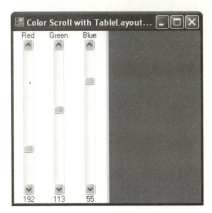

The client area of the form is filled with a *SplitContainer*. At the right, we see *Panel2* with a *BackColor* property governed by the three scroll bars. On the left is a 3-by-3 *TableLayoutPanel* with its *Dock* property set to *DockStyle.Fill*. The six labels have their *AutoSize* property set to *true* and their *Anchor* properties set to *AnchorStyles.None*. The three scroll bars do not have *AutoSize* enabled (the widths of the scroll bars are automatically appropriately sized anyway), and the *Anchor* properties are set to *AnchorStyles.Top | AnchorStyles.Bottom* to make them the height of the cell.

Another essential key to making this work right is the *RowStyles* collection. Three *RowStyle* objects are created at the very end of the constructor: The first and third rows with the labels have a *SizeType* of *AutoSize*. The middle row with the scroll bars has a *SizeType* of *Percent*, essentially instructing the *TableLayoutPanel* to use all available space for it. You might want to comment out those three statements to see the effect. (The default size of the scroll bar makes that row rather short, while all the leftover space is awarded to the third row.) Removing just the third *RowStyles.Add* statement has no effect—without an explicit *RowStyle*, that row would be tallied as *AutoSize* anyway.

Column and Row Spans

So far, I've shown programs that use *TableLayoutPanel* as a strict fixed grid of rows and columns. It's probably rare that a form can be squeezed into those constraints. Most forms will require a bit more flexibility with controls that spill over into multiple cells.

You accomplish this feat with column and row spans. For example:

```
table.SetColumnSpan(ctrl, 2);
```

The *ctrl* control must already be a child of the *table*. The second argument gives it a span of two cells. If *ctrl* occupied cell (2, 4) before the call, it will now occupy cells (2, 4) and (3, 4) after the call. If there was another control in cell (3, 4), that control will be bounced to an adjoining cell, perhaps shifting other controls and raising an exception if there aren't sufficient cells to accommodate everything. (It's probably best not to rely on cell-shifting logic if you want controls in specific locations.) If you're using cell borders, the border between cell (2, 4) and (3, 4) will *not* be removed.

The following control will be handled similarly:

```
table.SetRowSpan(ctrl, 3);
```

If *ctrl* occupied cell (2, 4) before this call, it will now occupy cells (2, 4), (2, 5), and (2, 6).

You can use both *SetColumnSpan* and *SetRowSpan* on the same control. The *GetColumnSpan* and *GetRowSpan* methods take a control argument and return an integer span value.

For a control that spans multiple rows and columns, *GetPositionFromControl* returns the uppermost and leftmost cell that the control occupies. *GetControlFromPosition* returns the same control for all the cell coordinates that it occupies.

Case Study: Font Dialog

Let's tackle more of a real-life project now and attempt to duplicate the standard font dialog box. Here's what an instance of *FontDialog* looks like with *ShowEffects* and *ShowColor* set to *true*.

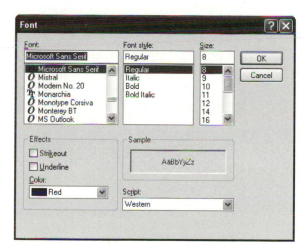

I see four columns here, the first three with the three combo boxes and the fourth with the two buttons. I see three rows, the first with the labels at the top, the second with the combo boxes, and the third with everything else. All other layout can be handled with *FlowLayout-Panel* and the *GroupPanel* control I presented earlier in this chapter.

I tried to make the new font dialog box have much of the functionality of the existing one. One petty annoyance is the way the font dialog box handles font styles. The *FontStyle* enumeration has members *Regular*, *Bold*, *Italic*, *Strikeout*, and *Underline*. But the standard font dialog box has a combo box with the items Regular, Bold, Italic, and Bold Italic. The Strikeout and Underline options appear as check boxes.

Another problem is that not all font families support all styles. Attempting to create a font from a font family and an unsupported font style raises an exception.

To isolate all the code involved in font styles, I made *StyleComboBox* its own class.

StyleComboBox.cs
```
//--------------------------------------------
// StyleComboBox.cs (c) 2005 by Charles Petzold
//--------------------------------------------
using System;
using System.Drawing;
using System.Windows.Forms;

class StyleComboBox : ComboBox
{
    public string FamilyName
    {
        set
        {
            TryStyle(value, FontStyle.Regular, "Regular");
            TryStyle(value, FontStyle.Italic, "Italic");
            TryStyle(value, FontStyle.Bold, "Bold");
            TryStyle(value, FontStyle.Bold | FontStyle.Italic, "Bold Italic");
            SelectedIndex = 0;
        }
    }
    public FontStyle FontStyle
    {
        set
        {
            if ((value & FontStyle.Bold & FontStyle.Italic) != 0)
                SelectedItem = "Bold Italic";

            else if ((value & FontStyle.Bold) != 0)
                SelectedItem = "Bold";

            else if ((value & FontStyle.Italic) != 0)
                SelectedItem = "Italic";
            else
                SelectedItem = "Regular";
        }
        get
        {
            if (SelectedItem.ToString() == "Bold Italic")
                return FontStyle.Bold | FontStyle.Italic;

            else if (SelectedItem.ToString() == "Bold")
                return FontStyle.Bold;
```

```
                else if (SelectedItem.ToString() == "Italic")
                    return FontStyle.Italic;

                return FontStyle.Regular;
            }
        }
    void TryStyle(string strFamilyName, FontStyle fntstyle, string strStyle)
    {
        int index = FindStringExact(strStyle);

        try
        {
            new Font(strFamilyName, 12, fntstyle);

            if (index == -1)
                Items.Add(strStyle);
        }
        catch
        {
            if (index != -1)
                Items.Remove(strStyle);
        }
    }
}
```

This combo box has a write-only *FamilyName* property that lets it add or delete any styles that might be supported or unsupported by that font family. The *FontStyle* property performs the necessary conversion between the *FontStyle* members and the combo box text.

Because the combo box showing the font colors should show the actual color, the combo box needs to be owner-drawn. That, too, became its own class.

ColorComboBox.cs

```
//-----------------------------------------------
// ColorComboBox.cs (c) 2005 by Charles Petzold
//-----------------------------------------------
using System;
using System.Drawing;
using System.Windows.Forms;

class ColorComboBox : ComboBox
{
    public ColorComboBox()
    {
        DataSource = new string[] { "Black", "Maroon", "Green", "Olive",
                                    "Navy", "Purple", "Teal", "Gray",
                                    "Silver", "Red", "Lime", "Yellow",
                                    "Blue", "Fuchsia", "Aqua", "White" };

        DropDownStyle = ComboBoxStyle.DropDownList;
        DrawMode = DrawMode.OwnerDrawFixed;
        ItemHeight = Font.Height;
```

```
    }
    public Color Color
    {
        get { return Color.FromName((string) SelectedItem); }
        set { SelectedText = value.Name; }
    }
    protected override void OnDrawItem(DrawItemEventArgs args)
    {
        Graphics grfx = args.Graphics;

        Rectangle rectColor =
            new Rectangle(args.Bounds.Left, args.Bounds.Top,
                          2 * args.Bounds.Height, args.Bounds.Height);

        rectColor.Inflate(-1, -1);

        Rectangle rectText =
            new Rectangle(args.Bounds.Left + 2 * args.Bounds.Height,
                          args.Bounds.Top,
                          args.Bounds.Width - 2 * args.Bounds.Height,
                          args.Bounds.Height);

        args.DrawBackground();
        grfx.DrawRectangle(Pens.Black, rectColor);
        grfx.FillRectangle(
            new SolidBrush(Color.FromName(Items[args.Index].ToString())),
            rectColor);
        grfx.DrawString(Items[args.Index].ToString(), Font,
            new SolidBrush(args.ForeColor), rectText);
    }
}
```

We're now ready to combine these two controls and others in a form.

NewFontDialog.cs

```
//---------------------------------------------
// NewFontDialog.cs (c) 2005 by Charles Petzold
//---------------------------------------------
using System;
using System.Drawing;
using System.Windows.Forms;

class NewFontDialog : Form
{
    ComboBox comboFont, comboSize;
    StyleComboBox comboStyle;
    CheckBox chkboxStrikeout, chkboxUnderline;
    ColorComboBox comboColor;
    Label lblColor, lblSample;

    public NewFontDialog()
    {
        FormBorderStyle = FormBorderStyle.FixedDialog;
```

```
MinimizeBox = MaximizeBox = ShowInTaskbar = false;
Text = "Font";
AutoSize = true;

TableLayoutPanel table = new TableLayoutPanel();
table.Parent = this;
table.AutoSize = true;
table.ColumnCount = 4;
table.RowCount = 3;
table.Padding = new Padding(base.Font.Height);

Label lbl = new Label();
lbl.Text = "&Font:";
lbl.AutoSize = true;
table.Controls.Add(lbl, 0, 0);

comboFont = new ComboBox();
comboFont.DropDownStyle = ComboBoxStyle.Simple;
comboFont.AutoSize = true;
comboFont.TextChanged += OnComboBoxTextChanged;
table.Controls.Add(comboFont, 0, 1);

// Fill the comboFont box with the font families.
foreach (FontFamily fntfam in FontFamily.Families)
    comboFont.Items.Add(fntfam.Name);

lbl = new Label();
lbl.Text = "&Font st&yle:";
lbl.AutoSize = true;
table.Controls.Add(lbl, 1, 0);

comboStyle = new StyleComboBox();
comboStyle.DropDownStyle = ComboBoxStyle.Simple;
comboStyle.AutoSize = true;
comboStyle.TextChanged += OnComboBoxTextChanged;
table.Controls.Add(comboStyle, 1, 1);

lbl = new Label();
lbl.Text = "&Size:";
lbl.AutoSize = true;
table.Controls.Add(lbl, 2, 0);

comboSize = new ComboBox();
comboSize.DropDownStyle = ComboBoxStyle.Simple;
comboSize.AutoSize = true;
comboSize.TextChanged += OnComboBoxTextChanged;
table.Controls.Add(comboSize, 2, 1);

// Add the font sizes to the combo box.
for (int i = 8; i < 12; i++)
    comboSize.Items.Add(i);

for (int i = 12; i < 30; i += 2)
    comboSize.Items.Add(i);
```

```
for (int i = 36; i <= 72; i += 12)
    comboSize.Items.Add(i);

comboSize.SelectedIndex = 0;

// Effects GroupPanel.
GroupPanel grppnl = new GroupPanel();
grppnl.Text = "Effects";
table.Controls.Add(grppnl, 0, 2);

// Strikeout CheckBox.
chkboxStrikeout = new CheckBox();
chkboxStrikeout.Text = "Stri&keout";
chkboxStrikeout.AutoSize = true;
chkboxStrikeout.Click += delegate { ShowNewFont(); };
grppnl.Controls.Add(chkboxStrikeout);

// Underline CheckBox.
chkboxUnderline = new CheckBox();
chkboxUnderline.Text = "&Underline";
chkboxUnderline.AutoSize = true;
chkboxUnderline.Click += delegate { ShowNewFont(); };
grppnl.Controls.Add(chkboxUnderline);

// Color Label.
lblColor = new Label();
lblColor.Text = "&Color:";
lblColor.AutoSize = true;
lblColor.Visible = false;
grppnl.Controls.Add(lblColor);

// Color ComboBox
comboColor = new ColorComboBox();
comboColor.Visible = false;
comboColor.AutoSize = true;
comboColor.TextChanged += OnComboBoxTextChanged;
grppnl.Controls.Add(comboColor);

// Flow panel for sample and script
FlowLayoutPanel flow = new FlowLayoutPanel();
flow.AutoSize = true;
flow.FlowDirection = FlowDirection.TopDown;
table.Controls.Add(flow, 1, 2);
table.SetColumnSpan(flow, 2);

// GroupPanel for sample.
grppnl = new GroupPanel();
grppnl.Text = "Sample";
flow.Controls.Add(grppnl);

// Sample label.
lblSample = new Label();
lblSample.Text = "AaBbYyZz";
lblSample.Font = base.Font;
lblSample.TextAlign = ContentAlignment.MiddleCenter;
```

```
    lblSample.BorderStyle = BorderStyle.Fixed3D;
    lblSample.Size = new Size(20 * base.Font.Height, 3 *
        base.Font.Height);
    grppnl.Controls.Add(lblSample);

    // Flow panel for buttons.
    flow = new FlowLayoutPanel();
    flow.AutoSize = true;
    flow.FlowDirection = FlowDirection.TopDown;
    table.Controls.Add(flow, 3, 1);

    // OK button.
    Button btn = new Button();
    btn.Text = "OK";
    btn.AutoSize = true;
    btn.DialogResult = DialogResult.OK;
    AcceptButton = btn;
    flow.Controls.Add(btn);

    // Cancel button.
    btn = new Button();
    btn.Text = "Cancel";
    btn.AutoSize = true;
    btn.DialogResult = DialogResult.Cancel;
    CancelButton = btn;
    flow.Controls.Add(btn);

    // Generate event for filling style box.
    comboFont.SelectedItem = base.Font.FontFamily.Name;
}

public new Font Font
{
    set
    {
        lblSample.Font = value;
        comboFont.SelectedItem = value.FontFamily.Name;

        comboStyle.FamilyName = value.FontFamily.Name;
        comboStyle.FontStyle = value.Style;

        chkboxStrikeout.Checked = (value.Style &
            FontStyle.Strikeout) != 0;
        chkboxUnderline.Checked = (value.Style &
            FontStyle.Underline) != 0;

        comboSize.SelectedItem = value.SizeInPoints;
        comboSize.Text = value.SizeInPoints.ToString();
    }
    get
    {
        return lblSample.Font;
    }
}
public Color Color
```

```
    {
        set
        {
            comboColor.Color = value;
        }
        get
        {
            return comboColor.Color;
        }
    }
    public bool ShowColor
    {
        set
        {
            lblColor.Visible = comboColor.Visible = value;
        }
        get
        {
            return comboColor.Visible;
        }
    }
    void OnComboBoxTextChanged(object objSrc, EventArgs args)
    {
        ComboBox combo = (ComboBox)objSrc;

        if (combo == comboColor)
        {
            lblSample.ForeColor = comboColor.Color;
            return;
        }

        if (combo == comboFont)
        {
            int index = comboFont.FindStringExact(comboFont.Text);

            if (index != -1)
            {
                comboFont.SelectedIndex = index;
                comboStyle.FamilyName = comboFont.Text;
            }
        }
        ShowNewFont();
    }
    void ShowNewFont()
    {
        FontStyle fntstyle;

        try
        {
            fntstyle = comboStyle.FontStyle;
        }
        catch
        {
            return;
        }
```

```
        if (chkboxStrikeout.Checked)
            fntstyle |= FontStyle.Strikeout;

        if (chkboxUnderline.Checked)
            fntstyle |= FontStyle.Underline;

        try
        {
            Font fnt = new Font(comboFont.Text, float.Parse(comboSize.Text),
                fntstyle);
            lblSample.Font = fnt;
        }
        catch
        {
            ;
        }
    }
}
```

It's basically a *TableLayoutPanel* with four columns and three rows. The Effects section uses a *GroupPanel*. The Sample and Script sections go into a *FlowPanel* (I didn't implement the Script combo box), with the Sample label inside a *GroupPanel*. A few explicit sizings are used: The *TableLayoutPanel* has *Padding* property equal to the height of the default font, and the Sample label is sized with the default font as well. Otherwise, everything is autosized.

These files as well as the next one are part of the FontDialogMimic project.

FontDialogMimic.cs

```
//-------------------------------------------------
// FontDialogMimic.cs (c) 2005 by Charles Petzold
//-------------------------------------------------
using System;
using System.Drawing;
using System.Windows.Forms;

class FontDialogMimic : Form
{
    [STAThread]
    public static void Main()
    {
        Application.EnableVisualStyles();
        Application.Run(new FontDialogMimic());
    }
    public FontDialogMimic()
    {
        Text = "FontDialog Mimic";
        ResizeRedraw = true;
        ForeColor = Color.Red;

        Menu = new MainMenu();
        Menu.MenuItems.Add("&Format");
        Menu.MenuItems[0].MenuItems.Add("&Old Font Dialog...", OnOldFont);
```

```
            Menu.MenuItems[0].MenuItems.Add("&New Font Dialog...", OnNewFont);
    }
    void OnOldFont(object objSrc, EventArgs args)
    {
        FontDialog fntdlg = new FontDialog();
        fntdlg.Font = Font;
        fntdlg.Color = ForeColor;
        fntdlg.ShowColor = true;

        if (fntdlg.ShowDialog() == DialogResult.OK)
        {
            Font = fntdlg.Font;
            ForeColor = fntdlg.Color;
            Invalidate();
        }
    }
    void OnNewFont(object objSrc, EventArgs args)
    {
        NewFontDialog fntdlg = new NewFontDialog();
        fntdlg.Font = Font;
        fntdlg.Color = ForeColor;
        fntdlg.ShowColor = true;

        if (fntdlg.ShowDialog() == DialogResult.OK)
        {
            Font = fntdlg.Font;
            ForeColor = fntdlg.Color;
            Invalidate();
        }
    }
    protected override void OnPaint(PaintEventArgs args)
    {
        Graphics grfx = args.Graphics;
        StringFormat strfmt = new StringFormat();
        strfmt.LineAlignment = strfmt.Alignment = StringAlignment.Center;
        grfx.DrawString(Font.ToString(), Font, new SolidBrush(ForeColor),
            ClientRectangle, strfmt);
    }
}
```

The program has menu items that let you choose the standard font dialog box or the new font dialog box. The new one looks like this:

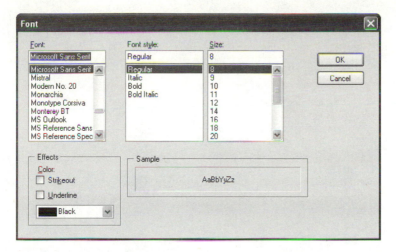

Testing Your Layouts

Every form and dialog box must be tested for functionality, but you should also test your forms for their resilience to device oddities. Try setting the screen resolution to a low or high value. (You can invoke the Display Properties dialog box from the Display item in Control Panel or by right-clicking the screen and selecting Properties. Click the Settings tab and the Advanced button to change the resolution of your display.) Also try giving your forms a smaller or larger font. All the controls should inherit this font, and they should size themselves appropriately.

Chapter 4

Custom Controls

Some people are never satisfied, and that probably goes double for programmers. Even with the many controls available under Windows Forms, it is still sometimes desirable to ascend a step (or perhaps several) beyond the customary controls into the realms of the custom control.

From a programming perspective, a custom control is a class that you define that derives—either directly or indirectly—from *Control*. A custom control can be an enhancement of an existing control or an entirely new control. Although you can perform a significant amount of customization just by installing event handlers on existing controls and processing those events, a new class is required if you need to *entirely* override default event handling. For example, you can add new visuals to a *Button* control by installing a *Paint* event handler, but you can't prevent the *Button* from displaying its own visuals as well unless you create a new class and override *OnPaint*.

You also need to create a new class if you want to add fields or properties to an existing control. However, if you just need to attach some arbitrary data to a control, you might consider using the *Tag* property provided specifically for this purpose. The property is defined as type *object*, so some casting will be required when you access it, but it's ideal for simple control identification and attaching arbitrary data.

As with most any programming job, the real benefit of custom controls comes with reusing them in multiple applications or in making them available to other programmers, either for cash or just glory.

Enhancing Existing Controls

A control is basically a filter through which user input is interpreted and consolidated into actions such as events. In most cases, a control must perform three crucial jobs. First, it displays something on a screen to identify itself to the user. Second, it handles user input, generally from the keyboard and mouse. (A control might also be specially programmed to handle stylus input on a Tablet PC, or even to respond to voice input.) Third, the control fires events to notify the application using the control of certain changes.

Because existing controls have already been designed and tested to perform these three functions, it is much easier to enhance an existing control (perhaps by deriving from *Button*, for example) rather than to start from scratch by deriving from *Control*.

Overriding Methods

Here's an extremely simple example, which is a button that beeps when it is clicked with the mouse:

```
BeepButton.cs
//------------------------------------------
// BeepButton.cs (c) 2005 by Charles Petzold
//------------------------------------------
using System;
using System.Drawing;
using System.Media;
using System.Windows.Forms;

class BeepButton : Button
{
    protected override void OnClick(EventArgs args)
    {
        SystemSounds.Exclamation.Play();
        base.OnClick(args);
    }
}
```

BeepButton simply inherits from *Button* and overrides the protected *OnClick* method. The overriding method makes a sound by using two of the three classes from the *System.Media* namespace, which is new in the .NET Framework 2.0. The *SystemsSounds* class contains several static properties—named *Asterisk*, *Beep*, *Exclamation*, *Hand*, and *Question*—associated with different sounds. These properties return objects of type *SystemSound*. Notice the difference in class names: the static methods in *SystemsSounds* (plural) return an object of type *SystemSound* (singular). The *SystemSound* class has a single method named *Play* to play the sound.

It is *imperative* that the *OnClick* method in your new class call the *OnClick* method in the base class:

```
base.OnClick(args);
```

Without this call, any program using the *BeepButton* control will not have access to the *Click* event. Here's why: *Button* inherits the *Click* event and the *OnClick* method from *Control*. The code in *Control* that defines the *Click* event probably looks something like this:

```
public event EventHandler Click;
```

The *EventHandler* part of that statement indicates that any event handlers installed for the *Click* event be defined in accordance with the *EventHandler* delegate.

The *Control* class doesn't have to worry about the mechanism for letting the program attach and detach event handlers. That happens behind the scenes. But *Control* is responsible for firing the *Click* event, and that happens in its *OnClick* method, which probably looks something like this:

```
protected virtual void OnClick(EventArgs args)
{
    ...
    if (Click != null)
        Click(this, args);
    ...
}
```

This *OnClick* method probably gets called from at least two places. The control's *OnMouse-Down* method—which occurs when the mouse cursor is positioned on top of the control and a mouse button is depressed—undoubtedly makes a call to *OnClick*. For buttons, *OnClick* is also called when the button has input focus and the user presses the spacebar or Enter key.

I've indicated with ellipses that *OnClick* might or might not perform some other duties, but it definitely triggers the *Click* event. The code I've shown can be translated like this: "If there are any *Click* event handlers installed, call those event handlers with the current object as the first argument and an *EventArgs* object as the second argument." If you define a class that inherits from *Control* (either directly or indirectly) and you override the *OnClick* method without call-ing the method in the base class, the code to call all the *Click* event handlers does not get exe-cuted. (Of course, if disabling the *Click* event is part of your nefarious strategy in creating a new control, don't bother calling the *OnClick* method in the base class.)

Code examples showing how an *OnClick* method calls the method in the base class usually put this call at the very beginning of the method:

```
protected override void OnClick(EventArgs args)
{
    base.OnClick(args);
    ...
}
```

Sometimes you might want the code in the base method executed first, but in this particular example, it didn't work well at all (and you'll see why shortly), so I put the call to *base.OnClick* at the end of *OnClick* in *ButtonBeep*.

Here's a simple "demo" program that creates an object of type *BeepButton* and installs a *Click* event handler on the button to display a message box:

```
BeepButtonDemo.cs
//-------------------------------------------------
// BeepButtonDemo.cs (c) 2005 by Charles Petzold
//-------------------------------------------------
using System;
using System.Drawing;
using System.Windows.Forms;
```

```
class BeepButtonDemo : Form
{
    [STAThread]
    public static void Main()
    {
        Application.EnableVisualStyles();
        Application.Run(new BeepButtonDemo());
    }
    public BeepButtonDemo()
    {
        Text = "BeepButton Demonstration";

        BeepButton btn = new BeepButton();
        btn.Parent = this;
        btn.Location = new Point(100, 100);
        btn.AutoSize = true;
        btn.Text = "Click the BeepButton";
        btn.Click += ButtonOnClick;
    }
    void ButtonOnClick(object objSrc, EventArgs args)
    {
        SilentMsgBox.Show("The BeepButton has been clicked", Text);
    }
}
```

Actually, I couldn't use the regular *MessageBox* class because that class itself makes a sound as the message box is displayed. Instead, I duplicated some of the functionality of *MessageBox* in this class:

SilentMsgBox.cs

```
//---------------------------------------------
// SilentMsgBox.cs (c) 2005 by Charles Petzold
//---------------------------------------------
using System;
using System.Drawing;
using System.Windows.Forms;

class SilentMsgBox
{
    public static DialogResult Show(string strMessage, string strCaption)
    {
        Form frm = new Form();
        frm.StartPosition = FormStartPosition.CenterScreen;
        frm.FormBorderStyle = FormBorderStyle.FixedDialog;
        frm.MinimizeBox = frm.MaximizeBox = frm.ShowInTaskbar = false;
        frm.AutoSize = true;
        frm.AutoSizeMode = AutoSizeMode.GrowAndShrink;
        frm.Text = strCaption;

        FlowLayoutPanel pnl = new FlowLayoutPanel();
        pnl.Parent = frm;
        pnl.AutoSize = true;
        pnl.FlowDirection = FlowDirection.TopDown;
```

```
        pnl.WrapContents = false;
        pnl.Padding = new Padding(pnl.Font.Height);

        Label lbl = new Label();
        lbl.Parent = pnl;
        lbl.AutoSize = true;
        lbl.Anchor = AnchorStyles.None;
        lbl.Margin = new Padding(lbl.Font.Height);
        lbl.Text = strMessage;

        Button btn = new Button();
        btn.Parent = pnl;
        btn.AutoSize = true;
        btn.Anchor = AnchorStyles.None;
        btn.Margin = new Padding(btn.Font.Height);
        btn.Text = "OK";
        btn.DialogResult = DialogResult.OK;

        return frm.ShowDialog();
    }
}
```

The BeepButton.cs, BeepButtonDemo.cs, and SilentMsgBox.cs files are all part of the Beep-ButtonDemo project.

Just to assure yourself that everything I said about the *Click* event handler is true, comment out the call to the *base.OnClick* method in *BeepButton*, recompile, and take careful note that *BeepButtonDemo* no longer gets notified of the *Click* event.

Now try this: in the *OnClick* method in *BeepButton*, swap the order of the two statements so that the *OnClick* method in the base class is called before the sound is played:

```
protected override void OnClick(EventArgs args)
{
    base.OnClick(args);
    SystemSounds.Exclamation.Play();
}
```

When you click the button with the mouse, this *OnClick* method is called—probably from the *OnMouseDown* method in *Control*. In this altered code, *BeepButton* first makes a call to the *OnClick* method in its base class. That base class is *Button*, but the *OnClick* method in *Button* calls the *OnClick* method in *its* base class, and so on, and eventually the *OnClick* method in *Control* is called. That *OnClick* method is responsible for executing the code that calls all the event handlers installed for *Click*. The *BeepButtonDemo* has installed such an event handler, so the *ButtonOnClick* method in *BeepButtonDemo* is called. That method calls the static *Show* method in *SilentMsgBox*, which (like *MessageBox*) displays a modal dialog box and waits for the user to dismiss it. When the user ends the message box, the *Show* call returns control back to *ButtonOnClick*, which in turn returns control back to the *OnClick* method in *BeepButton*, which finally (in the altered code) plays the sound—unfortunately, long after the user clicked the button.

The lesson is: You can choose when an *On* method calls the method in the base class. Choose wisely.

Adding New Properties

Besides demonstrating how to enhance existing controls, the *BeepButton* class also demonstrated the use of two of the three classes in the *System.Media* namespace. The third class in that namespace is *SoundPlayer*, which is used by the next program to create a new control called *SoundButton*. The *SoundButton* control is similar to *BeepButton* except that it plays a MicrosoftWindows waveform (.wav) file rather than a simple beep. This feature allows your buttons to be accompanied by the soothing voice of Bart Simpson, for example.

This class also inherits from *Button*. The first thing it does is create and store a *SoundPlayer* object as a field:

```
SoundButton.cs
//-------------------------------------------
// SoundButton.cs (c) 2005 by Charles Petzold
//-------------------------------------------
using System;
using System.Drawing;
using System.IO;
using System.Media;
using System.Windows.Forms;

class SoundButton : Button
{
    SoundPlayer sndplay = new SoundPlayer();

    public string WaveFile
    {
        set
        {
            sndplay.SoundLocation = value;
            sndplay.LoadAsync();
        }
        get
        {
            return sndplay.SoundLocation;
        }
    }
    public Stream WaveStream
    {
        set
        {
            sndplay.Stream = value;
            sndplay.LoadAsync();
        }
```

```
        get
        {
            return sndplay.Stream;
        }
    }
    protected override void OnClick(EventArgs args)
    {
        if (sndplay.IsLoadCompleted)
            sndplay.Play();

        base.OnClick(args);
    }
}
```

The class defines two new properties named *WaveFile* and *WaveStream*. These correspond to the *SoundPlayer* properties *SoundLocation* and *Stream*, which are the two ways that a program specifies to *SoundPlayer* the source of a waveform file. The *SoundLocation* property of *Sound-Player* (and the *WaveFile* property of *SoundButton*) is a string that indicates a local file or a URL. *Stream* (and *WaveStream*) is an object of type *Stream*, an abstract class defined in the *System.IO* namespace. The descendents of *Stream* include *FileStream*, which generally refers to an open file, and *MemoryStream*, which is a block of memory accessed as if it were a file. The *Stream* option is particularly useful for embedding waveform files into your executable file and accessing them as resources (as I'll demonstrate shortly). Whichever property is specified most recently is the one that *SoundPlayer* uses to access the waveform file.

Normally, *SoundPlayer* will not load a waveform file into memory until it needs to play it, which in this case occurs during the *OnClick* method. I was afraid that this loading process might slow down processing of *OnClick*, so the two properties load in the waveforms immediately in a separate thread by calling *LoadAsync*. (Using the *Load* method of *SoundPlayer* instead loads the waveform synchronously—that is, in the same thread—which might slow down initialization of the program.)

The normal *Play* command of *SoundPlayer* is asynchronous. The *OnClick* method starts the sound going and then does its other processing, which is a call to the base *OnClick* method and whatever else might happen as a result of that. (The alternative *PlaySync* method of *Sound-Player* doesn't return until a sound is finished. The *PlayLooping* method is asynchronous and plays the sound repeatedly until *Stop* is called.)

Here's a program that demonstrates three ways to use *SoundButton*: loading a local file (in this case the "ta-da" sound from the Windows Media directory), loading a file from the Internet (a lion's roar from the Oakland Zoo Web site), and using a resource. The SoundButtonDemo project also includes the SoundButton.cs file and a waveform file named MakeItSo.wav, which is my voice expressing the user's wish to "make it so."

SoundButtonDemo.cs

```
//-------------------------------------------------
// SoundButtonDemo.cs (c) 2005 by Charles Petzold
//-------------------------------------------------
using System;
using System.Drawing;
using System.IO;
using System.Windows.Forms;

class SoundButtonDemo : Form
{
    [STAThread]
    public static void Main()
    {
        Application.EnableVisualStyles();
        Application.Run(new SoundButtonDemo());
    }
    public SoundButtonDemo()
    {
        Text = "SoundButton Demonstration";

        SoundButton btn = new SoundButton();
        btn.Parent = this;
        btn.Location = new Point(50, 25);
        btn.AutoSize = true;
        btn.Text = "SoundButton with File";
        btn.Click += ButtonOnClick;
        btn.WaveFile = Path.Combine(
            Environment.GetEnvironmentVariable("windir"),
            "Media\\tada.wav");

        btn = new SoundButton();
        btn.Parent = this;
        btn.Location = new Point(50, 125);
        btn.AutoSize = true;
        btn.Text = "SoundButton with URI";
        btn.Click += ButtonOnClick;
        btn.WaveFile = "http://www.oaklandzoo.org/atoz/azlinsnd.wav";

        btn = new SoundButton();
        btn.Parent = this;
        btn.Location = new Point(50, 225);
        btn.AutoSize = true;
        btn.Text = "SoundButton with Resource";
        btn.Click += ButtonOnClick;
        btn.WaveStream = GetType().Assembly.GetManifestResourceStream(
                "SoundButtonDemo.MakeItSo.wav");
    }
    void ButtonOnClick(object objSrc, EventArgs args)
    {
        Button btn = objSrc as Button;
        SilentMsgBox.Show("The SoundButton has been clicked", btn.Text);
    }
}
```

None of these three approaches to obtaining waveform files is trivial. The tada.wav file is located in the *Media* subdirectory of your Windows directory, but that directory might be WINDOWS or WINNT. The program uses the *GetEnvironmentVariable* of the *Environment* class to obtain the directory name and then combines that with the *Media* subdirectory and tada.wav filename.

Specifying a URL is much easier of course, but only if you have complete confidence that the URL will not change over the commercial lifetime of your program, and that the program will have access to a live Internet connection.

The foolproof method for getting access to binary files is to make them part of your executable as resources. You do this by first adding the file to your project. When you click the file in the Solution Explorer in Microsoft Visual Studio, a Properties box will open at the bottom right. It is *very important* to change the Build Action to Embedded Resource. Otherwise, your program will not be able to load the resource at runtime, and you will go mad trying to figure out why.

The last statement of the constructor in *SoundButtonDemo* shows the code to load that binary resource into your program as a *Stream* object. The filename must be preceded with a "resource namespace," which Visual Studio normally sets to the name of the project. You can change that name through the Project Properties dialog box. In the Application section of that dialog box, it is identified by the label "Default namespace."

Control Paint Jobs

One of the most dramatic ways you can modify an existing control is by changing its entire visual appearance. At the very least, this requires that you override the *OnPaint* method. If your futuristic vision requires that the control be a different size than it would normally be, you'll also want to override *GetPreferredSize* and (perhaps) *OnResize*. With any luck, you might be able to leave the entire keyboard and mouse processing logic intact.

Windows Forms provides some assistance to programmers who implement control-drawing logic. Before you reinvent the button, you'll want to take a close look at *ControlPaint*. This class contains a number of static methods that perform various control-painting jobs and convert system colors into light and dark variations. System colors, pens, and brushes, by the way, are located in three classes in the *System.Drawing* namespace: *SystemColors*, *SystemPens*, and *SystemBrushes*. The *ProfessionalColors* and *ProfessionalColorTable* classes in *System.Windows.Forms* provide colors that are purportedly similar to those in Microsoft Office. *ProfessionalColors* is a collection of static properties, and *ProfessionalColorTable* contains identical instance properties that you can access after creating an instance of *ProfessionalColorTable*.

For the most part, I decided to forge my own drawing logic and choose my own colors in the *RoundButton* class. As the name suggests, *RoundButton* inherits from *Button* but creates a button that is round. This code also demonstrates how to make nonrectangular controls.

RoundButton.cs

```
//-------------------------------------------
// RoundButton.cs (c) 2005 by Charles Petzold
//-------------------------------------------
using System;
using System.Drawing;
using System.Drawing.Drawing2D;
using System.Windows.Forms;

class RoundButton : Button
{
    public RoundButton()
    {
        SetStyle(ControlStyles.UserPaint, true);
        SetStyle(ControlStyles.AllPaintingInWmPaint, true);
    }
    public override Size GetPreferredSize(Size szProposed)
    {
        // Base size on text string to be displayed.
        Graphics grfx = CreateGraphics();
        SizeF szf = grfx.MeasureString(Text, Font);
        int iRadius = (int)Math.Sqrt(Math.Pow(szf.Width / 2, 2) +
                                     Math.Pow(szf.Height / 2, 2));
        return new Size(2 * iRadius, 2 * iRadius);
    }
    protected override void OnResize(EventArgs args)
    {
        base.OnResize(args);

        // Circular region makes button non-rectangular.
        GraphicsPath path = new GraphicsPath();
        path.AddEllipse(ClientRectangle);
        Region = new Region(path);
    }
    protected override void OnPaint(PaintEventArgs args)
    {
        Graphics grfx = args.Graphics;
        grfx.SmoothingMode = SmoothingMode.AntiAlias;
        Rectangle rect = ClientRectangle;

        // Draw interior (darker if pressed).
        bool bPressed = Capture & ((MouseButtons & MouseButtons.Left) != 0) &
            ClientRectangle.Contains(PointToClient(MousePosition));

        GraphicsPath path = new GraphicsPath();
        path.AddEllipse(rect);
        PathGradientBrush pgbr = new PathGradientBrush(path);
        int k = bPressed ? 2 : 1;
        pgbr.CenterPoint = new PointF(k * (rect.Left + rect.Right) / 3,
                                      k * (rect.Top + rect.Bottom) / 3);
        pgbr.CenterColor = bPressed ? Color.Blue : Color.White;
        pgbr.SurroundColors = new Color[] { Color.SkyBlue };
        grfx.FillRectangle(pgbr, rect);
```

```
            // Display border (thicker for default button)
            Brush br = new LinearGradientBrush(rect,
                        Color.FromArgb(0, 0, 255), Color.FromArgb(0, 0, 128),
                        LinearGradientMode.ForwardDiagonal);
            Pen pn = new Pen(br, (IsDefault ? 4 : 2) * grfx.DpiX / 72);
            grfx.DrawEllipse(pn, rect);

            // Draw the text centered in the rectangle (grayed if disabled).
            StringFormat strfmt = new StringFormat();
            strfmt.Alignment = strfmt.LineAlignment = StringAlignment.Center;
            br = Enabled ? SystemBrushes.WindowText : SystemBrushes.GrayText;
            grfx.DrawString(Text, Font, br, rect, strfmt);

            // Draw dotted line around text if button has input focus.
            if (Focused)
            {
                SizeF szf = grfx.MeasureString(Text, Font, PointF.Empty,
                                        StringFormat.GenericTypographic);
                pn = new Pen(ForeColor);
                pn.DashStyle = DashStyle.Dash;
                grfx.DrawRectangle(pn,
                    rect.Left + rect.Width / 2 - szf.Width / 2,
                    rect.Top + rect.Height / 2 - szf.Height / 2,
                    szf.Width, szf.Height);
            }
        }
    }
}
```

The constructor sets two *ControlStyles* flags. For *Button*, these two flags happen to be *true* by default, but that can't be assumed for all controls. Setting the flags to *true* ensures that all painting logic is performed in the *OnPaint* method, so that overriding *OnPaint* is sufficient to replace all that drawing logic. (Alternatively, if the *AllPaintingInWmPaint* flag is *false*, you can paint the background of the control by overriding *OnPaintBackground*.)

GetPreferredSize is an important method in connection with autosizing. When *AutoSize* is set to *true*, a layout manager calls this method to obtain the size desired by the control. Whenever something happens that could affect the size—such as changes in the control's *Font* or *Text* properties—*GetPreferredSize* is called again to obtain an updated size. The *GetPreferredSize* method defined in *RoundButton* obtains the pixel dimensions of its *Text* property by calling *MeasureString*. It then calculates the distance from the center of that rectangle to a corner. This value is the desired radius of the round button.

The *OnResize* method is called whenever the size of the control changes, whether by autosizing or by explicit resizing. The code in the round button's *OnResize* method is also responsible for making the control nonrectangular by setting the *Region* property defined by the *Control* class. You set the *Region* property to an object of type *Region*, which is a class defined in *System.Drawing*. A graphical region defines an irregular area as a series of discontinuous scan lines. After setting the *Region* property, the control still has a rectangular dimension, but any part of the control lying outside the area defined by the region will be transparent—both visually and in regard to mouse activity.

If you work solely within the confines of the *Region* class, it is only possible to construct regions from Boolean combinations of multiple rectangles. A more general approach is to first construct a path using the *GraphicsPath* class. A path is a collection of lines and curves that might or might not be connected, and which might or might not enclose areas. (A full discussion of paths and regions can be found in Chapter 15 of my book *Programming Microsoft Windows with C#* [Microsoft Press, 2001].) The path that *RoundButton* creates is composed simply of an ellipse the size of the button's client area. This ellipse—or rather, the interior of an ellipse—is converted into a region, and then that region is set to the *Region* property of the button.

The only other method in *RoundButton* is *OnPaint*, and this method does *not* call the *OnPaint* method in the base class because it doesn't want that method to do anything. A call to *OnPaint* occurs whenever something about the button needs repainting.

The method begins by drawing the interior area of the button. I decided to use a *PathGradientBrush* to give the button a hemisphere-like appearance. (Brushes—gradient and otherwise—are discussed in Chapter 17 of *Programming Microsoft Windows with C#*.) However, the button should also provide visual feedback whenever it's "pressed" with the mouse. The code chooses a darker color if the *Capture* property is *true* (that is, mouse input is going to the control) and the left mouse button is down and the mouse pointer is over the control.

OnPaint next displays the border. This is a pen based on a *LinearGradientBrush*. A regular button generally draws a heavier border when the button is the default (that is, when it responds to the Enter key). *RoundButton* uses the *IsDefault* property to vary the width of the border.

OnPaint then displays the text. Once again, it's not quite as simple as it might at first seem. If the button is disabled, the text should appear in gray. The method chooses between the system brushes *SystemBrushes.WindowText* and *SystemBrushes.GrayText* for displaying the text. The *StringFormat* object helps position the text in the center of the button.

If the button has the input focus, a dashed line should appear around the text. That's the job of the final section of *OnPaint*. The method again calls *MeasureString* to obtain the width and height of the text string, and then constructs a rectangle from that to display the dashed line.

You'll notice that the calls to *MeasureString* in *GetPreferredSize* and *OnPaint* are a little different. In the latter method, an argument of *StringFormat.GenericTypographic* was passed to the method along with the text string and font. By default, *MeasureString* returns dimensions a little larger than the string. I thought that behavior was appropriate for determining the size of the button because it provides a little padding around the text. When I originally used the same *MeasureString* call to draw the dashed outline of the text, however, the left and right sides of the dashed rectangle were obscured by the border of the button. Passing *StringFormat.GenericTypographic* to *MeasureString* causes the dimensions to more closely approximate the actual text size, thus making a snugger dashed rectangle. (See Chapter 9 of *Programming Microsoft Windows with C#* for a fuller explanation of *GenericTypographic*.)

Here's a little program to test out the buttons. The RoundButtonDemo project includes both RoundButton.cs and this file.

RoundButtonDemo.cs

```csharp
//-------------------------------------------------
// RoundButtonDemo.cs (c) 2005 by Charles Petzold
//-------------------------------------------------
using System;
using System.Drawing;
using System.Windows.Forms;

class RoundButtonDemo : Form
{
    [STAThread]
    public static void Main()
    {
        Application.EnableVisualStyles();
        Application.Run(new RoundButtonDemo());
    }
    public RoundButtonDemo()
    {
        Text = "RoundButton Demonstration";
        Font = new Font("Times New Roman", 18);
        AutoSize = true;
        AutoSizeMode = AutoSizeMode.GrowAndShrink;

        FlowLayoutPanel flow = new FlowLayoutPanel();
        flow.Parent = this;
        flow.AutoSize = true;
        flow.FlowDirection = FlowDirection.TopDown;

        FlowLayoutPanel flowTop = new FlowLayoutPanel();
        flowTop.Parent = flow;
        flowTop.AutoSize = true;
        flowTop.Anchor = AnchorStyles.None;

        Label lbl = new Label();
        lbl.Parent = flowTop;
        lbl.AutoSize = true;
        lbl.Text = "Enter some text:";
        lbl.Anchor = AnchorStyles.None;

        TextBox txtbox = new TextBox();
        txtbox.Parent = flowTop;
        txtbox.AutoSize = true;

        FlowLayoutPanel flowBottom = new FlowLayoutPanel();
        flowBottom.Parent = flow;
        flowBottom.AutoSize = true;
        flowBottom.Anchor = AnchorStyles.None;
```

```
        RoundButton btnOk = new RoundButton();
        btnOk.Parent = flowBottom;
        btnOk.Text = "OK";
        btnOk.Anchor = AnchorStyles.None;
        btnOk.DialogResult = DialogResult.OK;
        AcceptButton = btnOk;

        RoundButton btnCancel = new RoundButton();
        btnCancel.Parent = flowBottom;
        btnCancel.AutoSize = true;
        btnCancel.Text = "Cancel";
        btnCancel.Anchor = AnchorStyles.None;
        btnCancel.DialogResult = DialogResult.Cancel;
        CancelButton = btnCancel;

        btnOk.Size = btnCancel.Size;
    }
}
```

This program simulates a little dialog box with a label, a *TextBox*, and two *RoundButton* controls for OK and Cancel. Three *FlowPanel* controls perform dynamic layout.

At first, I set the *AutoSize* property for both *RoundButton* controls to *true*, just as if they were normal buttons. The result looked very, very wrong:

This *had* to be fixed. I decided to set *AutoSize* to *true* for only the Cancel button. After both buttons are created, the OK button is set equal in size to Cancel:

```
btnOk.Size = btnCancel.Size;
```

The appearance is much better:

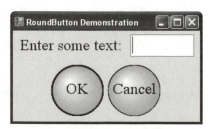

And, I guess I discovered why buttons aren't round by default.

Suppose a program wants to use the *RoundButton* control and also wants to add a little something to the visuals. It dutifully installs an event handler for *Paint* and . . . gets nothing. The problem is that *RoundButton* overrides *OnPaint*, but it doesn't call *OnPaint* in the base class because it doesn't want the base class doing anything. But that base class is responsible for firing the *Paint* event. Yet *RoundButton* can't fire the *Paint* event because only the class that defines the event can fire it.

The solution—if one is desired—is for *RoundButton* to define its own *Paint* event using the *new* keyword, and for the *OnPaint* method in *RoundButton* to fire that event.

Combining Existing Controls

One popular solution to creating new controls is by combining existing controls. To take advantage of much of the support of existing control logic, it is recommended that you derive such controls from the class *UserControl*. In particular, this class supports keyboard navigation among multiple controls.

As our first example, let's create a control not so different from a popular existing control. By whatever name they've gone under—spin buttons, up-down controls, the *NumericUpDown* class—I've always had a fundamental problem with controls that let you change numeric values using buttons sporting up and down arrows. On the one hand, the up-arrow might mean "higher," suggesting larger values, and the down-arrow might mean "lower." But when I visualize a list of numbers that I might be selecting from:

0

1

2

3

...

the up-arrow obviously means "toward 0" and the down-arrow means "toward infinity."

This ambiguity might be eliminated if the scroll bar were horizontal rather than vertical. Then, clearly, the left-arrow would signify smaller values and the right-arrow would move toward larger values, at least in cultures that read from left to right.

Because I am convinced that I am right about this issue and that the rest of the world need only see my example before universally adopting my design, I have decided to put my *NumericScan* control—as I've called it—into a dynamic-link library (DLL) named NumericScan.dll. I have also added some support so that this control will be more compliant with the Visual Studio designer.

Whether a collection of source code files becomes an executable (.exe) or a dynamic-link library (.dll) ultimately depends on the /target switch of the C# compiler. Set it to /target:exe or /target:winexe to create an executable, or set it to /target:library to create a DLL. Within Visual Studio, you specify whether you want an executable or a DLL in the project properties.

It's easy to make a dynamic-link library project rather than a program project. If you're using the predefined project types in Visual Studio, select a template of either Class Library or Windows Control Library. If you're using the Empty Project option, create the project normally, and then display the project properties. Under Output Type, select Class Library. Selecting this option will create a dynamic-link library (.dll) rather than an executable file (.exe). Add at least one source code file to the project, and begin.

The only problem is that a DLL can't be directly executed, so you might get to the point where your code compiles fine but you don't know whether the control is actually working. You need an actual program to test it out.

For that reason, it's common when creating a DLL to also have a test program handy. And the easiest way to do that is to put the DLL project *and* the test program in the same Visual Studio solution. Here's how I did it.

In Visual Studio, I selected New Project from the File menu to invoke the New Project dialog box, as usual. I chose a project name of NumericScan, but I also checked the Create Directory For Solution check box. Checking this box results in the creation of a solution directory named NumericScan and, within that directory, a project directory also named NumericScan. Then select New Project from the File menu again. In the New Project dialog box, type a project name of TestProgram and make sure the Solution combo box is Add To Solution. Now the NumericScan solution has two projects named NumericScan and TestProgram.

In the Project Properties for the NumericScan project, make sure the Output Type is Class Library. In the Solution Explorer, right-click TestProgram and select Set As Startup Project. That means that when Visual Studio recompiles the entire solution, it will then launch TestProgram. There's still a little more overhead involved in creating a DLL and testing it, but I'll get to that.

The *NumericScan* control that I'll present here will comprise a *TextBox* control and two buttons. However, the buttons aren't quite normal. If you click one of the arrows on a normal *NumericUpDown* control and hold down the mouse button, you'll find that the buttons have a repeating action much like a scroll bar. It's also similar to the typematic action of the keyboard, so I decided to call a button that exhibited this characteristic a *ClickmaticButton* control. This is the first file in the NumericScan project:

```
ClickmaticButton.cs
//-------------------------------------------------
// ClickmaticButton.cs (c) 2005 by Charles Petzold
//-------------------------------------------------
using System;
using System.Drawing;
using System.Windows.Forms;
```

```
namespace Petzold.ProgrammingWindowsForms
{
    class ClickmaticButton : Button
    {
        Timer tmr = new Timer();

        int iDelay = 250 * (1 + SystemInformation.KeyboardDelay);
        int iSpeed = 405 - 12 * SystemInformation.KeyboardSpeed;

        protected override void OnMouseDown(MouseEventArgs args)
        {
            base.OnMouseDown(args);

            if ((args.Button & MouseButtons.Left) != 0)
            {
                tmr.Interval = iDelay;
                tmr.Tick += TimerOnTick;
                tmr.Start();
            }
        }
        void TimerOnTick(object objSrc, EventArgs args)
        {
            OnClick(EventArgs.Empty);
            tmr.Interval = iSpeed;
        }
        protected override void OnMouseMove(MouseEventArgs args)
        {
            base.OnMouseMove(args);
            tmr.Enabled = Capture & ClientRectangle.Contains(args.Location);
        }
        protected override void OnMouseUp(MouseEventArgs args)
        {
            base.OnMouseUp(args);
            tmr.Stop();
        }
    }
}
```

Notice that this class is defined in a namespace. If you're going to be making DLLs, it's important to define the classes with a namespace so that they don't clash with class names used in any program using the DLL. I've chosen this namespace in rough accordance with common practice: company name first, followed by product name.

Regardless of the namespace, this particular class will *not* be visible from outside the DLL because the class definition does not include the *public* keyword. We haven't been worrying much about making classes public. It's really only an issue when you're putting classes in a DLL.

The class is fairly straightforward: it inherits from *Button* and overrides the *OnMouseDown* method to detect mouse clicks. Calling the method in the base class causes the normal call to *OnClick*, which then fires the *Click* event. *ClickmaticButton* continues processing *OnMouse-*

Down by starting a timer. The timer event handler makes additional calls to *OnClick* for repeated *Click* events. If the mouse button is down when the mouse moves away from the button, the timer should temporarily stop. The timer should also stop when the mouse button is released.

I was stuck for a little while about the proper *Interval* settings for the timer. There should be an initial delay when the button is clicked before the "clickmatic" action kicks in. Thereafter, the time interval should be shorter. Fortunately, I discovered some new .NET Framework 2.0 additions to the *SystemInformation* class. *SystemInformation.KeyboardDelay* is defined as "The keyboard repeat-delay setting, from 0 (approximately 250- millisecond delay) through 3 (approximately 1- second delay)." *SystemInformation.KeyboardSpeed* is defined as, "The keyboard repeat-speed setting, from 0 (approximately 2.5 repetitions per second) through 31 (approximately 30 repetitions per second)." These values worked just fine.

The *ArrowButton* class inherits from *ClickmaticButton* and overrides the *OnPaint* method to draw arrows using the *ControlPaint.DrawScrollButton* method. The direction of the arrow is specified through a public property.

```
ArrowButton.cs
//-------------------------------------------
// ArrowButton.cs (c) 2005 by Charles Petzold
//-------------------------------------------
using System;
using System.Drawing;
using System.Windows.Forms;

namespace Petzold.ProgrammingWindowsForms
{
    class ArrowButton : ClickmaticButton
    {
        ScrollButton scrbtn = ScrollButton.Right;

        public ArrowButton()
        {
            SetStyle(ControlStyles.Selectable, false);
        }
        public ScrollButton ScrollButton
        {
            set
            {
                scrbtn = value;
                Invalidate();
            }
            get { return scrbtn; }
        }
        protected override void OnPaint(PaintEventArgs args)
        {
            Graphics grfx = args.Graphics;
            ControlPaint.DrawScrollButton(grfx, ClientRectangle, scrbtn,
                !Enabled ? ButtonState.Inactive :
```

```
                    (Capture & ClientRectangle.Contains(
                                PointToClient(MousePosition))) ?
            ButtonState.Pushed : ButtonState.Normal);
    }
    protected override void OnMouseCaptureChanged(EventArgs args)
    {
        base.OnMouseCaptureChanged(args);
        Invalidate();
    }
  }
}
```

The *ArrowButton* class has a constructor that sets the *ControlStyles.Selectable* flag to *false*. When used in the *NumericScan* control, the buttons should not be selectable, which means they should not be able to get the input focus. The input focus should remain in the edit field.

Here's the public class *NumericScan* that inherits from *UserControl* and builds a control from a *TextBox* and two *ArrowButton* controls.

NumericScan.cs
```
//-------------------------------------------
// NumericScan.cs (c) 2005 by Charles Petzold
//-------------------------------------------
using System;
using System.ComponentModel;
using System.Drawing;
using System.Reflection;
using System.Windows.Forms;

[assembly: AssemblyTitle("NumericScan")]
[assembly: AssemblyDescription("NumericScan Control")]
[assembly: AssemblyConfiguration("")]
[assembly: AssemblyCompany("www.charlespetzold.com")]
[assembly: AssemblyProduct("NumericScan")]
[assembly: AssemblyCopyright("(c) Charles Petzold, 2005")]
[assembly: AssemblyTrademark("")]
[assembly: AssemblyVersion("1.0.*")]


namespace Petzold.ProgrammingWindowsForms
{
    [DefaultEvent("ValueChanged")]
    public class NumericScan : UserControl
    {
        public event EventHandler ValueChanged;

        TextBox txtbox;
        ArrowButton btn1, btn2;

        // These private fields have corresponding public properties.
        int iDecimalPlaces = 0;
        decimal mValue = 0;
        decimal mIncrement = 1;
```

```csharp
decimal mMinimum = 0;
decimal mMaximum = 100;

public NumericScan()
{
    txtbox = new TextBox();
    txtbox.Parent = this;
    txtbox.TextAlign = HorizontalAlignment.Right;
    txtbox.Text = ValueToText(mValue);
    txtbox.TextChanged += TextBoxOnTextChanged;
    txtbox.KeyDown += TextBoxOnKeyDown;

    btn1 = new ArrowButton();
    btn1.Parent = this;
    btn1.Text = "btn1";
    btn1.ScrollButton = ScrollButton.Left;
    btn1.Click += ButtonOnClick;

    btn2 = new ArrowButton();
    btn2.Parent = this;
    btn2.Text = "btn2";
    btn2.ScrollButton = ScrollButton.Right;
    btn2.Click += ButtonOnClick;

    Width = 4 * Font.Height;
    Height = txtbox.PreferredHeight +
                        SystemInformation.HorizontalScrollBarHeight;
}
string ValueToText(decimal mValue)
{
    return mValue.ToString("F" + DecimalPlaces);
}

[Category("Data"), Description("Value displayed in the control")]
public decimal Value
{
    set
    {
        txtbox.Text = ValueToText(mValue = value);
    }
    get
    {
        return mValue;
    }
}

[Category("Data"),
Description("The amount to increment or decrement on a button click")]
public decimal Increment
{
    set { mIncrement = value; }
    get { return mIncrement; }
}
```

```
[Category("Data"), Description("Minimum allowed value")]
public decimal Minimum
{
    set
    {
        if ((mMinimum = value) > Value)
            Value = mMinimum;
    }
    get { return mMinimum; }
}

[Category("Data"), Description("Maximum allowed value")]
public decimal Maximum
{
    set
    {
        if ((mMaximum = value) < Value)
            Value = mMaximum;
    }
    get { return mMaximum; }
}

[Category("Data"), Description("Number of decimal places to display")]
public int DecimalPlaces
{
    set { iDecimalPlaces = value; }
    get { return iDecimalPlaces; }
}
public override Size GetPreferredSize(Size szProposed)
{
    return new Size(4 * Font.Height, txtbox.PreferredHeight +
                        SystemInformation.HorizontalScrollBarHeight);
}
protected override void OnResize(EventArgs args)
{
    base.OnResize(args);

    txtbox.Height = txtbox.PreferredHeight;
    txtbox.Width = Width;
    btn1.Location = new Point(0, txtbox.Height);
    btn2.Location = new Point(Width / 2, txtbox.Height);
    btn1.Size = btn2.Size = new Size(Width / 2, Height - txtbox.Height);
}
void TextBoxOnTextChanged(object objSrc, EventArgs args)
{
    if (txtbox.Text.Length == 0)
        return;

    try
    {
        mValue = Decimal.Parse(txtbox.Text);
    }
    catch
    {
    }
```

```
        txtbox.Text = ValueToText(mValue);
    }
    void TextBoxOnKeyDown(object objSrc, KeyEventArgs args)
    {
        switch (args.KeyCode)
        {
            case Keys.Enter:
                OnValueChanged(EventArgs.Empty);
                break;
        }
    }
    void ButtonOnClick(object objSrc, EventArgs args)
    {
        ArrowButton btn = objSrc as ArrowButton;
        decimal mNewValue = Value;

        if (btn == btn1)
            if ((mNewValue -= Increment) < Minimum)
                return;

        if (btn == btn2)
            if ((mNewValue += Increment) > Maximum)
                return;

        Value = mNewValue;
        OnValueChanged(EventArgs.Empty);
    }
    protected override void OnLeave(EventArgs args)
    {
        base.OnLeave(args);
        OnValueChanged(EventArgs.Empty);
    }
    protected virtual void OnValueChanged(EventArgs args)
    {
        Value = Math.Max(Minimum, Value);
        Value = Math.Min(Maximum, Value);
        Value = Decimal.Round(Value, DecimalPlaces);

        if (ValueChanged != null)
            ValueChanged(this, args);
    }
  }
}
```

Everything in square brackets in the file is an attribute. The attributes at the beginning of the source code file are those I discussed in Chapter 1. The others are defined in the *System.ComponentModel* namespace. Preceding each of the public properties are *Category* and *Description* attributes. These are used by the *PropertyGrid* control to group related properties and to give a little description of them. Immediately preceding the class definition is a *DefaultEvent* attribute. Visual Studio uses this attribute in the designer to determine what event to use when you double-click a control to set up an event handler.

Notice also that the class is defined as *public*, so it will be visible from outside the DLL. The first member defined in the class is the public event *ValueChanged*.

NumericScan assembles one *TextBox* control and two *ArrowButton* controls on its surface. As in *NumericUpDown*, the control exposes public properties named *Value*, *Minimum*, *Maximum*, *Increment*, and *DecimalPlaces*. It's possible to implement more consistency checking than what I show here. (The .NET Framework *NumericUpDown* control throws some exceptions if a program sets *Value* outside the range of *Minimum* and *Maximum*, for example.) But what you should try to avoid are consistency checks that fail if a program sets properties in a particular order. For example, the default *Minimum* and *Maximum* properties are 0 and 100. A program might reset these two properties like this:

```
numscan.Minimum = 200;
numscan.Maximum = 300;
```

If the control threw an exception whenever *Minimum* is less than *Maximum*, the first statement would fail, and it really shouldn't.

Much of the remainder of the class is devoted to handling events from the *TextBox* and *Arrow-Button* controls. Whenever the text changes, the *TextBoxOnTextChanged* event handler determines whether it's still a number. If not, it changes it back to its previous value. This event handler does not try to enforce minimum and maximum boundaries. (Neither does the *NumericUpDown* control. You can type whatever number you want in the control.)

As with the *NumericUpDown* control, the *ValueChanged* event should be fired whenever the value is altered by the buttons, when the user presses the Enter key, or when the control loses input focus. This is when the minimum and maximum boundaries are imposed.

To determine when the Enter key is pressed, the control installs a *KeyDown* event handler for the *TextBox* control. At this time, I recognized the flaw in having the arrow buttons point to the left and right: the buttons should be mimicked by the left and right cursor keys, yet these are the same keys used to move within the *TextBox*. Perhaps the up and down arrows are the right way to implement a spin button after all!

At the very bottom of the class is the *OnValueChanged* method. It's defined as *virtual* so that programs wishing to derive from *NumericScan* can easily override the method. The method imposes the minimum and maximum boundaries, rounds it to the desired number of decimal places, and fires the *ValueChanged* event.

I mentioned earlier that the NumericScan solution has two projects: NumericScan, which creates the NumericScan.dll file, and TestProgram, which creates TestProgram.exe from the following source code file.

TestProgram.cs

```
//-------------------------------------------
// TestProgram.cs (c) 2005 by Charles Petzold
//-------------------------------------------
using Petzold.ProgrammingWindowsForms;
using System;
using System.Drawing;
using System.Windows.Forms;

class TestProgram : Form
{
    Label lbl;
    NumericScan numscan1, numscan2;

    [STAThread]
    public static void Main()
    {
        Application.EnableVisualStyles();
        Application.Run(new TestProgram());
    }
    public TestProgram()
    {
        Text = "Test Program";

        FlowLayoutPanel pnl = new FlowLayoutPanel();
        pnl.Parent = this;
        pnl.Dock = DockStyle.Fill;

        numscan1 = new NumericScan();
        numscan1.Parent = pnl;
        numscan1.AutoSize = true;
        numscan1.ValueChanged += NumericScanOnValueChanged;

        numscan2 = new NumericScan();
        numscan2.Parent = pnl;
        numscan2.AutoSize = true;
        numscan2.ValueChanged += NumericScanOnValueChanged;

        lbl = new Label();
        lbl.Parent = pnl;
        lbl.AutoSize = true;
    }
    void NumericScanOnValueChanged(object objSrc, EventArgs args)
    {
        lbl.Text = "First: " + numscan1.Value + ", Second: " + numscan2.Value;
    }
}
```

The test program is simply two *NumericScan* controls with event handlers installed and a *Label* that displays the two values.

When defining the references for the TestProgram project, you need the normal System, System.Drawing, and System.Windows.Forms dynamic-link libraries, but you also need to include NumericScan.dll. In the Add Reference dialog box, click the Projects tab and select NumericScan. As you'll note, TestProgram.cs also includes a *using* directive for the *Petzold.ProgrammingWindowsForms* namespace.

To add this control to Visual Studio's Toolbox, first right-click one of the tabs in the Toolbox and select Add Tab. You can name it More Controls, for example. Right-click that new tab and select Choose Items. The Choose Toolbox Items dialog box has a Browse button that lets you navigate to the NumericScan.dll file.

The following program gives the NumericScan control a more extensive workout. The first part of the program is a class that derives from *TableLayoutPanel* to display six *NumericScan* controls for setting the six fields of a .NET Framework matrix transform object. This class is quite similar to the MatrixElements program from the last chapter except that it's more generalized. The panel is given a public property named *Matrix* that allows setting the *NumericScan* controls and obtaining their values in the form of a *Matrix* object. The panel also defines a public event named *Change* that is fired whenever one of the *NumericScan* controls fires a *ValueChanged* event. Notice the first *using* directive for the namespace of the *NumericScan* control.

MatrixPanel.cs

```
//-------------------------------------------------
// MatrixPanel.cs (c) 2005 by Charles Petzold
//-------------------------------------------------
using Petzold.ProgrammingWindowsForms;
using System;
using System.Drawing;
using System.Drawing.Drawing2D;
using System.Windows.Forms;

class MatrixPanel: TableLayoutPanel
{
    public event EventHandler Change;

    NumericScan[] numscan = new NumericScan[6];

    public Matrix Matrix
    {
        set
        {
            for (int i = 0; i < 6; i++)
                numscan[i].Value = (decimal)value.Elements[i];
        }
        get
        {
            return new Matrix((float)numscan[0].Value, (float)numscan[1].Value,
                              (float)numscan[2].Value, (float)numscan[3].Value,
                              (float)numscan[4].Value, (float)numscan[5].Value);
        }
    }
    public MatrixPanel()
    {
```

```
        AutoSize = true;
        Padding = new Padding(Font.Height);
        ColumnCount = 2;

        SuspendLayout();

        for (int i = 0; i < 6; i++)
        {
            Label lbl = new Label();
            lbl.Parent = this;
            lbl.AutoSize = true;
            lbl.Anchor = AnchorStyles.Left;
            lbl.Text = new string[] { "X Scale:", "Y Shear:", "X Shear:",
                                      "Y Scale:", "X Translate:",
                                      "Y Translate:" }[i];

            numscan[i] = new NumericScan();
            numscan[i].Parent = this;
            numscan[i].AutoSize = true;
            numscan[i].Anchor = AnchorStyles.Right;
            numscan[i].Minimum = -1000;
            numscan[i].Maximum = 1000;
            numscan[i].DecimalPlaces = 2;
            numscan[i].ValueChanged += NumericScanOnValueChanged;
        }
        ResumeLayout();

        Matrix = new Matrix();
    }
    void NumericScanOnValueChanged(object objSrc, EventArgs args)
    {
        OnChange(EventArgs.Empty);
    }
    protected virtual void OnChange(EventArgs args)
    {
        if (Change != null)
            Change(this, args);
    }
}
```

Because *TableLayoutPanel* derives from *Control*, and because this new class derives from *TableLayoutPanel*, does that make this new class a custom control? Sure! Any class you derive directly or indirectly from *Control* can be treated as a custom control. Adding properties and events to the control certainly makes it more customized and more useful, and actually reusing the control in other applications is the crowning achievement.

Here's another "custom control" of sorts. This is a derivative of *Panel* that displays its *Text* property after setting a matrix transform delivered to it in its public *Transform* property. Some matrix transforms raise exceptions when the *Graphics* object is set to the transform. For invalid matrix transforms, the *Graphics* object raises an exception, and the panel displays the exception message.

DisplayPanel.cs

```
//-------------------------------------------
// DisplayPanel.cs (c) 2005 by Charles Petzold
//-------------------------------------------
using System;
using System.Drawing;
using System.Drawing.Drawing2D;
using System.Windows.Forms;

class DisplayPanel : Panel
{
    Matrix matx = new Matrix();

    public DisplayPanel()
    {
        ResizeRedraw = true;
    }
    public Matrix Transform
    {
        set
        {
            matx = value;
            Invalidate();
        }
        get
        {
            return matx;
        }
    }
    protected override void OnPaint(PaintEventArgs args)
    {
        Graphics grfx = args.Graphics;
        Brush brsh = new SolidBrush(ForeColor);

        try
        {
            grfx.Transform = matx;
            grfx.DrawString(Text, Font, brsh, Point.Empty);
        }
        catch (Exception exc)
        {
            StringFormat strfmt = new StringFormat();
            strfmt.Alignment = strfmt.LineAlignment = StringAlignment.Center;
            grfx.DrawString(exc.Message, Font, brsh, ClientRectangle, strfmt);
        }
        brsh.Dispose();
    }
}
```

Normally, panels don't display their *Text* properties, so nobody bothers setting a panel's *Text* property. It is the responsibility of a program using this *DisplayPanel* control to assign a valid *Text* property and perhaps a different *Font* property.

MatrixInteractive is not the name of a new movie (let's hope not, anyway) but a project that includes MatrixPanel.cs, DisplayPanel.cs, and the next file.

MatrixInteractive.cs

```
//--------------------------------------------------
// MatrixInteractive.cs (c) 2005 by Charles Petzold
//--------------------------------------------------
using System;
using System.Drawing;
using System.Windows.Forms;

class MatrixInteractive : Form
{
    MatrixPanel matxpnl;
    DisplayPanel disppnl;

    [STAThread]
    public static void Main()
    {
        Application.EnableVisualStyles();
        Application.Run(new MatrixInteractive());
    }
    public MatrixInteractive()
    {
        Text = "Matrix Interactive";

        TableLayoutPanel pnl = new TableLayoutPanel();
        pnl.Parent = this;
        pnl.Dock = DockStyle.Fill;
        pnl.ColumnCount = 2;

        matxpnl = new MatrixPanel();
        matxpnl.Parent = pnl;
        matxpnl.Anchor = AnchorStyles.Left | AnchorStyles.Right;
        matxpnl.Change += MatrixPanelOnChange;

        disppnl = new DisplayPanel();
        disppnl.Parent = pnl;
        disppnl.Dock = DockStyle.Fill;
        disppnl.BackColor = Color.White;
        disppnl.ForeColor = Color.Black;
        disppnl.Text = "Sample Text";
        disppnl.Font = new Font(FontFamily.GenericSerif, 24);

        Width = 3 * matxpnl.Width;
        Height = 3 * matxpnl.Height / 2;
    }
    void MatrixPanelOnChange(object objSrc, EventArgs args)
    {
        disppnl.Transform = matxpnl.Matrix;
    }
}
```

This program splits its client area into two parts using a *TableLayoutPanel*. At the left, centered vertically, is the *MatrixPanel*. At the right is a *DisplayPanel*, which is given a white background color, black foreground color, a *Text* property of "Sample Text," and a 24-point font. Whenever the *MatrixPanel* fires a *Change* event, this class obtains the matrix transform from the *MatrixPanel* and sets it to the *DisplayPanel*. Here's a sample screen shot:

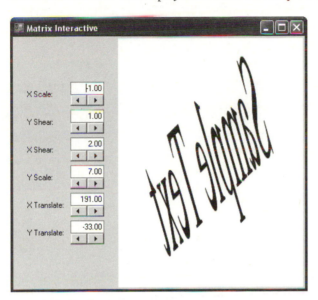

The Sheer Pleasure of Autoscroll

The *Form* class and various *Panel* classes have an interesting feature that's not used much because it's not quite acceptable as a general-purpose user interface technique. This feature is called "autoscroll," and you enable it simply by setting the *AutoScroll* property of these classes to *true*. Then, if the *Form* or *Panel* is not large enough to display all its child controls, scrollbars magically appear and the missing controls can be scrolled into view. Autoscroll is implemented in *ScrollableControl* and available in every control that derives from *ScrollableControl*. Not every control that has scrollbars derives from *ScrollableControl*, however. *TextBox*, *ListBox*, and *ScrollBar* do *not* derive from *ScrollableControl*, but *Form* and *Panel* do.

I don't think autoscroll is the best approach to fitting a lot of controls in a tiny dialog box. However, it can certainly make some custom controls a whole lot easier. For example, consider a control that displays an indeterminate number of thumbnails of image files. If you just put these thumbnails on a panel and enable autoscrolling, all the scrolling logic is handled for you.

The next custom control I'll show is called *ImageScan*, and it displays 1-inch-square thumbnails of all the image files in a particular disk directory in a single scrollable row. *ImageScan* itself derives from *FlowLayoutControl*, and the thumbnails are implemented using the *Picture-Box* control.

Once I started putting this control together, however, I ran into a basic problem. I wanted to navigate through the thumbnails using the Tab or arrow keys. The impediment was the *PictureBox* control itself, which is obstinately nonselectable. It cannot receive input focus, and (consequently) it cannot provide any feedback that it has input focus. The first step was to make a selectable picture box control and give it a simple keyboard interface.

SelectablePictureBox.cs

```
//---------------------------------------------------
// SelectablePictureBox.cs (c) 2005 by Charles Petzold
//---------------------------------------------------
using System;
using System.Drawing;
using System.Windows.Forms;

class SelectablePictureBox : PictureBox
{
    public SelectablePictureBox()
    {
        SetStyle(ControlStyles.Selectable, true);
        TabStop = true;
    }
    protected override void OnMouseDown(MouseEventArgs args)
    {
        base.OnMouseDown(args);
        Focus();
    }
    protected override void OnKeyPress(KeyPressEventArgs args)
    {
        if (args.KeyChar == '\r')
            OnClick(EventArgs.Empty);
        else
            base.OnKeyPress(args);
    }
    protected override void OnEnter(EventArgs args)
    {
        base.OnEnter(args);
        Invalidate();
    }
    protected override void OnLeave(EventArgs e)
    {
        base.OnLeave(e);
        Invalidate();
    }
    protected override void OnPaint(PaintEventArgs args)
    {
        base.OnPaint(args);

        if (Focused)
        {
```

```
            Graphics grfx = args.Graphics;
            grfx.DrawRectangle(new Pen(Brushes.Black, grfx.DpiX / 12),
                ClientRectangle);
        }
    }
}
```

The constructor sets the *ControlStyles.Selectable* flag and the *TabStop* property to *true*. An override of the *OnPaint* method lets the *OnPaint* method of the base class do its stuff, and then prints a black border around the control if the control has input focus. Several other *On* methods also needed some enhancements. When the control is clicked, the control gives itself input focus. When the Enter key is pressed, the control simulates an *OnClick* call. The *OnEnter* and *OnLeave* methods are called when the control gains input focus and loses it. My overrides simply invalidate the control to generate a call to *OnPaint* and ensure the control is painted correctly.

Here's the *ImageScan* control that inherits from *FlowLayoutPanel*. Notice the constructor that sets *WrapContents* to *false* and *AutoScroll* to *true*.

ImageScan.cs
```
//------------------------------------------
// ImageScan.cs (c) 2005 by Charles Petzold
//------------------------------------------
using System;
using System.ComponentModel;    // for AsyncCompletedEventArgs
using System.Drawing;
using System.IO;
using System.Windows.Forms;

class ImageScan : FlowLayoutPanel
{
    Size szImage;
    string strImageLocation;
    ToolTip tips = new ToolTip();

    public ImageScan()
    {
        FlowDirection = FlowDirection.LeftToRight;
        WrapContents = false;
        AutoScroll = true;

        // Create Size object of one square inch.
        Graphics grfx = CreateGraphics();
        szImage = new Size((int)grfx.DpiX, (int)grfx.DpiY); // 1" square
        grfx.Dispose();

        Height = szImage.Height + Font.Height +
                        SystemInformation.HorizontalScrollBarHeight;
    }
    public string Directory
    {
```

```
        set
        {
            Controls.Clear();
            tips.RemoveAll();

            string[] astrFiles = System.IO.Directory.GetFiles(value, "*.*");

            foreach (string strFile in astrFiles)
            {
                PictureBox picbox = new SelectablePictureBox();
                picbox.Parent = this;
                picbox.Size = szImage;
                picbox.SizeMode = PictureBoxSizeMode.Zoom;
                picbox.Click += PictureBoxOnClick;
                picbox.LoadCompleted += PictureBoxOnLoadCompleted;
                picbox.LoadAsync(strFile);
            }
        }
    }
    public string SelectedImageFile
    {
        get
        {
            return strImageLocation;
        }
    }
    void PictureBoxOnClick(object objSrc, EventArgs args)
    {
        PictureBox picbox = objSrc as PictureBox;
        strImageLocation = picbox.ImageLocation;

        OnClick(args);
    }

    // Don't generate Click events when user clicks the panel.
    protected override void OnMouseDown(MouseEventArgs args)
    {
    }
    void PictureBoxOnLoadCompleted(object objSrc, AsyncCompletedEventArgs args)
    {
        PictureBox picbox = objSrc as PictureBox;

        if (args.Error == null)
            tips.SetToolTip(picbox, Path.GetFileName(picbox.ImageLocation));
        else
            Controls.Remove(picbox);
    }
}
```

The control basically hosts a collection of *SelectablePictureBox* controls, each displaying a particular image in a directory. Also included is a *ToolTip* component for displaying file names as ToolTips. *ImageScan* implements a public property named *Directory* that specifies a disk directory. When this property is set, the control first clears out its existing collection of child controls and all the ToolTips. It then obtains all the files in the directory and creates a *SelectablePictureBox* object for each.

But wait: this control is supposed to display only *image* files, but a *SelectablePictureBox* is created for every file, whether it's an image file or not. Notice two things about these *SelectablePictureBox* controls: First, an event handler is installed for the *LoadCompleted* event, and second, the *LoadAsync* method of *PictureBox* is called for the file. This method loads the file in a secondary thread and fires the *LoadCompleted* event when it is completed. The event is accompanied by an object of type *AsyncCompletedEventArgs*. If the file loaded fine, the *Error* property of that object is *null*. If the file did not load correctly—and in this program that will happen a lot because the directory might contain a lot of nonimage files—the control removes that file from its child control collection.

And here's a program that uses *ImageScan*. The ImageDirectory project includes Selectable-PictureBox.cs, ImageScan.cs, and this file.

```
ImageDirectory.cs
//-------------------------------------------------
// ImageDirectory.cs (c) 2005 by Charles Petzold
//-------------------------------------------------
using System;
using System.Drawing;
using System.Windows.Forms;

class ImageDirectory: Form
{
    PictureBox picbox;
    ImageScan imgscan;
    Label lblDirectory;

    [STAThread]
    public static void Main()
    {
        Application.EnableVisualStyles();
        Application.Run(new ImageDirectory());
    }
    public ImageDirectory()
    {
        Text = "Image Directory";

        picbox = new PictureBox();
        picbox.Parent = this;
        picbox.Dock = DockStyle.Fill;
        picbox.SizeMode = PictureBoxSizeMode.Zoom;

        imgscan = new ImageScan();
        imgscan.Parent = this;
        imgscan.Dock = DockStyle.Top;
        imgscan.Click += ImageScanOnClick;
```

```
        FlowLayoutPanel pnl = new FlowLayoutPanel();
        pnl.Parent = this;
        pnl.AutoSize = true;
        pnl.Dock = DockStyle.Top;

        Button btn = new Button();
        btn.Parent = pnl;
        btn.AutoSize = true;
        btn.Anchor = AnchorStyles.Left;
        btn.Text = "Directory...";
        btn.Click += ButtonOnClick;

        lblDirectory = new Label();
        lblDirectory.Parent = pnl;
        lblDirectory.AutoSize = true;
        lblDirectory.Anchor = AnchorStyles.Right;

        // Initialize.
        imgscan.Directory = lblDirectory.Text =
            Environment.GetFolderPath(Environment.SpecialFolder.MyDocuments);
    }
    void ButtonOnClick(object objSrc, EventArgs args)
    {
        FolderBrowserDialog dlg = new FolderBrowserDialog();
        dlg.SelectedPath = lblDirectory.Text;
        dlg.ShowNewFolderButton = false;

        if (dlg.ShowDialog() == DialogResult.OK)
            imgscan.Directory = lblDirectory.Text = dlg.SelectedPath;
    }
    void ImageScanOnClick(object objSrc, EventArgs args)
    {
        picbox.ImageLocation = imgscan.SelectedImageFile;
    }
}
```

The program really just organizes controls into panels and hooks them together. A *Button* invokes a *FolderBrowserDialog* to let the user select a directory. A *Label* displays that directory. The *ImageScan* control shows the images in that directory, and the selected image occupies the remainder of the space in the program's client area. Here's a screen shot showing a selected image from the WINDOWS directory:

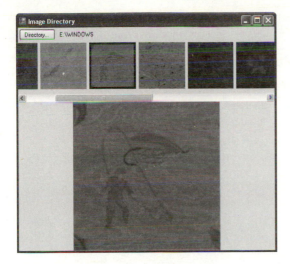

When selecting a directory containing a lot of nonimage files, the autoscroll facility of *Image-Scan* kicks in almost immediately in accordance with all the *SelectablePictureBox* controls added as children. As certain of these files are determined to be nonimage files, the scroll bar registers those changes and might disappear altogether! It's a little peculiar, but it seems to work.

Controls from Scratch

Some controls, of course, are so unlike any of the standard controls that they require significant amounts of custom drawing and processing of user input. For such controls, you'll probably just derive from *Control* and start coding. (Better get an early start.) As examples, I present two case studies: a ruler like the one that appears above documents in word-processing programs such as Windows WordPad and a simple color-selection grid.

An Interactive Ruler

Let's take a look at Windows WordPad. WordPad is built around the control known in the Windows API as the *RichEdit* control, and which is accessible in a Windows Forms program through the *RichTextBox* class. The *RichEdit* control saves documents in the Rich Text Format (RTF), which allows paragraph and character formatting to be applied to different parts of the document.

The ruler displayed by WordPad allows the user to interactively set a left indentation, right indentation, first-line indentation, and tabs that apply to the currently selected paragraph. (Alternatively, you can change these same formatting items in the Paragraph and Tabs dialog boxes accessible from the menu in WordPad Format.)

Now let's examine the ruler in a more sophisticated word-processing program. We'll pick one at random, say, Microsoft Office Word. Ostensibly, the ruler in Microsoft Word looks a lot like the ruler in WordPad, but it also lets you change the left and right *margins*. These margins apply to the entire document and can alternatively be altered through the Page Setup dialog box accessible through the File menu. The margins really only make sense in connection with a particular paper width. The margins denote areas on the right and left of the page—generally an inch or so wide—where text does not appear. The width of the text on the page is the page width minus the left and right margins. In Word, left and right paragraph indentation is normally 0, meaning that the paragraphs occupy the full width between the left and right margins. Indentation can be made larger for narrower paragraphs or made to be even less than zero to occupy space in the margin. It is also possible to set a different indentation for the first line of a paragraph, so that the line is either indented relative to the rest of the paragraph or "hanging" to the left beyond the paragraph.

By convention, the left margin is measured from the left edge of the page, the left indentation is relative to the left margin, and the first-line indentation is relative to the left indentation: positive for a normal indentation, negative for a hanging effect, and 0 for a flush first line. The right margin is measured from the right edge of the page, and the right indentation is measured from the right margin. Both numbers are normally non-negative.

My original intention was to create a *DocumentRuler* control (as I called it) similar to the one in Microsoft Word that lets you set margins and indentations. However, the *RichTextBox* control has a much weaker concept of margins than Word. The only thing in *RichTextBox* that comes close is a property named *RightMargin* that lets a program specify a pixel width of the text displayed by the control. (In conventional terminology, this property actually specifies something more akin to a page width minus the left and right margins.) By default, this property is 0, which means that the width of the text displayed by the control is governed by the width of the control itself. For awhile, I toyed with the idea of imposing traditional concepts of page widths and margins on the *RichTextBox*, but I eventually decided to go for a simpler approach. My ruler is similar to the WordPad implementation, but it also allows the text width to be changed.

Although *DocumentRuler* doesn't specifically *require* that it be used in conjunction with a *RichTextBox* control, it doesn't go beyond the capabilities of *RichTextBox* in any way. It would need some enhancements to be used with a real word-processing application such as Word.

Given a page width of 8 1/2 inches and margins of 1 1/4 inches, I figured that an initial default value of 6 inches for the *RightMargin* property seemed about right. It's customary to think of margins, indents, and tabs in terms of inches, particularly if there's a ruler sitting at the top of the document. But that's not the way *RichTextBox* does business. The *RightMargin* property and all the indentation properties in *RichTextBox* are instead specified in pixels.

I decided that the programming interface to the ruler must be in terms of inches. Thus, the ruler would have a set of properties with names such as *LeftIndent*, *RightIndent*, and *FirstLineIndent*, and these would be *float* values in inches. This decision resulted in a lot of conversion between inches and pixels throughout both the ruler control and the program using the control. Of course, because the ruler is displayed on the screen, the conversion between inches and pixels is based on the user's screen resolution, which is available from the *DpiX* and *DpiY* properties of the *Graphics* object. (Even more conversions go on behind the scenes. Rich Text Format maintains measurements in terms of "twips," which are 1/20 of a printer's point and equal to 1/1440 of an inch.)

Although the inch markings on *DocumentRuler* are based on the screen resolution, I was less successful in making other aspects of the ruler as device independent as I would have preferred. In particular, the little moveable markers showing the indentations are too tiny and precisely constructed to react well to sizes calculated based on screen resolution.

Inches and pixels weren't the only conversions required in this job. The three properties of *RichTextBox* connected with indentations are called *SelectionIndent*, *SelectionRightIndent*, and *SelectionHangingIndent*. Unfortunately, the first two of these properties work a little differently from the familiar conventions of paragraph formatting. *SelectionIndent* is the indentation of the first line of the paragraph from the left side of the text box. *SelectionHangingIndent* is the indentation of the remainder of the paragraph relative to the first line. A paragraph indented 100 pixels from the left side of the text box with the first line indented another 50 pixels would have a *SelectionIndent* of 150 and a *SelectionHangingIndent* of −50. I decided that *DocumentRuler* would implement indentations in the more familiar way. It is the responsibility of a program that creates both a *RichTextBox* and a *DocumentRuler* to convert between the two.

We are now ready to start looking at some code. The *DocumentRuler* control implements just one event that I called simply *Change*. The event is triggered whenever the user changes a margin, indentation, or tab on the ruler. I wanted the program using the ruler to know what had changed (for example, the left indentation), which implies that the event must deliver that information. The event could not be based on the standard *EventHandler* delegate but required a custom delegate. First, an enumeration is defined with fields for each of the items settable through the ruler.

```
RulerProperty.cs
//-----------------------------------------------
// RulerProperty.cs (c) 2005 by Charles Petzold
//-----------------------------------------------
public enum RulerProperty
{
    TextWidth,
    LeftIndent,
    RightIndent,
    FirstLineIndent,
    Tabs
}
```

The *Change* event will be accompanied by an object of type *RulerEventArgs*. This class derives from *EventArgs* but implements an additional property of type *RulerProperty*.

RulerEventArgs.cs

```
//---------------------------------------------
// RulerEventArgs.cs (c) 2005 by Charles Petzold
//---------------------------------------------
using System;

public class RulerEventArgs : EventArgs
{
    RulerProperty rlrprop;

    public RulerEventArgs(RulerProperty rlrprop)
    {
        this.rlrprop = rlrprop;
    }
    public RulerProperty RulerChange
    {
        get { return rlrprop; }
        set { rlrprop = value; }
    }
}
```

The class also defines a constructor to create a new *RulerEventArgs* object by specifying a member of *RulerProperty*.

Whenever you define a new class that will be used to deliver information to an event handler, you must also define a new delegate for the event handler. The code is simple.

RulerEventHandler.cs

```
//---------------------------------------------------
// RulerEventHandler.cs (c) 2005 by Charles Petzold
//---------------------------------------------------
public delegate void RulerEventHandler(object objSrc, RulerEventArgs args);
```

The ruler contains four little types of graphical pictures that denote the left indent, right indent, first-line indent, and tabs. These little items must be drawn, of course, but the ruler must also detect when the user clicks one of them with the mouse. I decided to implement these objects in separate classes, but all are based on one abstract class called *RulerSlider*.

RulerSlider.cs

```
//-------------------------------------------
// RulerSlider.cs (c) 2005 by Charles Petzold
//-------------------------------------------
using System;
using System.Drawing;
using System.Drawing.Drawing2D;
using System.Windows.Forms;

abstract class RulerSlider
{
```

```csharp
// Private fields.
RulerProperty rlrprop;
float fValue;
int x, y;
Bitmap bm;
Region rgn;

// Public properties.
public RulerProperty RulerProperty
{
    get { return rlrprop; }
    set { rlrprop = value; }
}
public float Value
{
    get { return fValue; }
    set { fValue = value; }
}
public int X
{
    get { return x; }
    set { x = value; }
}
public virtual Rectangle Rectangle
{
    get
    {
        return new Rectangle(X - bm.Width / 2, Y, bm.Width, bm.Height);
    }
}

// Protected property.
protected int Y
{
    get { return y; }
    set { y = value; }
}

// Public methods.
public virtual void Draw(Graphics grfx)
{
    grfx.DrawImage(bm, X - bm.Width / 2, Y);
}
public virtual bool HitTest(Point pt)
{
    return rgn.IsVisible(pt.X - x + bm.Width / 2, pt.Y - Y);
}
protected void CreateBitmap(int cx, int cy, Point[] apt)
{
    bm = new Bitmap(cx, cy);

    GraphicsPath path = new GraphicsPath();
    path.AddLines(apt);
    rgn = new Region(path);
```

```
            Graphics grfx = Graphics.FromImage(bm);
            grfx.FillPolygon(Brushes.LightGray, apt);
            grfx.Clip = rgn;

            Shading(grfx, Pens.White, 1, apt);
            Shading(grfx, Pens.Gray, -1, apt);

            grfx.ResetClip();
            grfx.DrawPolygon(Pens.Black, apt);
            grfx.Dispose();
        }
        void Shading(Graphics grfx, Pen pn, int iOffset, Point[] apt)
        {
            grfx.TranslateTransform(iOffset, 0);
            grfx.DrawPolygon(pn, apt);
            grfx.TranslateTransform(-iOffset, iOffset);
            grfx.DrawPolygon(pn, apt);
            grfx.TranslateTransform(0, -iOffset);
        }
    }
```

As you'll see shortly, the various classes that derive from *RulerSlider* themselves set the *Ruler-Property* property to an appropriate member of the *RulerProperty* enumeration. They also set the *Y* property to a fixed position of the slider relative to the top of the control. The *X* property varies as the user moves the slider from one place to another.

I also decided that these sliders should maintain a floating-point *Value* property that saves the current value in inches. In theory, *Value* and *X* are convertible between each other, but I wanted to keep the floating-point value intact to avoid rounding differences during conversions. I wanted to avoid situations in which a property such as *LeftIndent* might be set to one value but then return a slightly different value.

The *Draw* method of *RulerSlider* draws the slider at the *X* and *Y* coordinates. In *RulerSlider*, *Draw* is implemented to simply draw a bitmap—the same bitmap created in the protected *CreateBitmap* method. The *CreateBitmap* method requires a width and a height of the bitmap and an array of *Point* objects. This array defines a closed area on the bitmap that is filled with various colors and shading. In the process, a *Region* object is also created to be used in the *HitTest* method. If a mouse coordinate is passed to *HitTest*, the method returns *true* if the mouse is over the object.

The read-only *Rectangle* property returns a rectangle that encompasses the bitmap as displayed on the ruler. This is useful to invalidate areas of the ruler when the user is moving the slider.

Here's the *RightIndent* class that derives from *RulerSlider*.

RightIndent.cs

```
//-----------------------------------------------
// RightIndent.cs (c) 2005 by Charles Petzold
//-----------------------------------------------
using System;
using System.Drawing;
using System.Windows.Forms;

class RightIndent : RulerSlider
{
    public RightIndent()
    {
        RulerProperty = RulerProperty.RightIndent;
        Y = 9;
        CreateBitmap(9, 8, new Point[]
        {
            new Point(0, 7), new Point(0, 4), new Point(4, 0),
            new Point(8, 4), new Point(8, 7), new Point(0, 7)
        });
    }
}
```

The class simply sets two properties of *RulerSlider* and calls *CreateBitmap* to create an image that looks like a little house. The *LeftIndent* is similar except the image is a bit more elaborate.

LeftIndent.cs

```
//-----------------------------------------------
// LeftIndent.cs (c) 2005 by Charles Petzold
//-----------------------------------------------
using System;
using System.Drawing;
using System.Windows.Forms;

class LeftIndent : RulerSlider
{
    public LeftIndent()
    {
        RulerProperty = RulerProperty.LeftIndent;
        Y = 9;
        CreateBitmap(9, 14, new Point[]
        {
            new Point(0, 7), new Point(0, 4), new Point(4, 0), new Point(8, 4),
            new Point(8, 7), new Point(0, 7), new Point(0, 13), new Point(8, 13),
            new Point(8, 7), new Point(0, 7)
        });
    }
}
```

The *FirstLineIndent* is similar to *RightIndent* except that it's upside-down and positioned near the top of the control.

FirstLineIndent.cs

```
//-------------------------------------------
// FirstLineIndent.cs (c) 2005 by Charles Petzold
//-------------------------------------------
using System;
using System.Drawing;
using System.Windows.Forms;

class FirstLineIndent : RulerSlider
{
    public FirstLineIndent()
    {
        RulerProperty = RulerProperty.FirstLineIndent;
        Y = 1;
        CreateBitmap(9, 8, new Point[]
        {
            new Point(0, 0), new Point(8, 0), new Point(8, 3),
            new Point(4, 7), new Point(0, 3), new Point(0, 0)
        });
    }
}
```

The *Tab* character (an L shape) is better suited for a simple line. The class overrides the *Draw* and *HitTest* methods, as well as the *Rectangle* property.

Tab.cs

```
//-----------------------------------
// Tab.cs (c) 2005 by Charles Petzold
//-----------------------------------
using System;
using System.Drawing;
using System.Windows.Forms;

class Tab : RulerSlider
{
    public Tab()
    {
        RulerProperty = RulerProperty.Tabs;
        Y = 9;
    }
    public override void Draw(Graphics grfx)
    {
        Pen pn = new Pen(Color.Black, 2);

        grfx.DrawLine(pn, X, Y, X, Y + 4);
        grfx.DrawLine(pn, X, Y + 4, X + 4, Y + 4);
    }
    public override bool HitTest(Point pt)
    {
        return pt.X >= X - 1 && pt.X <= X + 1 && pt.Y >= Y - 1 && pt.Y <= Y + 6;
    }
    public override Rectangle Rectangle
```

```
    {
        get
        {
            return new Rectangle(X - 1, Y - 1, 6, 6);
        }
    }
}
```

The final class that inherits from *RulerSlider* is *TextWidth*. Changing the text width is a little different than moving little markers. The drawing logic needs to be handled in the main *OnPaint* method of the control, so the class doesn't do much.

TextWidth.cs

```
//-------------------------------------------------
// TextWidth.cs (c) 2005 by Charles Petzold
//-------------------------------------------------
using System;
using System.Drawing;
using System.Windows.Forms;

class TextWidth : RulerSlider
{
    public TextWidth()
    {
        RulerProperty = RulerProperty.TextWidth;
    }
    public override void Draw(Graphics grfx)
    {
    }
    public override bool HitTest(Point pt)
    {
        return (pt.X >= X - 2) && (pt.X <= X + 2);
    }
    public override Rectangle Rectangle
    {
        get { return Rectangle.Empty; }
    }
}
```

And now we're ready for the *RulerDocument* class itself. So that it won't be too overwhelming, I divided the class into two source code files using the *partial* keyword. The first installment has the constructor and all the properties.

DocumentRuler1.cs

```
//-------------------------------------------------
// DocumentRuler1.cs (c) 2005 by Charles Petzold
//-------------------------------------------------
using System;
using System.Collections.Generic;
using System.Drawing;
```

```
using System.Windows.Forms;

public partial class DocumentRuler : Control
{
    // Private fields.
    int iLeftMargin;
    float fDpi;
    Control ctrlDocument;

    // RulerSlider objects.
    LeftIndent rsLeftIndent = new LeftIndent();
    RightIndent rsRightIndent = new RightIndent();
    FirstLineIndent rsFirstIndent = new FirstLineIndent();
    TextWidth rsTextWidth = new TextWidth();
    List<RulerSlider> rsCollection = new List<RulerSlider>();

    // Constructor.
    public DocumentRuler()
    {
        Dock = DockStyle.Top;
        ResizeRedraw = true;
        TabStop = false;
        Height = 23;
        Font = new Font(Font.Name, 14, GraphicsUnit.Pixel);

        Graphics grfx = CreateGraphics();
        fDpi = grfx.DpiX;
        grfx.Dispose();

        rsCollection.Add(rsLeftIndent);
        rsCollection.Add(rsRightIndent);
        rsCollection.Add(rsFirstIndent);
        rsCollection.Add(rsTextWidth);
    }

    // Public properties.
    public float TextWidth
    {
        get { return rsTextWidth.Value; }
        set
        {
            rsTextWidth.Value = value;
            CalculateDisplayOffsets();
        }
    }
    public float LeftIndent
    {
        get { return rsLeftIndent.Value; }
        set
        {
            rsLeftIndent.Value = value;
            CalculateDisplayOffsets();
        }
    }
    public float RightIndent
```

```csharp
{
    get { return rsRightIndent.Value; }
    set
    {
        rsRightIndent.Value = value;
        CalculateDisplayOffsets();
    }
}
public float FirstLineIndent
{
    get { return rsFirstIndent.Value; }
    set
    {
        rsFirstIndent.Value = value;
        CalculateDisplayOffsets();
    }
}
public float[] Tabs
{
    get
    {
        List<float> fTabs = new List<float>();

        foreach (RulerSlider rs in rsCollection)
            if (rs is Tab)
                fTabs.Add(rs.Value);

        // RichTextBox wants tabs in numeric order
        float[] afTabs = fTabs.ToArray();
        Array.Sort(afTabs);
        return afTabs;
    }
    set
    {
        // First, delete tabs that aren't in value array.
        List<Tab> rsTabsDelete = new List<Tab>();

        foreach (RulerSlider rs in rsCollection)
            if (rs is Tab && (Array.IndexOf(value, rs.Value) == -1))
                rsTabsDelete.Add(rs as Tab);

        foreach (Tab tab in rsTabsDelete)
        {
            rsCollection.Remove(tab);
            Invalidate(tab.Rectangle);
        }

        // Second, add tabs that aren't in rsCollection.
        foreach (float fTab in value)
        {
            bool bAdd = true;

            foreach (RulerSlider rs in rsCollection)
                if (rs is Tab && rs.Value == fTab)
                    bAdd = false;
```

```
                    if (bAdd)
                    {
                        Tab tab = new Tab();
                        tab.Value = fTab;
                        tab.X = LeftMargin + InchesToPixels(fTab);
                        rsCollection.Add(tab);
                        Invalidate(tab.Rectangle);
                    }
                }
            }
        }
    }
    public int LeftMargin
    {
        get { return iLeftMargin; }
        set
        {
            iLeftMargin = value;
            CalculateDisplayOffsets();
        }
    }

    // For displaying a line when sliders are slid.
    public Control DocumentControl
    {
        get { return ctrlDocument; }
        set { ctrlDocument = value; }
    }

    // These two methods calculate X values for the four types of sliders
    //  (excluding tabs).  If the X values changes, invalidate the rectangle
    //  at the previous position and the new position.
    void CalculateDisplayOffsets()
    {
        CalculateDisplayOffsets2(rsTextWidth, LeftMargin +
                        InchesToPixels(rsTextWidth.Value));
        CalculateDisplayOffsets2(rsLeftIndent, LeftMargin +
                        InchesToPixels(rsLeftIndent.Value));
        CalculateDisplayOffsets2(rsRightIndent, LeftMargin +
                        InchesToPixels(TextWidth - rsRightIndent.Value));
        CalculateDisplayOffsets2(rsFirstIndent, LeftMargin +
                        InchesToPixels(LeftIndent + rsFirstIndent.Value));
    }
    void CalculateDisplayOffsets2(RulerSlider rs, int xNew)
    {
        if (rs.X != xNew)
        {
            Invalidate(rs.Rectangle);
            rs.X = xNew;
            Invalidate(rs.Rectangle);
        }
    }
    float PixelsToInches(int i)
    {
        return i / fDpi;
    }
```

```
    int InchesToPixels(float f)
    {
        return (int)Math.Round(f * fDpi);
    }
}
```

Fields define the various *RulerSlider* objects so that *rsLeftIndent* is an object of type *LeftIndent*, *rsRightIndent* is an object of type *RightIndent*, and so forth. Also created is a *List* collection of type *RulerSlider* named *rsCollection*. The constructor makes all these individual *RulerSlider* objects members of the collection. The collection must also eventually include multiple objects of type *Tab*.

Next in the file is a series of public properties named *TextWidth*, *LeftIndent*, and so forth. These provide access to the objects *rsTextWidth*, *rsLeftIndent*, and so on. For each of these properties, after the *Value* property is set for the *RulerSlider* object, a *CalculateDisplayOffsets* calculates the *X* properties.

The property named *Tabs* is more extensive than all the rest simply because it's plural rather than singular. Each paragraph may have its own series of tabs. In general, as the ruler displays information for different parts of the document, all the tabs in the *rsCollection* must be deleted and new ones added. My original code did literally that, and the constant erasing and redrawing during typing in the *RichTextBox* caused the markers to flicker. The current code doesn't delete and re-create tabs at the same location.

You'll also notice a public property named *LeftMargin* of type *int* that provides access to the *iLeftMargin* field, and you'll also notice that just about every calculation in the program uses this *LeftMargin* property. This property might better be called *Kludge*. Visually, the ruler needs a little space to the left of the 0 position to properly display the left indent slider. So, in the program coming up that puts the *RichTextBox* and *DocumentRuler* controls together, I did what WordPad does: I set the *ShowSelectionMargin* property of *RichTextBox* to *true*. This property opens up a little space to the left so that the user can select whole lines of text. But how much space? It seemed to be about 10 pixels, so that's what the program coming up sets as the *Left-Margin* property of *DocumentRuler*. I wasn't very happy, and I fear this is a decision that will haunt me for the rest of my days, but I wasn't sure of a better approach.

The final public property in *DocumentRuler* is named *DocumentControl*. This is set to the word-processing control associated with the *DocumentRuler*. The only reason *DocumentRuler* needs to know this is to draw a vertical line down the control when the user is sliding one of the sliders. All other interaction between the *DocumentRuler* and the *RichTextBox* takes place external to the two controls.

Although the first part of the *DocumentRuler* class is devoted to input and output for *programs* using the control, the second part of the *DocumentRuler* class is devoted to input and output for the *user*. It includes overrides of the *OnPaint*, *OnMouseDown*, *OnMouseMove*, and *OnMouseUp* methods.

DocumentRuler2.cs

```
//------------------------------------------------
// DocumentRuler2.cs (c) 2005 by Charles Petzold
//------------------------------------------------
using System;
using System.Collections.Generic;
using System.Drawing;
using System.Windows.Forms;

public partial class DocumentRuler : Control
{
    // Public event.
    public event RulerEventHandler Change;

    // Private fields used during mouse dragging.
    RulerSlider rsDragging;
    Point ptDown;
    int xOriginal;
    int xLineOverTextBox;

    // OnPaint method handles virtually all drawing.
    protected override void OnPaint(PaintEventArgs args)
    {
        Graphics grfx = args.Graphics;

        Rectangle rect = new Rectangle(LeftMargin, 0,
                            rsTextWidth.X - LeftMargin, Height - 4);
        grfx.FillRectangle(Brushes.White, rect);
        ControlPaint.DrawBorder3D(grfx, rect);

        for (int i = 1; i < 8 * PixelsToInches(Width); i++)
        {
            int x = LeftMargin + InchesToPixels(i / 8f);

            if (i % 8 == 0)
            {
                StringFormat strfmt = new StringFormat();
                strfmt.Alignment = strfmt.LineAlignment = StringAlignment.Center;
                grfx.DrawString((i / 8).ToString(), Font,
                            Brushes.Black, x, 9, strfmt);
            }
            else if (i % 4 == 0)
            {
                grfx.DrawLine(Pens.Black, x, 7, x, 10);
            }
            else
            {
                grfx.DrawLine(Pens.Black, x, 8, x, 9);
            }
        }

        // Display all sliders.
        foreach (RulerSlider rs in rsCollection)
            rs.Draw(grfx);
```

```
        return;
}

// OnMouseDown for moving sliders and creating tabs.
protected override void OnMouseDown(MouseEventArgs args)
{
    // Ignore if it's not the left button.
    if ((args.Button & MouseButtons.Left) == 0)
        return;

    // Loop through existing sliders looking for positive hit test.
    foreach (RulerSlider rs in rsCollection)
        if (rs.HitTest(args.Location))
        {
            rsDragging = rs;
            ptDown = args.Location;
            xOriginal = rsDragging.X;

            if (rsDragging is TextWidth)
                Cursor.Current = Cursors.SizeWE;

            DrawReversibleLine(xLineOverTextBox = args.X);
            return;
        }
    // If no hit, create a new tab.
    rsDragging = new Tab();
    rsCollection.Add(rsDragging);
    ptDown = args.Location;
    xOriginal = rsDragging.X = ptDown.X;

    Invalidate(rsDragging.Rectangle);
    DrawReversibleLine(xLineOverTextBox = args.X);
    return;
}

// OnMouseMove for moving sliders.
protected override void OnMouseMove(MouseEventArgs args)
{
    if (!Capture)    // i.e., mouse button not down.
    {
        // If over TextWidth end, change cursor.
        if (!rsRightIndent.HitTest(args.Location) &&
            rsTextWidth.HitTest(args.Location))
                Cursor.Current = Cursors.SizeWE;
        return;
    }

    // If rsDragging not null, we're in a drag operation.
    if (rsDragging != null)
    {
        if (rsDragging is TextWidth)
            Cursor.Current = Cursors.SizeWE;

        int xNow = xOriginal - ptDown.X + args.X;
```

```
                    // Don't let the sliders go out of bounds!
                    if (rsDragging is Tab && (xNow < LeftMargin || xNow > rsTextWidth.X))
                        return;

                    if ((rsDragging == rsLeftIndent || rsDragging == rsFirstIndent) &&
                            (xNow < LeftMargin || xNow > rsRightIndent.X))
                        return;

                    if (rsDragging == rsRightIndent && (xNow > rsTextWidth.X ||
                            xNow < rsLeftIndent.X || xNow < rsFirstIndent.X))
                        return;

                    if (rsDragging == rsTextWidth && xNow < rsRightIndent.X)
                        return;

                    if (rsDragging == rsTextWidth)
                    {
                        Invalidate(new Rectangle(Math.Min(rsDragging.X, xOriginal) - 1, 0,
                                        Math.Abs(rsDragging.X - xOriginal) + 2, Height));
                        rsDragging.X = xNow;
                    }
                    else
                    {
                        // Update the slider X property and invalidate old and new.
                        Invalidate(rsDragging.Rectangle);
                        rsDragging.X = xNow;
                        Invalidate(rsDragging.Rectangle);
                    }
                    // Move line over text box.
                    DrawReversibleLine(xLineOverTextBox);
                    DrawReversibleLine(xLineOverTextBox = args.X);
            }
        }

        // OnMouseUp is new position of slider.
        protected override void OnMouseUp(MouseEventArgs args)
        {
            if (rsDragging != null)
            {
                // Calculate new Value properties and trigger the event.
                if (rsDragging == rsLeftIndent || rsDragging == rsFirstIndent)
                {
                    rsLeftIndent.Value = PixelsToInches(rsLeftIndent.X - LeftMargin);
                    rsFirstIndent.Value =
                            PixelsToInches(rsFirstIndent.X - rsLeftIndent.X);
                    OnChange(new RulerEventArgs(rsDragging.RulerProperty));
                }
                else if (rsDragging == rsRightIndent || rsDragging == rsTextWidth)
                {
                    rsTextWidth.Value = PixelsToInches(rsTextWidth.X - LeftMargin);
                    rsRightIndent.Value =
                            PixelsToInches(rsTextWidth.X - rsRightIndent.X);
                    OnChange(new RulerEventArgs(rsTextWidth.RulerProperty));
                    OnChange(new RulerEventArgs(rsRightIndent.RulerProperty));
                }
```

```
            else if (rsDragging is Tab)
            {
                rsDragging.Value = PixelsToInches(rsDragging.X - LeftMargin);
                OnChange(new RulerEventArgs(rsDragging.RulerProperty));
            }
            // Cease drag operation.
            rsDragging = null;
            DrawReversibleLine(xLineOverTextBox);
        }
    }

    // Draw line down text box in screen coordinates.
    void DrawReversibleLine(int x)
    {
        if (ctrlDocument != null)
        {
            Point pt1 = ctrlDocument.PointToScreen(new Point(x, 0));
            Point pt2 = ctrlDocument.PointToScreen(
                             new Point(x, ctrlDocument.Height));
            ControlPaint.DrawReversibleLine(pt1, pt2, ctrlDocument.BackColor);
        }
    }

    // OnChange method triggers Change event.
    protected virtual void OnChange(RulerEventArgs args)
    {
        if (Change != null)
            Change(this, args);
    }
}
```

The *OnPaint* method is simpler than it might be because of the two lines of code near the bottom of the method:

```
foreach (RulerSlider rs in rsCollection)
    rs.Draw(grfx);
```

The *RulerSlider* objects draw themselves, so the *OnPaint* method doesn't need to bother.

Similarly, the *RulerSlider* objects perform their own hit-testing, and the *OnMouseDown* method uses those methods to determine whether the user is clicking an existing slider. If not, the user wants a new tab. In either case, *OnMouseDown* sets several private fields—*rsDragging* (the particular slider being dragged), *ptDown* (the original point where the mouse button was clicked), and *xOriginal* (the original position of the slider)—to assist in moving the sliders. The *OnMouseMove* method is mostly devoted to making sure the sliders don't get moved to illegal positions. The *SelectionRightIndent* property of *RichTextBox* cannot be negative, for example, which means that the right margin cannot be moved to the left of the right indent. *OnMouseUp* completes the dragging operation.

And now, here's the class that lets us actually look at the ruler and try it out. The *RichTextWith-Ruler* class inherits from *Form* and creates a *RichTextBox* control and a *DocumentRuler* control.

The RichTextWithRuler project includes this file and all other files starting with RulerProperty.cs.

RichTextWithRuler.cs

```
//--------------------------------------------------
// RichTextWithRuler.cs (c) 2005 by Charles Petzold
//--------------------------------------------------
using System;
using System.Drawing;
using System.Windows.Forms;

class RichTextWithRuler : Form
{
    DocumentRuler ruler;
    RichTextBox txtbox;
    float fDpi;

    [STAThread]
    public static void Main()
    {
        Application.EnableVisualStyles();
        Application.Run(new RichTextWithRuler());
    }
    public RichTextWithRuler()
    {
        Text = "RichText with Ruler";

        Graphics grfx = CreateGraphics();
        fDpi = grfx.DpiX;
        grfx.Dispose();

        txtbox = new RichTextBox();
        txtbox.Parent = this;
        txtbox.AcceptsTab = true;
        txtbox.Dock = DockStyle.Fill;
        txtbox.RightMargin = InchesToPixels(6);
        txtbox.ShowSelectionMargin = true;
        txtbox.SelectionChanged += TextBoxOnSelectionChanged;

        ruler = new DocumentRuler();
        ruler.Parent = this;
        ruler.LeftMargin = 10;
        ruler.TextWidth = PixelsToInches(txtbox.RightMargin);
        ruler.DocumentControl = txtbox;
        ruler.Change += RulerOnChange;

        // Initialize the ruler with text box values.
        TextBoxOnSelectionChanged(txtbox, EventArgs.Empty);
    }
    void TextBoxOnSelectionChanged(object objSrc, EventArgs args)
    {
        ruler.LeftIndent = PixelsToInches(txtbox.SelectionIndent +
                                          txtbox.SelectionHangingIndent);
        ruler.RightIndent = PixelsToInches(txtbox.SelectionRightIndent);
```

```
            ruler.FirstLineIndent = PixelsToInches(-txtbox.SelectionHangingIndent);

            float[] fTabs = new float[txtbox.SelectionTabs.Length];

            for (int i = 0; i < txtbox.SelectionTabs.Length; i++)
                fTabs[i] = PixelsToInches(txtbox.SelectionTabs[i]);

            ruler.Tabs = fTabs;
        }
        void RulerOnChange(object objSrc, RulerEventArgs args)
        {
            switch (args.RulerChange)
            {
                case RulerProperty.TextWidth:
                    txtbox.RightMargin = InchesToPixels(ruler.TextWidth);
                    break;

                case RulerProperty.LeftIndent:
                case RulerProperty.FirstLineIndent:
                    txtbox.SelectionIndent = InchesToPixels(ruler.LeftIndent +
                                                        ruler.FirstLineIndent);
                    txtbox.SelectionHangingIndent =
                        InchesToPixels(-ruler.FirstLineIndent);
                    break;

                case RulerProperty.RightIndent:
                    txtbox.SelectionRightIndent = InchesToPixels(ruler.RightIndent);
                    break;

                case RulerProperty.Tabs:
                    int[] iTabs = new int[ruler.Tabs.Length];

                    for (int i = 0; i < ruler.Tabs.Length; i++)
                        iTabs[i] = InchesToPixels(ruler.Tabs[i]);

                    txtbox.SelectionTabs = iTabs;
                    break;
            }
        }
        float PixelsToInches(int i)
        {
            return i / fDpi;
        }
        int InchesToPixels(float f)
        {
            return (int)Math.Round(f * fDpi);
        }
    }
```

As I promised, this file again contains a lot of converting between inches and pixels. The program must provide the interface between *RichTextBox* and *DocumentRuler*, and it does this largely in event handlers for the *SelectionChanged* event of the text box and the *Change* event of the ruler. Here's the program showing left and right indents of zero and a first-line indent of one inch:

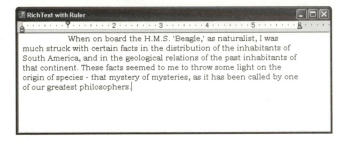

Color Selection

There are six million color-selection controls in .NET city, and this is one of them. *ColorGrid* displays an array of 40 colors in a grid. You can click one of the colors (of course), but you can also move through the color grid using the keyboard arrow keys. This control has the most extensive keyboard processing in this chapter.

```
ColorGrid.cs
//----------------------------------------
// ColorGrid.cs (c) 2005 by Charles Petzold
//----------------------------------------
using System;
using System.Drawing;
using System.Windows.Forms;

class ColorGrid : Control
{
    // Number of colors horizontally and vertically.
    const int xNum = 8;
    const int yNum = 5;

    // The colors.
    Color[,] aclr = new Color[yNum, xNum]
    {
        { Color.Black, Color.Brown, Color.DarkGreen, Color.MidnightBlue,
            Color.Navy, Color.DarkBlue, Color.Indigo, Color.DimGray },

        { Color.DarkRed, Color.OrangeRed, Color.Olive, Color.Green,
            Color.Teal, Color.Blue, Color.SlateGray, Color.Gray },

        { Color.Red, Color.Orange, Color.YellowGreen, Color.SeaGreen,
            Color.Aqua, Color.LightBlue, Color.Violet, Color.DarkGray },

        { Color.Pink, Color.Gold, Color.Yellow, Color.Lime,
            Color.Turquoise, Color.SkyBlue, Color.Plum, Color.LightGray },

        { Color.LightPink, Color.Tan, Color.LightYellow, Color.LightGreen,
            Color.LightCyan, Color.LightSkyBlue, Color.Lavender, Color.White }
    };
```

```
// Selected color as a private field.
Color clrSelected = Color.Black;

// Rectangles for displaying colors and borders.
Rectangle rectTotal, rectGray, rectBorder, rectColor;

// The coordinate currently highlighted by keyboard or mouse.
int xHighlight = -1;
int yHighlight = -1;

// Constructor.
public ColorGrid()
{
    AutoSize = true;

    // Obtain the resolution of the screen
    Graphics grfx = CreateGraphics();
    int xDpi = (int)grfx.DpiX;
    int yDpi = (int)grfx.DpiY;
    grfx.Dispose();

    // Calculate rectangles for color displays
    rectTotal = new Rectangle(0, 0, xDpi / 5, yDpi / 5);
    rectGray = Rectangle.Inflate(rectTotal, -xDpi / 72, -yDpi / 72);
    rectBorder = Rectangle.Inflate(rectGray, -xDpi / 48, -yDpi / 48);
    rectColor = Rectangle.Inflate(rectBorder, -xDpi / 72, -yDpi / 72);
}

// SelectedColor property -- access to clrSelected field
public Color SelectedColor
{
    get
    {
        return clrSelected;
    }
    set
    {
        clrSelected = value;
        Invalidate();
    }
}

// Required for autosizing.
public override Size GetPreferredSize(Size sz)
{
    return new Size(xNum * rectTotal.Width, yNum * rectTotal.Height);
}

// Draw all colors in the grid.
protected override void OnPaint(PaintEventArgs args)
{
    Graphics grfx = args.Graphics;

    for (int y = 0; y < yNum; y++)
        for (int x = 0; x < xNum; x++)
```

```
                    DrawColor(grfx, x, y, false);
}

// Draw an individual color. (grfx can be null)
void DrawColor(Graphics grfx, int x, int y, bool bHighlight)
{
    bool bDisposeGraphics = false;

    if (x < 0 || y < 0 || x >= xNum || y >= yNum)
        return;

    if (grfx == null)
    {
        grfx = CreateGraphics();
        bDisposeGraphics = true;
    }

    // Determine if the color is currently selected.
    bool bSelect = aclr[y, x].ToArgb() == SelectedColor.ToArgb();

    Brush br = (bHighlight | bSelect) ? SystemBrushes.HotTrack :
                    SystemBrushes.Menu;

    // Start draw rectangles.
    Rectangle rect = rectTotal;
    rect.Offset(x * rectTotal.Width, y * rectTotal.Height);
    grfx.FillRectangle(br, rect);

    if (bHighlight || bSelect)
    {
        br = bHighlight ? SystemBrushes.ControlDark :
                            SystemBrushes.ControlLight;
        rect = rectGray;
        rect.Offset(x * rectTotal.Width, y * rectTotal.Height);
        grfx.FillRectangle(br, rect);
    }

    rect = rectBorder;
    rect.Offset(x * rectTotal.Width, y * rectTotal.Height);
    grfx.FillRectangle(SystemBrushes.ControlDark, rect);

    rect = rectColor;
    rect.Offset(x * rectTotal.Width, y * rectTotal.Height);
    grfx.FillRectangle(new SolidBrush(aclr[y, x]), rect);

    if (bDisposeGraphics)
        grfx.Dispose();
}

// Methods for mouse movement and clicks.
protected override void OnMouseEnter(EventArgs args)
{
    xHighlight = -1;
    yHighlight = -1;
}
```

```csharp
protected override void OnMouseMove(MouseEventArgs args)
{
    int x = args.X / rectTotal.Width;
    int y = args.Y / rectTotal.Height;

    if (x != xHighlight || y != yHighlight)
    {
        DrawColor(null, xHighlight, yHighlight, false);
        DrawColor(null, x, y, true);

        xHighlight = x;
        yHighlight = y;
    }
}
protected override void OnMouseLeave(EventArgs args)
{
    DrawColor(null, xHighlight, yHighlight, false);

    xHighlight = -1;
    yHighlight = -1;
}
protected override void OnMouseDown(MouseEventArgs args)
{
    int x = args.X / rectTotal.Width;
    int y = args.Y / rectTotal.Height;
    SelectedColor = aclr[y, x];
    base.OnMouseDown(args);         // Generates Click event.
    Focus();
}

// Methods for keyboard interface.
protected override void OnEnter(EventArgs args)
{
    if (xHighlight < 0 || yHighlight < 0)
        for (yHighlight = 0; yHighlight < yNum; yHighlight++)
        {
            for (xHighlight = 0; xHighlight < xNum; xHighlight++)
            {
                if (aclr[yHighlight, xHighlight].ToArgb() ==
                            SelectedColor.ToArgb())
                    break;
            }
            if (xHighlight < xNum)
                break;
        }

    if (xHighlight == xNum && yHighlight == yNum)
        xHighlight = yHighlight = 0;

    DrawColor(null, xHighlight, yHighlight, true);
}
protected override void OnLeave(EventArgs args)
{
    DrawColor(null, xHighlight, yHighlight, false);
    xHighlight = yHighlight = -1;
```

```
    }
    protected override bool IsInputKey(Keys keyData)
    {
        return keyData == Keys.Home || keyData == Keys.End ||
               keyData == Keys.Up || keyData == Keys.Down ||
               keyData == Keys.Left || keyData == Keys.Right;
    }
    protected override void OnKeyDown(KeyEventArgs args)
    {
        DrawColor(null, xHighlight, yHighlight, false);
        int x = xHighlight, y = yHighlight;

        switch (args.KeyCode)
        {
            case Keys.Home:
                x = y = 0;
                break;

            case Keys.End:
                x = xNum - 1;
                y = yNum - 1;
                break;

            case Keys.Right:
                if (++x == xNum)
                {
                    x = 0;
                    if (++y == yNum)
                    {
                        Parent.GetNextControl(this, true).Focus();
                    }
                }
                break;

            case Keys.Left:
                if (--x == -1)
                {
                    x = xNum - 1;
                    if (--y == -1)
                    {
                        Parent.GetNextControl(this, false).Focus();
                    }
                }
                break;

            case Keys.Down:
                if (++y == yNum)
                {
                    y = 0;
                    if (++x == xNum)
                    {
                        Parent.GetNextControl(this, true).Focus();
                    }
                }
                break;
```

```
        case Keys.Up:
            if (--y == -1)
            {
                y = 0;
                if (--x == -1)
                {
                    Parent.GetNextControl(this, false).Focus();
                }
            }
            break;

        case Keys.Enter:
        case Keys.Space:
            SelectedColor = aclr[y, x];
            OnClick(EventArgs.Empty);
            break;

        default:
            base.OnKeyDown(args);
            return;
    }
    DrawColor(null, x, y, true);

    xHighlight = x;
    yHighlight = y;
}
}
```

The control defines one new public property named *SelectedColor*. A program using the control is notified when the *SelectedColor* has changed by the normal *Click* event.

The constructor defines four rectangles used for displaying each of the colors in the grid. The dimensions of these rectangles are based entirely upon the vertical and horizontal resolution of the display. *ColorGrid* is one control (at least) that won't need recoding when people begin using 300-DPI displays. The *OnPaint* method simply calls *DrawColor* for each of the 40 colors in the grid; the *DrawColor* method does the real work. The drawing logic distinguishes between the *selected* color, which is the color available from the *SelectedColor* property, and the *highlighted* color. The highlighted control changes when the mouse pointer passes over the control, or when the control has input focus and the arrow keys are pressed. A color is converted from highlighted to selected when the mouse button is depressed or when the Enter key or spacebar is pressed.

Changing the highlight based on the mouse pointer is the responsibility of the *OnMouseEnter*, *OnMouseMove*, and *OnMouseLeave* overrides. The *OnMouseDown* method sets a new selected color and calls the base method to generate a *Click* event.

The keyboard processing is more extensive. First, the control must determine when it gets and loses input focus. If the mouse pointer is not over the control, a color is highlighted only when the control has the input focus. *ColorGrid* uses the *OnEnter* and *OnLeave* methods for this job.

Another problem: many of the keys that *ColorGrid* wants—the arrow keys in particular—are used by the parent control to shift input focus among its children. *ColorGrid* must override the *IsInputKey* and return *true* for any key that it wants exclusive use of. These keys are then processed in the *OnKeyDown* method. The arrow keys move through the rows and columns of the grid until the color is reached at the upper-left or lower-right corner. At that point, input focus passes to the previous or next sibling control. Notice also the processing of the Enter and spacebar keys to change the selection.

The ColorGridDemo project includes ColorGrid.cs and the next file.

```
ColorGridDemo.cs
//----------------------------------------------
// ColorGridDemo.cs (c) 2005 by Charles Petzold
//----------------------------------------------
using System;
using System.Drawing;
using System.Windows.Forms;

class ColorGridDemo : Form
{
    Label lbl;

    [STAThread]
    public static void Main()
    {
        Application.EnableVisualStyles();
        Application.Run(new ColorGridDemo());
    }
    public ColorGridDemo()
    {
        Text = "Custom Color Control";
        AutoSize = true;

        TableLayoutPanel table = new TableLayoutPanel();
        table.Parent = this;
        table.AutoSize = true;
        table.ColumnCount = 3;

        Button btn = new Button();
        btn.Parent = table;
        btn.AutoSize = true;
        btn.Text = "Button One";

        ColorGrid clrgrid = new ColorGrid();
        clrgrid.Parent = table;
        clrgrid.Click += ColorGridOnClick;

        btn = new Button();
        btn.Parent = table;
        btn.AutoSize = true;
        btn.Text = "Button Two";
```

```
        lbl = new Label();
        lbl.Parent = table;
        lbl.AutoSize = true;
        lbl.Font = new Font("Times New Roman", 24);
        lbl.Text = "Sample Text";

        table.SetColumnSpan(lbl, 3);
        clrgrid.SelectedColor = lbl.ForeColor;
    }
    void ColorGridOnClick(object objSrc, EventArgs args)
    {
        ColorGrid clrgrid = (ColorGrid) objSrc;
        lbl.ForeColor = clrgrid.SelectedColor;
    }
}
```

The *ColorGridDemo* class creates a *ColorGrid* control, and it puts the control between two *Button* controls just to test the transfer of input focus. When a new color is selected, that color is used as the foreground color of a *Label* control:

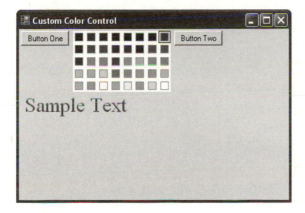

If you think that color grid resembles something you've seen in the Format | Background menu in a Microsoft Office application, I must confess that was the source of my inspiration. Putting that control into a menu and toolbar will be one of the challenges facing us in the next chapter.

Chapter 5
Cruisin' the Strip

There was once a time when menus and toolbars were easy to distinguish. Menus were a hierarchical collection of text items, while toolbars consisted of simple bitmapped buttons. But when toolbars started supporting drop-down menus and menus acquired graphics, the differences became less obvious. This overlapping of functionality between menus and toolbars has progressed to such a point that they have become basically the same, as witnessed by this partial Microsoft .NET Framework 2.0 class hierarchy:

Object

    MarshalByRefObject

        Component

            Control

                ScrollableControl

                    ToolStrip

                      MenuStrip

                      StatusStrip

ToolStrip, *MenuStrip*, and *StatusStrip* are the new classes in the .NET Framework 2.0 for toolbars, menus, and status bars, respectively. The .NET Framework 1.x classes *ToolBar*, *MainMenu*, and *StatusBar* continue to be supported, of course, and they are discussed in Chapters 14 and 20 of my book *Programming Microsoft Windows with C#* (Microsoft Press, 2002). But the new classes are just as easy (if not easier) to use, so there's really no reason not to take advantage of them for new applications that will run under the .NET Framework 2.0.

The *ToolStrip* control provides most of the flexibility and modern features we've come to expect from using toolbars in sophisticated applications such as Microsoft Office. *ToolStrip* supports bitmapped buttons, of course, but it also allows text-edit fields, combo boxes, and drop-down menus. You can have multiple *ToolStrip* controls and let the user move them around, even to the left, right, and bottom sides of the window. You can also allow the user to move *ToolStrip* items from one *ToolStrip* to another. (What the .NET Framework 2.0 does *not* directly support, however, is the *floating toolbar*, which is essentially a toolbar converted to a modeless dialog box.)

The new *MenuStrip* is unlike the .NET Framework 1.x *MainMenu* class in a fundamental way: The *MainMenu* class provides programmatic access to the normal menu that is part of the standard window. It's the same old menu that's accessible through the Windows API, and if you want to put a bitmap next to a menu item, you need to use owner-draw, which is rarely pleasant. The *MenuStrip*, however, is a new control, and it can do everything *ToolStrip* can do, including mixing text and bitmaps. The only real difference between *ToolStrip* and *MenuStrip* is that the *MenuStrip* is activated when the user presses the Alt key.

The fact that *MenuStrip* (unlike *MainMenu*) is a control rather than part of the window has another profound implication: Using the *MainMenu* class in your program results in the client area becoming smaller to accommodate the menu. The *MenuStrip*, however, is a control that sits on the client area—usually at the very top. If you want to put other controls on your client area, you'll need to take account of the space occupied by the *MenuStrip* (as well as any *Tool-Strip* and *StatusStrip* controls you might have). In most cases, you'll want to put a panel in the center of your client area with a *Dock* property of *DockStyle.Fill*.

Even with the visual embellishments of bitmaps, the most important type of menu a program can have is the one that shows all the program options in a hierarchy of text strings. Let's begin with that job first.

Menus and Menu Items

Menus, like toolbars and status bars, usually contain multiple "items." Each item is commonly identified by a short text string, such as "File" or "Save As." Some items—often "File," "Edit," "View," and so on—are always visible. These are called "top-level" menu items, and they can be selected with either the keyboard or mouse. Selecting a top-level item often results in the display of a "submenu" or "drop-down menu" containing more items, often more text strings and sometimes accompanied by bitmaps and keyboard shortcuts (such as Ctrl+V for Paste). These menu items can carry out commands or invoke other submenus. Submenus can be nested as deep as you believe the user will tolerate. Menus also often contain horizontal lines called "separators" that help congregate related commands on a single submenu.

The *MenuStrip* class is a control that has a default *Dock* property of *DockStyle.Top* and which displays the top-level menu items horizontally across the window. Each of these menu items— as well as all other items in the menu—is a separate object. For simple menus, the two types of menu items you're likely to use most often are based on classes called (rather perversely) *Tool-StripMenuItem* and *ToolStripSeparator*. These are not controls, but instead derive from *Component* and the abstract *ToolStripItem* class, as shown in the following partial class hierarchy:

Object

    MarshalByRefObject

        Component

            ToolStripItem (abstract)

                ToolStripDropDownItem

                    ToolStripMenuItem

                ToolStripSeparator

The *MenuStrip* class inherits a property from *ToolStrip* named *Items* that is of type *ToolStrip-ItemCollection*, which (as the name suggests) is a collection of *ToolStripItem* objects. The *Items* collection of *MenuStrip* contains the top-level menu items. These are generally *ToolStripMenu-Item* objects, and in a traditional application, they would be commonly associated with the text strings "File", "Edit", "View", and eventually "Help".

The *ToolStripMenuItem* class is descended from *ToolStripDropDownItem*. That class implements a property named *DropDownItems* that is also of type *ToolStripItemCollection*. Thus, for each of the top-level items, the *DropDownItems* property contains the items in the submenu. Further nesting can be accomplished by using the *DropDownItems* properties of those items.

Just so we don't get too far adrift in details, let's quickly look at a program that builds a simple menu.

SimpleMenu.cs

```
//---------------------------------------------
// SimpleMenu.cs (c) 2005 by Charles Petzold
//---------------------------------------------
using System;
using System.Drawing;
using System.Windows.Forms;

class SimpleMenu: Form
{
    [STAThread]
    public static void Main()
    {
        Application.EnableVisualStyles();
        Application.Run(new SimpleMenu());
    }
    public SimpleMenu()
    {
        Text = "Simple Menu";

        // Main menu.
        MenuStrip menu = new MenuStrip();
        menu.Parent = this;

        // File item.
        ToolStripMenuItem itemFile = new ToolStripMenuItem();
        itemFile.Text = "&File";
        menu.Items.Add(itemFile);

        // Open item.
        ToolStripMenuItem itemOpen = new ToolStripMenuItem();
        itemOpen.Text = "&Open...";
        itemOpen.ShortcutKeys = Keys.Control | Keys.O;
        itemOpen.Click += OpenOnClick;
        itemFile.DropDownItems.Add(itemOpen);
```

```
            // Separator.
            ToolStripSeparator itemSep = new ToolStripSeparator();
            itemFile.DropDownItems.Add(itemSep);

            // Exit item.
            ToolStripMenuItem itemExit = new ToolStripMenuItem();
            itemExit.Text = "E&xit";
            itemExit.Click += ExitOnClick;
            itemFile.DropDownItems.Add(itemExit);

            // Help item.
            ToolStripMenuItem itemHelp = new ToolStripMenuItem();
            itemHelp.Text = "&Help";
            menu.Items.Add(itemHelp);

            // About item.
            ToolStripMenuItem itemAbout = new ToolStripMenuItem();
            itemAbout.Text = "&About...";
            itemAbout.Click += AboutOnClick;
            itemHelp.DropDownItems.Add(itemAbout);
        }
        void OpenOnClick(object objSrc, EventArgs args)
        {
            MessageBox.Show("\"Open\" feature not yet implemented", Text);
        }
        void ExitOnClick(object objSrc, EventArgs args)
        {
            Close();
        }
        void AboutOnClick(object objSrc, EventArgs args)
        {
            MessageBox.Show("(c) 2005 by Charles Petzold", Text);
        }
    }
```

The program creates an object of type *MenuStrip* and makes it a child of the form. Each item that gets added to the menu is an instance of either *ToolStripMenuItem* or *ToolStripSeparator*. If it's an instance of the former, the program sets the *Text* property and the *Click* event, which is triggered when the item is clicked. The menu is built up using the *Add* method of either the *Items* collection (for the top-level items) or the *DropDownItems* collection.

Menu Items in General

The *ToolStripItem* class (from which *ToolStripMenuItem* derives) is not derived from *Control*, but it implements some of the properties and events associated with controls. The class has *Size*, *Width*, and *Height* properties, for example. (There is no *Location* property, but there is a read-only *Bounds* property.) Like controls, *ToolStripItem* objects have *Margin*, *Padding*, *Dock*, and *Anchor* properties.

The *ToolStripItem* class contains *Font*, *ForeColor*, and *BackColor* properties. If, for example, you want to give one particular menu item (or toolbar item) a 24-point Times New Roman font, you can do it as simply as this:

```
item.Font = new Font("Times New Roman", 24);
```

Perhaps more immediately useful are the Boolean properties *Enabled* and *Visible*. Setting *Enabled* to *false* grays out the item and makes it unresponsive to user input. Setting *Visible* to *false* makes it invisible.

ToolStripItem is capable of displaying a text string (indicated by the *Text* property) or an image (indicated by the *Image* property), or both. The *ToolStripMenuItem* always displays the bitmap to the left of the text in a separate column of the drop-down menu. (The use of bitmaps in tool strips is more flexible.)

Rather than setting the *Image* property directly, a program can set the *ImageList* property of the *ToolStrip* to a collection of images in an *ImageList* object, and then reference these images using the *ToolStripItem* properties *ImageIndex* and *ImageKey*.

Keep in mind that the .NET Framework *Image* class is parent to the two classes *Bitmap* and *Metafile*. It's just as easy to put a metafile in your menu (or toolbar) as a bitmap. You can load these images from files or resources, or you can create them right in your program.

The *ToolStripMenuItem* class adds a couple of expected features to the *ToolStripItem*. You specify a keyboard shortcut in the *ShortCutKeys* property using one or more members of the *Keys* enumeration combined with the bitwise OR operator—for example:

```
item.ShortCutKeys = Key.Control | Keys.O;
```

Normally, the item will construct an appropriate text string for display (such as "Ctrl+O"), but you can override that by setting the *ShortcutKeyDisplayString* property to an alternative string you want displayed, or you can suppress the display entirely by setting *ShowShortcutKeys* to *false*.

Menu items can also display check marks, governed by the *Checked* or *CheckState* properties. *Checked* is a Boolean; *CheckState* is a member of the *CheckState* enumeration, which includes the members *Checked*, *Unchecked*, and *Indeterminate*. If the *Checked* property is *true* for a menu item that has an associated image, the image is boxed to indicate the item is checked. The *CheckOnClick* property causes check marks to be automatically toggled when the user clicks the item.

Like *Control*, *ToolStripItem* defines a *Paint* event and a corresponding *OnPaint* method. You can create your own visuals for a toolbar or menu item by defining a class that inherits from *ToolStripItem* and which overrides the *GetPreferredSize* and *OnPaint* methods.

The *ToolStripItem* class implements mouse events but not keyboard events. (The *ToolStrip* or *MenuStrip* itself is responsible for managing the keyboard interface to the items on the toolbar or menu.) In particular, *ToolStripItem* implements a *Click* event, which is the primary way a program knows that a user has triggered a command on the *ToolStrip* or *MenuStrip*.

Click is one of two events you'll probably be handling when working with menus. The other is *DropDownOpening*, which is implemented by *ToolStripDropDownItem* and inherited by *ToolStripMenuItem*. This event occurs when a drop-down menu is about to be displayed, and it's the perfect opportunity to enable or disable menu items. For example, the Cut, Copy, and Delete items on the Edit menu must be disabled if there's no selection currently defined, and Paste should be disabled if there's no appropriate data in the clipboard.

Assembling the Menu

A menu consists of one *MenuStrip* object and multiple *ToolStripMenuItem* objects, perhaps interspersed with a few *ToolStripSeparator* objects. The top-level items are assembled in the *Items* collection of *MenuStrip*. The *ToolStripMenuItem* class includes a property named *DropDownItems* for continued nesting.

You create a *MenuStrip* object and make it a child of your form like so:

```
MenuStrip menu = new MenuStrip();
menu.Parent = this;
```

The default *Dock* property is already set to *DockStyle.Top*.

The options you have in assembling the menu from the menu items are ridiculously plentiful. Each item on the menu requires that you create (either explicitly or implicitly) an object of type *ToolStripMenuItem*. Perhaps the clearest, most explicit, code is something like this:

```
ToolStripMenuItem itemOpen = new ToolStripMenuItem();
itemOpen.Text = "&Open...";
itemOpen.Image = bmOpen;
itemOpen.ShortcutKeys = Keys.Control | Keys.O;
itemOpen.Click += OpenOnClick;
```

Notice the ampersand in the text string. That indicates the character will be underlined when the user presses the Alt key, and it will let the user choose that item when navigating the menu from the keyboard. The ellipsis (...) is a convention for indicating that the menu item invokes a dialog box. *OpenOnClick* is an event handler.

ToolStripMenuItem also has five other constructors that let you specify the text string, the image, the text string *and* the image, the text string and the image *and* the *Click* event handler, or all three of those plus the shortcut key combination:

```
ToolStripMenuItem itemOpen =
    new ToolStripMenuItem("&Open...", bmOpen,
    OpenOnClick, Keys.Control | Keys.O);
```

It's less code, certainly, but it's not quite as clear. I tend to favor the constructor that requires only the text string:

```
ToolStripMenuItem itemFile = new ToolStripMenuItem("&File");
```

For top-level menu items, you'll probably also want to install an event handler for the *Drop-DownOpening* event:

```
itemFile.DropDownOpening += FileOnDropDown;
```

You can make the "Open" item part of the "File" drop-down menu with the following code:

```
itemFile.DropDownItems.Add(itemOpen);
```

and you can make the "File" item part of the main *MenuStrip* with the following code:

```
menu.Items.Add(itemFile);
```

You don't have to call those two *Add* methods in that particular order. You can continue to set properties of a *ToolStripMenuItem* object after it's been added to a collection. You use the *Items* collection only to add the top-level items to the menu. To add items to each of those top-level items, you use the *DropDownItems* collection. The order that you add them to the collection is the order in which they appear on the menu.

Both *Items* and *DropDownItems* are of type *ToolStripItemCollection*. This class implements additional *Add* methods that implicitly create *ToolStripMenuItem* objects. Rather than explicitly creating the "File" item and adding it to the menu like this:

```
ToolStripMenuItem itemFile = new ToolStripMenuItem("&File");
menu.Items.Add(itemFile);
```

you can do it in one statement like this:

```
ToolStripMenuItem itemFile = menu.Items.Add("&File");
```

The *Add* method conveniently returns the object it creates in case you need to do more with it, like add a *DropDownOpening* event handler. (Although the documentation of the *Add* method indicates that it returns an object of type *ToolStripItem*, when adding an item to a *MenuStrip*, it actually creates and returns a *ToolStripMenuItem* object. It couldn't create a *ToolStripItem* object even if it wanted to because that class is abstract.)

ToolStripItemCollection also includes *Add* methods that let you specify an image, text *and* an image, or text and an image and a *Click* event handler. Moreover, *ToolStripItemCollection* includes an *AddRange* method that lets you add multiple items in one shot. The method exists in two versions: one has another *ToolStripItemCollection* argument, and the other requires an array of *ToolStripItem* objects. You can use the latter version of the *AddRange* method like this:

```
menu.Items.AddRange(new ToolStripMenuItem[] { itemFile, itemEdit,
                                              itemView, itemHelp });
```

There's also another *ToolStripMenuItem* constructor that I haven't mentioned yet. This one requires a string, an image, and an array of *ToolStripItem* objects, letting you create and assemble a drop-down menu like this:

```
itemFile = new ToolStripMenuItem("&File", null,
    new ToolStripMenuItem[] { itemOpen, itemSave, itemSaveAs, itemClose });
```

If you enjoy nested array creations, you can construct an entire menu in a single statement, as demonstrated in the following program. Just be sure to keep all those parentheses and curly brackets properly paired!

CrazyMenuAssemblage.cs

```
//-------------------------------------------------------
// CrazyMenuAssemblage.cs (c) 2005 by Charles Petzold
//-------------------------------------------------------
using System;
using System.Drawing;
using System.Windows.Forms;

class CrazyMenuAssemblage : Form
{
    [STAThread]
    public static void Main()
    {
        Application.EnableVisualStyles();
        Application.Run(new CrazyMenuAssemblage());
    }
    public CrazyMenuAssemblage()
    {
        Text = "Crazy Menu Assemblage";

        MenuStrip menu = new MenuStrip();
        menu.Parent = this;

        menu.Items.AddRange(new ToolStripMenuItem[]
            {
                new ToolStripMenuItem("&File", null, new ToolStripMenuItem[]
                {
                    new ToolStripMenuItem("&Open...", null, DefaultOnClick,
                                        Keys.Control | Keys.O),
                    new ToolStripMenuItem("&Save", null, DefaultOnClick,
                                        Keys.Control | Keys.S),
                    new ToolStripMenuItem("&Close", null, DefaultOnClick)
                }),
                new ToolStripMenuItem("&Edit", null, new ToolStripMenuItem[]
                {
                    new ToolStripMenuItem("Cu&t", null, DefaultOnClick,
                                        Keys.Control | Keys.X),
                    new ToolStripMenuItem("&Copy", null, DefaultOnClick,
                                        Keys.Control | Keys.C),
                    new ToolStripMenuItem("&Paste", null, DefaultOnClick,
                                        Keys.Control | Keys.V)
                }),
```

```
                     new ToolStripMenuItem("&Help", null, new ToolStripMenuItem[]
                     {
                          new ToolStripMenuItem("&Help", null, DefaultOnClick,
                                                Keys.F1),
                          new ToolStripMenuItem("&About...", null, DefaultOnClick)
                     })
               });
     }
     void DefaultOnClick(object obj, EventArgs args)
     {
          MessageBox.Show("Menu item not yet implemented", Text);
     }
}
```

Although none of these menu items have bitmaps—that particular argument of the *ToolStrip-MenuItem* constructor has been set to *null* in this code—they certainly could if the bitmaps had been loaded prior to this code. (We'll see how to do that shortly.) Each of the menu items could also have been assigned its own *Click* event handler rather than sharing a single handler.

This method of assembling the menu does not give you immediate access to the individual *ToolStripMenuItem* objects. If you wanted to disable some menu items or check them, or install *DropDownOpening* event handlers, you'd be stuck with accessing all the menu items through the collections of *ToolStripMenuItem* objects stored as the *Items* and *DropDownItems* properties.

A cleaner, certainly saner, approach to assembling the menu is to create every object explicitly. This is the approach used by Microsoft Visual Studio if you choose to let the Designer generate your menu code. (As with controls, Visual Studio indulges in that hideous programming practice of making every *ToolStripMenuItem* a field.) Visual Studio then uses *AddRange* rather than *Add* in assembling the items into the drop-down menus and the top-level menu.

Here's my rendition of sane menu assemblage:

SaneMenuAssemblage.cs

```
//-------------------------------------------------
// SaneMenuAssemblage.cs (c) 2005 by Charles Petzold
//-------------------------------------------------
using System;
using System.Drawing;
using System.Windows.Forms;

class SaneMenuAssemblage : Form
{
     [STAThread]
     public static void Main()
     {
          Application.EnableVisualStyles();
          Application.Run(new SaneMenuAssemblage());
     }
```

```csharp
public SaneMenuAssemblage()
{
    Text = "Sane Menu Assemblage";

    MenuStrip menu = new MenuStrip();
    menu.Parent = this;

    // Assemble File menu.
    ToolStripMenuItem itemFile = new ToolStripMenuItem("&File");
    menu.Items.Add(itemFile);

    ToolStripMenuItem item = new ToolStripMenuItem("&Open...");
    item.ShortcutKeys = Keys.Control | Keys.O;
    item.Click += DefaultOnClick;
    itemFile.DropDownItems.Add(item);

    item = new ToolStripMenuItem("&Save");
    item.ShortcutKeys = Keys.Control | Keys.S;
    item.Click += DefaultOnClick;
    itemFile.DropDownItems.Add(item);

    item = new ToolStripMenuItem("&Close");
    item.Click += DefaultOnClick;
    itemFile.DropDownItems.Add(item);

    // Assemble Edit menu.
    ToolStripMenuItem itemEdit = new ToolStripMenuItem("&Edit");
    menu.Items.Add(itemEdit);

    item = new ToolStripMenuItem("Cu&t");
    item.ShortcutKeys = Keys.Control | Keys.X;
    item.Click += DefaultOnClick;
    itemEdit.DropDownItems.Add(item);

    item = new ToolStripMenuItem("&Copy");
    item.ShortcutKeys = Keys.Control | Keys.C;
    item.Click += DefaultOnClick;
    itemEdit.DropDownItems.Add(item);

    item = new ToolStripMenuItem("&Paste");
    item.ShortcutKeys = Keys.Control | Keys.V;
    item.Click += DefaultOnClick;
    itemEdit.DropDownItems.Add(item);

    // Assemble Help menu.
    ToolStripMenuItem itemHelp = new ToolStripMenuItem("&Help");
    menu.Items.Add(itemHelp);

    item = new ToolStripMenuItem("&Help");
    item.ShortcutKeys = Keys.F1;
    item.Click += DefaultOnClick;
    itemHelp.DropDownItems.Add(item);

    item = new ToolStripMenuItem("&About...");
    item.Click += DefaultOnClick;
```

```
        itemHelp.DropDownItems.Add(item);
    }
    void DefaultOnClick(object obj, EventArgs args)
    {
        MessageBox.Show("Menu item not yet implemented", Text);
    }
}
```

Fields or Fishing

The SaneMenuAssemblage program reuses the *item* variable for every item on every drop-down menu. In a real-life program, this practice is fine for many menu items but probably not for all. Your program will need to reference some menu items later, and the easiest way to do that is to store the items as fields.

For example, in a real-life program, the Cut, Copy, and Delete items on the Edit menu should be enabled only when there is something selected in the program that can be copied to the clipboard. Similarly, the Paste item should be enabled only when the clipboard contains something of interest to your program. Items that must be enabled only under certain circumstances can be stored as fields:

```
ToolStripMenuItem itemCut, itemCopy, itemPaste, itemDelete;
```

You'll also need to install a *DropDownOpening* event handler for the drop-down item on which this items appear, in this case Edit:

```
itemEdit.DropDownOpening += EditOnDropDownOpening;
```

The *EditOnDropDownOpening* method then enables or disables the *itemCut*, *itemCopy*, *item-Paste*, and *itemDelete* items appropriately. (An example is coming up shortly.)

Even if you don't save the menu item objects as fields, you still have access to them by fishing around in the *Items* and *DropDownItems* collections. You can index these collections as if they were arrays to pull out the items you need. This can be a little tricky because some casting is required. Both *Items* and *DropDownItems* are collections of type *ToolStripItem*, and *ToolStrip-Item* doesn't have a *DropDownItems* property. That property is implemented by *ToolStripDrop-DownItem*, from which *ToolStripMenuItem* is descended.

Suppose you've saved the *MenuStrip* object *menu* as a field. In either the CrazyMenuAssemblage or SaneMenuAssemblage program, you can later fish out the *ToolStripMenuItem* for Paste with the following code:

```
ToolStripMenuItem item = (ToolStripMenuItem)
    ((ToolStripMenuItem) menu.Items[1]).DropDownItems[2];
```

From the *Items* collection in *menu*, you can extract the Edit item with an index of 1. (The collection is zero-based, of course; an index of 0 references the File item.) This item is then cast to a *ToolStripMenuItem* object to allow obtaining the *DropDownItems* collection. The index of 2 fishes out the Paste item, and the result is again cast to an object of type *ToolStripMenuItem*.

Although the casting is a nuisance, the use of explicit numeric indices is potentially a more serious problem. If you ever add menu items or change the order of existing items, these indices might need to be changed. There is a better way: If you look at the documentation for *ToolStripItemCollection*, you'll find that items can alternatively be indexed using a text string. This text string refers to the *Name* property of the item. To use this feature, you'll have to assign the *Name* property when you create each menu item:

```
ToolStripMenuItem itemEdit = new ToolStripMenuItem("&Edit");
itemEdit.Name = "Edit";
...
item = new ToolStripMenuItem("&Paste");
item.Name = "Paste";
```

I suggest using a *Name* property that is identical (or nearly so) to the menu item text, but without any ampersands or ellipses. You can then later fish out the Paste item like this:

```
ToolStripMenuItem item = (ToolStripMenuItem)
    ((ToolStripMenuItem)menu.Items["Edit"]).DropDownItems["Paste"];
```

Controls, Items, and Owners

Only controls—that is, instances of classes descended from *Control*—can occupy visual space on the screen. Instances of *MenuStrip*, *ToolStrip*, and *StatusStrip* are such controls, and they occupy rectangular space on the screen.

A *MenuStrip* control displays top-level items that are included in its *Items* collection. These items are *not* controls. Any space they seemingly occupy on the screen is actually space controlled by the *MenuStrip* to which the items belong. When the *MenuStrip* redraws itself (perhaps as a result of the program being restored after being minimized), the items end up drawing themselves, but they draw themselves on the surface of the *MenuStrip* control.

When you click a top-level menu item, a rectangular drop-down menu appears containing everything in that top-level item's *DropDownItems* collection. Because this drop-down menu occupies visual space on the screen, it must be a control. Yet the item you clicked is an object of type *ToolStripMenuItem*, which is not a control. The items displayed on the drop-down are also *ToolStripMenuItem* objects. Somehow a control has been created behind the scenes to host these items. How does this work?

The *ToolStripDropDownItem* class (from which *ToolStripMenuItem* descends) includes a property named *DropDown*, which is of type *ToolStripDropDown*, which is descended from *Control*. This is the control that's used to display drop-down menus.

More explicitly, whenever you create an object of type *ToolStripMenuItem*, the object creates a control of type *ToolStripDropDownMenu* (which inherits from *ToolStripDropDown*). The *Visible* property of this *ToolStripDropDownMenu* object is initially set to *false;* the object is saved in the *DropDown* property of the *ToolStripMenuItem*. When the item is clicked, the item checks whether any items are stored in its *DropDownItems* collection. If so, it must use the control stored in its *DropDown* property to display these items to the screen.

Here's a class hierarchy showing *all* the descendents of *ToolStrip:*

Object

    MarshalByRefObject

        Component

            Control

                ScrollableControl

                    ToolStrip

                        BindingNavigator

                        MenuStrip

                        StatusStrip

                        ToolStripDropDown

                            ToolStripDropDownMenu

                            ContextMenuStrip

                        ToolStripOverflow

Notice *ToolStripDropDown* and *ToolStripDropDownMenu*. These are the controls used to display items not permanently displayed on the *ToolStrip* or *MenuStrip*. (The *BindingNavigator* control is a special toolbar used for navigating through databases. I'll demonstrate its use in the next chapter.)

These preliminaries are necessary to understand the concept of the "owner" in menu items. *ToolStripItem* has a property named *Owner* that is defined to be of type *ToolStrip*. This property indicates the control on which the item is displayed. For a top-level menu item, the *Owner* property indicates the *MenuStrip* on which the top-level item is displayed. For any other *ToolStripMenuItem* object, the *Owner* property indicates the *ToolStripDropDownMenu* on which the item is displayed.

ToolStripItem also has a protected *Parent* property. Generally, this property returns the same object as the *Owner* property. However, if a *ToolStrip* does not have sufficient space to display all its items, the other items end up on an overflow drop-down menu. That overflow drop-down menu becomes the *Parent* of those items, but the *Owner* remains the same.

ToolStripDropDown has a property named *OwnerItem* that is defined to be of type *ToolStripItem*. This property indicates the item that invokes the drop-down menu.

If *item* is an instance of *ToolStripMenuItem*, the expression

```
item == item.DropDown.OwnerItem
```

is always *true*. The *OwnerItem* of the drop-down menu that an item invokes is always the item. If *itemFile* and *itemOpen* are instances of *ToolStripMenuItem*, and *itemOpen* has been added to the *DropDownItems* collection of *itemFile* (as is normal), the expression

```
itemFile.DropDown == itemOpen.Owner
```

is *true*. Both expressions refer to the *ToolStripDropDownMenu* that is invoked by File and on which Open appears. This expression requires some casting but is also *true*:

```
itemFile == ((ToolStripDropDownMenu) itemOpen.Owner).OwnerItem
```

The owner of the Open item is the *ToolStripDropDownMenu* on which it appears. The *OwnerItem* of that is the File item that invokes the drop-down menu.

And this expression is *true* as well:

```
itemFile == (ToolStripDropDownMenu) itemFile.DropDownItems[0].Owner).OwnerItem
```

Checking and Unchecking

Although you rarely interact with it directly, the *ToolStripDropDownMenu* class is obviously important to the appearance of menus. It is the responsibility of this class to display a margin to the left of menu items that (by default) is used for both images and check marks.

To display a check mark next to an item, set the *Checked* property to *true* or the *CheckState* property to the enumeration value *CheckState.Checked*. To remove the check mark, set the *Checked* property to *false* or the *CheckState* property to *CheckState.Unchecked*. The only advantage of using *CheckState* rather than *Checked* is the option *CheckState.Indeterminate*, which displays a dot rather than a check mark to indicate that the item has been neither checked nor unchecked. You can change the *Checked* or *CheckState* property in a *Click* event handler for the menu item.

If you set the *CheckOnClick* property to *true*, the menu item check mark is automatically toggled on and off with each click. You'll probably still need to install an event handler for the item if your program needs to do something in response to the change in the check state.

CheckOnClick won't work well when you're using check marks to indicate one selected item out of several mutually exclusive items. Almost always, in such cases, you'll want to share a single *Click* event handler among all the items. Generally, you'll use this event handler to uncheck the currently checked item and check the item generating the *Click* event. What else you do at this point depends on the nature of the menu items.

Here's a program with a Font menu that lists all the available font family names. In most systems, the entire menu won't fit on the screen. The *ToolStripDropDownMenu* object is responsible for displaying arrows on the top and bottom that let you navigate the whole drop-down menu. A panel with a *Dock* property of *DockStyle.Fill* displays the selected font.

FontMenu.cs

```csharp
//-----------------------------------------
// FontMenu.cs (c) 2005 by Charles Petzold
//-----------------------------------------
using System;
using System.Drawing;
using System.Windows.Forms;

class FontMenu : Form
{
    Panel pnl;
    ToolStripMenuItem itemSelectedFont;

    [STAThread]
    public static void Main()
    {
        Application.EnableVisualStyles();
        Application.Run(new FontMenu());
    }
    public FontMenu()
    {
        Text = "Font Menu";

        pnl = new Panel();
        pnl.Parent = this;
        pnl.Dock = DockStyle.Fill;
        pnl.Paint += PanelOnPaint;

        MenuStrip menu = new MenuStrip();
        menu.Parent = this;

        ToolStripMenuItem itemFormat = new ToolStripMenuItem("&Format");
        menu.Items.Add(itemFormat);

        ToolStripMenuItem itemFont = new ToolStripMenuItem("&Font");
        itemFormat.DropDownItems.Add(itemFont);

        Graphics grfx = CreateGraphics();

        foreach (FontFamily fntfam in FontFamily.GetFamilies(grfx))
        {
            if (fntfam.IsStyleAvailable(FontStyle.Regular))
            {
                ToolStripMenuItem item = new ToolStripMenuItem(fntfam.Name);
                item.Click += FontOnClick;
                itemFont.DropDownItems.Add(item);

                if (fntfam.Name == Font.Name)
```

```
                    {
                        itemSelectedFont = item;
                        itemSelectedFont.Checked = true;
                    }
                }
            }
        grfx.Dispose();
    }
    void PanelOnPaint(object objSrc, PaintEventArgs args)
    {
        Graphics grfx = args.Graphics;
        Font fnt = new Font(itemSelectedFont.Text, 48);
        grfx.DrawString(fnt.Name, fnt, new SolidBrush(ForeColor), 0, 0);
    }
    void FontOnClick(object objSrc, EventArgs args)
    {
        ToolStripMenuItem item = (ToolStripMenuItem)objSrc;
        itemSelectedFont.Checked = false;
        itemSelectedFont = item;
        itemSelectedFont.Checked = true;
        pnl.Invalidate();
    }
}
```

This program demonstrates a rather conventional method of checking and unchecking menu items. The currently checked item is saved as a field named *itemSelectedFont*. The *Click* handler simply unchecks *itemSelectedFont*, sets *itemSelectedFont* to the item generating the *Click* event, checks that item, and then calls *Invalidate* to invalidate the panel and generate a *Paint* event. The *Paint* handler uses the *Text* property of the selected item to obtain the font family name and create a font.

By the way, you might be tempted to display each item in the font menu using a different font. It's certainly possible to do this. Simply add the following line after the *new* statement that creates each item in that drop-down menu:

```
item.Font = new Font(fntfam.Name, item.Font.SizeInPoints);
```

The problem, however, is that it takes quite a bit of time, both when the program is initializing and when the drop-down menu is first displayed. You're also not guaranteed that every font contains definitions for the characters required to display the font name.

This program can actually be written without explicitly saving any information about the checked menu item. The program really implicitly "knows" which item is checked because it's part of the *Font* object associated with the panel. Here's a different approach to checking and unchecking menu items:

FontMenu2.cs

```csharp
//-------------------------------------------
// FontMenu2.cs (c) 2005 by Charles Petzold
//-------------------------------------------
using System;
using System.Drawing;
using System.Windows.Forms;

class FontMenu2 : Form
{
    Panel pnl;

    [STAThread]
    public static void Main()
    {
        Application.EnableVisualStyles();
        Application.Run(new FontMenu2());
    }
    public FontMenu2()
    {
        Text = "Font Menu #2";

        pnl = new Panel();
        pnl.Parent = this;
        pnl.Dock = DockStyle.Fill;
        pnl.Font = new Font(pnl.Font.Name, 24);
        pnl.Paint += PanelOnPaint;

        MenuStrip menu = new MenuStrip();
        menu.Parent = this;

        ToolStripMenuItem itemFormat = new ToolStripMenuItem("&Format");
        menu.Items.Add(itemFormat);

        ToolStripMenuItem itemFont = new ToolStripMenuItem("&Font");
        itemFormat.DropDownItems.Add(itemFont);

        Graphics grfx = CreateGraphics();

        foreach (FontFamily fntfam in FontFamily.GetFamilies(grfx))
        {
            if (fntfam.IsStyleAvailable(FontStyle.Regular))
            {
                ToolStripMenuItem item = new ToolStripMenuItem(fntfam.Name);
                item.Click += FontOnClick;
                itemFont.DropDownItems.Add(item);

                if (fntfam.Name == Font.Name)
                    item.Checked = true;
            }
        }
        grfx.Dispose();
    }
    void PanelOnPaint(object objSrc, PaintEventArgs args)
```

```
    {
        Graphics grfx = args.Graphics;
        grfx.DrawString(pnl.Font.Name, pnl.Font, new SolidBrush(ForeColor), 0, 0);
    }
    void FontOnClick(object objSrc, EventArgs args)
    {
        ToolStripMenuItem itemClick = (ToolStripMenuItem)objSrc;
        ToolStripMenuItem itemFont = (ToolStripMenuItem)
            ((ToolStripDropDownMenu) itemClick.Owner).OwnerItem;

        foreach (ToolStripMenuItem item in itemFont.DropDownItems)
            item.Checked = false;

        itemClick.Checked = true;
        pnl.Font = new Font(itemClick.Text, 24);
    }
}
```

This program obtains the Font menu item from the item that was clicked. It then unchecks every item in the *DropDownItems* collection and then checks the clicked item. I figured that unchecking every item was just as fast as searching through all the items for the currently checked item and then just unchecking that one.

Both FontMenu and FontMenu2 relied on the *Text* property of the item to be exactly what was needed to create a new font. That's not always possible, of course. Another approach (coming up in the next sample program) involves use of the *Tag* property to save information along with each menu item. The next program also doesn't check and uncheck items during the *Click* handler; instead, it waits until the drop-down menu is displayed.

Adding Images

It might seem odd that the menus in Microsoft Office applications display the Paste item (for example) accompanied by an image that illustrates a tiny clipboard with a still tinier document. Surely the word "Paste" conveys much more information than the superfluous bitmap. But the image on the menu doesn't exist in isolation. Such images become significant only when the program incorporates the same images into a toolbar. Through the use of the menu, the user can become accustomed to the images associated with each command, and then eventually switch to the toolbar for speed.

A large collection of standard toolbar and menu bitmaps is included with Visual Studio 2005. Check the directory *Program Files**Microsoft Visual Studio 8**Common7**VS2005ImageLibrary* for a ZIP file named VS2005ImageLibrary.zip. (Unfortunately, the Visual C# 2005 Express Edition doesn't contain this library.) You can unzip the file in either the same directory or another directory. In either case, you'll want to preserve the directory structure of the items.

The most common images for menus will be found in the *bitmaps\commands* subdirectory, which is further divided into subdirectories for various color depths. Unless you think your program will be running on a lot of 16-color video displays and you'd like the images to look best for those displays, you can probably stick to the 24-bit or 32-bit images.

It's easiest to use the images in your program as *resources*. Resources are binary data that are embedded into the .EXE file and easily accessible by the program. When you have a project open in Visual Studio, select Add Existing Item from the Project menu, or right-click the Project name and select Add and then Existing Item from the menu. Then navigate to the bitmap you want and click the Add button.

The bitmap becomes part of the project and is listed with the source code files in the Solution Explorer at the upper right. When you click each bitmap, Visual Studio displays the Properties window at the lower right.

This is *very* important: In the Properties window for the bitmap, change the Build Action to Embedded Resource.

If your project contains a file named Paste.bmp (for example) and that bitmap has been marked as an Embedded Resource, you can load the image into your program as a *Bitmap* object by using the following code:

```
Bitmap bmPaste = new Bitmap(GetType(), "namespace.Paste.bmp");
```

The first argument to the *Bitmap* constructor must refer to any class defined by the program. Within any instance method or constructor in any class defined by the program, you can simply use *GetType* method. The second argument is the filename of the image preceded by the resource namespace of the program (indicated by *namespace* in italics). Don't confuse this resource namespace with .NET Framework namespaces. The resource namespace is used solely in connection with resources, and by default Visual Studio sets it to the project name. You can set it to whatever you want by viewing project properties, selecting the Application tab, and changing the Default Namespace field.

You set the *Image* property of the menu item like this:

```
itemPaste.Image = bmPaste;
```

and that's all that's needed to display the image in the menu. The image is displayed in the same column to the left of the menu text used for check marks.

Here's a program that illustrates much of what we've learned so far in this chapter. It lets you load and save image files, copy and paste them with the clipboard, and display them in four different ways.

ImageFiler.cs

```
//-------------------------------------------
// ImageFiler.cs (c) 2005 by Charles Petzold
//-------------------------------------------
using System;
using System.Drawing;
using System.Drawing.Imaging;
using System.IO;
using System.Windows.Forms;

class ImageFiler : Form
{
    PictureBox picbox;
    ToolStripMenuItem itemSaveAs, itemCut, itemCopy, itemPaste, itemDelete;

    [STAThread]
    public static void Main()
    {
        Application.EnableVisualStyles();
        Application.Run(new ImageFiler());
    }
    public ImageFiler()
    {
        Text = "Image Filer";

        // Create picture box.
        picbox = new PictureBox();
        picbox.Parent = this;
        picbox.Dock = DockStyle.Fill;

        // Load bitmaps.
        Bitmap bmOpen = new Bitmap(GetType(), "ImageFiler.Open.bmp");
        Bitmap bmCut = new Bitmap(GetType(), "ImageFiler.Cut.bmp");
        Bitmap bmCopy = new Bitmap(GetType(), "ImageFiler.Copy.bmp");
        Bitmap bmPaste = new Bitmap(GetType(), "ImageFiler.Paste.bmp");
        Bitmap bmDelete = new Bitmap(GetType(), "ImageFiler.Delete.bmp");

        // Create menu.
        MenuStrip menu = new MenuStrip();
        menu.Parent = this;

        // Assemble File menu.
        ToolStripMenuItem itemFile = new ToolStripMenuItem("&File");
        itemFile.DropDownOpening += FileOnDropDown;
        menu.Items.Add(itemFile);

        ToolStripMenuItem item = new ToolStripMenuItem("&Open...");
        item.Image = bmOpen;
        item.ImageTransparentColor = Color.Magenta;
        item.ShortcutKeys = Keys.Control | Keys.O;
        item.Click += OpenOnClick;
        itemFile.DropDownItems.Add(item);

        itemSaveAs = new ToolStripMenuItem("Save &As...");
```

```
itemSaveAs.Click += SaveAsOnClick;
itemFile.DropDownItems.Add(itemSaveAs);

itemFile.DropDownItems.Add(new ToolStripSeparator());

item = new ToolStripMenuItem("E&xit");
item.Click += ExitOnClick;
itemFile.DropDownItems.Add(item);

// Assemble Edit menu.
ToolStripMenuItem itemEdit = new ToolStripMenuItem("&Edit");
itemEdit.DropDownOpening += EditOnDropDown;
menu.Items.Add(itemEdit);

itemCut = new ToolStripMenuItem("Cu&t");
itemCut.Image = bmCut;
itemCut.ImageTransparentColor = Color.Magenta;
itemCut.ShortcutKeys = Keys.Control | Keys.X;
itemCut.Click += CutOnClick;
itemEdit.DropDownItems.Add(itemCut);

itemCopy = new ToolStripMenuItem("&Copy");
itemCopy.Image = bmCopy;
itemCopy.ImageTransparentColor = Color.Magenta;
itemCopy.ShortcutKeys = Keys.Control | Keys.C;
itemCopy.Click += CopyOnClick;
itemEdit.DropDownItems.Add(itemCopy);

itemPaste = new ToolStripMenuItem("&Paste");
itemPaste.Image = bmPaste;
itemPaste.ImageTransparentColor = Color.Magenta;
itemPaste.ShortcutKeys = Keys.Control | Keys.V;
itemPaste.Click += PasteOnClick;
itemEdit.DropDownItems.Add(itemPaste);

itemDelete = new ToolStripMenuItem("&Delete");
itemDelete.Image = bmDelete;
itemDelete.ImageTransparentColor = Color.Magenta;
itemDelete.ShortcutKeys = Keys.Delete;
itemDelete.Click += DeleteOnClick;
itemEdit.DropDownItems.Add(itemDelete);

// Create and assemble View menu items.
ToolStripMenuItem itemView = new ToolStripMenuItem("&View");
itemView.DropDownOpening += ViewOnDropDown;
menu.Items.Add(itemView);

item = new ToolStripMenuItem("&Normal");
item.Tag = PictureBoxSizeMode.Normal;
item.Click += ViewItemOnClick;
itemView.DropDownItems.Add(item);

item = new ToolStripMenuItem("&Center");
item.Tag = PictureBoxSizeMode.CenterImage;
item.Click += ViewItemOnClick;
```

```
            itemView.DropDownItems.Add(item);

        item = new ToolStripMenuItem("&Stretch");
        item.Tag = PictureBoxSizeMode.StretchImage;
        item.Click += ViewItemOnClick;
        itemView.DropDownItems.Add(item);

        item = new ToolStripMenuItem("&Zoom");
        item.Tag = PictureBoxSizeMode.Zoom;
        item.Click += ViewItemOnClick;
        itemView.DropDownItems.Add(item);
    }
    void FileOnDropDown(object obj, EventArgs args)
    {
        itemSaveAs.Enabled = picbox.Image != null;
    }
    void EditOnDropDown(object obj, EventArgs args)
    {
        itemCut.Enabled = itemCopy.Enabled = itemDelete.Enabled =
            picbox.Image != null;

        IDataObject data = Clipboard.GetDataObject();

        itemPaste.Enabled = data.GetDataPresent(typeof(Bitmap)) ||
                            data.GetDataPresent(typeof(Metafile));
    }
    void ViewOnDropDown(object obj, EventArgs args)
    {
        ToolStripMenuItem itemView = (ToolStripMenuItem)obj;

        foreach (ToolStripItem item in itemView.DropDownItems)
        {
            ToolStripMenuItem mitem = (ToolStripMenuItem)item;
            mitem.Checked = (PictureBoxSizeMode)mitem.Tag == picbox.SizeMode;
        }
    }
    void OpenOnClick(object obj, EventArgs args)
    {
        OpenFileDialog dlg = new OpenFileDialog();
        dlg.Filter = "All Image Files|*.bmp;*.ico;*.gif;*.jpeg;*.jpg;" +
                        "*.jfif;*.png;*.tif;*.tiff;*.wmf;*.emf|" +
                    "Windows Bitmap (*.bmp)|*.bmp|" +
                    "Windows Icon (*.ico)|*.ico|" +
                    "Graphics Interchange Format (*.gif)|*.gif|" +
                    "JPEG File Interchange Format (*.jpg)|" +
                        "*.jpg;*.jpeg;*.jfif|" +
                    "Portable Network Graphics (*.png)|*.png|" +
                    "Tag Image File Format (*.tif)|*.tif;*.tiff|" +
                    "Windows Metafile (*.wmf)|*.wmf|" +
                    "Enhanced Metafile (*.emf)|*.emf|" +
                    "All Files (*.*)|*.*";

        if (dlg.ShowDialog() == DialogResult.OK)
        {
            try
```

```
            {
                picbox.Image = Image.FromFile(dlg.FileName);
            }
            catch (Exception exc)
            {
                MessageBox.Show(exc.Message, Text);
                return;
            }
        }
    }
}
void SaveAsOnClick(object obj, EventArgs args)
{
    SaveFileDialog savedlg = new SaveFileDialog();
    savedlg.AddExtension = true;
    savedlg.Filter = "Windows Bitmap (*.bmp)|*.bmp|" +
                     "Graphics Interchange Format (*.gif)|*.gif|" +
                     "JPEG File Interchange Format (*.jpg)|" +
                        "*.jpg;*.jpeg;*.jfif|" +
                     "Portable Network Graphics (*.png)|*.png|" +
                     "Tagged Imaged File Format (*.tif)|*.tif;*.tiff";

    ImageFormat[] aif = { ImageFormat.Bmp,  ImageFormat.Gif,
                          ImageFormat.Jpeg, ImageFormat.Png,
                          ImageFormat.Tiff };

    if (savedlg.ShowDialog() == DialogResult.OK)
    {
        try
        {
            picbox.Image.Save(savedlg.FileName, aif[savedlg.FilterIndex - 1]);
        }
        catch (Exception exc)
        {
            MessageBox.Show(exc.Message, Text);
            return;
        }
    }
}
void CutOnClick(object obj, EventArgs args)
{
    CopyOnClick(obj, args);
    DeleteOnClick(obj, args);
}
void CopyOnClick(object obj, EventArgs args)
{
    Clipboard.SetDataObject(picbox.Image, true);
}
void PasteOnClick(object obj, EventArgs args)
{
    IDataObject data = Clipboard.GetDataObject();

    if (data.GetDataPresent(typeof(Metafile)))
        picbox.Image = (Image)data.GetData(typeof(Metafile));

    else if (data.GetDataPresent(typeof(Bitmap)))
```

```
            picbox.Image = (Image)data.GetData(typeof(Bitmap));
    }
    void DeleteOnClick(object obj, EventArgs args)
    {
        picbox.Image = null;
    }
    void ViewItemOnClick(object obj, EventArgs args)
    {
        ToolStripMenuItem item = (ToolStripMenuItem)obj;
        picbox.SizeMode = (PictureBoxSizeMode) item.Tag;
    }
    void ExitOnClick(object obj, EventArgs args)
    {
        Close();
    }
}
```

Besides the *MenuStrip*, the client area of the program contains a *PictureBox* control with a *Dock* property of *DockStyle.Fill*. The program need not explicitly retain an *Image* object because the *PictureBox* stores the image and displays it, as well.

The program has *DropDownOpening* event handlers for all three drop-down menus. For the File drop-down menu, the Save As item is enabled only if an image is present. For the Edit drop-down menu, Cut, Copy, and Delete items are enabled similarly, and Paste is enabled only if clipboard contains a *Bitmap* or *Metafile* object.

The *SizeMode* property of *PictureBox* governs how the control displays the image—whether in actual size, centered, stretched to the size of the control, or stretched without distortion. For each of the four items on the View drop-down menu, the *Tag* property is assigned the corresponding *PictureBoxSizeMode* enumeration value. In the *ViewOnDropDown* handler, the *Checked* property of each item is set to an expression comparing the *Tag* property of the item with the *SizeMode* property of the *PictureBox*. The *Click* event handler for these four items (*ViewItemOnClick*) thus doesn't need to bother with unchecking or checking items. It simply sets *SizeMode* to the *Tag* property of the clicked item.

The ImageFiler program sets the *Image* properties of several of the items to *Bitmap* objects loaded from resources. These bitmaps use magenta to represent transparency, and the menu item must know about that.

Another approach in using bitmaps is more involved but might be better for managing large numbers of images. You first need to create an *ImageList* object:

```
ImageList imglst = new ImageList();
```

As each image is loaded, you add it to the image list with a key name:

```
imglst.Images.Add("Paste", new Bitmap(GetType(), "Paste.bmp"));
```

The image list itself is associated with the *MenuStrip*:

```
menu.ImageList = imglst;
```

and the image is referenced in the menu item by the key name you assigned:

```
itemPaste.ImageKey = "Paste";
```

If you'll be using a lot of images, you might even want to define a class that inherits from *ImageList* and use the constructor of that class to load all the image resources your program will need.

Regardless of which method you use, you'll also need to specify which color in the bitmaps has been used to represent transparency. For the images supplied with Visual Studio 2005, that color is magenta. If you're using an *ImageList* approach, you can just specify that color once:

```
imglst.TransparentColor = Color.Magenta;
```

Otherwise, you'll need to specify it for each menu item that uses an image:

```
itemPaste.ImageTransparentColor = Color.Magenta;
```

as the ImageFiler program does. To me, the ease of specifying the transparent color just once indicates that the *ImageList* is the way to go.

The column at the left of drop-down menus is normally used to display both images and check marks. The functionality and appearance of this column is governed by two properties of the *ToolStripDropDownMenu* class: *ShowImageMargin*, which is *true* by default, and *ShowCheckMargin*, which is *false*. With this default configuration, the images and check marks share the same column. If an item has both an image and a check mark, the check mark will not be displayed but the image is boxed.

If you set *ShowImageMargin* to *false* and *ShowCheckMargin* to *true*, images are suppressed in that drop-down menu but check marks are shown normally. Set both properties to *false* to suppress all images and check marks, and set both properties to *true* to display two columns—one for images and the other for check marks.

Custom Menu Items

If we're going to be using Microsoft Office as our standard for creating menus and toolbars, we'll have to do a little better than menu items consisting of text and images. In Microsoft Word, for example, the Background item on the Format menu contains an actual grid of colors. Let's see if we can duplicate that.

It is possible to create a custom menu item by inheriting from *ToolStripItem* and overriding at the very least *GetPreferredSize* and *OnPaint*. However, there's a better way. You can put any control on a *MenuStrip* or *ToolStrip* by "wrapping" it in the *ToolStripControlHost* class. This class is derived from *ToolStripItem* and has a single constructor that requires a *Control* object. That control then magically becomes usable as a menu toolbar item.

Fortunately, to implement the Word-like color grid, we already have exactly the control we need. It's the *ColorGrid* control from the ColorGridDemo project in the previous chapter. Here's a class named *ToolStripColorGrid* that derives from *ToolStripControlHost* to wrap that *ColorGrid* control.

```
ToolStripColorGrid.cs
//-------------------------------------------------
// ToolStripColorGrid.cs (c) 2005 by Charles Petzold
//-------------------------------------------------
using System;
using System.Drawing;
using System.Windows.Forms;

class ToolStripColorGrid : ToolStripControlHost
{
    public ToolStripColorGrid() : base(new ColorGrid())
    {
    }
    public Color SelectedColor
    {
        get
        {
            return ((ColorGrid)Control).SelectedColor;
        }
        set
        {
            ((ColorGrid)Control).SelectedColor = value;
        }
    }
    protected override void OnClick(EventArgs args)
    {
        base.OnClick(args);
        ((ToolStripDropDown)Owner).Close(
            ToolStripDropDownCloseReason.ItemClicked);
    }
}
```

Although the constructor of a class that derives from *ToolStripControlHost* could do more, this one merely invokes the constructor of the base class, which requires an object of type *Control*. If you need access to that control later (and you probably will), it is stored in the read-only property of *ToolStripControlHost* named *Control*. The *ColorGrid* class, you'll recall, implements a public property named *SelectedColor* that provides access to the selected color. A program using a *ToolStripColorGrid* item could get access to that property by casting the *Control* property to an object of type *ColorGrid*, but it's cleaner for the *ToolStripColorGrid* class itself to duplicate that property. (It's common also to have a read-only property that returns the control directly. Such a property would have a name of *ColorGrid* and return an object of type *ColorGrid*.)

A class that inherits from *ToolStripControlHost* might want to expose some events of the underlying control. It does this by defining a public event (probably with the same name as the event in the control) and an event handler for the control's event. The event handler for the control's event triggers the event defined in the class. The class also overrides the *OnSubscribeControlEvents* and *OnUnsubscribeControlEvents* methods, during which the class installs and removes the event handler. In these methods, it's also necessary to call the *OnSubscribeControlEvents* and *OnUnsubscribeControlEvents* methods in the base class to ensure that other events in *ToolStripControlHost* are properly installed.

After some experimentation with *ToolStripColorGrid*, I found it necessary to override the *OnClick* handler to explicitly close the menu. Without this call, the drop-down menu stayed in place after being clicked.

Here's a program that makes use of this *ToolStripColorGrid* in a menu. The menu allows only changing the background color of the form, but it also includes a menu item that brings up the standard *ColorDialog* for more extensive color selection.

```
CustomColorMenu.cs
//-------------------------------------------------
// CustomColorMenu.cs (c) 2005 by Charles Petzold
//-------------------------------------------------
using System;
using System.Drawing;
using System.Windows.Forms;

class CustomColorMenu : Form
{
    ToolStripColorGrid clrgrd;
    ColorDialog clrdlg = new ColorDialog();

    [STAThread]
    public static void Main()
    {
        Application.EnableVisualStyles();
        Application.Run(new CustomColorMenu());
    }
    public CustomColorMenu()
    {
        Text = "Custom Color Menu";

        MenuStrip menu = new MenuStrip();
        menu.Parent = this;

        ToolStripMenuItem itemFormat = new ToolStripMenuItem("&Format");
        itemFormat.DropDownOpening += FormatOnDropDownOpening;
        menu.Items.Add(itemFormat);
```

```
        ToolStripMenuItem itemBackground = new ToolStripMenuItem(
            "&Background Color");
        itemFormat.DropDownItems.Add(itemBackground);

        clrgrd = new ToolStripColorGrid();
        clrgrd.Click += ColorGridOnClick;
        itemBackground.DropDownItems.Add(clrgrd);

        itemBackground.DropDownItems.Add(new ToolStripSeparator());

        ToolStripMenuItem item = new ToolStripMenuItem("&More Colors...");
        item.Click += MoreColorsOnClick;
        itemBackground.DropDownItems.Add(item);
    }
    void FormatOnDropDownOpening(object objSrc, EventArgs args)
    {
        clrgrd.SelectedColor = BackColor;
    }
    void ColorGridOnClick(object objSrc, EventArgs args)
    {
        BackColor = clrgrd.SelectedColor;
    }
    void MoreColorsOnClick(object objSrc, EventArgs args)
    {
        clrdlg.Color = BackColor;

        if (clrdlg.ShowDialog() == DialogResult.OK)
            BackColor = clrdlg.Color;
    }
}
```

Notice that the *ColorDialog* object is created just once and stored in a field. This ensures that any custom colors the user selects in this dialog box are retained when the dialog box is displayed next. (Of course, the custom color won't be retained when the user ends the program. See the discussion on pages 762 through 770 of *Programming Microsoft Windows with C#* for a fuller analysis with solutions.)

Context Menus

The most recent class hierarchy in this chapter showed a class named *ContextMenuStrip* that is descended from *ToolStripDropDownMenu*, the control that's created behind the scenes to display drop-down menus. Context menus are generally displayed when the user right-clicks something on the screen. The items on a *ContextMenuStrip* are generally *ToolStripMenuItem* objects, but you can use any object of any class that descends from *ToolStripItem*.

There are basically two ways to use a context menu. The *Control* class defines a *ContextMenuStrip* property that you can set to a particular *ContextMenuStrip* object. Whenever the user right-clicks the control, the context menu is displayed. (If you set the *ContextMenuStrip* property, don't also set the *ContextMenu* property—that's the property used with .NET Framework 1.x menus.)

Here's an example of a *ContextMenuStrip* that shows yet another approach to color selection. This one lists all the .NET Framework colors in seven submenus and lets you change the background color of the form:

ContextMenuStripDemo.cs

```
//-----------------------------------------------------
// ContextMenuStripDemo.cs (c) 2005 by Charles Petzold
//-----------------------------------------------------
using System;
using System.Drawing;
using System.Reflection;
using System.Windows.Forms;

class ContextMenuStripDemo : Form
{
    ToolStripMenuItem itemChecked;

    [STAThread]
    public static void Main()
    {
        Application.EnableVisualStyles();
        Application.Run(new ContextMenuStripDemo());
    }
    public ContextMenuStripDemo()
    {
        Text = "ContextMenuStrip Demo";
        BackColor = Color.White;

        // Division of colors alphabetically.
        int[] iMenu = { 0,0,0,1,2,2,2,2,2,2,2,2,3,4,5,5,5,5,5,6,6,6,6,6,6,6,6 };

        // Create ContextMenuStrip and attach to this form via the
        //   ContextMenuStrip property of Control.
        ContextMenuStrip menu = new ContextMenuStrip();
        ContextMenuStrip = menu;

        // Top level items show a range of letters.
        for (int i = 0; i <= 6; i++)
        {
            ToolStripMenuItem item = new ToolStripMenuItem();
            char chFirst = Convert.ToChar(Array.IndexOf(iMenu, i) + 'A');
            char chLast = Convert.ToChar(Array.LastIndexOf(iMenu, i) + 'A');
            item.Text = String.Format("Colors {0} to {1}", chFirst, chLast);
            ((ToolStripDropDownMenu)item.DropDown).ShowCheckMargin = true;
            menu.Items.Add(item);
        }

        // Obtain array of PropertyInfo objects with Color properties.
        PropertyInfo[] api = typeof(Color).GetProperties();

        // Make each color into a ToolStripMenuItem.
        foreach (PropertyInfo pi in api)
        {
            if (pi.CanRead && pi.PropertyType == typeof(Color))
```

```
        {
            Color clr = (Color)pi.GetValue(null, null);
            int i = iMenu[clr.Name[0] - 'A'];

            ToolStripMenuItem item = new ToolStripMenuItem();
            item.Text = CamelSpaceOut(clr.Name);
            item.Name = clr.Name;
            item.Image = CreateBitmap(clr);
            item.Click += ColorOnClick;
            ((ToolStripMenuItem)menu.Items[i]).DropDownItems.Add(item);

            if (clr.Equals(BackColor))
                (itemChecked = item).Checked = true;
        }
    }
}
void ColorOnClick(object objSrc, EventArgs args)
{
    ToolStripMenuItem item = (ToolStripMenuItem) objSrc;
    itemChecked.Checked = false;
    (itemChecked = item).Checked = true;
    BackColor = Color.FromName(itemChecked.Name);
}
Bitmap CreateBitmap(Color clr)
{
    Bitmap bm = new Bitmap(16, 16);
    Graphics grfx = Graphics.FromImage(bm);
    grfx.FillRectangle(new SolidBrush(clr), 0, 0, 16, 16);
    grfx.Dispose();
    return bm;
}
string CamelSpaceOut(string str)
{
    for (int i = 1; i < str.Length; i++)
        if (Char.IsUpper(str[i]))
            str = str.Insert(i++, " ");
    return str;
}
}
```

The *iMenu* array contains 26 integers corresponding to the 26 letters of the alphabet to apportion the standard 128 colors into seven submenus. The *for* loop creates the top-level menu items. These display the range of colors in each submenu. Notice also that the *ShowCheckMargin* property of the drop-down menu has been set to *true* to display separate columns for images and check marks.

The *foreach* loop goes through all the colors obtained as a *PropertyInfo* array. The *Name* property of each *ToolStripMenuItem* gets the color name, but the *Text* property gets a text string processed by the *CamelSpaceOut* method. This method takes a name using so-called camel casing with embedded capitals (such as "LightGoldenrodYellow") and inserts spaces before each capital, turning it into "Light Goldenrod Yellow." The *CreateBitmap* method creates a simple bitmap showing the color.

This context menu is displayed if you right-click on any part of the form's client area. If you'd prefer more control over the display of the context menu, you can instead install event handlers for right-clicks and then display the context menu with the *Show* method that *Context-MenuStrip* inherits from *ToolStripDropDown*. Arguments to the *Show* method let you specify where the context menu is to appear.

Tool Strips and Their Components

The big advantage that comes with the merging of menu and toolbar functionality in .NET Framework 2.0 is the ability to leverage your knowledge. It's fairly easy to start using the *Tool-Strip* after having explored the *MenuStrip*. The types of items found on toolbars are generally more varied than those on menus, but the principles are the same. Here, at long last, is the complete class hierarchy that derives from *ToolStripItem*:

Object

    MarshalByRefObject

        Component

            ToolStripItem (abstract)

                ToolStripButton

                ToolStripControlHost

                    ToolStripComboBox

                    ToolStripProgressBar

                    ToolStripTextBox

                ToolStripDropDownItem

                    ToolStripDropDownButton

                        ToolStripOverflowButton

                    ToolStripMenuItem

                    ToolStripSplitButton

                ToolStripLabel

                    StatusStripPanel

                    ToolStripStatusLabel

                ToolStripSeparator

Although you've seen how menu items can display bitmaps along with text, you've also seen that the bitmap is always to the left of the text. With items on tool strips you have more flexibility. If you want to display both text and an image, the visual relationship is governed by the

TextImageRelation property. Set the property to a member of the *TextImageRelation* enumeration: *TextAboveImage*, *ImageAboveText*, *TextBeforeImage*, *ImageBeforeText* (the default), or *Overlay*.

Toolbars often don't display much text at all, and the images can be rather cryptic, so ToolTips are essential. ToolTips are small phrases that appear in a balloon when the mouse cursor hovers over the item. Normally the item's *Text* property will be displayed, but you can override that by setting the *ToolTipText* property to the ToolTip text you want. Set the *AutoToolTip* property to *false* to suppress the ToolTip.

Tool Strip Buttons

Three types of button classes show up in the class hierarchy descending from *ToolStripItem*. Perhaps the most common is the *ToolStripButton*, which generally carries out a particular command, such as a Cut, Copy, or Paste. As usual, install an event handler for the *Click* event to be notified when the user clicks the button.

Should you use the same *Click* event handlers for menu items and toolbar items? Yes, definitely, absolutely, without a doubt. Your program should have one *PasteOnClick* handler, and it should be invoked by both the menu item and the toolbar item.

Enabling and disabling *ToolStripButton* objects is a little different than enabling and disabling menu items. Menu items on a drop-down menu don't need to be enabled until the drop-down menu is displayed. Many toolbar items, however, are visible all the time. For Cut, Copy, and Delete, for example, you'll probably need to install an event handler to determine when your program has data it can copy to the clipboard. The Paste button is particularly tricky. For that, you'll probably start a timer going and check the clipboard every one-tenth of a second or so to see whether there's anything of use in there.

The *ToolStripButton* can also function as a toggle, such as the Bold and Italic buttons found in text-formatting toolbars. Like the *ToolStripMenuItem*, the *ToolStripButton* has a Boolean *Checked* property and also a *CheckState* property that you can set to a member of the *CheckState* enumeration. Setting the *CheckOnClick* property to *true* causes the button to toggle itself whenever it's clicked. Multiple *ToolStripButton* items can also be used like radio buttons to indicate one choice out of several.

If you want a button to invoke a drop-down item, use *ToolStripDropDownButton*. Like *ToolStripMenuItem*, this class inherits from *ToolStripDropDownItem*, and it has a property named *DropDownItems* that is a collection of *ToolStripItem* objects. You probably don't need to install a handler for the *Click* event, but you'll want to install a handler for the *DropDownOpening* event if you need to enable or disable particular items on the drop-down menu.

If you use any Microsoft Office application, you're probably accustomed to buttons that perform certain default actions but are also accompanied by little triangles that display a drop-down menu. This style of button is implemented by the *ToolStripSplitButton* class, which is also descended from *ToolStripDropDownItem*. You add drop-down items to this button just like with *ToolStripDropDownButton*. You probably do not want to install a handler for the *Click* event, however, because that event is triggered when the user clicks *anywhere* on the button. To be notified when the user clicks the part of the button that does not invoke the drop-down menu, install a handler for the *ButtonClick* event.

Controls as *ToolStrip* Items

Besides buttons (and the fairly trivial *ToolStripLabel*), the other major category of items available for tool strips includes *ToolStripComboBox*, *ToolStripProgressBar*, and *ToolStripTextBox*. These three classes are all descended from *ToolStripControlHost*, and we've already seen how *ToolStripControlHost* provides a wrapper for controls that lets them be used in menus and tool strips. As you might expect, the *ToolStripComboBox*, *ToolStripProgressBar*, and *ToolStripTextBox* classes let you use the normal *ComboBox*, *ProgressBar*, and *TextBox* on tool strips. (The *ToolStripProgressBar*, however, is most commonly found on *StatusStrip* controls at the bottom of windows.)

Rather than demonstrate each of these tool strip items separately, let's look at something approaching a "real-life" program that has a *ToolStrip* that includes *ToolStripComboBox*, *ToolStripButton*, *ToolStripSplitButton*, *ToolStripLabel*, *ToolStripTextBox*, and our own custom *ToolStripColorGrid*.

A Text-Formatting *ToolStrip*

It is common in word processing applications such as Microsoft Word or Microsoft WordPad to have a toolbar that includes items for common text and paragraph formatting.

WordPad, of course, is built around the RichEdit control supported by the Windows API. This control is available to .NET Framework programmers through the *RichTextBox* class. Unlike the simpler *TextBox* control, *RichTextBox* allows a single document to have multiple fonts and paragraph formatting. As I discussed in the previous chapter, *RichTextBox* has several properties that let you obtain the current formatting and set new formatting. All these formatting properties begin with the word *Selection* and pertain to the text currently selected in the document. Selecting text is normally something the user does (either with the mouse or the keyboard cursor keys with the Shift key depressed), so setting character and paragraph formatting based on the current selection sounds ideal. (In real life, it doesn't quite work that way.)

For example, if *txtbox* is a *RichTextBox* control, a program can set the font for the current selection using the *SelectionFont* property:

```
txtbox.SelectionFont = new Font("Times New Roman", 24, FontStyle.Italic);
```

If there is no current selection, the new font is applied at the position of the keyboard caret within the text—called the "insertion point"—and will apply to new text typed at that point.

Obtaining the font for the current selection is similar:

```
Font fnt = txtbox.SelectionFont;
```

This is the only way to obtain the font that applies to a particular part of the document. If your program needs to obtain the font for a part of the document that is not currently selected, it must set the selection itself using the *Select* method. The program will probably want to save the user's selection during this process and later restore it. (We'll see an example shortly.)

Suppose the user has selected some text and wants to make it bold. After the program has used the *SelectionFont* property to obtain the current font (perhaps with the line of code just shown), it must create and set a new font with the desired style. The *FontStyle* enumeration is a combination of bit flags indicating bold, italic, underline, and strikeout. To add a new style, *FontStyle.Bold* must be combined with the current style by the bitwise OR operator:

```
txtbox.SelectionFont = new Font(fnt, fnt.Style | FontStyle.Bold);
```

The process is similar if the user wants to remove bold from a selection. The existing font style must be bitwise AND-ed with the bitwise complement of *FontStyle.Bold*:

```
txtbox.SelectionFont = new Font(fnt, fnt.Style & ~FontStyle.Bold);
```

What if the current selection contains two or more fonts? For example, part of the selection is italic and part is not. You want the part of the selection that's italic to become bold-italic, and the part that is not italic to become just bold.

According to the documentation of *SelectionFont*, "If the current text selection has more than one font specified, this property is *null*." My experience contradicts that. I have found that *SelectionFont* returns *null* only when the selection encompasses two or more fonts with different face names (for example, Times New Roman and Arial). If the face name is the same but part of the selection is bold and part is not, *SelectionFont* returns a font without bold. If the selection encompasses two different sizes of the same face name, *SelectionFont* returns a 13-point font.

As you might imagine, properly modifying a selection that encompasses multiple fonts drains much of the simplicity from the job. The program must save the two integers marking the beginning and length of the current selection, and then scan through the user's selection character by character by setting a series of one-character selections. At the end of the job, the user's original selection must be restored.

Besides supporting fonts, the *RichTextBox* supports other character formatting. The *Selection-Color* and *SelectionBackColor* properties refer to the text and background colors of the selected text. If these properties are not used, the text and background will be colored with the normal *ForeColor* and *BackColor* properties implemented by *Control*. *SelectionCharOffset* is a vertical offset in pixels that you can use for subscripting or superscripting. You'll probably want to combine this character offset with a smaller font size.

All other formatting properties involve paragraph formatting. *SelectionAlignment* is a member of the *HorizontalAlignment* enumeration—*Center*, *Left*, or *Right*—and governs how the paragraph is aligned within the control. *SelectionBullet* is a Boolean indicating whether the paragraph is to be preceded by a bullet. The *SelectionTabs* property is an array of integers that indicate tab stops in pixels.

SelectionIndent, *SelectionRightIndent*, and *SelectionHangingIndent* are integer pixel values that govern the left and right indentations of the paragraph and the first line of that paragraph. You'll recall from the previous chapter that these properties work a little differently from the familiar conventions of paragraph formatting.

The sample program coming up contains a *RichTextBox* control and a *ToolStrip* that lets you change all the formatting items except horizontal character offsets and tabs. Changing character and paragraph formatting is about *all* that the program does. To illustrate the *ToolStrip* with maximum clarity, the program can't load or save files. (However, the *RichTextBox* responds to the normal keyboard commands—Ctrl+X, Ctrl+C, Ctrl+V, and Ctrl+Z—to cut, copy, paste, and undo.)

There's not exactly a one-to-one correspondence between the *RichTextBox* formatting properties and the *ToolStrip* items. The *SelectionFont* property, for example, corresponds to six items on the *ToolStrip*—two combo boxes and four buttons. The danger with such a situation is that you could end up with a lot of event handlers that do basically the same thing with just slight variations. I use a variety of techniques (mostly involving the *Tag* property) to avoid duplication of that sort. For example, the same event handlers handle both foreground color and background color.

The program uses the *ToolStripColorGrid* class for color selection, so both the ToolStripColorGrid.cs file from this chapter and the ColorGrid.cs file from Chapter 4 must also be included as part of this project.

FormattingToolStrip.cs

```
//-------------------------------------------------------
// FormattingToolStrip.cs (c) 2005 by Charles Petzold
//-------------------------------------------------------
using System;
using System.Drawing;
using System.Reflection;
using System.Windows.Forms;

class FormattingToolStrip : Form
{
    protected RichTextBox txtbox;
    ToolStripComboBox comboName, comboSize;
    ToolStripButton btnBold, btnItalic, btnUnderline, btnStrikeout;
    ToolStripButton btnLeft, btnRight, btnCenter, btnBullets;
    ToolStripTextBox txtLeftIndent, txtRightIndent, txtFirstLine;
    ColorDialog clrdlg = new ColorDialog();
    float xDpi;
```

```
bool bSuspendSelectionChanged = false;

[STAThread]
public static void Main()
{
    Application.EnableVisualStyles();
    Application.Run(new FormattingToolStrip());
}
public FormattingToolStrip()
{
    Text = "Formatting ToolStrip";
    Width = 800;

    // Obtain the horizontal resolution of the screen in dots per inch.
    Graphics grfx = CreateGraphics();
    xDpi = grfx.DpiX;
    grfx.Dispose();

    // Load in many bitmaps for the tool strip.
    ImageList imglst = new ImageList();
    imglst.TransparentColor = Color.Magenta;
    imglst.Images.Add("BackColor", new Bitmap(GetType(), "ChooseColor.bmp"));
    imglst.Images.Add("ForeColor", new Bitmap(GetType(), "Forecolor.bmp"));
    imglst.Images.Add("Left",
        new Bitmap(GetType(), "AlignTableCellMiddleLeftJustHS.bmp"));
    imglst.Images.Add("Right",
        new Bitmap(GetType(), "AlignTableCellMiddleRight.bmp"));
    imglst.Images.Add("Center",
        new Bitmap(GetType(), "AlignTableCellMiddleCenter.bmp"));
    imglst.Images.Add("Bullets", new Bitmap(GetType(), "List_Bullets.bmp"));

    // Create a few more bitmaps.
    imglst.Images.Add("Bold", FontStyleBitmap("B", FontStyle.Bold));
    imglst.Images.Add("Italic", FontStyleBitmap("I", FontStyle.Italic));
    imglst.Images.Add("Underline", FontStyleBitmap("U", FontStyle.Underline));
    imglst.Images.Add("Strikeout", FontStyleBitmap("S", FontStyle.Strikeout));

    // Create the RichTextBox control that dominates the client area.
    txtbox = new RichTextBox();
    txtbox.Parent = this;
    txtbox.Dock = DockStyle.Fill;
    txtbox.SelectionChanged += TextBoxOnSelectionChanged;

    // Create the ToolStrip control.
    ToolStrip tool = new ToolStrip();
    tool.Parent = this;
    tool.ImageList = imglst;

    // Create and fill the font name combo box.
    comboName = new ToolStripComboBox();
    comboName.ToolTipText = "Font Name";
    comboName.SelectedIndexChanged += NameOnSelectionChanged;
    tool.Items.Add(comboName);
```

```csharp
foreach (FontFamily fntfam in FontFamily.Families)
    comboName.Items.Add(fntfam.Name);

// Create and fill the font size combo box.
comboSize = new ToolStripComboBox();
comboSize.ToolTipText = "Font Size";
comboSize.SelectedIndexChanged += SizeOnSelectionChanged;
tool.Items.Add(comboSize);

for (int i = 8; i <= 10; i++)
    comboSize.Items.Add(i.ToString());
for (int i = 12; i <= 28; i += 2)
    comboSize.Items.Add(i.ToString());
for (int i = 36; i <= 72; i += 12)
    comboSize.Items.Add(i.ToString());

// Create the bold, italic, underline, and strikeout buttons.
btnBold = new ToolStripButton();
btnBold.ImageKey = "Bold";
btnBold.ToolTipText = "Bold";
btnBold.Tag = FontStyle.Bold;
btnBold.CheckOnClick = true;
btnBold.Click += FontStyleOnClick;
tool.Items.Add(btnBold);

btnItalic = new ToolStripButton();
btnItalic.ImageKey = "Italic";
btnItalic.ToolTipText = "Italic";
btnItalic.Tag = FontStyle.Italic;
btnItalic.CheckOnClick = true;
btnItalic.Click += FontStyleOnClick;
tool.Items.Add(btnItalic);

btnUnderline = new ToolStripButton();
btnUnderline.ImageKey = "Underline";
btnUnderline.ToolTipText = "Underline";
btnUnderline.Tag = FontStyle.Underline;
btnUnderline.CheckOnClick = true;
btnUnderline.Click += FontStyleOnClick;
tool.Items.Add(btnUnderline);

btnStrikeout = new ToolStripButton();
btnStrikeout.ImageKey = "Strikeout";
btnStrikeout.ToolTipText = "Strikeout";
btnStrikeout.CheckOnClick = true;
btnStrikeout.Tag = FontStyle.Strikeout;
btnStrikeout.Click += FontStyleOnClick;
tool.Items.Add(btnStrikeout);
tool.Items.Add(new ToolStripSeparator());

// Create background color drop-down button.
ToolStripSplitButton spltbtn = new ToolStripSplitButton();
spltbtn.ImageKey = "BackColor";
spltbtn.ToolTipText = "Background Color";
spltbtn.ButtonClick += delegate
```

```
{
    txtbox.SelectionBackColor = txtbox.BackColor;
};
spltbtn.DropDownOpening += ColorOnDropDownOpening;
tool.Items.Add(spltbtn);

// Create PropertyInfo for background color.
PropertyInfo pi = typeof(RichTextBox).GetProperty("SelectionBackColor");

// Add Color Grid to drop down.
ToolStripColorGrid clrgrid = new ToolStripColorGrid();
clrgrid.Name = "ColorGrid";
clrgrid.Tag = pi;
clrgrid.Click += ColorGridOnClick;
spltbtn.DropDownItems.Add(clrgrid);
spltbtn.DropDownItems.Add(new ToolStripSeparator());

// Add "More Colors" item to drop down.
ToolStripMenuItem item = new ToolStripMenuItem("More colors...");
item.Tag = pi;
item.Click += MoreColorsOnClick;
spltbtn.DropDownItems.Add(item);

// Create foreground color button likewise.
spltbtn = new ToolStripSplitButton();
spltbtn.ImageKey = "ForeColor";
spltbtn.ToolTipText = "Font Color";
spltbtn.ButtonClick += delegate
{
    txtbox.SelectionColor = txtbox.ForeColor;
};
spltbtn.DropDownOpening += ColorOnDropDownOpening;
tool.Items.Add(spltbtn);

// Create PropertyInfo for foreground color.
pi = typeof(RichTextBox).GetProperty("SelectionColor");

// Add Color Grid and "More Colors" items.
clrgrid = new ToolStripColorGrid();
clrgrid.Name = "ColorGrid";
clrgrid.Tag = pi;
clrgrid.Click += ColorGridOnClick;
spltbtn.DropDownItems.Add(clrgrid);
spltbtn.DropDownItems.Add(new ToolStripSeparator());

item = new ToolStripMenuItem("More colors...");
item.Tag = pi;
item.Click += MoreColorsOnClick;
spltbtn.DropDownItems.Add(item);

tool.Items.Add(new ToolStripSeparator());

// Create buttons for left, right, and center alignment.
btnLeft = new ToolStripButton();
btnLeft.ImageKey = "Left";
```

```csharp
btnLeft.ToolTipText = "Align Left";
btnLeft.Tag = HorizontalAlignment.Left;
btnLeft.Checked = true;
btnLeft.Click += AlignOnClick;
tool.Items.Add(btnLeft);

btnRight = new ToolStripButton();
btnRight.ImageKey = "Right";
btnLeft.ToolTipText = "Align Right";
btnRight.Tag = HorizontalAlignment.Right;
btnRight.Click += AlignOnClick;
tool.Items.Add(btnRight);

btnCenter = new ToolStripButton();
btnCenter.ImageKey = "Center";
btnLeft.ToolTipText = "Align Center";
btnCenter.Tag = HorizontalAlignment.Center;
btnCenter.Click += AlignOnClick;
tool.Items.Add(btnCenter);

// Create button for bullets.
btnBullets = new ToolStripButton();
btnBullets.ImageKey = "Bullets";
btnBullets.ToolTipText = "Bullets";
btnBullets.CheckOnClick = true;
btnBullets.Click += BulletsOnClick;
tool.Items.Add(btnBullets);
tool.Items.Add(new ToolStripSeparator());

// Create labels and text boxes for indentation.
ToolStripLabel lbl = new ToolStripLabel("Left:");
tool.Items.Add(lbl);

txtLeftIndent = new ToolStripTextBox();
txtLeftIndent.ToolTipText = "Left Indentation in Inches";
txtLeftIndent.TextChanged += IndentOnTextChanged;
tool.Items.Add(txtLeftIndent);

lbl = new ToolStripLabel("Right:");
tool.Items.Add(lbl);

txtRightIndent = new ToolStripTextBox();
txtRightIndent.ToolTipText = "Right Indentation in Inches";
txtRightIndent.TextChanged += IndentOnTextChanged;
tool.Items.Add(txtRightIndent);

lbl = new ToolStripLabel("First line:");
tool.Items.Add(lbl);

txtFirstLine = new ToolStripTextBox();
txtFirstLine.ToolTipText = "First Line Indentation in Inches";
txtFirstLine.TextChanged += IndentOnTextChanged;
tool.Items.Add(txtFirstLine);
```

```
        // Initialize the ToolStrip.
        TextBoxOnSelectionChanged(txtbox, EventArgs.Empty);
}

// Creates buttons for Bold, Italic, Underline, and Strikeout
Bitmap FontStyleBitmap(string str, FontStyle fntstyle)
{
    Bitmap bm = new Bitmap(16, 16);
    Font fnt = new Font("Times New Roman", 14, fntstyle, GraphicsUnit.Pixel);
    StringFormat strfmt = new StringFormat();
    strfmt.Alignment = StringAlignment.Center;

    Graphics grfx = Graphics.FromImage(bm);
    grfx.DrawString(str, fnt, Brushes.Black, 8, 0, strfmt);
    grfx.Dispose();
    return bm;
}

// whenever the RichTextBox selection changes, alter the ToolStrip items.
void TextBoxOnSelectionChanged(object objSrc, EventArgs args)
{
    if (bSuspendSelectionChanged)
        return;

    Font fnt = txtbox.SelectionFont;

    if (fnt != null)
    {
        comboName.SelectedItem = fnt.Name;
        comboSize.Text = fnt.Size.ToString();

        btnBold.Checked = (fnt.Style & FontStyle.Bold) != 0;
        btnItalic.Checked = (fnt.Style & FontStyle.Italic) != 0;
        btnUnderline.Checked = (fnt.Style & FontStyle.Underline) != 0;
        btnStrikeout.Checked = (fnt.Style & FontStyle.Strikeout) != 0;
    }
    else
    {
        comboName.SelectedItem = null;
        comboSize.SelectedItem = null;

        btnBold.CheckState = CheckState.Unchecked;
        btnItalic.CheckState = CheckState.Unchecked;
        btnUnderline.CheckState = CheckState.Unchecked;
        btnStrikeout.CheckState = CheckState.Unchecked;
    }

    HorizontalAlignment hAlign = txtbox.SelectionAlignment;
    btnLeft.Checked = hAlign == HorizontalAlignment.Left;
    btnRight.Checked = hAlign == HorizontalAlignment.Right;
    btnCenter.Checked = hAlign == HorizontalAlignment.Center;
    btnBullets.Checked = txtbox.SelectionBullet;

    txtLeftIndent.Text = ((txtbox.SelectionIndent +
                    txtbox.SelectionHangingIndent) / xDpi).ToString();
```

```csharp
            txtRightIndent.Text = (txtbox.SelectionRightIndent / xDpi).ToString();
            txtFirstLine.Text = (-txtbox.SelectionHangingIndent / xDpi).ToString();
}


// Change the font family name.
void NameOnSelectionChanged(object objSrc, EventArgs args)
{
    ChangeFont(comboName.Text, 0, 0, false);
}


// Change the font size.
void SizeOnSelectionChanged(object objSrc, EventArgs args)
{
    float fSize = float.Parse(comboSize.Text);
    ChangeFont(null, fSize, 0, false);
}


// Change the font style.
void FontStyleOnClick(object objSrc, EventArgs args)
{
    ToolStripButton btn = (ToolStripButton)objSrc;
    FontStyle fntstyle = (FontStyle)btn.Tag;
    ChangeFont(null, 0, (FontStyle)btn.Tag, btn.Checked);
}


// Master method to change the font.
void ChangeFont(string strName, float fSize, FontStyle fntsty, bool bAdd)
{
    bSuspendSelectionChanged = true;

    int iSelStart = txtbox.SelectionStart;
    int iSelLength = txtbox.SelectionLength;

    for (int iStart1 = iSelStart; iStart1 < iSelStart + iSelLength; )
    {
        txtbox.Select(iStart1, 1);
        Font fnt = txtbox.SelectionFont;

        for (int iStart2 = iStart1 + 1; iStart2 <= iSelStart + iSelLength;
            iStart2++)
        {
            txtbox.Select(iStart2, 1);
            Font fntNext = txtbox.SelectionFont;

            if (iStart2 == iSelStart + iSelLength || !fnt.Equals(fntNext))
            {
                txtbox.Select(iStart1, iStart2 - iStart1);

                if (strName != null)
                    txtbox.SelectionFont = new Font(strName, fnt.Size,
                        fnt.Style);
                else if (fSize != 0)
                    txtbox.SelectionFont = new Font(fnt.Name, fSize,
                        fnt.Style);
                else if (bAdd)
```

```
                            txtbox.SelectionFont = new Font(fnt, fnt.Style | fntsty);
                    else
                            txtbox.SelectionFont = new Font(fnt, fnt.Style & ~fntsty);

                    iStart1 = iStart2;
                    break;
                }
            }
        }
    bSuspendSelectionChanged = false;
    txtbox.Select(iSelStart, iSelLength);
}


// Initialize the color grid when the drop down is opening.
void ColorOnDropDownOpening(object objSrc, EventArgs args)
{
    ToolStripSplitButton btn = (ToolStripSplitButton)objSrc;
    ToolStripColorGrid clrgrid =
        (ToolStripColorGrid)btn.DropDownItems["ColorGrid"];
    PropertyInfo pi = (PropertyInfo) clrgrid.Tag;
    clrgrid.SelectedColor = (Color)pi.GetValue(txtbox, null);
}


// Obtain a new color from the color grid.
void ColorGridOnClick(object objSrc, EventArgs args)
{
    ToolStripColorGrid clrgrid = (ToolStripColorGrid)objSrc;
    PropertyInfo pi = (PropertyInfo)clrgrid.Tag;
    pi.SetValue(txtbox, clrgrid.SelectedColor, null);
}


// Display the standard color dialog.
void MoreColorsOnClick(object objSrc, EventArgs args)
{
    ToolStripMenuItem item = (ToolStripMenuItem)objSrc;
    PropertyInfo pi = (PropertyInfo)item.Tag;
    clrdlg.Color = (Color)pi.GetValue(txtbox, null);

    if (clrdlg.ShowDialog() == DialogResult.OK)
        pi.SetValue(txtbox, clrdlg.Color, null);
}


// Change the alignment based on the button pressed.
void AlignOnClick(object objSrc, EventArgs args)
{
    ToolStripButton btn = (ToolStripButton)objSrc;
    btnLeft.Checked = btnRight.Checked = btnCenter.Checked = false;
    btn.Checked = true;
    txtbox.SelectionAlignment = (HorizontalAlignment) btn.Tag;
}


// Change the bullet formatting.
void BulletsOnClick(object objSrc, EventArgs args)
{
    ToolStripButton btn = (ToolStripButton)objSrc;
```

```
        txtbox.SelectionBullet = btn.Checked;
}


// Change the indents based on the number in the text boxes.
void IndentOnTextChanged(object objSrc, EventArgs args)
{
    try
    {
        int iLeftIndent = (int)(xDpi * float.Parse(txtLeftIndent.Text));
        int iRightIndent = (int)(xDpi * float.Parse(txtRightIndent.Text));
        int iFirstLine = (int)(xDpi * float.Parse(txtFirstLine.Text));

        txtbox.SelectionIndent = iLeftIndent + iFirstLine;
        txtbox.SelectionHangingIndent = -iFirstLine;
        txtbox.SelectionRightIndent = iRightIndent;
    }
    catch
    {
    }
}
}
```

The constructor begins by loading some bitmaps into an *ImageList*. (I set the Default Namespace of the project to a blank string because the last program in this chapter inherits from this form and would normally have a different Default Namespace, so the images wouldn't be loaded properly.) These bitmaps are from the stash shipped with Visual Studio; they have been made part of the project and flagged as Embedded Resources. Although the Visual Studio bitmap collection includes Bold.bmp, Italic.bmp, and Underline.bmp, it does not include Strikeout.bmp. For consistency, I decided to generate all four of these images myself in the *FontStyleBitmap* method following the constructor.

The rest of the constructor is dedicated to creating the *RichTextBox* and *ToolStrip* controls. The remainder of the program contains event handlers for the controls and *ToolStrip* items. It will be useful to explore the creation logic and corresponding event handlers in tandem.

The program installs a handler for only one event of the *RichTextBox*. This is the *Selection-Changed* event, which is handled by the *TextBoxOnSelectionChanged* method in the program. The event handler obtains the current *SelectionFont*, *SelectionAlignment*, *SelectionIndent*, and so forth, and it sets the *ToolStrip* items based on those values.

The constructor next creates the *ToolStrip* itself and two *ToolStripComboBox* items for the font name and font size. For both combo boxes, event handlers are installed for the *SelectedIndex-Changed* event. These handlers (called *NameOnSelectionChanged* and *SizeOnSelectionChanged*) are quite short and just call *ChangeFont*, which is the master font-changing method.

Next come four buttons for Bold, Italic, Underline, and Strikeout. In each case, the *Tag* property is set to the corresponding *FontStyle* member: *FontStyle.Bold*, *FontStyle.Italic*, and so forth. The setting of the *Tag* property allows these buttons to use the same *Click* event handler, which is called *FontStyleOnClick*. *FontStyleOnClick* is also quite short, and again is designed primarily to call *ChangeFont*.

ChangeFont must change the font for the current selection, but that font might not be the same for the entire selection. *ChangeFont* will need to alter and analyze the selection to properly change the font. The method begins by setting the *bSuspendSelectionChanged* field to *true*. The *TextBoxOnSelectionChanged* method uses this variable to avoid changing the *ToolStrip* items while the *ChangeFont* method is changing the selection.

ChangeFont begins by saving the user's current selection in *iSelStart* and *iSelLength*. It then changes the selection one character at a time and compares the fonts. When it finds a string of characters with the same font, it then changes that font based on the existing font and the arguments to the *ChangeFont* method.

Back to the constructor: both the background color and foreground color are represented by a *ToolStripSplitButton*. The part of the split button that *doesn't* have a drop-down menu generally performs a default action. In this case, I thought the color of the selection should be restored to the *BackColor* and *ForeColor* properties of the *RichTextBox*. This job seemed small enough to be suitable for an anonymous method right there in the constructor:

```
spltbtn.ButtonClick += delegate
{
    txtbox.SelectionBackColor = txtbox.BackColor;
};
```

The drop-down part of the button displays a *ToolStripColorGrid* and a *ToolStripMenuItem* with the text "More colors…" These two items both have *Click* event handlers (called *ColorGridOnClick* and *MoreColorsOnClick*), and both items are added to the *DropDownItems* collection of the *ToolStripSplitButton*.

I wanted to use the same *Click* event handlers for both the background color and font color. One possible approach is to assign the *Name* property of the two *ToolStripColorGrid* items "Foreground" and "Background." Then the *ColorGridOnClick* event handler might have code that looked something like this:

```
if (clrgrid.Name == "Background")
    txtbox.SelectionBackColor = clrgrid.SelectedColor;
else
    txtbox.SelectionColor = clrgrid.SelectedColor;
```

There's nothing wrong with that code, and it certainly meets the objective of having one event handler for both the foreground and background colors. But I decided to do something a bit more unusual. I created *PropertyInfo* objects that refer to the two particular properties of the *RichTextBox* I was interested in. For the background color, I used:

```
PropertyInfo pi = typeof(RichTextBox).GetProperty("SelectionBackColor");
```

For the foreground color, I used:

```
pi = typeof(RichTextBox).GetProperty("SelectionColor");
```

I then set the *Tag* property of both the *ToolStripColorGrid* and the *ToolStripMenuItem* (the one that invokes the standard color dialog box) to that *PropertyInfo* object. The *PropertyInfo* class is most commonly used in connection with reflection to obtain the various properties of a class that your program might be interested in. By creating a *PropertyInfo*, the program is able to treat a particular property of a particular class as an object. The *ColorGridOnClick* event handler uses this *PropertyInfo* object to set the actual property of the *txtbox* object:

```
pi.SetValue(txtbox, clrgrid.SelectedColor, null);
```

If the *pi* object was created for the *SelectionBackColor* property, this code is basically equivalent to:

```
txtbox.SelectionBackColor = clrgrid.SelectedColor;
```

The rest of the program is simple in comparison. The three alignment buttons (Left, Right, and Center) use the same event handler (*AlignOnClick*) and identify themselves by setting the appropriate enumeration member (*HorizontalAlignment.Left*, and so forth) to the *Tag* property. The Bullets button corresponds to a single Boolean property of the *RichTextBox* and has its own *Click* event handler.

Finally, three *ToolStripLabel* items identify three *ToolStripTextBox* items for the left, right, and first-line indentation. Because two of these items—the left and first-line indentation—are intertwined in the *RichTextBox* properties anyway, I decided again to have a single event handler for the *TextChanged* event. This event handler gets all three text items, converts them to integer pixels, and sets the appropriate properties.

Handling Multiple Tool Strips

What is a programmer's ultimate aspiration? To write an application with so many toolbars that it becomes necessary for the user to move them around? Perhaps.

If this is where your application is going, you have a few options. If you want all the toolbars to remain at the top of the window (or any other particular side of the window), you can create a *ToolStripPanel* as a child of your form. The *ToolStripPanel* must be explicitly docked to one edge of the window. All your *ToolStrip* objects are then made children of this panel. Use the *Join* method of *ToolStripPanel* to put the *ToolStrip* objects in particular places on the *ToolStripPanel*. The user can then move the various tool strips around on the panel.

You can also put the *MenuStrip* on this panel as well, and (as in Microsoft Office applications) the user has the option of moving the menu underneath the toolbar. You'll want to set the *GripStyle* property of the *MenuStrip* object to *ToolStripGripStyle.Visible*. This approach provides a little dotted handle at the far left of the *MenuStrip* so that it can be moved with the mouse.

The next higher level of flexibility allows the user to move *ToolStrip* and *MenuStrip* controls to all four sides of the window—or at least to the top and bottom. This job involves making a *ToolStripContainer* control a child of your form. Assign its *Dock* property to *DockStyle.Fill*. The *ToolStripContainer* divides its surface into five areas. At the top, left, bottom, and right are four *ToolStripPanel* objects identified by the properties *TopToolStripPanel*, *LeftToolStripPanel*, *BottomToolStripPanel*, and *RightToolStripPanel*. You put your *ToolStrip* and *MenuStrip* objects on these panels by making them children or using the *ToolStripPanel* method *Join*. You can suppress the use of any of these panels with the property *TopToolStripPanelVisible*, and so on.

In the center of its four *ToolStripPanel* controls, *ToolStripContainer* puts a *ToolStripContentPanel* control, which is accessible through the property *ContentPanel*. Here's where you put the other controls that populate your form.

You can also let the user rearrange the individual items on a *ToolStrip* by setting the *AllowItemReorder* property to *true*. The user can use the mouse (with the Alt key pressed on the keyboard) to drag-and-drop items within that tool strip. If there are multiple toolbars, the user can also drag items between toolbars, but only if both the source and destination toolbars have its *AllowItemReorder* property set to *true*.

It is the program's responsibility to retain the user's *ToolStrip* preferences for the next time the program is run. You can accomplish this by handling the *ItemRemoved* and *ItemAdded* events for each tool strip that has reordering enabled. When the user moves an item from one location to another, these two events occur in succession as the item settles into its new position. (These events will also be triggered if the program itself adds or removes a tool strip item.) The object accompanying the event is the tool strip from which the item is being removed or added. The events are accompanied by *ToolStripItemEventArgs* objects, which has a property named *Item* that identifies the particular item.

Status Strips

After menu strips and tool strips, the *StatusStrip* class is a snap. Status bars are customarily displayed at the very bottom of the window; consequently, the *StatusStrip* control has a default *Dock* property of *DockStyle.Bottom*. If you're docking other controls at the bottom (a *ToolStripPanel*, for example), you'll want to add the status strip to the form *after* that control.

Although multiple status bars are uncommon, there's no reason why you can't use them if you need them. Normally, a *StatusStrip* object displays a "sizing grip" in the lower right corner that gives the user a larger target to drag the corner of the form, but you can suppress it by setting the *SizingGrip* property to *false*.

You can also put one or more *StatusStrip* objects on a *ToolStripPanel*. You'll probably want to set the *GripStyle* property to *ToolStripGripStyle.Visible* to let the user move them around.

The items appearing on a status strip will customarily be limited to *ToolStripStatusLabel* (which simply displays some text) and *ToolStripProgressBar*. These are the only components that the Visual Studio designer lets you put on the status bar. However, if contrarianism is your creed, you can decorate the status bar with other items.

Status Labels

The *AutoSize* property of a *ToolStripStatusLabel* object is *true* by default, so the width of the label is based on its content. By default, the labels do not have borders. Text displayed by multiple *ToolStripStatusLabel* objects, therefore, just follow each other without any real differentiation.

One solution is to set *AutoSize* to *false* and explicitly set the *Width* property of the label. The text will normally be centered within the label, but you can change that with the *TextAlign* property.

A better solution is the *Margin* property. The label will still adjust itself to the size of its content, but with some additional space. Although you can set a margin on all four sides, you'll probably want to restrict yourself to the left and right sides.

Another popular solution is bordering the labels. Set the *BorderSides* property of the label to one or more members of the *ToolStripStatusLabelBorderSides* enumeration, which has members *None*, *Left*, *Top*, *Right*, *Bottom*, and *All*. Set the appearance of the border by setting the *BorderStyle* property to a member of the *Border3DStyle* enumeration. The default is *Border3D-Style.Flat*.

Often you'll want some labels at the left of the status strip, some labels to the right (by setting the *Alignment* property), and something in the middle. If you set the *Spring* property of that middle label to *true*, the label will use all the remaining space and give you the effect you want. If there is not sufficient room for all the items, however, entire items will not be displayed beginning at the right.

Here's a program that inherits from FormattingToolStrip and adds a *StatusStrip* to the bottom. The label on the left displays the current selection; the one on the right displays the current date and time.

```
RichTextWithStatus.cs
//----------------------------------------------------
// RichTextWithStatus.cs (c) 2005 by Charles Petzold
//----------------------------------------------------
using System;
using System.Drawing;
using System.Windows.Forms;

class RichTextWithStatus: FormattingToolStrip
{
    ToolStripStatusLabel lblSelection, lblDateTime;

    [STAThread]
    public static new void Main()
    {
```

```csharp
            Application.EnableVisualStyles();
            Application.Run(new RichTextWithStatus());
        }
    public RichTextWithStatus()
    {
        Text = "Rich Text with Status";

        txtbox.SelectionChanged += TextBoxOnSelectionChanged;

        StatusStrip stat = new StatusStrip();
        stat.Parent = this;

        lblSelection = new ToolStripStatusLabel();
        stat.Items.Add(lblSelection);

        lblDateTime = new ToolStripStatusLabel();
        lblDateTime.Alignment = ToolStripItemAlignment.Right;
        stat.Items.Add(lblDateTime);

        Timer tmr = new Timer();
        tmr.Interval = 1000;
        tmr.Enabled = true;
        tmr.Tick += TimerOnTick;

        // Initialize labels.
        TextBoxOnSelectionChanged(txtbox, EventArgs.Empty);
        TimerOnTick(tmr, EventArgs.Empty);
    }
    void TextBoxOnSelectionChanged(object objSrc, EventArgs args)
    {
        RichTextBox txtbox = (RichTextBox) objSrc;

        int iSelStart = txtbox.SelectionStart;
        int iSelLength = txtbox.SelectionLength;
        int iSelEnd = iSelStart + iSelLength;

        int iLine = txtbox.GetLineFromCharIndex(iSelStart);
        int iChar = iSelStart - txtbox.GetFirstCharIndexFromLine(iLine);
        lblSelection.Text = String.Format("Line {0} Character {1}",
            iLine + 1, iChar + 1);

        if (iSelLength > 0)
        {
            iLine = txtbox.GetLineFromCharIndex(iSelEnd);
            iChar = iSelEnd - txtbox.GetFirstCharIndexFromLine(iLine);
            lblSelection.Text += String.Format(" - Line {0} Character {1}",
                iLine + 1, iChar + 1);
        }
    }
    void TimerOnTick(object objSrc, EventArgs args)
    {
        lblDateTime.Text = DateTime.Now.ToString("G");
    }
}
```

Chapter 6

Data Binding and Data Views

Sample programs shown in books like this one are usually small and tidy and self-contained. Programs in the real world, however, are often large and sprawling and deal with external data. Controls must often display data, and a user interacts with controls to effect changes to the data. In many cases, these changes by the user to the control need to be acknowledged and assimilated, and the controls themselves often need to be updated to reflect the changes.

Establishing a connection between controls and data can be facilitated through the use of *data binding*. Binding is the process of linking a property of a control with a property of some other object (called a "data source") so that changes in the control can be reflected in the data source, and vice versa. Data bindings always occur between properties of the two objects.

Linking Controls and Data

The *Binding* class defined in the *System.Windows.Forms* namespace is the basic tool to establish a data binding between a control and a data source. A Windows Forms program generally interacts with *Binding* objects through the *DataBindings* property defined by *Control*. *DataBindings* is an instance of the *ControlBindingsCollection* class, which inherits from *BindingsCollection* and (as the name implies) is a collection of *Binding* objects.

Here's a program that contains a *Label* control whose *Text* property is bound to the window's *ClientSize* property. As you change the size of the window, the text in the label control is continually updated to show the new size of the window's client area.

```
WhatClientSize.cs
//-------------------------------------------------
// WhatClientSize.cs (c) 2005 by Charles Petzold
//-------------------------------------------------
using System;
using System.Drawing;
using System.Windows.Forms;

class WhatClientSize: Form
{
    [STAThread]
    public static void Main()
    {
        Application.EnableVisualStyles();
        Application.Run(new WhatClientSize());
    }
    public WhatClientSize()
    {
```

```
        Text = "What Client Size?";

        Label lbl = new Label();
        lbl.Parent = this;
        lbl.AutoSize = true;
        lbl.DataBindings.Add("Text", this, "ClientSize");
    }
}
```

That last statement shows a binding added to the *DataBindings* collection of the *Label* control. It essentially says, "I want the *Text* property of the label control to be set to the *ClientSize* property of the object *this*." In this class, of course, the keyword *this* refers to the program's form. This program treats the form as a data source.

You can have multiple bindings on the same control. Add the following statement:

```
lbl.DataBindings.Add("Location", this, "Location");
```

Recompile. Now when you run the program, you probably won't be able to see the label. But move the window toward the upper left corner of the display, and you'll see the *Label* control move relative to the upper left corner of the client area. The *Location* property of *Label* (the first argument to *Add*) is tracking the *Location* property of the form (indicated by the second and third arguments to *Add*).

The *Add* method shown in the program is one of seven *Add* methods implemented by the *ControlBindingsCollection* class. It is equivalent to the following code, which uses another of the *Add* methods:

```
Binding bind = new Binding("Text", this, "ClientSize");
lbl.DataBindings.Add(bind);
```

Like the *Add* method shown in the WhatClientSize program, the remaining *Add* methods all result in the creation of a new *Binding* object and have additional arguments that set various properties of the *Binding* object they create. The *Binding* class itself has six constructors that parallel these *Add* methods.

How It Works

The *Binding* constructor—and the corresponding *Add* method of *ControlBindingsCollection*—require that the two linked properties be specified as strings. The use of strings might seem odd until you realize that there's no other convenient way to refer to a particular property itself rather than (as is usually the case when you're working with objects) the *value* of a particular property.

Behind the scenes, these strings are converted into objects of type *PropertyInfo* (a class defined in the *System.Reflection* namespace) probably using code that looks something like the following, where *obj* is a particular object and *str* is the name of a property defined by that object:

```
PropertyInfo propinfo = obj.GetType().GetProperty(str);
```

GetType obtains the type of the object and returns an object of type *Type*, which implements many properties and methods for obtaining information about the type, including *GetProperty*.

An instance of *PropertyInfo* refers to a particular property of a particular *class*, not a property of a particular *object*. Rather than using *obj.GetType()* to obtain the type, you could have used *typeof(Form)*, for example, if you were interested in a property of the *Form* class.

The value of that property for a particular object (again, *obj*) can then be obtained using the *GetValue* method defined in *PropertyInfo*:

```
object objValue = propinfo.GetValue(obj, null);
```

For example, within a class derived from *Form*, the current value of the *ClientSize* property can be obtained using this normal code:

```
Size sz = ClientSize;
```

Or it can be obtained by using reflection, like this:

```
Size sz = (Size) GetType().GetProperty("ClientSize").GetValue(this, null);
```

or like this:

```
Size sz = (Size) typeof(Form).GetProperty("ClientSize").GetValue(this, null);
```

A similar method named *SetValue* allows the value of a property to be set.

So, when the WhatClientSize program adds the following data binding to the *Label* control,

```
lbl.DataBindings.Add("Text", this, "ClientSize");
```

it shouldn't be much of a mystery how the current *ClientSize* property of the form can be obtained, converted to text, and set to the *Text* property of the label. But there's more work that needs to be done (and much of it is probably performed by the *PropertyManager* class).

The *Label* control doesn't just show the form's *ClientSize* property when the data binding is first set; the display changes as you change the size of the form's window. *PropertyManager* performs this feat by taking the name of the property you're interested in ("ClientSize") and appending the word "Changed" to get "ClientSizeChanged." Not coincidentally, that happens to be the name of an event defined by *Control* and inherited by *Form*. *PropertyManager* then installs an event handler for that event so that it can be notified whenever the *ClientSize* property changes and change the label accordingly.

What if *Form* did not implement an event named *ClientSizeChanged*? Well, then, an event handler would not be installed, and the *PropertyManager* could not be informed when the *ClientSize* property changed. The *Label* control would not be updated in that case.

Let's try it: in WhatClientSize.cs, change "ClientSize" to "ClientRectangle" in the call to *Add*, recompile, and run. Now the *Label* control will display the initial value of the form's *ClientRectangle* property, but it won't be kept updated when you change the size of the window, and that's because an event named *ClientRectangleChanged* does not exist.

Control Bites Data

Can we go the other way? Can we make the data source respond to changes in the control? Absolutely, and in fact, that's the most common way in which bindings are used. A control is initialized by a data source when the binding is first hooked up, and then the control changes the data source. The control could also respond to changes in the data source for a two-way link, but that would require that the data source also have *Changed* events for the bound properties.

Here's a program with three *CheckBox* controls that again treats the program's form as a data source. In this case, the *CheckBox* controls change the data source through bindings to the *MinimizeBox*, *MaximizeBox*, and *ControlBox* properties of the form.

```
BooleanToggle.cs
//-------------------------------------------
// BooleanToggle.cs (c) 2005 by Charles Petzold
//-------------------------------------------
using System;
using System.Drawing;
using System.Windows.Forms;

class BooleanToggle : Form
{
    [STAThread]
    public static void Main()
    {
        Application.EnableVisualStyles();
        Application.Run(new BooleanToggle());
    }
    public BooleanToggle()
    {
        Text = "Boolean Toggle";

        FlowLayoutPanel flow = new FlowLayoutPanel();
        flow.Parent = this;
        flow.Dock = DockStyle.Fill;
        flow.FlowDirection = FlowDirection.TopDown;

        CheckBox chkbox = new CheckBox();
        chkbox.Parent = flow;
        chkbox.Text = "Minimize Box";
        chkbox.AutoSize = true;
        chkbox.DataBindings.Add("Checked", this, "MinimizeBox");
        chkbox.DataBindings[0].DataSourceUpdateMode =
            DataSourceUpdateMode.OnPropertyChanged;
```

```
        chkbox = new CheckBox();
        chkbox.Parent = flow;
        chkbox.Text = "Maximize Box";
        chkbox.AutoSize = true;
        chkbox.DataBindings.Add("Checked", this, "MaximizeBox");
        chkbox.DataBindings[0].DataSourceUpdateMode =
            DataSourceUpdateMode.OnPropertyChanged;

        chkbox = new CheckBox();
        chkbox.Parent = flow;
        chkbox.Text = "Control Box";
        chkbox.AutoSize = true;
        chkbox.DataBindings.Add("Checked", this, "ControlBox");
        chkbox.DataBindings[0].DataSourceUpdateMode =
            DataSourceUpdateMode.OnPropertyChanged;
    }
}
```

When the program starts up, the *Checked* property of each *CheckBox* is set to the Boolean value of the form property that it's linked to. In all cases, the check boxes will be checked. Then, by manually clicking the check boxes, you can disable the minimize box and maximize box, and you can even make all caption bar buttons go away by unchecking the "Control Box" check box.

You'll notice that each binding is followed by the statement

```
chkbox.DataBindings[0].DataSourceUpdateMode = DataSourceUpdateMode.OnPropertyChanged;
```

By indexing the *DataBindings* collection, this statement accesses the *Binding* object created in the previous statement. The *Binding* class has two properties named *ControlUpdateMode* and *DataSourceUpdateMode* that govern how controls and data sources are updated from one another.

The *ControlUpdateMode* property governs how the data source updates the control. You set this property to a member of the *ControlUpdateMode* enumeration, which, by default, is *OnPropertyChanged*. This means that the control is updated whenever the property of the data source changes. That's why the WhatClientSize program was able to work without setting the *ControlUpdateMode* property. (The other member of the *ControlUpdateMode* enumeration is *Never*, which means the control is never updated from the data source.)

The *DataSourceUpdateMode* property of *Binding* governs how the control updates the data source. You set this property to a member of the *DataSourceUpdateMode* enumeration: *OnPropertyChanged*, *OnValidation*, or *Never*. The default is *OnValidation*, which refers to the *Validating* and *Validated* events implemented by *Control*. These events are generated when a control is losing input focus, and they give a program the opportunity to assure itself that the user has entered valid information in a control.

If a program handles the *Validating* event of a control, it has the option of setting the *Cancel* property of the *CancelEventArgs* accompanying the event to *true*, and that prevents the control from losing input focus. (The program would probably also want to inform the user in some way why focus can't be shifted to the next control.) If *Cancel* remains set at *false*, the *Validating* event is followed by a *Validated* event, and the control loses input focus.

By making the *DataSourceUpdateMode* property have a default value of *DataSourceUpdate-Mode.OnValidation*, the designers of Windows Forms are suggesting that you might want to validate the value of a control before it's used to change the data source. If that's not necessary, set the property to *DataSourceUpdateMode.OnPropertyChanged* like the BooleanToggle program does. If you remove those three statements from the program, you'll still be able to change the data source (the form) from the check boxes, but each change takes effect only when the particular check box loses input focus.

Because *Form* also descends from *Control*, it's possible to set data bindings on the form as well as any controls in the form. Here's a program that establishes two one-way data bindings between a scrollbar and the form. As you change the value of the scrollbar, the form's width changes, and as you change the form's width, the scrollbar thumb moves up and down.

```
ChangeWidth.cs
//-------------------------------------------
// ChangeWidth.cs (c) 2005 by Charles Petzold
//-------------------------------------------
using System;
using System.Drawing;
using System.Windows.Forms;

class ChangeWidth: Form
{
    [STAThread]
    public static void Main()
    {
        Application.EnableVisualStyles();
        Application.Run(new ChangeWidth());
    }
    public ChangeWidth()
    {
        Text = "Change Width";

        VScrollBar scrl = new VScrollBar();
        scrl.Parent = this;
        scrl.Dock = DockStyle.Left;
        scrl.Minimum = SystemInformation.MinimumWindowSize.Width;
        scrl.Maximum = SystemInformation.MaxWindowTrackSize.Width;
        scrl.Value = Width;

        // Changes in Size.Width change scrollbar Value.
        scrl.DataBindings.Add("Value", this, "Size.Width");
        scrl.DataBindings[0].DataSourceUpdateMode = DataSourceUpdateMode.Never;
```

```
        // Changes in scrollbar Value change width.
        DataBindings.Add("Width", scrl, "Value");
        DataBindings[0].DataSourceUpdateMode = DataSourceUpdateMode.Never;
    }
}
```

For both bindings, the *DataSourceUpdateMode* is set to *Never* just to clarify that the control is not updating the data source. You can change those properties to *OnPropertyChanged*, and the program will work exactly the same.

The first data binding is added to the scrollbar collection:

```
scrl.DataBindings.Add("Value", this, "Size.Width");
```

It looks as if the *Value* property of the scrollbar can change the *Size.Width* property of the form, but that's not so. If you put a statement like this

```
Size.Width = 800;
```

in your form, you'll get a compile error of "Cannot modify the return value of 'System.Window.Forms.Form.Size' because it is not a variable." However, even though the data binding can't change *Size.Width*, the binding does install an event handler for the form's *Size* event and changes the scrollbar *Value* property accordingly.

The second data binding is added to the form collection:

```
DataBindings.Add("Width", scrl, "Value");
```

In this data binding, the scrollbar is being treated as a data source. This is how the scrollbar *Value* property changes the form's *Width* property. There is no *WidthChanged* event implemented by *Form*, so the binding can't change the scrollbar based on changes in the form's width.

ColorScroll Revisited

In Chapter 3, I presented a program named ColorScrollTable that used a *TableLayoutPanel* control to display three scrollbars and some labels. The three scrollbars changed the red, green, and blue components of the background color of a panel. I used a little data binding in that program to keep three *Label* controls updated with the current value of the corresponding scrollbar:

```
alblValue[col].DataBindings.Add("Text", vscrl, "Value");
```

However, I wasn't able to use as much data binding as I wanted in that program because of the nature of the *Color* structure. Once you create a *Color* value, you can't change it. The individual *R*, *G*, and *B* fields are read-only, and *Color* does not implement any events.

The first step to making a totally data-bound program is creating a new color class with the required features. The following *Rgb* class maintains a color as red, green, and blue properties that are both gettable *and* settable through public properties. A *Color* property provides a conversion between the normal *Color* structure and these three color components.

```
Rgb.cs
//-----------------------------------
// Rgb.cs (c) 2005 by Charles Petzold
//-----------------------------------
using System;
using System.Drawing;
using System.Windows.Forms;

class Rgb
{
    public event EventHandler ColorChanged;
    int r, g, b;

    public int Red
    {
        get { return r; }
        set
        {
            r = value;
            OnColorChanged(this, EventArgs.Empty);
        }
    }
    public int Green
    {
        get { return g; }
        set
        {
            g = value;
            OnColorChanged(this, EventArgs.Empty);
        }
    }
    public int Blue
    {
        get { return b; }
        set
        {
            b = value;
            OnColorChanged(this, EventArgs.Empty);
        }
    }
    public Color Color
    {
        get { return Color.FromArgb(Red, Green, Blue); }
        set
        {
            r = value.R;
            g = value.G;
            b = value.B;
```

```
                OnColorChanged(this, EventArgs.Empty);
        }
    }
    protected virtual void OnColorChanged(object objSrc, EventArgs args)
    {
        if (ColorChanged != null)
            ColorChanged(objSrc, args);
    }
}
```

This *Rgb* class also includes a *ColorChanged* event that is triggered whenever the color stored by the class changes in any way.

Here's the *RgbScroll* class that makes use of *Rgb* to implement color scrolling with no explicit event handling.

RgbScroll.cs

```
//-------------------------------------------
// RgbScroll.cs (c) 2005 by Charles Petzold
//-------------------------------------------
using System;
using System.Drawing;
using System.Windows.Forms;

class ColorScrollTable : Form
{
    [STAThread]
    public static void Main()
    {
        Application.EnableVisualStyles();
        Application.Run(new ColorScrollTable());
    }
    public ColorScrollTable()
    {
        Text = "Rgb Scroll with TableLayoutPanel";

        // Create a SplitContainer that fills the client area.
        SplitContainer splt = new SplitContainer();
        splt.Parent = this;
        splt.Dock = DockStyle.Fill;
        splt.SplitterDistance = ClientSize.Width / 2;

        // The TableLayoutPanel is on the left of the splitter.
        TableLayoutPanel table = new TableLayoutPanel();
        table.Parent = splt.Panel1;
        table.Dock = DockStyle.Fill;
        table.BackColor = Color.White;
        table.ColumnCount = 3;
        table.RowCount = 3;

        // Create the right SplitterPanel for displaying the color.
        Panel pnlColor = splt.Panel2;
```

```
    // Create an Rgb object and give it the pnlColor color.
    Rgb rgb = new Rgb();
    rgb.Color = pnlColor.BackColor;

    // Bind the background color to rgb.
    pnlColor.DataBindings.Add("BackColor", rgb, "Color");

    // Array for color names.
    string[] astrColors = { "Red", "Green", "Blue" };

    // Loop through the three columns (red, green, blue).
    for (int col = 0; col < 3; col++)
    {
        // Label at the top identifies red, green, or blue.
        Label lbl = new Label();
        lbl.AutoSize = true;
        lbl.Anchor = AnchorStyles.None;
        lbl.Text = astrColors[col];
        lbl.ForeColor = Color.FromName(astrColors[col]);
        table.Controls.Add(lbl, col, 0);

        // Scrollbar to set new values is bound to rgb.
        VScrollBar vscrl = new VScrollBar();
        vscrl.Parent = table;
        vscrl.Anchor = AnchorStyles.Top | AnchorStyles.Bottom;
        vscrl.TabStop = true;
        vscrl.LargeChange = 16;
        vscrl.Maximum = 255 + vscrl.LargeChange - 1;
        vscrl.DataBindings.Add("Value", rgb, astrColors[col]);
        vscrl.DataBindings[0].DataSourceUpdateMode =
                                DataSourceUpdateMode.OnPropertyChanged;
        table.Controls.Add(vscrl, col, 1);

        // Label showing color value is bound to scrollbar.
        Label lblValue = new Label();
        lblValue.AutoSize = true;
        lblValue.Anchor = AnchorStyles.None;
        lblValue.ForeColor = Color.FromName(astrColors[col]);
        lblValue.DataBindings.Add("Text", vscrl, "Value");
        table.Controls.Add(lblValue, col, 2);

        // ColumnStyles allocate three columns equally.
        table.ColumnStyles.Add(new ColumnStyle(SizeType.Percent, 33));
    }

    // RowStyles let the middle row be as large as possible.
    table.RowStyles.Add(new RowStyle(SizeType.AutoSize));
    table.RowStyles.Add(new RowStyle(SizeType.Percent, 100));
    table.RowStyles.Add(new RowStyle(SizeType.AutoSize));
    }
}
```

This program has several data bindings. The first one binds the *BackColor* property of the panel to the *Color* property of the *Rgb* object:

```
pnlColor.DataBindings.Add("BackColor", rgb, "Color");
```

The panel's background color is updated from the data source (the *rgb* object) during *Color-Changed* events.

For each of the scrollbars, the *Value* property of the scrollbar is bound to the particular *Red*, *Green*, or *Blue* property of the *Rgb* object:

```
vscrl.DataBindings.Add("Value", rgb, astrColors[col]);
```

In this case, the control changes the data source (the *rgb* object), and the *DataSourceUpdate-Mode* property of the *Binding* object needs to be set to *OnPropertyChanged*.

The *Label* controls at the bottom are bound to the values of the scroll bars:

```
lblValue.DataBindings.Add("Text", vscrl, "Value");
```

That particular binding was accomplished in the earlier version.

By eliminating all explicit event handling, we've created a program that appears to have no moving parts. No moving parts means smoother operation and less maintenance.

The *ComboBox* Difference

With *ListBox* and *ComboBox*, you can still peg properties to data sources, but you generally do something a little different. Both these controls derive from the abstract *ListControl*, which is where the pertinent properties are defined. I'll be referring to *ComboBox* in the following discussion, but what I say also applies to *ListBox*.

Let's review a little. Generally, you fill up a *ComboBox* by multiple calls to the *Add* method of the *Items* property. You can fill up the control with any type of object. The control uses the object's *ToString* method to display the object in the list.

You generally also install an event handler for the control's *SelectedIndexChanged* or *Selected-ValueChanged* event. When the event is triggered, you can determine the user's current selection by getting the *SelectedIndex* property to index the *Items* collection, or you can obtain the *SelectedItem* property directly.

Notice the difference in names between the event and property: you're installing an event handler for *SelectedValueChanged*, but you're accessing the *SelectedItem* property. If you want to be notified when the *SelectedItem* property has changed, it might make more sense to install a handler for the *SelectedItemChanged* event, but there is no event of that name.

There *is* a property named *SelectedValue*, but if you fill up the list box using the *Items* property, you will find that *SelectedValue* always equals *null*. With this conventional way of filling up the list box, the *SelectedValueChanged* event is triggered even when *SelectedValue* hasn't changed at all.

This means that if you try to bind to the *SelectedValue* property of a *ComboBox* control like this:

```
combo.DataBindings.Add("SelectedValue", obj, "SomeProperty");
```

you won't have much luck, because *SelectedValue* always returns *null*.

The *ListControl* class (from which both *ListBox* and *ComboBox* derive) implements an alternative method for filling up the control. This is by use of the *DataSource* property. You can set this property to an instance of any class that implements the *IList* or *IListSource* interface, and that includes arrays, *ArrayList* objects, and *List* objects. Once you do set *DataSource*, however, you can't add more items to the control using the *Items* property.

For example, you can fill up a *ComboBox* like this:

```
combo.DataSource = Enum.GetValues(typeof(KnownColor));
```

The *Enum.GetValues* method returns an array of all enumeration values, so this code fills the *ComboBox* with all the members of the *KnownColor* enumeration. Now the *SelectedValue* property returns the same value as the *SelectedItem* property—in this case, a particular member of the enumeration.

However, you *still* can't install a data binding for the *SelectedValue* property. If you try, an exception will be thrown that indicates a problem with the *ValueMember* property.

The *DataSource* property is documented as an object that implements the *IList* or *IListSource* interface, and this includes arrays. But what this property *really* wants is an array of objects that have at least one public property, and preferably two. One of these properties is treated as the actual "value" of the object, and the second (if it's available) is probably a text string used to display the object in the control. After you set the *DataSource* property of the *ComboBox* to the array (or whatever), you also set the *ValueMember* property of the control to the name of the first of these properties of the array objects, and you set *DisplayMember* to the second of these properties.

For example, suppose you have a class named *Doodle*, and this class has a property named *DoodleValue* and a property of type *string* named *DoodleName*. You have an array of *Doodle* objects named *adoodle*. You set up your *ComboBox* like this:

```
combo.DataSource = adoodle;
combo.ValueMember = "DoodleValue";
combo.DisplayMember = "DoodleName".
```

The *ComboBox* uses the *DoodleName* properties to display the items in the list. The *SelectedValue* property of *Combobox* is an object of the same type as the *DoodleValue* property.

Let's define a simple class suitable for use with the *DataSource* property of *ComboBox*. This class is based on the *KnownColor* enumeration, which includes the names of all the color in the *Color* structure (such as *AliceBlue* and *PapayaWhip*) and also the names of the system colors (such as *HighlightText* and *InactiveCaption*).

KnownColorClass.cs

```csharp
//-------------------------------------------------
// KnownColorClass.cs (c) 2005 by Charles Petzold
//-------------------------------------------------
using System;
using System.Drawing;

class KnownColorClass
{
    KnownColor kc;

    public KnownColorClass(KnownColor kc)
    {
        this.kc = kc;
    }
    public Color Color
    {
        get { return Color.FromKnownColor(kc); }
    }
    public string Name
    {
        get
        {
            string str = Enum.GetName(typeof(KnownColor), kc);

            for (int i = 1; i < str.Length; i++)
                if (Char.IsUpper(str[i]))
                    str = str.Insert(i++, " ");

            return str;
        }
    }
    public static KnownColorClass[] KnownColorArray
    {
        get
        {
            // Create an array of KnownColorClass objects.
            KnownColor[] akc = (KnownColor[])Enum.GetValues(typeof(KnownColor));
            KnownColorClass[] akcc = new KnownColorClass[akc.Length];

            for (int i = 0; i < akc.Length; i++)
                akcc[i] = new KnownColorClass(akc[i]);

            return akcc;
        }
    }
}
```

The class stores a *KnownColor* member as a private field. The public *Color* property returns a *Color* object based on that *KnownColor* enumeration member, and the *Name* property returns a string with the color name broken into separate words based on the camel casing.

For convenience, a static property named *KnownColorArray* returns an array of *KnownColor-Class* objects based on all the members of the *KnownColor* enumeration.

The ComboBoxBind project includes KnownColorClass.cs and the following file.

ComboBoxBind.cs

```
//-------------------------------------------
// ComboBoxBind.cs (c) 2005 by Charles Petzold
//-------------------------------------------
using System;
using System.Drawing;
using System.Windows.Forms;

class ComboBoxBind : Form
{
    [STAThread]
    public static void Main()
    {
        Application.EnableVisualStyles();
        Application.Run(new ComboBoxBind());
    }
    public ComboBoxBind()
    {
        Text = "ComboBox Bind";

        // Create the ComboBox.
        ComboBox combo = new ComboBox();
        combo.Parent = this;
        combo.DropDownStyle = ComboBoxStyle.DropDownList;
        combo.AutoSize = true;
        combo.Width = 12 * Font.Height;

        // Set the data source, display and value members.
        combo.DataSource = KnownColorClass.KnownColorArray;
        combo.ValueMember = "Color";
        combo.DisplayMember = "Name";

        // Bind the ComboBox with the form background color.
        combo.DataBindings.Add("SelectedValue", this, "BackColor");
        combo.DataBindings[0].DataSourceUpdateMode =
                            DataSourceUpdateMode.OnPropertyChanged;
    }
}
```

After the *ComboBox* is created, its *DataSource* property is assigned an array of *KnownColorClass* objects created by the static *KnownColorArray* property in that class. The *ValueMember* property is assigned "Color," which is the name of the property in *KnownColorClass* that returns a *Color* value, and *DisplayMember* is assigned "Name," which is the name of the property in *KnownColorClass* that returns a string identifying the color.

Finally, the form constructor concludes by establishing a binding between the *SelectedValue* property of the *ComboBox* and the *BackColor* property of the form. By default, the *BackColor* of the form is the *Color* value obtained from the static property *SystemColors.Control*. This is a *Color* value that does *not* correspond to any of the static read-only properties in the *Color* structure, but it corresponds to the member of the *KnownColor* enumeration also named *Control*.

When you run the program, it does indeed display the proper initial color in the *ComboBox*:

And, of course, changing the value in the *ComboBox* also changes the background color of the form.

Entry-Level Data Entry

Data entry is one of the most common jobs for real-world programmers. Through the process of data binding, data entry has gone through a quiet revolution. The enhancements to Windows Forms in the .NET Framework 2.0—particularly the *BindingNavigator* and the momentous *DataGridView* control—will continue to ease the job of data entry. This is an enormous topic, and I can really only scratch the surface here. I will stop short of exploring anything in the *System.Data* namespace, which is really best pursued in books dedicated to working with databases.

The Traditional Approach

Let's assume we want to maintain a database of people of some sort. For each person, we want to store a first name, a last name, and a birth date. One good way to begin is by defining a class containing public properties for these three items. The properties simply provide a public interface to private fields.

Person.cs

```
//--------------------------------------
// Person.cs (c) 2005 by Charles Petzold
//--------------------------------------
using System;

public class Person
{
    // Private fields.
    string strFirstName, strLastName;
    DateTime dtBirth = new DateTime(1800, 1, 1);

    // Public properties.
    public string FirstName
    {
        get { return strFirstName; }
        set { strFirstName = value; }
    }
    public string LastName
    {
        get { return strLastName; }
        set { strLastName = value; }
    }
    public DateTime BirthDate
    {
        get { return dtBirth; }
        set { dtBirth = value; }
    }
}
```

The next step is designing a form containing controls that will allow us to enter this information. Rather than populate an object of type *Form*, let's instead put all the controls on a panel, an approach that might allow us to reuse the panel in various settings. To keep the layout simple, let's derive from *FlowLayoutPanel*. The following class contains three labels, two *TextBox* controls, and a *DateTimePicker*. I call the class *PersonPanelNoBinding* because it doesn't use any of the data-binding features I showed earlier in this chapter.

PersonPanelNoBinding.cs

```
//----------------------------------------------------
// PersonPanelNoBinding.cs (c) 2005 by Charles Petzold
//----------------------------------------------------
using System;
using System.Drawing;
using System.Windows.Forms;

class PersonPanelNoBinding : FlowLayoutPanel
{
    TextBox txtboxFirstName, txtboxLastName;
    DateTimePicker dtPicker;
```

```csharp
// Public property.
public Person Person
{
    set
    {
        txtboxFirstName.Text = value.FirstName;
        txtboxLastName.Text = value.LastName;
        dtPicker.Value = value.BirthDate;
    }
    get
    {
        Person pers = new Person();
        pers.FirstName = txtboxFirstName.Text;
        pers.LastName = txtboxLastName.Text;
        pers.BirthDate = dtPicker.Value;
        return pers;
    }
}

// Constructor.
public PersonPanelNoBinding()
{
    Label lbl = new Label();
    lbl.Parent = this;
    lbl.Text = "First Name: ";
    lbl.AutoSize = true;
    lbl.Anchor = AnchorStyles.Left;

    txtboxFirstName = new TextBox();
    txtboxFirstName.Parent = this;
    txtboxFirstName.AutoSize = true;

    this.SetFlowBreak(txtboxFirstName, true);

    lbl = new Label();
    lbl.Parent = this;
    lbl.Text = "Last Name: ";
    lbl.AutoSize = true;
    lbl.Anchor = AnchorStyles.Left;

    txtboxLastName = new TextBox();
    txtboxLastName.Parent = this;
    txtboxLastName.AutoSize = true;

    this.SetFlowBreak(txtboxLastName, true);

    lbl = new Label();
    lbl.Parent = this;
    lbl.Text = "Birth Date: ";
    lbl.AutoSize = true;
    lbl.Anchor = AnchorStyles.Left;

    dtPicker = new DateTimePicker();
    dtPicker.Parent = this;
```

```
        dtPicker.Format = DateTimePickerFormat.Long;
        dtPicker.AutoSize = true;
    }
}
```

The class defines a public property named *Person* of type *Person*. Take careful note how the property is implemented: the *set* accessor sets the *Text* properties of the two *TextBox* controls from the *FirstName* and *LastName* properties of the *Person* object, and the *Value* property of the *DateTimePicker* from the *BirthDate* property. The *get* accessor creates a new object of type *Person*, sets the properties of that object from the three controls, and returns it.

A program using this panel can initialize all the controls from a *Person* object just by setting the *Person* property, and it can obtain the user's entry from the *Person* property. One could easily imagine a program maintaining an array of *Person* objects, with additional controls separate from this panel that let a user navigate through the array, add a new *Person* object, or delete an existing one. At any time, the user sees only one of these *Person* objects, and that's the one displayed by the panel.

We will, of course, aim for (and achieve) that goal, but for now let's see if we can successfully load and save a single *Person* object.

XML Serialization

A few years ago, I might have been showing you at this point how to use the .NET Framework file I/O classes to write the *Person* properties to a file in a simple comma-separated text format. These days, however, using anything other than XML for this purpose might leave me vulnerable to public humiliation and even imprisonment.

For storing a single *Person* object (which is our immediate goal), such an XML file might look something like this:

```
<Person>
  <FirstName>
    Johannes
  </FirstName>
  <LastName>
    Brahms
  </LastName>
  <BirthDate>
    1833-05-07T00:00:00
  </BirthDate>
</Person>
```

There are a couple ways you can write and read such a file. Because XML files are ultimately just text files, you might decide to descend down to the level of writing and reading the actual angle brackets and slashes using the *StreamWriter* and *StreamReader* classes defined in the *System.IO* namespace.

A mighty step above that approach is taking advantage of the classes defined in the *System.Xml* namespace. The *XmlTextWriter* class lets you write XML with methods such as *WriteStartElement*, *WriteString*, and *WriteEndElement*. The *XmlTextReader* class is a bit trickier: you generally use the *Read* method to read the next node (which could be an element, an attribute, content, or something scarier), and then you figure out what that node is from the *NodeType*, *Name*, and *Value* properties.

While the *XmlTextWriter* and *XmlTextReader* classes provide much ease and safety over *StreamWriter* and *StreamReader*, by far the easiest way to read and write XML is with methods in the *XmlSerializer* class defined in the *System.Xml.Serialization* namespace. (The term *serialization* refers to the process of converting an object into a transportable form—in this case, a stream of XML.)

The XML just shown exactly parallels the *Person* class. The *FirstName*, *LastName*, and *BirthDate* elements in the XML are nested in the *Person* element just like the *FirstName*, *LastName*, and *BirthDate* properties are members of the *Person* class. Some clever code ought to be able to translate an object of type *Person* into an XML file and back again. That clever code is the *XmlSerializer* class. It sometimes doesn't work quite the way you want, but it's usually worth a try. Keep in mind that you can always fall back on having total control by using *XmlTextWriter* and *XmlTextReader*.

The first step is to create an object of type *XmlSerializer* by specifying the type of the class you want it to work with, for example:

```
XmlSerializer xmlser = new XmlSerializer(typeof(Person));
```

You can then save an object of type *Person* in XML by calling the *Serialize* method. No overload of the *Serialize* method lets you specify just a filename, however. You need at least an object of *Stream*, *XmlWriter*, or *TextWriter* (from which *StreamWriter* descends). There is a considerable amount of flexibility here. If you create an object of type *StringWriter* (which also inherits from *TextWriter*), you can write the XML to a *string* variable. If you create an instance of *NetworkStream* or *MemoryStream* (both of which inherit from *Stream*), you can write the XML to a destination on the network or to a block of memory. If you just want to write a *Person* object named *pers* to an ordinary local file, one simple approach is:

```
StreamWriter sw = new StreamWriter(strFileName);
xmlser.Serialize(sw, pers);
sw.Close();
```

The *Deserialize* method of the *XmlSerializer* class converts XML into an object of the type you specified in the *XmlSerializer* constructor. In the current example, *Deserialize* creates an object of type *Person*. Because *Deserialize* is defined as returning an *object*, you must cast the return value if you're storing that object in an object of type *Person*. Here's some simple code:

```
StreamReader sr = new StreamReader(strFileName);
pers = xmlser.Deserialize(sr) as Person;
sr.Close();
```

As you might guess, the *XmlSerializer* uses reflection to look inside the class you specify in the constructor and examine its members. According to the documentation, *XmlSerializer* actually generates code that is executed outside of your application space. For that reason, any class you want serialized must be defined as *public*. (You might have noticed that I defined the *Person* class that way.)

XmlSerializer serializes and deserializes only fields and properties that are defined as *public*, and it ignores any read-only or write-only members. When deserializing, the *Deserialize* method creates an object of the proper type using the class's parameterless constructor and then sets the object's properties from the XML elements. For that reason, the class must have a parameterless constructor (which the *Person* class does).

If any serializable members of the class are complex data types (that is, other classes or structures), those classes and structures must also be defined as public and have parameterless constructors. The *XmlSerializer* will treat the public read/write properties and fields of these other classes and structures as nested elements. *XmlSerializer* can also handle properties that are arrays and *List* objects.

The *System.Xml.Serialization* namespace also provides a number of attributes that you can use to control the serialization and deserialization process. For example, if you include the attribute

```
[XmlIgnore]
```

before any public read-write field or property, that field or property will *not* be serialized.

We are now ready for the *DataEntryNoBinding* class, which completes the *DataEntryNoBinding* project. The project requires a reference to the *System.Xml* dynamic-link library in addition to the others normally used with Windows Forms programming. The program creates an object of type *PersonPanelNoBinding* and a File menu with New, Open, and Save. The *XmlSerializer* is defined as a field because it is used in both the File Open and File Save event handlers.

```
DataEntryNoBinding.cs
//-------------------------------------------------
// DataEntryNoBinding.cs (c) 2005 by Charles Petzold
//-------------------------------------------------
using System;
using System.Drawing;
using System.IO;
using System.Windows.Forms;
using System.Xml.Serialization;

class DataEntryNoBinding : Form
{
    const string strFilter = "Person XML files (*.PersonXml)|" +
                             "*.PersonXml|All files (*.*)|*.*";
    PersonPanelNoBinding personpnl;
    XmlSerializer xmlser = new XmlSerializer(typeof(Person));
```

```csharp
[STAThread]
public static void Main()
{
    Application.EnableVisualStyles();
    Application.Run(new DataEntryNoBinding());
}
public DataEntryNoBinding()
{
    Text = "Simple Data Entry (No Binding)";

    // Create the panel.
    personpnl = new PersonPanelNoBinding();
    personpnl.Parent = this;
    personpnl.Dock = DockStyle.Fill;

    // Create the menu.
    MenuStrip menu = new MenuStrip();
    menu.Parent = this;
    ToolStripMenuItem item = (ToolStripMenuItem)menu.Items.Add("&File");
    item.DropDownItems.Add("&New", null, FileNewOnClick);
    item.DropDownItems.Add("&Open...", null, FileOpenOnClick);
    item.DropDownItems.Add("Save &As...", null, FileSaveAsOnClick);
}
void FileNewOnClick(object objSrc, EventArgs args)
{
    personpnl.Person = new Person();
}
void FileOpenOnClick(object objSrc, EventArgs args)
{
    OpenFileDialog dlg = new OpenFileDialog();
    dlg.Filter = strFilter;

    if (dlg.ShowDialog() == DialogResult.OK)
    {
        StreamReader sr = new StreamReader(dlg.FileName);
        personpnl.Person = xmlser.Deserialize(sr) as Person;
        sr.Close();
    }
}
void FileSaveAsOnClick(object objSrc, EventArgs args)
{
    SaveFileDialog dlg = new SaveFileDialog();
    dlg.Filter = strFilter;

    if (dlg.ShowDialog() == DialogResult.OK)
    {
        StreamWriter sw = new StreamWriter(dlg.FileName);
        xmlser.Serialize(sw, personpnl.Person);
        sw.Close();
    }
}
}
```

And here it is with some data filled in:

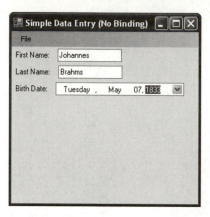

You'll want to experiment with filling in the fields, saving files, and reloading them, and perhaps examining them in NotePad, Internet Explorer, or some other XML viewer or editor. Files are saved with an extension of PersonXml.

The File New and File Open event handlers both create a new object of type *Person* (the New handler directly and the Open handler implicitly) and set that object to the *Person* property of *PersonPanelNoBinding*. The File Save event handler obtains the *Person* property from *Person-PanelNoBinding* and saves it to a file. Only when the File New or File Open event handler executes does the program create an object of type *Person*. This accounts for a peculiarity in the program: When you first run the program, the *DateTimePicker* displays the current date. When you select New from the File menu, the date January 1, 1800, is displayed. The current date is what *DateTimePicker* displays when its *Value* property hasn't been initialized. The other date is what the *BirthDate* field of the *Person* class is initialized to when a new *Person* object is created. To avoid this difference, you might want to have code in the constructor of *Data-EntryNoBinding* to initialize the *PersonPanelNoBinding* object with a new object of type *Person*:

```
personpnl.Person = new Person();
```

Or you could simulate a call to the File New event handler from the constructor:

```
FileNewOnClick(null, EventArgs.Empty);
```

The latter approach is ideal if the event handler has multiple lines of code.

Not Quite Bindable

For what it does, the *DataEntryNoBinding* program works fine. But I'm not happy with it. What if I wanted to add a new property? Obviously, I'd have to change the *Person* class. I expect that, and I can live with it. I'd also have to add an additional control or two to the panel. That job, too, is to be expected. But I better not forget to also add a couple lines of code to both the *set* and *get* accessors of the *Person* property of the panel. That kind of maintenance, it seems, should be part of what goes away when you start using data bindings.

So let's try to add a data binding to *PersonPanelNoBinding*, and see what happens.

Data bindings for the two *TextBox* controls and the *DateTimePicker* would look like this:

```
txtboxFirstName.DataBindings.Add("Text", pers, "FirstName");
txtboxLastName.DataBindings.Add("Text", pers, "LastName");
dtPicker.DataBindings.Add("Value", pers, "BirthDate");
```

The second argument to the *Add* method is an object of type *Person*. This object must exist (that is, *pers* must be non-*null*) when the *Binding* object is created by the *Add* method. You'll probably want to define it as a field:

```
Person pers = new Person();
```

The *Person* property is now simplified to something like what we were hoping for:

```
public Person Person
{
    set { pers = value; }
    get { return pers; }
}
```

And so we try it out. We enter something into the fields, select Save from the File menu, and examine the resultant XML file, which seems fine. However, the New and Open options don't work at all.

One problem here is that the data binding has no way of knowing when the data source (the *Person* object) changes, so it can't update the controls. We might add *FirstNameChanged*, *Last-NameChanged*, and *BirthDateChanged* events to the *Person* class, but that seems a bit excessive. One possibility is to update the controls manually using this *set* accessor in the *Person* property:

```
set
{
    pers = value;

    foreach (Control ctrl in Controls)
        foreach (Binding bind in ctrl.DataBindings)
            bind.ReadValue();
}
```

This code steps through all the controls in the *Controls* collection of the panel and then through all the *Binding* objects in each control's *DataBindings* collection, and it calls *ReadValue* to update the control from the new data value.

But there's another problem. The bindings we've defined for each of the three controls is *not* to the variable *pers*, but to the *Person* object originally created as a field and stored as *pers*:

```
Person pers = new Person();
```

In the first statement of the *set* accessor, that object is replaced with another one created somewhere in File New or File Open event handlers of the *DataEntryNoBinding* class. What's really required is copying all the fields of the value passed to the accessor into the original *Person* object:

```
set
{
    pers.FirstName = value.FirstName;
    pers.LastName = value.LastName;
    pers.BirthDate = value.BirthDate;

    foreach (Control ctrl in Controls)
        foreach (Binding bind in ctrl.DataBindings)
            bind.ReadValue();
}
```

This code works (finally), but we haven't quite simplified the program to the desired level. Another approach might be to use a single *Person* object throughout the entire program, and to share that object between *PersonPanelNoBinding* and *DataEntryNoBinding*. However, the File New event handler would have to explicitly set all the properties of *Person* to default values, and the File Open handler would involve another copying job.

What we *really* need is an intermediary between the controls and the *Person* object. We need to bind the controls to one object that remains constant throughout the life of the program, and we need to plug various *Person* objects into that *whatever-it-is*.

The magic class we're looking for is called *BindingSource*, which is new in the .NET Framework 2.0. *BindingSource* takes care of this particular job and has versatility to spare.

The *BindingSource* Intermediary

Let's look first at how the panel with the controls can use *BindingSource*. The *PersonPanel* class shown next includes a constructor with a parameter that provides a *BindingSource* object to the class. (Obviously, this *BindingSource* object will be created by the program that also creates the *PersonPanel* object.)

```
PersonPanel.cs
//-------------------------------------------
// PersonPanel.cs (c) 2005 by Charles Petzold
//-------------------------------------------
using System;
using System.Drawing;
using System.Windows.Forms;

class PersonPanel : FlowLayoutPanel
{
    // Constructor.
    public PersonPanel(BindingSource bindsrc)
    {
```

```
Label lbl = new Label();
lbl.Parent = this;
lbl.Text = "First Name: ";
lbl.AutoSize = true;
lbl.Anchor = AnchorStyles.Left;

TextBox txtboxFirstName = new TextBox();
txtboxFirstName.Parent = this;
txtboxFirstName.AutoSize = true;
txtboxFirstName.DataBindings.Add("Text", bindsrc, "FirstName");
txtboxFirstName.DataBindings[0].DataSourceUpdateMode =
    DataSourceUpdateMode.OnPropertyChanged;

this.SetFlowBreak(txtboxFirstName, true);

lbl = new Label();
lbl.Parent = this;
lbl.Text = "Last Name: ";
lbl.AutoSize = true;
lbl.Anchor = AnchorStyles.Left;

TextBox txtboxLastName = new TextBox();
txtboxLastName.Parent = this;
txtboxLastName.AutoSize = true;
txtboxLastName.DataBindings.Add("Text", bindsrc, "LastName");
txtboxLastName.DataBindings[0].DataSourceUpdateMode =
    DataSourceUpdateMode.OnPropertyChanged;

this.SetFlowBreak(txtboxLastName, true);

lbl = new Label();
lbl.Parent = this;
lbl.Text = "Birth Date: ";
lbl.AutoSize = true;
lbl.Anchor = AnchorStyles.Left;

DateTimePicker dtPicker = new DateTimePicker();
dtPicker.Parent = this;
dtPicker.Format = DateTimePickerFormat.Long;
dtPicker.AutoSize = true;
dtPicker.DataBindings.Add("Value", bindsrc, "BirthDate");
dtPicker.DataBindings[0].DataSourceUpdateMode =
    DataSourceUpdateMode.OnPropertyChanged;
    }
}
```

This code includes data bindings for the two *TextBox* controls and the *DateTimePicker*. Here's the first one:

```
txtboxFirstName.DataBindings.Add("Text", bindsrc, "FirstName");
```

The first argument of the *Add* method certainly looks normal: the data is attached to the *Text* property of the *TextBox*. The second argument is the *BindingSource* object passed to the constructor, and the third argument is the string "FirstName," and that seems very peculiar. Although we don't know much about the *BindingSource* class yet, of one thing we can be pretty sure: The *BindingSource* class does *not* define a *FirstName* property. However, as you'll see, we *can* bind the *BindingSource* to an object (of type *Person*, say) that *does* include *FirstName*, *Last-Name*, and *BirthDate* properties, and that's how *BindingSoruce* provides this information. We'll see how this works shortly.

Meanwhile, there's much to admire in *PersonPanel*. It has no moving parts (that is, no event handlers) and no *Person* property. In fact, *PersonPanel* doesn't know anything about the *Person* class. All it knows is that it gets its data from a *BindingSource* object.

The DataEntryWithBinding project has a link to Person.cs and also includes PersonPanel.cs and the following file.

DataEntryWithBinding.cs

```
//---------------------------------------------------
// DataEntryWithBinding.cs (c) 2005 by Charles Petzold
//---------------------------------------------------
using System;
using System.Drawing;
using System.IO;
using System.Windows.Forms;
using System.Xml.Serialization;

class DataEntryWithBinding : Form
{
    const string strFilter = "Person XML files (*.PersonXml)|" +
                            "*.PersonXml|All files (*.*)|*.*";
    XmlSerializer xmlser = new XmlSerializer(typeof(Person));
    BindingSource bindsrc = new BindingSource();

    [STAThread]
    public static void Main()
    {
        Application.EnableVisualStyles();
        Application.Run(new DataEntryWithBinding());
    }
    public DataEntryWithBinding()
    {
        Text = "Simple Data Entry with Binding";

        // Initialize BindingSource object.
        bindsrc.Add(new Person());

        // Create the panel.
        PersonPanel personpnl = new PersonPanel(bindsrc);
        personpnl.Parent = this;
        personpnl.Dock = DockStyle.Fill;

        // Create the menu.
        MenuStrip menu = new MenuStrip();
        menu.Parent = this;
```

```
        ToolStripMenuItem item = (ToolStripMenuItem) menu.Items.Add("&File");
        item.DropDownItems.Add("&New", null, FileNewOnClick);
        item.DropDownItems.Add("&Open...", null, FileOpenOnClick);
        item.DropDownItems.Add("Save &As...", null, FileSaveAsOnClick);
    }
    void FileNewOnClick(object objSrc, EventArgs args)
    {
        bindsrc[0] = new Person();
    }
    void FileOpenOnClick(object objSrc, EventArgs args)
    {
        OpenFileDialog dlg = new OpenFileDialog();
        dlg.Filter = strFilter;

        if (dlg.ShowDialog() == DialogResult.OK)
        {
            StreamReader sr = new StreamReader(dlg.FileName);
            bindsrc[0] = xmlser.Deserialize(sr);
            sr.Close();
        }
    }
    void FileSaveAsOnClick(object objSrc, EventArgs args)
    {
        SaveFileDialog dlg = new SaveFileDialog();
        dlg.Filter = strFilter;

        if (dlg.ShowDialog() == DialogResult.OK)
        {
            StreamWriter sw = new StreamWriter(dlg.FileName);
            xmlser.Serialize(sw, bindsrc[0]);
            sw.Close();
        }
    }
}
```

The *BindingSource* object is defined as a field because it's used in multiple methods in the class:

```
BindingSource bindsrc = new BindingSource();
```

The constructor initializes the *BindingSource* by simply calling the *Add* method with an object of type *Person*:

```
bindsrc.Add(new Person());
```

BindingSource actually maintains a collection of objects of the same type, and the call to this *Add* method establishes that type as *Person*. An alternative to the *Add* method in this program is:

```
bindsrc.DataSource = new Person();
```

In either case, the *BindingSource* now stores a collection of one object of type *Person*. (This particular program doesn't require that *BindingSource* store more than one object, so it never does.) It is now possible for the *BindingSource* object to be passed to the *PersonPanel* constructor:

```
personpnl = new PersonPanel(bindsrc);
```

The data bindings in *PersonPanel* are successful because the *BindingSource* is storing an object of type *Person* and that object has properties named *FirstName*, *LastName*, and *BirthDate*.

Rather than calling the *Add* method of *BindingSource* or setting the *DataSource* to an instance of *Person*, it is also possible to initialize the *BindingSource* object like this before passing it to the *PersonPanel* constructor:

```
bindsrc.DataSource = typeof(Person);
```

The data bindings in *PersonPanel* will be successful even though the *BindingSource* object isn't yet storing any actual objects of type *Person*. It only knows that the type of the objects it will be storing are *Person*. If you actually make this change, you'll see the current date displayed in the *DateTimePicker* rather than January 1, 1800. Also, none of the menu commands will work because they all expect the *BindingSource* to be storing at least one object. You can fix that problem by making this call after setting the *DataSource* property:

```
bindsrc.AddNew();
```

Using reflection, the *BindingSource* will create a new object of type *Person* and add it to its collection.

BindingSource implements an indexer that allows the collection to be referenced like an array. For that reason, the File New command can be implemented simply by setting the first item of the collection (the only item we're using) to a new object of type *Person*:

```
bindsrc[0] = new Person();
```

Similarly, the File Open handler sets this item from the return value of the *Deserialize* call:

```
bindsrc[0] = xmlser.Deserialize(sr);
```

Notice that no casting is required as in the previous program. For either File New or File Open, the controls are updated to reflect the new values. The File Save handler references the first item in the collection:

```
xmlser.Serialize(sw, bindsrc[0]);
```

Obviously, by storing only *one* object of type *Person*, we're not taking full advantage of *BindingSource*. Much of *BindingSource* is devoted to maintaining a collection of objects. The class has methods to *Add* and *Remove* items, *Find* particular items based on the values of certain properties, and to apply a sort to the items.

BindingSource also keeps track of a *current* item of the collection, which is indicated by the *Position* property (an integer index) and the *Current* property (an object). Calls to the *MoveNext* and *MovePrevious* methods of *BindingSource* change which item is the current one. Typically, a program lets the user page through the objects, edit them, add a new object, or delete an existing object. Properties and methods of *BindingSource* let you do this.

You can implement this logic yourself, or you can use the *BindingNavigator* control. The *BindingNavigator* inherits from *ToolStrip*, and it is the only custom toolbar provided in the Windows Forms library.

Navigating the Data

The first job is to decide how we want our multiple-person data to be stored. Here's one possibility:

```
<PersonFile>
  <CreationDate>2005-08-13T14:44:32.7528768-04:00</CreationDate>
  <Persons>
    <Person>
      <FirstName>Johannes</FirstName>
      <LastName>Brahms</LastName>
      <BirthDate>1833-05-07T00:00:00</BirthDate>
    </Person>
    <Person>
      <FirstName>Franz</FirstName>
      <LastName>Schubert</LastName>
      <BirthDate>1797-01-31T00:00:00</BirthDate>
    </Person>
  </Persons>
</PersonFile>
```

The root element is PersonFile. It contains two sub-elements named CreationDate and Persons (plural). Within Persons are multiple Person (singular) elements. This format allows us to continue using the *Person* class. We also need a new class named *PersonFile*.

```
PersonFile.cs
//-------------------------------------------
// PersonFile.cs (c) 2005 by Charles Petzold
//-------------------------------------------
using System;
using System.Collections.Generic;

public class PersonFile
{
    DateTime dtCreation = DateTime.Now;
    List<Person> persons = new List<Person>();

    public DateTime CreationDate
    {
        get { return dtCreation; }
```

```
        set { dtCreation = value; }
    }

    public List<Person> Persons
    {
        get { return persons; }
        set { persons = value; }
    }
}
```

The *Persons* property is defined as a *List* of *Person* objects. This class happens to serialize in exactly the format shown above. (It could be that you prefer an XML format where multiple Person elements are sub-elements of PersonFile, and the Persons element doesn't exist. In that case, you can preface the definition of the *Persons* property with the attribute *[XmlElement("Person")]*.

The DataEntryWithNavigation project includes Person.cs, PersonFile.cs, PersonPanel.cs, and the following file.

DataEntryWithNavigation.cs

```
//-------------------------------------------------------
// DataEntryWithNavigation.cs (c) 2005 by Charles Petzold
//-------------------------------------------------------
using System;
using System.Drawing;
using System.IO;
using System.Windows.Forms;
using System.Xml.Serialization;

class DataEntryWithNavigation : Form
{
    const string strFilter = "Person File files (*.PersonFileXml)|" +
                             "*.PersonFileXml|All files (*.*)|*.*";
    XmlSerializer xmlser = new XmlSerializer(typeof(PersonFile));
    BindingSource bindsrc = new BindingSource();

    [STAThread]
    public static void Main()
    {
        Application.EnableVisualStyles();
        Application.Run(new DataEntryWithNavigation());
    }
    public DataEntryWithNavigation()
    {
        Text = "Simple Data Entry with Navigation";

        // Initialize the BindingSource.
        FileNewOnClick(null, EventArgs.Empty);

        // Create the panel.
        PersonPanel personpnl = new PersonPanel(bindsrc);
        personpnl.Parent = this;
        personpnl.Dock = DockStyle.Fill;
```

```
        // Create the menu.
        MenuStrip menu = new MenuStrip();
        menu.Parent = this;
        ToolStripMenuItem item = (ToolStripMenuItem) menu.Items.Add("&File");
        item.DropDownItems.Add("&New", null, FileNewOnClick);
        item.DropDownItems.Add("&Open...", null, FileOpenOnClick);
        item.DropDownItems.Add("Save &As...", null, FileSaveAsOnClick);

        // Create the BindingNavigator.
        BindingNavigator bindnav = new BindingNavigator(true);
        bindnav.Parent = this;
        bindnav.Dock = DockStyle.Bottom;
        bindnav.BindingSource = bindsrc;
    }
    void FileNewOnClick(object objSrc, EventArgs args)
    {
        PersonFile persfile = new PersonFile();
        persfile.Persons.Add(new Person());

        bindsrc.DataSource = persfile;
        bindsrc.DataMember = "Persons";
    }
    void FileOpenOnClick(object objSrc, EventArgs args)
    {
        OpenFileDialog dlg = new OpenFileDialog();
        dlg.Filter = strFilter;

        if (dlg.ShowDialog() == DialogResult.OK)
        {
            StreamReader sr = new StreamReader(dlg.FileName);
            bindsrc.DataSource = xmlser.Deserialize(sr);
            sr.Close();
        }
    }
    void FileSaveAsOnClick(object objSrc, EventArgs args)
    {
        SaveFileDialog dlg = new SaveFileDialog();
        dlg.Filter = strFilter;

        if (dlg.ShowDialog() == DialogResult.OK)
        {
            StreamWriter sw = new StreamWriter(dlg.FileName);
            xmlser.Serialize(sw, bindsrc.DataSource);
            sw.Close();
        }
    }
}
```

As in the previous program, the *BindingSource* object is created as a field, but now the constructor of this class calls the File New event handler to initialize the *BindingSource* object. That method first creates an object of type *PersonFile* with a single *Person* object in the *Persons* collection.

```
PersonFile persfile = new PersonFile();
persfile.Persons.Add(new Person());
```

That *PersonFile* object is then set to the *DataSource* property of the *BindingSource*:

```
bindsrc.DataSource = persfile;
```

However, we're really only interested in having the *BindingSource* maintain part of this object, which is the collection of *Person* objects identified by the *Persons* property. That *Persons* property (in text string form) is set to the *DataMember* property of the *BindingSource*:

```
bindsrc.DataMember = "Persons";
```

The File Open handler simply resets the *DataSource* property to the deserialized XML file:

```
bindsrc.DataSource = xmlser.Deserialize(sr);
```

Similarly, the File Save handler serializes the *PersonFile* object saved in the *DataSource* property:

```
xmlser.Serialize(sw, bindsrc.DataSource);
```

Notice also that this program saves files with the extension PersonFileXml rather than Person-Xml. If you try to load a PersonXml file into this program, an exception will be raised. A real-life program would put the *Deserialize* call in a *try* block to catch any problems that might arise with invalid files.

The final statements of the *DataEntryWithNavigation* constructor create an object of type *Bind-ingNavigator* and dock it at the bottom of the client area:

```
BindingNavigator bindnav = new BindingNavigator(true);
bindnav.Parent = this;
bindnav.Dock = DockStyle.Bottom;
bindnav.BindingSource = bindsrc;
```

The final statement sets the *BindingSource* property of the *BindingNavigator* to the *Binding-Source* object. (It's like they were made for each other.) And here's what it looks like:

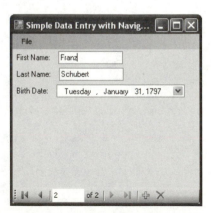

The buttons on the *BindingNavigator* let you move to the beginning or end, step backward or forward, add a new item, or delete the current item. These buttons are customizable, of course, and because *BindingNavigator* derives from *ToolStrip*, you can add other buttons and allow the user to move the control to another area of the window.

You can, of course, implement your own navigation. The left two buttons on the *Binding-Navigator* simply call the *MoveFirst* and *MovePrevious* methods of *BindingSource*. The edit field shows the *Position* property and the text field that follows shows the *Count* property. The remaining four buttons on *BindingNavigator* call the *BindingSource* methods *MoveNext*, *Move-Last*, *AddNew*, and *RemoveCurrent*.

The *BindingNavigator* provides access to the *ToolStripItem* objects that it creates on its surface. For example, if you feel that the Delete button is too close to the New button and might accidentally be clicked, you can shift the button over using

```
bindnav.DeleteItem.Alignment = ToolStripItemAlignment.Right;
```

Direct to Data

Going beyond the DataEntryWithNavigation program is also possible. Although that program might seem about as tidy as we can imagine, and it shows the basics of data entry and editing, there's potentially another step. If you think about it, once we have an XML file of the desired format, the *Person* and *PersonFile* classes shouldn't be necessary. It should be possible for a program to get all the information about the data from the XML and go from there. (Well, not quite. Because everything in an XML file is stored as strings, the typing is not as strong as we might require. There is no real way of knowing just from looking at the XML that the Birth-Date element should really be a *DateTime* object. You'll probably need an XML Schema to help define the types.)

At that point, however, you can make use of the *DataSet* class defined in the *System.Data* namespace. *DataSet* has two methods named *ReadXml* and *WriteXml*, and, just as importantly, you can set a *DataSet* object to the *DataSource* property of the *BindingSource* object. But exploring the *DataSet* class is just a bit beyond the scope of this book.

The *DataGridView* Control

The *DataGridView* control is enormous. It implements 118 of its own events in addition to the 69 events it inherits from *Control*, and yet, it also seems to be a work in progress. Already a cottage industry has sprung up supplying enhancements, and I'm sure that one day someone will write a book with the title *Programming DataGridView*. Obviously, all I can do here is scratch the surface.

The *DataGridView* can often serve as a complete solution for data viewing or data entry. The control organizes cells in a grid of rows and columns. (For purposes of class hierarchy, rows and columns are both types of *bands*.) There is a header above each column and a "header" at the left of each row. In database terminology, columns are fields, and rows are records.

DataGridView is extensibly customizable, but I will be focusing more on some simple basic uses.

DataGridView and Text

Let's look at a simple implementation of *DataGridView* that allows the entry of names and e-mail addresses.

```
SimpleDataGridView.cs
//-----------------------------------------------------
// SimpleDataGridView.cs (c) 2005 by Charles Petzold
//-----------------------------------------------------
using System;
using System.Drawing;
using System.Windows.Forms;

class SimpleDataGridView : Form
{
    [STAThread]
    public static void Main()
    {
        Application.EnableVisualStyles();
        Application.Run(new SimpleDataGridView());
    }
    public SimpleDataGridView()
    {
        Text = "Simple DataGridView";

        DataGridView grid = new DataGridView();
        grid.Parent = this;
        grid.AutoSize = true;
        grid.Dock = DockStyle.Fill;
        grid.ColumnCount = 3;
        grid.Columns[0].HeaderText = "First Name";
        grid.Columns[1].HeaderText = "Last Name";
        grid.Columns[2].HeaderText = "Email Address";
    }
}
```

After setting a few common properties (*Parent*, *AutoSize*, and *Dock*), the program initializes the *DataGridView* control by setting a number of columns and the text that appears in the column headings.

DataGridView has both *ColumnCount* and *RowCount* properties, and properties named *Columns* and *Rows*. *Columns* is an object of type *DataGridViewColumnCollection*, which is a collection of *DataGridViewColumn* objects. Generally, the *ColumnCount* is set during initialization of the control, either explicitly (as in this program) or as a result of adding columns to the control. The code to set the *ColumnCount* and the *HeaderText* can be replaced with the following:

```
grid.Columns.Add("", "First Name");
grid.Columns.Add("", "Last Name");
grid.Columns.Add("", "Email Address");
```

Both blocks of code result in the creation of three *DataGridViewColumn* objects. The first argument to the *Add* method becomes the *Name* property of the *DataGridViewColumn* object. I'll give that property actual values and make use of it shortly.

Following this initialization, the *DataGridView* displays itself like this:

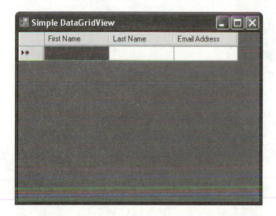

Initially, the *DataGridView* has one row capped by column headers. Each row is preceded by a "row header" at the left that shows a little graphic. The triangular arrow indicates the current row—the row you're typing in. The asterisk indicates a new row in which nothing has been entered. As soon as you start typing in the first cell, a new row is created:

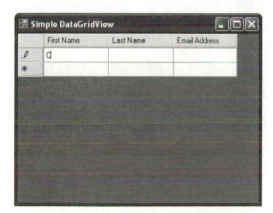

The little pencil at the left indicates that a cell is in edit mode. Only when you press Tab to go to the next cell (or an arrow key to move to another cell) are the typed contents of the first cell potentially validated and saved by the control in its cell collection. (The contents are said to be "committed.") Now the second column has the input focus, and the user can begin to enter text there:

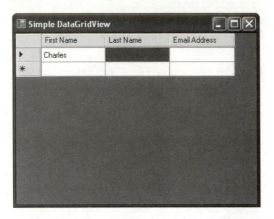

At this point, the *RowCount* property of the control would indicate two, and the *Rows* collection stores two, *DataGridViewRow* objects. However, a property of *DataGridViewRow* named *IsNewRow* indicates whether one of the rows is a new row (indicated visually by the asterisk) in which nothing has been entered. After you've entered text in the last column, a press of the Tab key moves the focus down to the second row, and you can keep entering data pretty much as long as you want.

A program can assign the *RowCount* property of the *DataGridView* control to give the control a certain number of initial rows. It can also use the *Add* method of the *Rows* collection to assign explicit values to the cells, but this is probably not a common way to initialize the control.

The *DataGridView* implements a two-dimensional indexer. If *grid* is an object of *DataGridView*, the expression

```
grid[col][row]
```

is an object of type *DataGridViewCell* at the specified column and row. The *col* index must be less than *ColumnCount*, and *row* less than *RowCount*. The *Value* property of *DataGridViewCell* is an object of type *object* that indicates the value of the cell. In the simple program just shown, the *Value* of each cell is *null* until text has been entered and committed, in which case *Value* becomes the *string* object displayed in the cell.

You can also index the *DataGridView* using the name of a column, for example:

```
grid["first"][row]
```

You would have needed to assign the *Name* property of the column at some point, perhaps like this:

```
grid.Columns[0].Name = "first";
```

Or you could have done it in an *Add* method:

```
grid.Columns.Add("first", "First Name");
```

If all you need out of *DataGridView* is the ability to enter text strings, you'll probably do quite well. However, most data requirements are more complex than that. Text is important, of course, but so are dates and other data types.

The Class Hierarchy

As you can confirm by browsing the documentation of the *System.Windows.Forms* namespace, many classes begin with the prefix *DataGridView* and are used in connection with *DataGrid-View* controls. *DataGridView* itself inherits directly from *Control*. Many other important classes inherit from *DataGridViewElement*, as shown in this partial class hierarchy:

object

    DataGridViewElement

        DataGridViewBand

            DataGridViewColumn

            DataGridViewRow

        DataGridViewCell (abstract)

A *DataGridView* control that displays three columns and four rows of data stores 3 instances of *DataGridViewColumn*, 4 instances of *DataGridViewRow*, and 20 instances of *DataGridView-Cell*. That 20 includes the 12 data cells, plus three column headers, plus four row headers (which actually appear at the left of each row) and a top-left header in the corner. These headers are objects of classes that descend from *DataGridViewCell*:

DataGridViewCell (abstract)

    DataGridViewHeaderCell

        DataGridViewColumnHeaderCell

            DataGridViewTopLeftHeaderCell

        DataGridViewRowHeaderCell

DataGridViewCell has six other descendents for various types of data cells:

DataGridViewCell (abstract)

    DataGridViewButtonCell

    DataGridViewCheckBoxCell

    DataGridViewComboBoxCell

    DataGridViewImageCell

DataGridViewLinkCell

DataGridViewTextBoxCell

By default, data cells are of type *DataGridViewTextBoxCell*, which of course are designed for entering text. If you want cells of other types, you need to work at it a bit.

It is very, very common for all data cells in a particular column to be associated with the same kind of data. Therefore, rather than require the program to set the type of the data cell on a cell-by-cell basis, it is possible to set the data type of an entire column using these descendents of *DataGridViewColumn*:

DataGridViewColumn

 DataGridViewButtonColumn

 DataGridViewCheckBoxColumn

 DataGridViewComboBoxColumn

 DataGridViewImageColumn

 DataGridViewLinkColumn

 DataGridViewTextBoxColumn

The default is the last one on the list.

Expanding Our Data Horizons

Let's begin constructing a database just a little broader than the one we worked with earlier in this chapter. A class named *School* consists of a collection of *Student* objects.

```
School.cs
//---------------------------------------
// School.cs (c) 2005 by Charles Petzold
//---------------------------------------
using System.Collections.Generic;

public class School
{
    List<Student> studentlist = new List<Student>();

    public List<Student> Students
    {
        set { studentlist = value; }
        get { return studentlist; }
    }
}
```

Each student is an instance of the *Student* class.

Student.cs

```csharp
//------------------------------------------
// Student.cs (c) 2005 by Charles Petzold
//------------------------------------------
using System;

public class Student
{
    CourtesyTitle court = CourtesyTitle.None;
    string strFirstName = "<first name>";
    string strLastName = "<last name>";
    DateTime dtBirth = new DateTime(1985, 1,1);
    bool bEnrolled = false;

    public CourtesyTitle Courtesy
    {
        set { court = value; }
        get { return court; }
    }
    public string FirstName
    {
        set { strFirstName = value; }
        get { return strFirstName; }
    }
    public string LastName
    {
        set { strLastName = value; }
        get { return strLastName; }
    }
    public DateTime BirthDate
    {
        set { dtBirth = value; }
        get { return dtBirth; }
    }
    public bool Enrolled
    {
        set { bEnrolled = value; }
        get { return bEnrolled; }
    }
}
```

The *Courtesy* property is a member of the *CourtesyTitle* enumeration.

CourtesyTitle.cs

```csharp
//------------------------------------------------
// CourtesyTitle.cs (c) 2005 by Charles Petzold
//------------------------------------------------

public enum CourtesyTitle
{
    None,
    Mr,
```

```
        Ms,
        Mrs,
        Miss
    }
```

So, with the *Student* class, we're dealing with objects of type *string*, *bool*, *CourtesyTitle*, and *DateTime*. We already know how to create a *DataGridView* control for entering *string* values. A *DataGridViewCheckBoxColumn* might be good for *bool* values, and a *DataGridViewComboBoxColumn* might be good for picking a value from the *CourtesyTitle* enumeration. For the *Birth-Date* property, we'd probably want a *DataGridViewDateTimePickerColumn*, but unfortunately, that class does not exist. For now we'll have to make do with entering dates in text form.

The strategy here is first to create a *DataGridView* control, and then to explicitly create objects of type *DataGridViewComboBoxColumn*, *DataGridViewTextBoxColumn*, and *DataGrid-ViewCheckBoxColumn*, and add those objects to the *Columns* collection of the control. This program is called UnboundDataGridView because the control is not bound to a data source. In the next descendent of this program, we'll be putting data into the control and extracting it "manually."

UnboundDataGridView.cs
```csharp
//-----------------------------------------------------
// UnboundDataGridView.cs (c) 2005 by Charles Petzold
//-----------------------------------------------------
using System;
using System.Drawing;
using System.Windows.Forms;

class UnboundDataGridView : Form
{
    protected DataGridView grid;

    [STAThread]
    public static void Main()
    {
        Application.EnableVisualStyles();
        Application.Run(new UnboundDataGridView());
    }
    public UnboundDataGridView()
    {
        Text = "Unbound DataGridView";
        Width *= 2;

        grid = new DataGridView();
        grid.Parent = this;
        grid.AutoSize = true;
        grid.Dock = DockStyle.Fill;

        DataGridViewComboBoxColumn colCombo = new DataGridViewComboBoxColumn();
        colCombo.Name = "Courtesy";
        colCombo.HeaderText = "Courtesy";
        colCombo.DataSource = Enum.GetValues(typeof(CourtesyTitle));
```

```
        colCombo.ValueType = typeof(CourtesyTitle);
        grid.Columns.Add(colCombo);

        DataGridViewTextBoxColumn colText = new DataGridViewTextBoxColumn();
        colText.Name = "FirstName";
        colText.HeaderText = "First Name";
        grid.Columns.Add(colText);

        colText = new DataGridViewTextBoxColumn();
        colText.Name = "LastName";
        colText.HeaderText = "Last Name";
        grid.Columns.Add(colText);

        colText = new DataGridViewTextBoxColumn();
        colText.Name = "BirthDate";
        colText.HeaderText = "Birth Date";
        grid.Columns.Add(colText);

        DataGridViewCheckBoxColumn colCheck = new DataGridViewCheckBoxColumn();
        colCheck.Name = "Enrolled";
        colCheck.HeaderText = "Enrolled?";
        grid.Columns.Add(colCheck);
    }
}
```

Although the UnboundDataGridView project includes the School.cs and Student.cs source code files, they are not required by this program and serve only as reference in defining the columns of the control. As you'll note, each of the columns gets assigned a *Name* property that is the same as the corresponding property in the *Student* class, and a slightly friendlier *HeaderText* property for the actual display. Notice also that the *DataSource* property of the *DataGridViewComboBoxColumn* is assigned an array of the *CourtesyTitle* enumeration members. When using enumeration members in the combo box, the *ValueType* property must also be set to the type of the enumeration.

And here's the program running with one row entered and the combo box pulled down for beginning the second row:

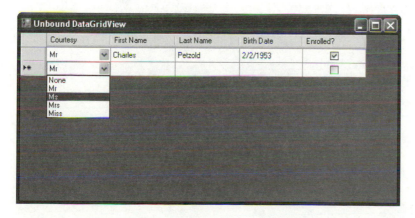

Saving to XML

The next step, of course, is to implement a File menu, save the entered data to an XML file using serialization of the *School* class, and then load the data back in. The major hitch is that fourth column, which is a string that must be converted to a *DateTime* object. The static *DateTime.Parse* method does that job, and it will accept a date in any of several formats, but it will throw an exception if the date isn't acceptable. We really should be verifying proper date values at the time they're entered. (Don't worry. We'll fix that problem eventually.)

The *UndboundDataGridViewWithFileIO* class inherits from *UnboundDataGridView* and implements File New, File Open, and File Save As commands. The files are saved with an extension of StudentXml. The UnboundDataGridViewWithFileIO project includes links to all the files in the UnboundDataGridView project plus the following file.

```
UnboundDataGridViewWithFileIO.cs
//-------------------------------------------------------------
// UnboundDataGridViewWithFileIO.cs (c) 2005 by Charles Petzold
//-------------------------------------------------------------
using System;
using System.Drawing;
using System.IO;
using System.Windows.Forms;
using System.Xml.Serialization;

class UnboundDataGridViewWithFileIO : UnboundDataGridView
{
    const string strFilter = "School files (*.SchoolXml)|" +
                             "*.SchoolXml|All files (*.*)|*.*";
    XmlSerializer xmlser = new XmlSerializer(typeof(School));

    [STAThread]
    public new static void Main()
    {
        Application.EnableVisualStyles();
        Application.Run(new UnboundDataGridViewWithFileIO());
    }
    public UnboundDataGridViewWithFileIO()
    {
        Text = "Unbound DataGridView with File IO";

        // Create the menu.
        MenuStrip menu = new MenuStrip();
        menu.Parent = this;
        ToolStripMenuItem item = (ToolStripMenuItem) menu.Items.Add("&File");
        item.DropDownItems.Add("&New", null, FileNewOnClick);
        item.DropDownItems.Add("&Open...", null, FileOpenOnClick);
        item.DropDownItems.Add("Save &As...", null, FileSaveAsOnClick);
    }
    void FileNewOnClick(object objSrc, EventArgs args)
    {
        grid.Rows.Clear();
```

```csharp
}
void FileOpenOnClick(object objSrc, EventArgs args)
{
    OpenFileDialog dlg = new OpenFileDialog();
    dlg.Filter = strFilter;

    if (dlg.ShowDialog() == DialogResult.OK)
    {
        // Read the School object in as XML.
        StreamReader sr = new StreamReader(dlg.FileName);
        School sch = (School) xmlser.Deserialize(sr);
        sr.Close();

        // Clear the existing rows from the DataGridView.
        grid.Rows.Clear();

        // Add rows to the DataGridView for each student.
        foreach (Student sdt in sch.Students)
        {
            int index = grid.Rows.Add();

            grid["Courtesy", index].Value = sdt.Courtesy;
            grid["FirstName", index].Value = sdt.FirstName;
            grid["LastName", index].Value = sdt.LastName;
            grid["BirthDate", index].Value =
                                    sdt.BirthDate.ToShortDateString();
            grid["Enrolled", index].Value = sdt.Enrolled;
        }
    }
}
void FileSaveAsOnClick(object objSrc, EventArgs args)
{
    SaveFileDialog dlg = new SaveFileDialog();
    dlg.Filter = strFilter;

    if (dlg.ShowDialog() == DialogResult.OK)
    {
        // End any editing still in progress.
        grid.EndEdit();

        // Create a new School object.
        School sch = new School();

        // Add Student objects from rows in the DataGridView.
        foreach (DataGridViewRow row in grid.Rows)
        {
            if (row.IsNewRow)
                continue;

            Student sdt = new Student();
            sdt.Courtesy = (CourtesyTitle) row.Cells["Courtesy"].Value;
            sdt.FirstName = (string) row.Cells["FirstName"].Value;
            sdt.LastName = (string)row.Cells["LastName"].Value;
            sdt.BirthDate =
```

```
                        DateTime.Parse((string) row.Cells["BirthDate"].Value);
            sdt.Enrolled = (bool)row.Cells["Enrolled"].Value;

            sch.Students.Add(sdt);
        }

        // Write the School object out as XML.
        StreamWriter sw = new StreamWriter(dlg.FileName);
        xmlser.Serialize(sw, sch);
        sw.Close();
    }
  }
}
```

Here's what I want you to do: Enter at least two complete rows. Select a courtesy title from the combo box, enter a first name and last name, and enter a valid date in the format shown in the screen shot shown earlier. If you want to have the check box be unchecked, click it (either with the mouse or by pressing the spacebar) and click it again to turn it off. If you don't click it at least once, the cell considers itself to be uninitialized, and you won't be able to tab down to another row. At the end of the second or third record, leave the highlight sitting in the check box cell. Select Save As from the File menu and specify a name. If you've been good about entering the data, the program will not go down with an unhandled exception. Consider yourself lucky.

Let's look at the Save As logic first. After obtaining a filename, the method terminates any cell editing that might still be going on in the control:

```
grid.EndEdit();
```

For this particular program, I told you to leave the highlight in the cell with the check box. If you've just tabbed to that cell for the first time, it will have no value. The *Value* property of the *DataGridViewCell* object will be *null*. Even if you've checked the check box, you'll still be in edit mode. (See the pencil at the left?) Later on in the Save As logic, that *Value* property is cast to a *bool*, and that won't work if the *Value* is *null*. The call to *EndEdit* commits the changes you've made to the cell.

The Save As logic then creates a new object of type *School* and loops through all the rows in the *DataGridView* control. Skipping the new row, the method creates an object of type *Student* for each row and sets the properties from the cell *Value* properties. (It accesses the cells by indexing the *Cells* property in the *DataGridViewRow* object.) This is straightforward except for the Birth Date column, which is a string that must be passed to *DateTime.Parse*. Each *Student* object is then added to the *Students* collection of *School*. The *School* object is then serialized as XML.

The File Open logic reverses that. It creates a new *School* object by deserializing the XML. For each *Student* object in the *Students* list, a new row is created in the *DataGridView*, and the columns of that row are set from the properties of the student.

Validation and Initialization

You'll surely agree that the previous program simply should not crash as much as it does. One big problem is the date. If the date is not in a valid format, the *DateTime.Parse* method will raise an exception. It would be very nice for the program to catch that exception and deal with it gracefully. But you don't want the program alerting you to date formatting problems when you're saving the file. You want to be alerted much earlier when the cursor is still sitting in the cell. This is a problem of *validation*.

Suppose you fill in a proper date but leave the cursor sitting in the Birth Date field while you select Save As from the menu. The value in the check-box cell will be *null*, and an exception will be raised when that is cast to a *bool*. If you don't bother selecting a courtesy title from the combo box, that cell will also be *null*, and consequently will raise an exception. These are both problems of *initialization*.

We can deal with these two problems by installing event handlers for two of the many, many events that *DataGridView* implements. These are *OnDefaultValuesNeeded* (which solves the initialization problem) and *OnValidating*. The following file is part of the UnboundDataGrid-ViewWithValidation project that includes all the earlier files in this exercise.

```
UnboundDataGridViewWithValidation.cs
//-------------------------------------------------------------------
// UnboundDataGridViewWithValidation.cs (c) 2005 by Charles Petzold
//-------------------------------------------------------------------
using System;
using System.Drawing;
using System.Windows.Forms;

class UnboundDataGridViewwithValidation: UnboundDataGridViewwithFileIO
{
    [STAThread]
    public new static void Main()
    {
        Application.EnableVisualStyles();
        Application.Run(new UnboundDataGridViewwithValidation());
    }
    public UnboundDataGridViewwithValidation()
    {
        Text = "Unbound DataGridView with Validation";

        grid.DefaultValuesNeeded += OnDefaultValuesNeeded;
        grid.CellValidating += OnValidating;
    }
    void OnDefaultValuesNeeded(object objSrc, DataGridViewRowEventArgs args)
    {
        // Create Student object with default values.
        Student sdt = new Student();

        args.Row.Cells["Courtesy"].Value = sdt.Courtesy;
        args.Row.Cells["FirstName"].Value = sdt.FirstName;
```

```
            args.Row.Cells["LastName"].Value = sdt.LastName;
            args.Row.Cells["BirthDate"].Value = sdt.BirthDate.ToShortDateString();
            args.Row.Cells["Enrolled"].Value = sdt.Enrolled;
        }
        void OnValidating(object objSrc, DataGridViewCellValidatingEventArgs args)
        {
            DataGridView grid = objSrc as DataGridView;
            DateTime dtResult;

            grid.Rows[args.RowIndex].ErrorText = "";

            if (args.ColumnIndex != grid.Columns["BirthDate"].Index)
                return;

            // Check if the BirthDate value parses.
            if (!DateTime.TryParse(args.FormattedValue.ToString(), out dtResult))
            {
                args.Cancel = true;
                grid.Rows[args.RowIndex].ErrorText =
                    "Enter the date like: September 4, 1985\r\n" +
                    "or: 9/4/1985";
            }
        }
    }
}
```

The *DefaultValuesNeeded* event handler delivers a new *DataGridViewRow* object named *Row* and requests that it be initialized. The event handler simply creates a new *Student* object (which itself initializes the properties of the object) and sets the row from those.

The event handler for *Validating* is interested only in the column with a *Name* property of "Birth-Date." If the *TryParse* method of *DateTime* fails to convert the date, the handler sets the *Cancel* property of the event arguments to *true* and the *ErrorText* property of the row to a helpful hint.

Now when you run the program, the Courtesy and Birth Date columns are initialized with valid values. If you enter an invalid date, you can't move the input focus from that cell and a red icon with an exclamation point appears at the row header:

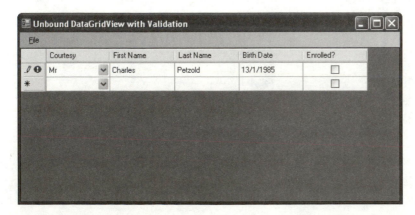

Passing the mouse pointer over the icon shows a ToolTip containing the *ErrorText*. It's satisfactory, I suppose, but what we really, really, really need is a *DateTimePicker* control in the *DataGridView*.

Implementing a Calendar Column

I mentioned that there is no *DataGridViewDateTimePickerColumn*. However, there does exist a topic included with the .NET Framework 2.0 documentation titled "How to: Host Controls in Windows Forms DataGridView Cells," which shows precisely what we need. I blatantly stole the source code from that topic and separated it into three files for the classes *CalendarEditingControl* (which derives from *DateTimePicker* and implements the *IDataGridViewEditingControl* interface), *CalendarCell* (which derives from *DataGridViewTextBoxCell*), and *CalendarColumn* (which derives from *DataGridViewColumn*). Those three files are included with the downloadable source code for this book. Those three files—plus CourtesyTitle.cs—are part of the UnboundDataGridViewWithCalendar project along with the following file.

```
UnboundDataGridViewWithCalendar.cs
//-----------------------------------------------------------------
// UnboundDataGridViewWithCalendar.cs (c) 2005 by Charles Petzold
//-----------------------------------------------------------------
using System;
using System.Drawing;
using System.Windows.Forms;

class UnboundDataGridViewWithCalendar: Form
{
    [STAThread]
    public static void Main()
    {
        Application.EnableVisualStyles();
        Application.Run(new UnboundDataGridViewWithCalendar());
    }
    public UnboundDataGridViewWithCalendar()
    {
        Text = "Unbound DataGridView with Calendar";
        Width *= 2;

        DataGridView grid = new DataGridView();
        grid.Parent = this;
        grid.AutoSize = true;
        grid.Dock = DockStyle.Fill;

        DataGridViewComboBoxColumn colCombo = new DataGridViewComboBoxColumn();
        colCombo.Name = "Courtesy";
        colCombo.HeaderText = "Courtesy";
        colCombo.DataSource = Enum.GetValues(typeof(CourtesyTitle));
        colCombo.ValueType = typeof(CourtesyTitle);
        grid.Columns.Add(colCombo);
```

```
        DataGridViewTextBoxColumn colText = new DataGridViewTextBoxColumn();
        colText.Name = "FirstName";
        colText.HeaderText = "First Name";
        grid.Columns.Add(colText);

        colText = new DataGridViewTextBoxColumn();
        colText.Name = "LastName";
        colText.HeaderText = "Last Name";
        grid.Columns.Add(colText);

        CalendarColumn colBirth = new CalendarColumn();
        colBirth.Name = "BirthDate";
        colBirth.HeaderText = "Birth Date";
        grid.Columns.Add(colBirth);

        DataGridViewCheckBoxColumn colCheck = new DataGridViewCheckBoxColumn();
        colCheck.Name = "Enrolled";
        colCheck.HeaderText = "Enrolled?";
        grid.Columns.Add(colCheck);
    }
}
```

To keep things simple, this program doesn't implement file I/O or validation. It just shows how to use the *CalendarColumn* when creating the *DataGridView*. When the control comes up, the cell looks like a text-entry cell, but clicking it makes the arrow appear for the *DataTime-Picker*. Because the *Value* of the cell is set to the *Value* property of the underlying control, and that *Value* is an instance of *DateTime*, no conversions would be needed when saving or loading a file, and no validation is required.

DataGridView and Data Binding

Linking a *DataGridView* with a data source should be fairly easily. You would first define a *BindingSource* something like this:

```
BindingSource bindsrc = new BindingSource();
bindsrc.DataSource = typeof(School);
bindsrc.DataMember = "Students";
```

You then create the *DataGridView* in a form like we've been doing:

```
DataGridView grid = new DataGridView();
grid.Parent = this;
grid.AutoSize = true;
grid.Dock = DockStyle.Fill;
```

The final step is to link the *DataGridView* with the *BindingSource*:

```
grid.DataSource = bindsrc;
```

This code works, and yet it doesn't. It works to the extent that the *DataGridView* control obtains the column headings from the properties of the *Student* class and then allows you to enter information in the grid. However, my experience is that this code creates a *DataGridView* control that looks like this:

As you can see, the columns are not in the right order. Moreover, the Courtesy column is implemented as text input, and the BirthDate column doesn't use our new *CalendarColumn* object (but you probably never expected it to). This means that the *DataGridView* needs to be initialized a little differently.

Here's the approach used in the final program of this chapter: before setting the *DataSource* property of the *DataGridView* to the *BindingSource*, set the *AutoGenerateColumns* property to *false*. That prevents columns from being created for each property of the binding source. We don't want those columns because they're not adequate for our needs. Then, explicitly create all the columns just like in the UnboundDataGridView program, and set the *DataProperty-Name* property of each column to the property of *Student* you want associated with that column. For the combo box, for example, here's the code:

```
DataGridViewComboBoxColumn colCombo = new DataGridViewComboBoxColumn();
colCombo.DataPropertyName = "Courtesy";
colCombo.DataSource = Enum.GetValues(typeof(CourtesyTitle));
colCombo.HeaderText = "Courtesy";
grid.Columns.Add(colCombo);
```

You could assign the *Name* property as well, but this program no longer needs it because it doesn't have to reference the columns to insert and remove data. All it needs is the *Binding-Source* object. The DataGridViewWithBinding project includes School.cs, Student.cs, and CourtesyTitle.cs—the three files associated with the *CalendarColumn* class—and the following file.

DataGridViewWithBinding.cs

```
//-----------------------------------------------------------
// DataGridViewWithBinding.cs (c) 2005 by Charles Petzold
//-----------------------------------------------------------
using System;
using System.Drawing;
using System.IO;
using System.Windows.Forms;
using System.Xml.Serialization;

class DataGridViewWithBinding : Form
{
    const string strFilter = "School files (*.SchoolXml)|" +
                        "*.SchoolXml|All files (*.*)|*.*";
```

```
XmlSerializer xmlser = new XmlSerializer(typeof(School));
BindingSource bindsrc = new BindingSource();

[STAThread]
public static void Main()
{
    Application.EnableVisualStyles();
    Application.Run(new DataGridViewWithBinding());
}
public DataGridViewWithBinding()
{
    Text = "DateGridView with Binding";
    Width *= 2;

    // Initialize the BindingSource.
    FileNewOnClick(null, EventArgs.Empty);

    // Create DataGridView control.
    DataGridView grid = new DataGridView();
    grid.Parent = this;
    grid.AutoSize = true;
    grid.Dock = DockStyle.Fill;

    // Bind the control to the data source.
    grid.AutoGenerateColumns = false;
    grid.DataSource = bindsrc;

    // Create desired columns for DataGridView.
    DataGridViewComboBoxColumn colCombo = new DataGridViewComboBoxColumn();
    colCombo.DataPropertyName = "Courtesy";
    colCombo.DataSource = Enum.GetValues(typeof(CourtesyTitle));
    colCombo.HeaderText = "Courtesy";
    grid.Columns.Add(colCombo);

    DataGridViewTextBoxColumn colText = new DataGridViewTextBoxColumn();
    colText.DataPropertyName = "FirstName";
    colText.HeaderText = "First Name";
    grid.Columns.Add(colText);

    colText = new DataGridViewTextBoxColumn();
    colText.DataPropertyName = "LastName";
    colText.HeaderText = "Last Name";
    grid.Columns.Add(colText);

    CalendarColumn colBirth = new CalendarColumn();
    colBirth.DataPropertyName = "BirthDate";
    colBirth.HeaderText = "Birth Date";
    grid.Columns.Add(colBirth);

    DataGridViewCheckBoxColumn colCheck = new DataGridViewCheckBoxColumn();
    colCheck.DataPropertyName = "Enrolled";
    colCheck.HeaderText = "Enrolled?";
    grid.Columns.Add(colCheck);
```

```
        // Create the menu.
        MenuStrip menu = new MenuStrip();
        menu.Parent = this;
        ToolStripMenuItem item = (ToolStripMenuItem)menu.Items.Add("&File");
        item.DropDownItems.Add("&New", null, FileNewOnClick);
        item.DropDownItems.Add("&Open...", null, FileOpenOnClick);
        item.DropDownItems.Add("Save &As...", null, FileSaveAsOnClick);
    }
    void FileNewOnClick(object objSrc, EventArgs args)
    {
        bindsrc.DataSource = new School();
        bindsrc.DataMember = "Students";
    }
    void FileOpenOnClick(object objSrc, EventArgs args)
    {
        OpenFileDialog dlg = new OpenFileDialog();
        dlg.Filter = strFilter;

        if (dlg.ShowDialog() == DialogResult.OK)
        {
            // Read the School object in as XML.
            StreamReader sr = new StreamReader(dlg.FileName);
            bindsrc.DataSource = xmlser.Deserialize(sr);
            sr.Close();
        }
    }
    void FileSaveAsOnClick(object objSrc, EventArgs args)
    {
        SaveFileDialog dlg = new SaveFileDialog();
        dlg.Filter = strFilter;

        if (dlg.ShowDialog() == DialogResult.OK)
        {
            // Write the School object out as XML.
            StreamWriter sw = new StreamWriter(dlg.FileName);
            xmlser.Serialize(sw, bindsrc.DataSource);
            sw.Close();
        }
    }
}
```

Although "manually" creating all the columns is a nuisance, there are still several advantages to data binding. First, the program doesn't have to install any event handlers for the *DataGrid-View* to initialize the data for each new row. Second, the File Open and File Save routines need only refer to the *BindingSource* rather than the *School* object or the properties of the *Student* class. It is, perhaps, asking a little too much of *DataGridView* that it correctly create each column using a *DataGridViewColumn* object perfectly suited to the data type. As more varied descendents of *DataGridViewColumn* become available, you'll want the opportunity to hand-pick them for the jobs they need to perform.

Chapter 7
Two Real Applications

Often programming tutorials like this one show numerous tiny programs but nothing that can be termed a "real application." Real applications are more than just tiny programs made larger. In this era of object-oriented programming, a real application consists of numerous classes that optimally fit together like cogs in a machine. A quite substantial application would probably require a whole book to discuss, but in this chapter, I'd like to present two smaller real applications as case studies. These are:

- A developer tool named ControlExplorer that I discussed in Chapter 2. ControlExplorer lets you create any control in Microsoft Windows Forms and experiment with its properties and events.

- A multiple-document interface Web browser named MdiBrowser. MdiBrowser makes use of the *WebBrowser* control to achieve (without much sweat) much of the functionality of Internet Explorer.

Aside from being larger than earlier programs in this book, these applications have been given a few accoutrements that aren't necessary in smaller sample programs:

- Both programs have icons and "about" boxes.

- The accompanying console windows have been removed, and they have all been compiled in the non-default Release configuration under Microsoft Visual Studio.

- In the case of MdiBrowser, a small help file has been prepared.

- Both programs have been prepared for installation. I have used the new ClickOnce installation procedure, and the programs can be downloaded and installed from my Web site. Go to the "Programming Microsoft Windows Forms" page at *www.charlespetzold.com/winforms.*

Case Study 1: ControlExplorer

The ControlExplorer program's main form contains *MenuStrip* and *Panel* controls. The menu has a top-level item named Control. From that item descends a menu with a hierarchy that parallels the class hierarchy of all the Windows Forms controls that derive from *Control*. When you select a control from the menu, ControlExplorer creates a control of that type as a child of the panel and displays a large modeless dialog box:

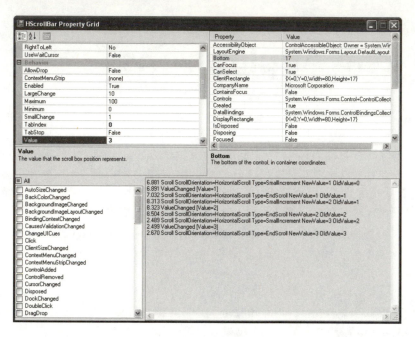

This dialog box contains three controls separated by splitters. At the upper left is a standard Windows Forms *PropertyGrid* control that lets you view and change read-write properties of the control. The upper-right quadrant contains a similar control that I wrote called *Read-OnlyPropertyGrid* to display the values of all the read-only properties. The bottom half is another custom control, called *EventLogger*, that lets you view any or all events defined by the control. This control has several parts. Most of the left part is a *CheckedListBox* control listing all the control's events. The part at the right is a *TextBox* configured to display console output. Each event is accompanied by the time (in seconds and milliseconds only), the event name, and the values of all the public properties delivered with the event. If the name of the event ends in the word "Changed," the value of the property being changed is shown in brackets. When you close this dialog box, the control is destroyed. You can create several sibling controls, and each one will have its own modeless dialog box.

Obviously, almost every inch, nook, and cranny of this program relies upon *reflection*, which is the process of obtaining information about classes and objects during runtime and using that information to create or manipulate the objects. Even the About dialog box uses reflection.

I will be presenting the source code for this program in a "bottom-up" fashion—that is, beginning with the most elementary controls, and then the assembly of these controls into dialog boxes, and finally the main application form.

The *Control* Class Hierarchy

The top-level menu item labeled Control mimics the hierarchy of classes that descend from the *Control* class and which are located in the System.Windows.Forms assembly. The Control menu item with its children is created in this subclass of *ToolStripMenuItem*.

```
ControlMenuItem.cs
//-----------------------------------------------
// ControlMenuItem.cs (c) 2005 by Charles Petzold
// From ControlExplorer program
//-----------------------------------------------
using System;
using System.Collections.Generic;
using System.Drawing;
using System.Reflection;
using System.Windows.Forms;

class ControlMenuItem : ToolStripMenuItem
{
    public ControlMenuItem(EventHandler evtClick)
    {
        // Obtain the assembly in which the Control class is defined.
        Assembly asbly = Assembly.GetAssembly(typeof(Control));

        // This is an array of all the types in that class
        Type[] atype = asbly.GetTypes();

        // We're going to store descendents of Control in a sorted list.
        SortedList<string, ToolStripMenuItem> sortlst =
            new SortedList<string, ToolStripMenuItem>();

        Text = "Control";
        Tag = typeof(Control);
        sortlst.Add("Control", this);

        // Enumerate all the types in the array.
        // For Control and its descendents, create menu items and
        //  add to the SortedList object.
        // Notice the menu item Tag property is the associated Type object.
        foreach (Type typ in atype)
        {
            if (typ.IsPublic && (typ.IsSubclassOf(typeof(Control))))
            {
                ToolStripMenuItem item = new ToolStripMenuItem(typ.Name);
                item.Click += evtClick;
                item.Tag = typ;
                sortlst.Add(typ.Name, item);
            }
        }

        // Go through the sorted list and set menu item parents.
        foreach (KeyValuePair<string, ToolStripMenuItem> kvp in sortlst)
        {
```

```
                    if (kvp.Key != "Control")
                    {
                        string strParent = ((Type)kvp.Value.Tag).BaseType.Name;
                        ToolStripMenuItem itemParent = sortlst[strParent];
                        itemParent.DropDownItems.Add(kvp.Value);

                        // itemParent shouldn't have event handler!
                        itemParent.Click -= evtClick;
                    }
                }

                // Scan through again:
                //   If abstract and selectable, disable.
                //   If not abstract and not selectable, add a new item.
                foreach (KeyValuePair<string, ToolStripMenuItem> kvp in sortlst)
                {
                    Type typ = (Type) kvp.Value.Tag;

                    if (typ.IsAbstract && kvp.Value.DropDownItems.Count == 0)
                        kvp.Value.Enabled = false;

                    if (!typ.IsAbstract && kvp.Value.DropDownItems.Count > 0)
                    {
                        ToolStripMenuItem item = new ToolStripMenuItem(kvp.Value.Text);
                        item.Click += evtClick;
                        item.Tag = typ;
                        kvp.Value.DropDownItems.Insert(0, item);
                    }
                }
            }
        }
    }
```

The class begins by obtaining all types (that is, classes, structures, delegates, interfaces, and enumerations) from the particular assembly that *Control* is located in. (That assembly, of course, is System.Windows.Forms.dll.) The first *foreach* loop accumulates every public class that derives from *Control* in a *SortedList* object. The *SortedList* stores data in pairs of keys and values, and sorts on the key. For each class stored in the *SortedList* object, the key is the text name of the class (such as "Button") while the value is a *ToolStripMenuItem* for that class. The *Tag* property of each *ToolStripMenuItem* is the *Type* object for the particular control class.

Following the creation of all these *ToolStripMenuItem* objects, it's necessary to link them together in a hierarchy. That's the job of the second *foreach* loop. The code obtains the base class from each *ToolStripMenuItem Tag* property, and then it uses the *SortedList* to find the corresponding *ToolStripMenuItem*, to whose *DropDownItems* collection the item is added.

But we're not quite finished. Although some parent classes (such as *ButtonBase*) are abstract, others (for example, *Label*) are not. It's all right that *ButtonBase* invokes a submenu with *Button*, *CheckBox*, and *RadioButton*, because we can't create an object of type *ButtonBase* even if we wanted to. But it's not good that *Label* invokes a submenu with just *LinkLabel* on it. How do we then create a *Label* control? For each control that is a parent to other controls and *not* abstract, the third *foreach* loop creates a new *ToolStripMenuItem* in the submenu with text the same as the parent. The *Label* item, for example, invokes a submenu that also includes *Label* as well as *LinkLabel*.

I originally wrote this program using the *MainMenu* and *MenuItem* classes from the .NET Framework 1.0, and when I revised the program to use *MenuStrip* and *ToolStripMenuItem*, I discovered an interesting oddity: A *MenuItem* that displays a drop-down menu could have a *Click* event handler, but it's basically inoperative. However, a *ToolStripMenuItem* invokes its *Click* event handler regardless of whether it's a parent to a submenu or not. I didn't really need to add another *Label* item to the *Label* submenu. But I decided that items that are parents to submenus should not have *Click* event handlers, so I added code to remove the event handlers added earlier.

Read-Only Properties

The *ReadOnlyPropertyGrid* control is mostly a *ListView* control in *View.Details* mode, with two columns that display the read-only properties and their values. But *ReadOnlyPropertyGrid* contains other controls, as well: The *ListView* actually occupies the top part of a *SplitterContainer*. The bottom part contains two labels that display the currently selected property in the *ListView* and a brief description of it. This description originates in the source code of the control as a *Description* attribute prefacing the property.

Because there's no general way to be notified when a property of an object changes, the control starts up a *Timer* object and refreshes the control every tenth of a second.

```
ReadOnlyPropertyGrid.cs
//----------------------------------------------------
// ReadOnlyPropertyGrid.cs (c) 2005 by Charles Petzold
// From ControlExplorer program
//----------------------------------------------------
using System;
using System.ComponentModel; // for DescriptionAttribute
using System.Drawing;
using System.Reflection;
using System.Windows.Forms;

class ReadOnlyPropertyGrid: Control
{
    object objSelected;
    ListView lvProps;
    Label labProp, labDesc;
    Timer tmr;

    // Public property.
    public object SelectedObject
    {
        get
        {
            return objSelected;
        }
    }
```

```
            set
            {
                objSelected = value;
                FullRefresh();
                tmr.Enabled = objSelected != null;
            }
    }
    // Constructor.
    public ReadOnlyPropertyGrid()
    {
        ClientSize = new Size(30 * Font.Height, 30* Font.Height);

        SplitContainer sc = new SplitContainer();
        sc.Parent = this;
        sc.Dock = DockStyle.Fill;
        sc.Orientation = Orientation.Horizontal;
        sc.FixedPanel = FixedPanel.Panel2;
        sc.SplitterDistance = Height - 4 * Font.Height;

        // ListView displays properties and values.
        lvProps = new ListView();
        lvProps.Parent = sc.Panel1;
        lvProps.Dock = DockStyle.Fill;
        lvProps.View = View.Details;
        lvProps.HeaderStyle = ColumnHeaderStyle.Nonclickable;
        lvProps.GridLines = true;
        lvProps.FullRowSelect = true;
        lvProps.MultiSelect = false;
        lvProps.HideSelection = false;
        lvProps.Activation = ItemActivation.OneClick;
        lvProps.SelectedIndexChanged += ListViewOnSelectedIndexChanged;

        lvProps.Columns.Add("Property", 12 * Font.Height,
            HorizontalAlignment.Left);
        lvProps.Columns.Add("Value", 18 * Font.Height,
            HorizontalAlignment.Left);

        // Labels show selected property and value.
        labDesc = new Label();
        labDesc.Parent = sc.Panel2;
        labDesc.Dock = DockStyle.Fill;

        labProp = new Label();
        labProp.Parent = sc.Panel2;
        labProp.Dock = DockStyle.Top;
        labProp.Height = Font.Height;
        labProp.Font = new Font(labProp.Font, FontStyle.Bold);

        tmr = new Timer();
        tmr.Interval = 100;
        tmr.Tick += TimerOnTick;
    }
    // Fill the ListView with properties and values.
    void FullRefresh()
    {
        lvProps.Items.Clear();
```

```csharp
        if (SelectedObject == null)
            return;

    PropertyInfo[] api = SelectedObject.GetType().GetProperties();

    foreach (System.Reflection.PropertyInfo pi in api)
    {
        if (pi.CanRead && !pi.CanWrite)
        {
            ListViewItem lvi = new ListViewItem(pi.Name);
            lvi.Tag = pi;
            object objValue = pi.GetValue(SelectedObject, null);
            lvi.SubItems.Add(objValue == null ? "" : objValue.ToString());
            lvProps.Items.Add(lvi);
            lvi.Selected = pi.Name == "Bottom";
        }
    }
}
// Refresh the value of each property that has changed.
void ValueRefresh()
{
    foreach (ListViewItem lvi in lvProps.Items)
    {

        PropertyInfo pi = (PropertyInfo) lvi.Tag;
        object objValue = pi.GetValue(SelectedObject, null);
        string strNew = objValue == null ? "" : objValue.ToString();

        if (strNew != lvi.SubItems[1].Text)
            lvi.SubItems[1].Text = strNew;
    }
}
// Change the labels based on the ListView selection.
void ListViewOnSelectedIndexChanged(object objSrc, EventArgs args)
{
    ListView lv = (ListView)objSrc;

    if (lv.SelectedItems.Count == 0)
    {
        labProp.Text = labDesc.Text = "";
        return;
    }
    ListViewItem lvi = lv.SelectedItems[0];
    PropertyInfo pi = (PropertyInfo)lvi.Tag;
    DescriptionAttribute dattr = (DescriptionAttribute)
        Attribute.GetCustomAttribute(pi, typeof(DescriptionAttribute));

    labProp.Text = pi.Name;
    labDesc.Text = dattr == null ? "" : dattr.Description;
}
// On timer tick, refresh all property values.
void TimerOnTick(object objSrc, EventArgs args)
{
    ValueRefresh();
}
}
```

The control defines a public property named *SelectedObject*—I used the same name as the relevant property of *PropertyGrid*—and calls *FullRefresh* when the property needs to update the *ListView* with a new object. The *GetProperties* method of the *Type* class obtains an array of *PropertyInfo* objects; only the read-only properties are selected for the *ListView*. The *GetValue* method of *PropertyInfo* obtains the particular property's value.

The *ListViewOnSelectedIndexChanged* event handler keeps the two *Label* controls updated. The code obtains the *Description* attribute from the static *Attribute.GetCustomAttribute* method.

Dynamic Event Trapping

The third control in the modeless dialog box displayed by ControlExplorer lets you view a control's events. The right part of this control is a control that mimics the display of console output.

```
ConsoleControl.cs
//-------------------------------------------------
// ConsoleControl.cs (c) 2005 by Charles Petzold
// From ControlExplorer program
//-------------------------------------------------
using System;
using System.Drawing;
using System.Windows.Forms;

class ConsoleControl: Control
{
    TextBox txtbox;

    public ConsoleControl()
    {
        txtbox = new TextBox();
        txtbox.Parent = this;
        txtbox.Multiline = true;
        txtbox.WordWrap = false;
        txtbox.ScrollBars = ScrollBars.Both;
        txtbox.ReadOnly = true;
        txtbox.Dock = DockStyle.Fill;
        txtbox.TabStop = false;
        txtbox.HideSelection = false;
    }
    public void Clear()
    {
        txtbox.Clear();
    }
    public void WriteLine()
    {
        Output("\r\n");
    }
    public void Write(object obj)
    {
        Output(obj.ToString());
```

```
    }
    public void WriteLine(object obj)
    {
        Output(obj + "\r\n");
    }
    public void Write(string strFormat, params object[] aobj)
    {
        Output(String.Format(strFormat, aobj));
    }
    public void WriteLine(string strFormat, params object[] aobj)
    {
        Output(String.Format(strFormat, aobj) + "\r\n");
    }
    void Output(string str)
    {
        txtbox.SelectionStart = txtbox.TextLength;
        txtbox.AppendText(str);
    }
}
```

This control is undoubtedly one of the easiest parts of the whole program. It is simply a *Text-Box* to which text is appended based on arguments to a couple *Write* and *WriteLine* methods.

The *EventLogger* class that uses this console-output control is not so simple, however. It is easy enough to obtain all the events defined for a class: Simply call the *GetEvents* method of the *Type* object associated with the class to obtain an array of *EventInfo* objects. However, if you want to do anything with an event, you need to install an event handler. For many events, such a handler must be defined in accordance with the *EventHandler* delegate defined in the *System* namespace:

```
public delegate void EventHandler(object objSrc, EventArgs args);
```

You could define a suitable method in your code and attach it to an event by calling the *Add-EventHandler* method of the particular *EventInfo* object. But some events (such as *MouseMove*) are associated with different delegates:

```
public delegate void MouseEventHandler(object objSrc, MouseEventArgs args);
```

In previous versions of C#, it would be necessary to have a method defined like this delegate if you wanted to install a handler for the *MouseMove* event. In C# 2.0, it is possible for *Mouse-Move* to use a method defined in accordance with *EventHandler*. The method could then obtain the actual type of *args* and use reflection to obtain any additional properties of that argument.

However, if *EventLogger* defined a method in accordance with the *EventHandler* delegate, it would need to use that single method as the event handler for multiple events. To properly display information about the event, the event handler would need to identify the particular event (such as *MouseMove*). How can this single handler identify the event that it's currently processing? It cannot.

I came to realize that for each event that *EventLogger* was called upon to log, the control would have to dynamically generate a method in memory to handle that event. This sounds like some of the crazy stuff we used to do in C and assembly language, but with the .NET Framework, you can generate methods in memory while still maintaining managed code. The two classes I used are defined in the *System.Reflection.Emit* namespace and are named *DynamicMethod* and *ILGenerator* (which stands for "Intermediate Language Generator").

We're now ready to look at *EventLogger*.

```
EventLogger.cs
//-------------------------------------------
// EventLogger.cs (c) 2005 by Charles Petzold
// From ControlExplorer program
//-------------------------------------------
using System;
using System.Collections.Generic;
using System.Drawing;
using System.Reflection;
using System.Reflection.Emit;
using System.Windows.Forms;

class EventLogger: SplitContainer
{
    object objSelected;
    CheckBox chkbox;
    CheckedListBox lstbox;
    ConsoleControl cons;
    Dictionary<string, Delegate> deledict = new Dictionary<string, Delegate>();
    static Dictionary<object, ConsoleControl> consdict =
        new Dictionary<object, ConsoleControl>();

    // Public property for SelectedObject.
    public object SelectedObject
    {
        get
        {
            return objSelected;
        }
        set
        {
            if (objSelected != null)
                consdict.Remove(objSelected);

            objSelected = value;

            if (objSelected != null)
                consdict.Add(objSelected, cons);

            FullRefresh();
        }
    }
    // Constructor.
    public EventLogger()
```

```
{
    // CheckedListBox displays all events supported by control.
    lstbox = new CheckedListBox();
    lstbox.Parent = Panel1;
    lstbox.Dock = DockStyle.Fill;
    lstbox.CheckOnClick = true;
    lstbox.Sorted = true;
    lstbox.ItemCheck += ListBoxOnItemCheck;

    // CheckBox for checking or unchecking all events.
    chkbox = new CheckBox();
    chkbox.Parent = Panel1;
    chkbox.AutoSize = true;
    chkbox.AutoCheck = false;
    chkbox.ThreeState = true;
    chkbox.Text = "All";
    chkbox.Dock = DockStyle.Top;
    chkbox.Click += CheckBoxOnClick;

    // ConsoleControl for logging events.
    cons = new ConsoleControl();
    cons.Parent = Panel2;
    cons.Dock = DockStyle.Fill;
}
// ListBoxOnItemCheck: Attach and detach event handlers
void ListBoxOnItemCheck(object objSrc, ItemCheckEventArgs args)
{
    if (args.CurrentValue == args.NewValue)
        return;

    CheckedListBox lstbox = (CheckedListBox) objSrc;
    string strEvent = lstbox.Items[args.Index].ToString();

    // Attach a handler if the item is being checked.
    if (args.NewValue == CheckState.Checked)
    {
        AttachHandler(strEvent);

        if (lstbox.CheckedIndices.Count + 1 == lstbox.Items.Count)
            chkbox.CheckState = CheckState.Checked;
        else
            chkbox.CheckState = CheckState.Indeterminate;
    }
    // Detach a handler otherwise.
    else
    {
        RemoveHandler(strEvent);

        if (lstbox.CheckedIndices.Count == 1)
            chkbox.CheckState = CheckState.Unchecked;
        else
            chkbox.CheckState = CheckState.Indeterminate;
    }
}
```

```
    // When "All" CheckBox checked or unchecked, apply change to list box.
    void CheckBoxOnClick(object objSrc, EventArgs args)
    {
        CheckBox chkbox = (CheckBox)objSrc;

        // Let ListBoxOnItemChecked change the state of the check box check.
        if (chkbox.CheckState == CheckState.Unchecked)
        {
            for (int i = 0; i < lstbox.Items.Count; i++)
                lstbox.SetItemChecked(i, true);
        }
        else
        {
            for (int i = 0; i < lstbox.Items.Count; i++)
                lstbox.SetItemChecked(i, false);
        }
    }
    // FullRefresh called when SelectedProperty changes.
    void FullRefresh()
    {
        cons.Clear();
        lstbox.Items.Clear();

        if (SelectedObject == null)
            return;

        // Fill an array with all the events.
        EventInfo[] aevtinfo = SelectedObject.GetType().GetEvents();

        lstbox.BeginUpdate();

        // Loop through the events.
        foreach (EventInfo evtinfo in aevtinfo)
        {
            bool bChecked = false;

            // Check the event if the SelectedObject is a Control.
            if (SelectedObject.GetType() == typeof(Control))
                bChecked = true;

            // Otherwise, check if the event is not implemented by Control.
            else if (SelectedObject is Control)
                bChecked = typeof(Control).GetEvent(evtinfo.Name) == null;

            lstbox.Items.Add(evtinfo.Name, bChecked);
        }
        lstbox.EndUpdate();
    }
    // AttachHandler
    void AttachHandler(string strEvent)
    {
        // Information about the particular event.
        EventInfo evtinfo = SelectedObject.GetType().GetEvent(strEvent);
```

```
        // The type of the event handler.
        Type htype = evtinfo.EventHandlerType;

        // Information about the event handler method.
        MethodInfo[] methinfo = htype.GetMethods();

        // Arguments to the event handler.
        ParameterInfo[] parminfo = methinfo[0].GetParameters();

        // Create a method with a name like "ClickEventHandler"
        //  with the proper return type and arguments.
        DynamicMethod dynameth =
            new DynamicMethod(strEvent + "EventHandler", typeof(void),
                            new Type[] { typeof(object),
                                parminfo[1].ParameterType },
                            GetType());

        // The ILGenerator allows generating code for this method.
        ILGenerator ilg = dynameth.GetILGenerator();

        // The event handler will call the EventDump static method below.
        MethodInfo miEventDump = GetType().GetMethod("EventDump");

        // Generate code to push event name and two arguments on stack,
        //  and then call the EventDump method.
        ilg.Emit(OpCodes.Ldstr, strEvent);
        ilg.Emit(OpCodes.Ldarg_0);
        ilg.Emit(OpCodes.Ldarg_1);
        ilg.EmitCall(OpCodes.Call, miEventDump, null);
        ilg.Emit(OpCodes.Ret);

        // Create a delegate based on the event handler type.
        Delegate dynadele = dynameth.CreateDelegate(htype);

        // Finally, install the event handler.
        evtinfo.AddEventHandler(SelectedObject, dynadele);

        // Add the delegate to a dictionary for later detachment.
        deledict.Add(strEvent, dynadele);
    }
    // Remove event handler.
    void RemoveHandler(string strEvent)
    {
        EventInfo evtinfo = SelectedObject.GetType().GetEvent(strEvent);
        evtinfo.RemoveEventHandler(SelectedObject, deledict[strEvent]);
        deledict.Remove(strEvent);
    }
    // This static method displays the event.
    // Because the method must be static, it has to obtain the correct
    //  ConsoleControl object from the ConsoleControl dictionary (consdict).
    // Although the last argument is defined as EventArgs, for many events it
    //  will actually be a descendent of EventArgs.
    public static void EventDump(string strEvent, object objSrc, EventArgs args)
    {
```

```
        // Fish the correct ConsoleControl from the static dictionary.
        ConsoleControl cons = consdict[objSrc];

        // Display the event with the seconds and milliseconds.
        DateTime dt = DateTime.Now;
        cons.Write("{0}.{1:D3} {2}", dt.Second % 10, dt.Millisecond, strEvent);

        // Display all the properties in the EventArgs (or descendent).
        PropertyInfo[] api = args.GetType().GetProperties();

        foreach (PropertyInfo pi in api)
            cons.Write(" {0}={1}", pi.Name, pi.GetValue(args, null));

        // If the event ends with "Changed", display the new property.
        if (strEvent.EndsWith("Changed"))
        {
            string strProperty = strEvent.Substring(0, strEvent.Length - 7);
            PropertyInfo pi = objSrc.GetType().GetProperty(strProperty);
            cons.Write(" [{0}={1}]", strProperty, pi.GetValue(objSrc, null));
        }
        // End the line.
        cons.WriteLine();
    }
}
```

In the *AttachHandler* method, the *DynamicMethod* and *ILGenerator* methods essentially create a static method in memory. For the *MouseMove* event, for example, this fabricated method might be visualized in C# code like this:

```
static void MouseMoveEventHandler(object obj, MouseEventArgs args)
{
    EventLogger.EventDump("MouseMove", obj, args);
}
```

It simply passes its own arguments along with the name of the event to the static *EventDump* method in *EventLogger*, which then displays the event information on the *ConsoleControl*. However, because *EventDump* is necessarily static (because the generated event handler method is static) it can't simply access the *ConsoleControl* that was created in the constructor. That's the reason for the static *Dictionary* object named *consdict* ("console dictionary"). The event handler has to obtain the *ConsoleControl* associated with the particular control whose events are being logged.

Wrapping It Up

With the *EventLogger* control out of the way, we're home free. The *PropertiesAndEventsDialog* class is the modeless dialog box that displays the *PropertyGrid*, *ReadOnlyPropertyGrid*, and *EventLogger* controls all nicely separated by splitters.

PropertiesAndEventsDialog.cs

```
//-----------------------------------------------------------
// PropertiesAndEventsDialog.cs (c) 2005 by Charles Petzold
// From ControlExplorer program
//-----------------------------------------------------------
using System;
using System.Drawing;
using System.Windows.Forms;

class PropertiesAndEventsDialog : Form
{
    PropertyGrid propgrid;
    ReadOnlyPropertyGrid ropropgrid;
    EventLogger evtlst;

    // SelectedObject distributes property to other controls.
    public object SelectedObject
    {
        get
        {
            return propgrid.SelectedObject;
        }
        set
        {
            propgrid.SelectedObject = value;
            ropropgrid.SelectedObject = value;
            evtlst.SelectedObject = value;
        }
    }
    // Constructor.
    public PropertiesAndEventsDialog()
    {
        MaximizeBox = false;
        ShowInTaskbar = false;
        ClientSize = new Size(800, 600);

        SplitContainer sc1 = new SplitContainer();
        sc1.Parent = this;
        sc1.Dock = DockStyle.Fill;
        sc1.SplitterDistance = ClientSize.Height / 2;
        sc1.Orientation = Orientation.Horizontal;

        SplitContainer sc2 = new SplitContainer();
        sc2.Parent = sc1.Panel1;
        sc2.Dock = DockStyle.Fill;
        sc2.SplitterDistance = ClientSize.Width / 2;

        // PropertyGrid control.
        propgrid = new PropertyGrid();
        propgrid.Parent = sc2.Panel1;
        propgrid.Dock = DockStyle.Fill;

        // ReadOnlyPropertyGrid control.
        ropropgrid = new ReadOnlyPropertyGrid();
```

```
        roropgrid.Parent = sc2.Panel2;
        roropgrid.Dock = DockStyle.Fill;

        // EventLogger controls.
        evtlst = new EventLogger();
        evtlst.Parent = sc1.Panel2;
        evtlst.Dock = DockStyle.Fill;
    }
}
```

The dialog box itself has a *SelectedObject* property that it uses to distribute the object to its three children.

The second dialog box included with the ControlExplorer project is *AboutDialog*.

AboutDialog.cs

```
//-------------------------------------------
// AboutDialog.cs (c) 2005 by Charles Petzold
//-------------------------------------------
using System;
using System.Diagnostics;
using System.Drawing;
using System.Reflection;
using System.Windows.Forms;

class AboutDialog : Form
{
    protected FlowLayoutPanel flow;
    protected Button btnOk;

    public AboutDialog(string strResource)
    {
        // Get current assembly.
        Assembly a = GetType().Assembly;

        // Get program title.
        AssemblyTitleAttribute asmblytitle = (AssemblyTitleAttribute)
            a.GetCustomAttributes(typeof(AssemblyTitleAttribute), false)[0];
        string strTitle = asmblytitle.Title;

        // Get program version.
        AssemblyFileVersionAttribute asmblyvers = (AssemblyFileVersionAttribute)
            a.GetCustomAttributes(typeof(AssemblyFileVersionAttribute), false)[0];
        string strVersion = asmblyvers.Version.Substring(0, 3);

        // Get program copyright.
        AssemblyCopyrightAttribute asmblycopy = (AssemblyCopyrightAttribute)
            a.GetCustomAttributes(typeof(AssemblyCopyrightAttribute), false)[0];
        string strCopyright = asmblycopy.Copyright;

        // Set multititudes of attributes.
        Text = "About " + strTitle;
        AutoSize = true;
```

```
          AutoSizeMode = AutoSizeMode.GrowAndShrink;
          FormBorderStyle = FormBorderStyle.FixedDialog;
          ControlBox = false;
          MinimizeBox = false;
          MaximizeBox = false;
          ShowInTaskbar = false;
          Icon = ActiveForm.Icon;
          StartPosition = FormStartPosition.Manual;
          Location = ActiveForm.Location + SystemInformation.CaptionButtonSize +
                                        SystemInformation.FrameBorderSize;
          // Create controls.
          flow = new FlowLayoutPanel();
          flow.Parent = this;
          flow.AutoSize = true;
          flow.FlowDirection = FlowDirection.TopDown;

          FlowLayoutPanel flow2 = new FlowLayoutPanel();
          flow2.Parent = flow;
          flow2.AutoSize = true;
          flow2.Margin = new Padding(Font.Height);

          PictureBox picbox = new PictureBox();
          picbox.Parent = flow2;
          picbox.Image = Icon.ToBitmap();
          picbox.SizeMode = PictureBoxSizeMode.AutoSize;
          picbox.Anchor = AnchorStyles.None;

          Label lbl = new Label();
          lbl.Parent = flow2;
          lbl.AutoSize = true;
          lbl.Anchor = AnchorStyles.None;
          lbl.Text = strTitle + " Version " + strVersion;
          lbl.Font = new Font(FontFamily.GenericSerif, 24, FontStyle.Italic);

          lbl = new Label();
          lbl.Parent = flow;
          lbl.Text = "From the Microsoft Press book:";
          lbl.AutoSize = true;
          lbl.Anchor = AnchorStyles.None;
          lbl.Margin = new Padding(Font.Height);
          lbl.Font = new Font(FontFamily.GenericSerif, 16);

          picbox = new PictureBox();
          picbox.Parent = flow;
          picbox.Image = new Bitmap(GetType(), strResource + ".BookCover.png");
          picbox.SizeMode = PictureBoxSizeMode.AutoSize;
          picbox.Anchor = AnchorStyles.None;

          LinkLabel lnk = new LinkLabel();
          lnk.Parent = flow;
          lnk.AutoSize = true;
          lnk.Anchor = AnchorStyles.None;
          lnk.Margin = new Padding(Font.Height);
          lnk.Text = "\x00A9 2005 by Charles Petzold";
          lnk.Font = lbl.Font; // new Font(FontFamily.GenericSerif, 16);
```

```
        lnk.LinkArea = new LinkArea(10, 15);
        lnk.LinkClicked +=
            delegate { Process.Start("http://www.charlespetzold.com"); };

        btnOk = new Button();
        btnOk.Text = "OK";
        btnOk.Parent = flow;
        btnOk.AutoSize = true;
        btnOk.Anchor = AnchorStyles.None;
        btnOk.Margin = new Padding(Font.Height);
        btnOk.DialogResult = DialogResult.OK;
    }
}
```

I mentioned earlier that even the About box uses reflection, and you'll note at the outset of the constructor the use of the *GetCustomAttributes* method to get information about the assembly—in particular, the program name, file version, and copyright information. (Some of this information is available from static methods in *Application* named *CompanyName*, *ProductName*, and *ProductVersion*.) I wanted to use the same dialog box for both programs in this chapter, so obtaining this information from the assembly provided a suitable approach to generalizing the code.

The constructor sets the *Icon* property of the dialog box from the *Icon* property of the *ActiveForm*, which is the program that invoked the dialog box. The constructor also has an argument indicating the resource namespace. (You'll recall that Visual Studio sets this resource namespace to be the same as the project name.) The constructor of *AboutDialog* requires this information to load the BookCover.png file, which was added to the project and flagged as an Embedded Resource.

Also included in the project and flagged as an Embedded Resource is ControlExplorer.ico. A single icon file can contain multiple images in a variety of resolutions. When you create an icon in Visual Studio, two common sizes are created: 16 pixels square and 32 pixels square. The small size is used in the form's title bar, the taskbar, and the start menu. The larger size is used for the desktop. Depending on the view, Windows Explorer displays either the large or small icon. Here's the large size of the icon I created as displayed in Visual Studio. The icon displays a button with the text "foo," which I thought was suitably descriptive of the way developers would use this program:

Finally, here's the *ControlExplorer* class itself. It begins with several assembly attributes that help identify the EXE file.

ControlExplorer.cs

```
//-----------------------------------------------
// ControlExplorer.cs (c) 2005 by Charles Petzold
//-----------------------------------------------
using System;
using System.Drawing;
using System.Reflection;
using System.Windows.Forms;

[assembly: AssemblyTitle("Control Explorer")]
[assembly: AssemblyDescription("Developer Tool for Windows Forms")]
[assembly: AssemblyCompany("www.charlespetzold.com")]
[assembly: AssemblyProduct("Control Explorer")]
[assembly: AssemblyCopyright("(c) 2005 by Charles Petzold")]
[assembly: AssemblyVersion("1.0.*")]
[assembly: AssemblyFileVersion("1.0.0.0")]

class ControlExplorer: Form
{
    const string strResource = "ControlExplorer";
    Panel pnl;

    [STAThread]
    public static void Main()
    {
        Application.EnableVisualStyles();
        Application.Run(new ControlExplorer());
    }

    public ControlExplorer()
    {
        Text = "Control Explorer";
        Icon = new Icon(GetType(), strResource + ".ControlExplorer.ico");

        pnl = new Panel();
        pnl.Parent = this;
        pnl.Dock = DockStyle.Fill;

        MenuStrip menu = new MenuStrip();
        menu.Parent = this;
        menu.Items.Add(new ControlMenuItem(MenuItemOnClick));

        ToolStripMenuItem itemHelp = new ToolStripMenuItem("&Help");
        menu.Items.Add(itemHelp);
        ToolStripMenuItem itemAbout = new ToolStripMenuItem();
        itemAbout.Text = "&About Control Explorer...";
        itemAbout.Click += AboutOnClick;
        itemHelp.DropDownItems.Add(itemAbout);
    }
```

```
void MenuItemOnClick(object objSrc, EventArgs args)
{
    // Obtain the menu Item and the class it refers to.
    ToolStripMenuItem item = objSrc as ToolStripMenuItem;
    Type typ = (Type)item.Tag;

    // Get ready to create an object of that type.
    ConstructorInfo ci = typ.GetConstructor(System.Type.EmptyTypes);
    Control ctrl;

    // Try creating an object of that type.
    try
    {
        ctrl = (Control)ci.Invoke(null);
    }
    catch (Exception exc)
    {
        MessageBox.Show(exc.Message, Text);
        return;
    }

    // Create a dialog box that contains a PropertyGrid control.
    PropertiesAndEventsDialog dlg = new PropertiesAndEventsDialog();
    dlg.Owner = this;
    dlg.Text = item.Text + " Property Grid";
    dlg.SelectedObject = ctrl;
    dlg.Closed += new EventHandler(DialogOnClosed);
    dlg.Show();

    // If the Parent property can't be assigned, it's probably
    //   a Form, so just call Show for it.
    try
    {
        ctrl.Parent = pnl;
    }
    catch
    {
        ctrl.Show();
    }
}

// When the Properties dialog box is closed,
//   get rid of the control.
void DialogOnClosed(object objSrc, EventArgs args)
{
    PropertiesAndEventsDialog dlg = (PropertiesAndEventsDialog)objSrc;
    Control ctrl = (Control)dlg.SelectedObject;
    ctrl.Dispose();
}
void AboutOnClick(object objSrc, EventArgs args)
{
    new AboutDialog(strResource).ShowDialog();
}
}
```

The constructor loads the icon and creates the panel and menu. When the user picks an item from the Control menu, the *MenuItemOnClick* handler creates an object of that type and creates a *PropertiesAndEventsDialog* to accompany it. When the dialog box is closed, the control is disposed.

When a program has an icon resource, the program can load the icon and set it to the *Icon* property of the form. That causes the icon to be displayed in the caption bar of the program. In Visual Studio, you'll also want to bring up the project properties dialog box, select the Application tab, and set the Icon field to the application icon. Doing this allows other programs (such as the Windows shell) to extract the icon from the .EXE file for display.

ClickOnce Installation

One subject of vital importance in the creation of real applications is *deployment*. How do you get your program on the user's machine? With a programming tool such as ControlExplorer, the users are programmers, so it's tempting to just hand out a ControlExplorer.exe file and let the user worry about what they're going to do with it.

However, for real applications targeted to users less handy than programmers, you'll want an actual installation process. You could use Microsoft Installer (MSI), which takes the user through a series of familiar dialog boxes. MSI (or a similar installation utility) is probably best for applications that need to mess around with the registry to set file extension associations and whatnot. But for simpler applications, there's a new installation procedure available with the .NET Framework 2.0 called ClickOnce, and that's what I'm going to discuss here.

ClickOnce automates several routine jobs in program installation: If the .NET Framework 2.0 is not installed on the user's machine, it will give the user the opportunity to install it. Click-Once will handle other program prerequisites (such as Microsoft SQL Server) similarly. Click-Once puts a program shortcut on the user's Start menu and allows the program to be uninstalled through the Control Panel. ClickOnce also determines whether a later version of the program is available, and it will handle all the downloading and installation of that newer version. The Control Panel Add Or Remove Programs applet also allows rolling back to the previous version.

ClickOnce does not store programs in the Program Files directory like a normal installation. Instead, the programs are installed on a per-user basis and saved to the ClickOnce application cache, which is the Apps subdirectory of the user's Local Settings directory.

Although you can use ClickOnce to prepare a disk file for CD-ROM installation, ClickOnce really makes most sense when you provide downloading of the application from a Web site. Although you can create the necessary files manually or using the "manifest generator and editor" utilities mage.exe or mageui.exe, Visual Studio does a good job in preparing the files and copying them to your Web server. These files include setup.exe, which is sometimes referred to as a "bootstrapper" because it will install the .NET Framework 2.0 if necessary so that the rest of the installation can take place. Visual Studio also optionally creates an HTML page (named publish.htm in some beta versions of Visual Studio 2005) that contains JavaScript to check whether the prerequisites are required on the user machine. Also included are XML files with the extensions .application and .manifest, and binary files with the extension .deploy that contain the actual .exe files and any other files required by the application (such as help).

Creating a ClickOnce installation procedure for the user is called "publishing" the application. I'll walk through the process I used to publish ControlExplorer on my Web site. Publishing a program on your own Web site will be a little different, of course.

With the project loaded in Visual Studio, bring up the project properties dialog box and select the Publish tab. The opening screen requires several pieces of information. The Publishing Location indicates where the application files are to be stored. This could be a local file or a local HTTP server. In my case, I wanted to copy the files to my Web site, which I normally do by copying the files to an EarthLink FTP address. I used:

ftp://ftp.business.earthlink.net/www/winforms/ControlExplorer/

That address indicates a subdirectory named *ControlExplorer* (which Visual Studio will create for me) of the *winforms* directory of my Web site. Visual Studio uses the next field, labeled Installation URL to run the installation once it's completed. In my case, that address is:

http://www.charlespetzold.com/winforms/ControlExplorer/

Under Install Mode And Settings, you have two options: to require the user to always run the program from your Web page, or to install it on the user's machine and add a shortcut to the Start menu. I chose the latter.

The Publish Version is completely independent of any other version number you might have set, including the assembly version and file version. To avoid inordinately confusing users, you should probably keep at least the Major and Minor version numbers consistent. Visual Studio will bump up the Revision number each time you publish another version of the application, but not past the number 9.

There are also four buttons. The Application Files button lets you add additional files to the installation. (I'll show you how to use this button later with the MdiBrowser program.) For Prerequisites, you'll want to make sure the .NET Framework 2.0 is selected, and (unless you know that all your users will have the .NET Framework 2.0 installed) you'll probably want a setup file to be created to install the prerequisites. You'll also want to stipulate that the prerequisites should be downloaded from the vendor's site (that is, Microsoft's).

For Updates, you have a few options. You can avoid having the program check for updates entirely, or it can check for updates before it starts or after it has started running. Checking for updates before the program starts ensures that the user is always running the most recent version, but doing so might slow down startup time. If you choose to check for updates after the application starts running (which is my preference), the user might run an out-of-date version, but the next time the user runs the program, a dialog box will pop up asking the user whether he or she wants to download a newer version.

The Options dialog box requests a Publisher Name and a Product Name. These two names are used on the Web page that Visual Studio creates and also on the Start menu when the program is installed. If you leave these fields blank, Visual Studio will use a Publisher Name that is the same as the company name you specified when installing Windows, and a Product Name that is the same as the project name. I chose a Publisher Name of "Petzold Programming Windows Forms" and a Product Name of "Control Explorer"—that is, a friendlier two-word version rather than one.

You can also enter a Support URL. Visual Studio puts a link to the URL on the Web page that it creates and also puts it on the Start menu alongside the program. I chose to leave this option blank.

For Deployment Web Page, I entered *publish.htm*. (Some beta versions of Visual Studio 2005 entered this name by default.) Under that field, I selected the two check boxes to generate the HTML file automatically and display it after publishing has completed. The other check boxes I left in their default values.

Security Issues

Some special considerations accompany the process of publishing an application on a Web site. The two main issues are what the program does and where it comes from. Users want to be assured that a downloaded program isn't going to wreck their systems, and part of this assurance involves trusting the particular Web site where they obtain the program.

Click the Security tab in the Project Properties dialog box. By default, the Enable ClickOnce Security Settings check box should be checked. You have a choice of flagging your application as "full trust" or "partial trust." These terms apply to the user's trust of your application. Do you require the user to have "full trust" that the application won't do anything bad, or do you just require the user to have "partial trust" and let the .NET common language runtime prevent the application from harming the system?

By default, the Full Thrust radio button is selected. It is likely that most Windows Forms applications will need to perform certain actions (such as accessing files) that require full trust from the user. If you want to attempt to write a partial trust application, you must take heed of the .NET Framework Security section in the documentation of classes, methods, and properties that your program uses. This section of documentation (if present) tells you what types of permissions your program requires. For a partial trust application downloaded over the Internet, a program has only *FileDialogPermission*, *IsolatedStorageFilePermission*, *SecurityPermission*, *UIPermission*, and *PrintingPermission*. (These are classes in the *System.Security.Permissions* and *System.Drawing.Printing* namespaces.) The ControlExplorer program uses some methods requiring *ReflectionPermission*, so ControlExplorer cannot be a partial trust application.

Most applications will require full trust from the user. For that reason, you'll want to persuade potential users that the program comes from a reputable source and hasn't been altered since it was published. You do this by using a process called "code signing" with Microsoft's Authenticode technology. You first obtain a code-signing digital certificate from a certificate authority (or CA). Perhaps the best-known certificate authority is VeriSign, but if you're like me (an unincorporated freelancer), VeriSign doesn't want your business. Other companies (such as Comodo at *www.instantssl.com*) will sell certificates to individuals.

For me, the process of obtaining a code-signing certificate resulted in the creation of two files on my local computer: an .SPC ("software publisher certificate") file and a .PVK ("private key") file, which is password protected. Visual Studio wants a .PFX ("personal information exchange") file. You can create a .PFX file from .SPC and .PVK files using the PVK Digital Certificate Files Importer (pvkimprt.exe), a utility available at *http://office.microsoft.com/downloads/2000/pvkimprt.aspx*.

To use this .PFX file to sign your application, select the Signing tab in the Project Properties dialog box. Check the Sign The ClickOnce Manifests check box. Click the Select From File button to specify the .PFX file. The certificate authority should also have provided a URL that you can enter in the Timestamp Server URL field.

If you do not provide a code-signing certificate, Visual Studio will manufacture a temporary one for you during the publishing process, but to the user it will seem as if the code has not been signed.

Publishing the Application

We're now ready to go back to the Publish tab of the Project Properties dialog box. The final step is to click the Publish Now button. While attempting to connect to your FTP site, Visual Studio will probably request a user ID and password. After installation is complete, you might want to explore the directories and files that Visual Studio creates on your Web site. Aside from *publish.htm* and *setup.exe*, you'll see XML files with the filename extensions .application and .manifest, and a binary .deploy file. Directories are created for each new version you publish.

One warning: Your Web server must know about the MIME type of the .application and .manifest files. You'll probably need to add the following two lines to the *.htaccess* file in the root directory of your Web site:

```
AddType application/x-ms-application application
AddType application/x-ms-application manifest
```

Of course, I also needed to change the *index.html* page located in my *winforms* directory to invoke the *publish.htm* page in the *ControlExplorer* subdirectory. That simply required some HTML that looked like this:

```
Install <a href="ControlExplorer/publish.htm">Control Explorer</a> ...
```

At some point in the future, I might want to design my own *publish.htm* page that more closely resembles the rest of my Web site, but for now this one does the job.

When installing the ClickOnce program, the user sees a dialog box labeled "Application Install – Security Warning." If you have not signed the application, this dialog box will contain warnings such as "Publisher cannot be verified" and "Publisher of this software is unknown." If you have signed the application, no such warnings appear, and you (the publisher) are identified to the user. If the application requires full trust, the dialog box contains warnings such as "Application requires potentially unsafe access to your computer." For partial trust applications, the dialog box informs the user that "Application can only access your computer in ways deemed safe."

Case Study 2: MdiBrowser

The Windows Forms control known as *WebBrowser* incorporates so much of the functionality of Internet Explorer that I almost feel guilty using it. To get a little idea of its basic capabilities, just create a *WebBrowser* control in ControlExplorer, type a URL into the *Url* property, and start playing. Although there's no Back button—a problem that at first seems to inhibit navigation a bit—you can press the Backspace key or right-click the control and select Back from the context menu. The context menu also allows you to print the page, so it's evident that printing functionality is built in, as well. (Of course, the *WebBrowser* control, which is built around an ActiveX control, is basically Internet Explorer, so none of this is surprising.)

The next program I describe is a Web browser that uses the Multiple Document Interface (MDI), a program structure that has fallen out of favor in recent years, but which is supported under Windows Forms and seems to be one good approach for a browser application. (The Web browser Opera uses MDI.) The program hosts multiple child windows, each of which can display a different Web page and be independently navigated.

In many other respects, I shamelessly mimic the user interface of Internet Explorer, for better or worse. MdiBrowser contains a toolbar that displays buttons for Back, Forward, Stop, Refresh, Home, and Print, and an "address bar" (actually a second *ToolStrip*) that allows entering a URL and clicking a Go button.

The status bar, however, I decided would be more properly implemented on the child window so that each child window has its own status bar. If you consider that multiple child windows can be engaged in different downloads, they should really be marking download progress on separate status bars. Here's the program as it appears the first time you run it:

Of course, as the creator of this program, I have the prerogative to set the default Home page to whatever I see fit.

The Multiple Document Interface

An MDI program has a main application window, but the client area is host to child forms, each containing its own document. These children look much like application windows except they generally have no menus. As you switch among the children, the program's main menu and toolbar (if any) show settings and options that reflect the currently active child window. For example, a browser toolbar probably has Back and Forward buttons. The Back button is enabled only if the page is capable of backing up, and the Forward button is enabled only if the user already backed up from a page. As you switch between the child windows, these buttons should change to reflect whether or not the currently active child can go back or forward.

An application form becomes an MDI container by setting its *IsMdiContainer* property to *true*. Setting this flag results in the creation of a control of type *MdiClient* that fills the client area and is the actual parent to the child documents. Generally, however, you don't interact with the *MdiClient* control directly. A child window is an instance of *Form* or a class that derives from *Form*. When you create a child form, you set its *MdiParent* to the application form and call its *Show* method.

If you minimize a child window, it is displayed at the bottom of the application client area collapsed to a degree where just part of the caption bar is visible. If you maximize a child window, the caption bar of the child disappears. The text that appeared in that caption bar is surrounded by square brackets and appended to the caption bar text of the application. The icon, minimize box, maximize box, and close box of the child become part of the application menu. If you're using a *MenuStrip* control rather than the older *MainMenu*, you should set the *MainMenuStrip* property of the application form to the *MenuStrip* object to get this to work the way it should.

A child window can determine whether it is an MDI child by examining its *IsMdiChild* property. An application window can obtain a collection of its children through the *MdiChildren* property.

The child window that is in front of all the others with a highlighted caption bar is called the *active* child. An application form can activate a particular child by calling the *ActivateMdiChild* method. An application form can obtain the currently active child by examining the *ActiveMdiChild* property. An application form can be notified when the active child changes by installing an event handler for the *MdiChildActivate* event or (probably more commonly) overriding the *OnMdiChildActivate* method.

It is common for an MDI program to have a top-level menu item labeled Window. This is usually the last item on the menu before Help. Generally, this menu contains items to Cascade, Tile, or Minimize the children. You can implement these menu items with the *LayoutMdi* method.

By convention, the Window menu also contains a list of all the current children so the user can select among them. If there are more than nine children, an option at the bottom of the menu brings up a little dialog box that lets you choose the child you want. You do *not* need to implement this feature. All you need to do is set the *MdiWindowListItem* property of the *MenuStrip* to the *ToolStripMenuItem* for the Window item.

Solution and Project

Until now, I've been creating projects in Visual Studio so that the project file (.csproj) and solution file (.sln) both end up in the same directory, which is given the name of the project. It is also possible, when creating a new project, to select the Create Directory For Solution check box in the New Project dialog box. You'll then get a solution directory (by default, the same name as the project you're creating) and a project directory as a subdirectory of the solution.

That's how I created the MdiBrowser project. Later in this chapter, we'll see how to create a Help file for the program. I wanted the files for Help to be located in a directory named Help that is a subdirectory of the MdiBrowser solution directory but a sibling of the MdiBrowser project directory.

Favorites and Settings

If I were seriously interested in writing a Web browser that would compete with Internet Explorer, I'd try to integrate with Internet Explorer's storage of Favorites, or at least provide an import option. Because MdiBrowser is really just for pedagogical purposes, I thought it would be more instructive to implement my own logic to save and display Favorites rather than try to integrate with Internet Explorer. (As a result, the program is somewhat inconsistent: If you use the menu to set a Favorite, MdiBrowser saves it. But if you use the *WebBrowser* control context menu, the Favorite is saved with the Internet Explorer Favorites.) My Favorites logic does not permit directories, and it does not allow changing the text identifying the Favorite to something other than the title of the Web page.

A Favorite is encapsulated by the *Favorite* class.

```
Favorite.cs
//----------------------------------------
// Favorite.cs (c) 2005 by Charles Petzold
// From MdiBrowser Program
//----------------------------------------
using System;

public class Favorite : IComparable<Favorite>
{
    string strTitle, strUrl;

    // Public properties.
    public string Title
    {
        get { return strTitle; }
        set { strTitle = value; }
    }
    public string Url
    {
        get { return strUrl; }
        set { strUrl = value; }
    }
    // Constructors.
    public Favorite()
    {
    }
    public Favorite(string strTitle, string strUrl)
    {
        Title = strTitle;
        Url = strUrl;
    }
    // Method to implement IComparable interface.
    public int CompareTo(Favorite fav)
    {
        return Title.CompareTo(fav.Title);
    }
}
```

It's really just two strings. The class implements the *IComparable* interface so that the favorites can be sorted by the *Title* property. The class is defined as *public* and contains a parameterless constructor, so it is serializable by the *XmlSerializer* class.

The main class for saving and retrieving program settings is called *MdiBrowserSettings*.

MdiBrowserSettings.cs

```
//---------------------------------------------------
// MdiBrowserSettings.cs (c) 2005 by Charles Petzold
// From MdiBrowser Program
//---------------------------------------------------
using System;
using System.Collections.Generic;
using System.Drawing;
using System.IO;
using System.Windows.Forms;
using System.Xml.Serialization;

public class MdiBrowserSettings
{
    // Default settings.
    public Rectangle WindowBounds = new Rectangle(0, 0, 800, 600);
    public FormWindowState WindowState = FormWindowState.Normal;

    public Rectangle ChildWindowBounds = new Rectangle(0, 0, 660, 400);
    public FormWindowState ChildWindowState = FormWindowState.Normal;

    public string Home = "http://www.charlespetzold.com";
    public bool ViewToolBar = true;
    public bool ViewAddressBar = true;

    // Lists of favorites and typed-in URLs.
    public List<Favorite> Favorites = new List<Favorite>();
    public List<string> ManualUrls = new List<string>();

    // Load settings from file.
    public static MdiBrowserSettings Load(string strAppData)
    {
        StreamReader sr;
        MdiBrowserSettings settings;
        XmlSerializer xmlser =
            new XmlSerializer(typeof(MdiBrowserSettings));

        try
        {
            sr = new StreamReader(strAppData);
            settings = (MdiBrowserSettings)xmlser.Deserialize(sr);
            sr.Close();
        }
        catch
        {
            settings = new MdiBrowserSettings();
        }
        return settings;
    }
    // Save settings to file.
    public void Save(string strAppData)
    {
```

```
            Directory.CreateDirectory(Path.GetDirectoryName(strAppData));
            StreamWriter sw = new StreamWriter(strAppData);
            XmlSerializer xmlser = new XmlSerializer(GetType());
            xmlser.Serialize(sw, this);
            sw.Close();
        }
    }
```

Just for simplicity and clarity, the settings are maintained as public fields rather than properties. *WindowBounds* and *WindowState* refer to the initial size of the application window and whether it's minimized, maximized, or normal. The *ChildWindowBounds* and *ChildWindowState* are the same properties for the child windows (although the program currently doesn't change these settings).

The next field is the default Home page. The next two fields govern the display of the toolbar and address bar.

Two *List* objects are also maintained—one of *Favorite* objects and another called *ManualUrls* that consists of all the URLs entered manually by the user in the address bar or the File Open dialog box.

The class concludes with *Load* and *Save* methods—the former is used to load in an existing XML file with the settings, and the latter is used to save the current *MdiBrowserSettings* object. The filename used by these methods is defined by the *MdiBrowser* class coming up.

The Child Window

The class for the child window is called *BrowserChild*, and it inherits from *Form*. The constructor creates both a *WebBrowser* control to fill most of its client area and a *StatusStrip* at the bottom.

BrowserChild.cs
```
//-------------------------------------------
// BrowserChild.cs (c) 2005 by Charles Petzold
// From MdiBrowser Program
//-------------------------------------------
using System;
using System.Drawing;
using System.Windows.Forms;

class BrowserChild : Form
{
    WebBrowser wb;
    ToolStripStatusLabel statlbl;
    ToolStripProgressBar statprog;

    // Constructor.
    public BrowserChild()
    {
```

```csharp
        wb = new WebBrowser();
        wb.Parent = this;
        wb.Dock = DockStyle.Fill;

        StatusStrip status = new StatusStrip();
        status.Parent = this;

        statlbl = new ToolStripStatusLabel();
        statlbl.TextAlign = ContentAlignment.MiddleLeft;
        statlbl.Spring = true;
        status.Items.Add(statlbl);

        statprog = new ToolStripProgressBar();
        statprog.Visible = false;
        status.Items.Add(statprog);

        // Now that the StatusStrip is in place, it's safe to install
        //   event handlers for the WebBrowser.
        wb.DocumentTitleChanged += OnDocumentTitleChanged;
        wb.StatusTextChanged += OnStatusTextChanged;
        wb.ProgressChanged += OnProgressChanged;
    }
    // Public property.
    public WebBrowser WebBrowser
    {
        get { return wb; }
    }
    // Event handlers for caption bar and status bar.
    void OnDocumentTitleChanged(object objSrc, EventArgs args)
    {
        WebBrowser wb = objSrc as WebBrowser;
        Text = wb.DocumentTitle;

        if (wb.Url != null && wb.Url.ToString().Length > 0)
            Text += " \x2014 " + wb.Url.ToString();
    }
    void OnStatusTextChanged(object objSrc, EventArgs args)
    {
        WebBrowser wb = objSrc as WebBrowser;
        statlbl.Text = wb.StatusText;
    }
    void OnProgressChanged(object obj, WebBrowserProgressChangedEventArgs args)
    {
        if (statprog.Visible = (args.CurrentProgress != args.MaximumProgress))
            statprog.Value = (int)(100 * args.CurrentProgress /
                                        args.MaximumProgress);
    }
    protected override void OnClosed(EventArgs args)
    {
        base.OnClosed(args);
        WebBrowser.Dispose();
    }
}
```

This class is responsible for keeping the caption bar and status bar of the window up to date, but this isn't much work: three events implemented by *WebBrowser* called *DocumentTitleChanged*, *StatusTextChanged*, and *ProgressChanged* inform the class when any changes have occurred.

The Application Form

As I was developing this program, the application form class (which of course I named *MdiBrowser*) got larger and larger. This class normally contains code to create the menu and toolbars, and it also defines handlers for menu and toolbar *Click* events. To the rescue came the *partial* keyword introduced with C# 2.0. The *partial* keyword lets you divide a class among multiple source code files. A program can thus have multiple class definitions that look like this:

```
partial class MdiBrowser
{
    ...
}
```

I decided that each top-level menu item would be implemented in a separate file. These files are named MdiBrowser.FileMenu.cs, MdiBrower.ViewMenu.cs, MdiBrowser.FavoritesMenu.cs, MdiBrowser.WindowMenu.cs, and MdiBrowser.HelpMenu.cs. Each of these files contains a method that creates that part of the menu and also the event handlers for that part of the menu. The toolbar and address bar are also implemented in separate files named MdiBrowser.ToolBar.cs and MdiBrowser.AddrBar.cs.

Moving all those jobs to other files left MdiBrowser.cs with almost nothing to do.

MdiBrowser.cs

```
//------------------------------------------
// MdiBrowser.cs (c) 2005 by Charles Petzold
// From MdiBrowser Program
//------------------------------------------
using System;
using System.Drawing;
using System.IO;
using System.Reflection;
using System.Windows.Forms;

[assembly: AssemblyTitle("MDI Browser")]
[assembly: AssemblyDescription("Multiple Document Interface Web Browser")]
[assembly: AssemblyCompany("www.charlespetzold.com")]
[assembly: AssemblyProduct("MDI Browser")]
[assembly: AssemblyCopyright("(c) 2005 by Charles Petzold")]
[assembly: AssemblyVersion("1.0.*")]
[assembly: AssemblyFileVersion("1.0.0.0")]

partial class MdiBrowser : Form
{
```

```csharp
static string strAppData = Path.Combine(
    Environment.GetFolderPath(
        Environment.SpecialFolder.LocalApplicationData),
            "Petzold\\MdiBrowser\\MdiBrowser.Settings.xml");


MdiBrowserSettings settings;
MenuStrip menu;
ToolStrip addr, tool;

[STAThread]
public static void Main()
{
    Application.EnableVisualStyles();
    Application.Run(new MdiBrowser());
}
public MdiBrowser()
{

    // Set basic Form properties.
    Text = "MDI Browser";
    Icon = new Icon(GetType(), "MdiBrowser.MdiBrowser.ico");
    IsMdiContainer = true;

    // Load settings.
    settings = MdiBrowserSettings.Load(strAppData);

    // Set window size and state.
    Bounds = settings.WindowBounds;
    WindowState = settings.WindowState;

    // Create Address bar ToolStrip
    addr = CreateAddressBar("MdiBrowser");  // in MdiBrowser.AddrBar.cs

    // Create Toolbar ToolStrip
    tool = CreateToolBar("MdiBrowser");  // in MdiBrowser.ToolBar.cs

    // Create MenuStrip
    menu = new MenuStrip();
    menu.Parent = this;
    MainMenuStrip = menu;              // This is good for MDI.

    menu.Items.Add(FileMenu());        // in MdiBrowser.FileMenu.cs
    menu.Items.Add(ViewMenu());        // in MdiBrowser.ViewMenu.cs
    menu.Items.Add(FavoritesMenu());// in MdiBrowser.FavoritesMenu.cs
    menu.Items.Add(WindowMenu());      // in MdiBrowser.WindowMenu.cs
    menu.Items.Add(HelpMenu());        // in MdiBrowser.HelpMenu.cs

    // Load a child window with the Home page.
    Go(settings.Home, false);
}
// The Go method goes to a URL and optionally adds it to the list.
void Go(string strUrl, bool bAddToList)
{
    BrowserChild bcNew = new BrowserChild();
    bcNew.MdiParent = this;
    bcNew.Icon = Icon;
```

```
        bcNew.WebBrowser.Navigate(strUrl);

        // We're setting these from the settings object, but not
        //  updating them. That would require installing event
        //  handlers for Resize and saving the user's last
        //  preference.
        bcNew.Bounds = settings.ChildWindowBounds;
        bcNew.WindowState = settings.ChildWindowState;
        bcNew.Show();

        // If the URL was typed in manually, add it to the list
        //  to be displayed by the combo boxes.
        if (bAddToList)
        {
            if (settings.ManualUrls.IndexOf(strUrl) == -1)
            {
                settings.ManualUrls.Add(strUrl);
                settings.ManualUrls.Sort();
                settings.Save(strAppData);
            }
        }
    }
    // Save settings when the form is closing.
    protected override void OnClosed(EventArgs args)
    {
        settings.WindowState = WindowState;
        settings.WindowBounds = WindowState ==
            FormWindowState.Normal ? Bounds : RestoreBounds;
        settings.Save(strAppData);

        base.OnClosed(args);
    }
}
```

Notice that the class sets the *IsMdiContainer* property to *true*, which is the necessary prerequisite to implementing the Multiple Document Interface.

The program then attempts to load a settings file. Where are program settings saved? Generally, applications store per-user program settings in the area of isolated storage known as "user application data." For a program named MdiBrowser, distributed by a company named Petzold and installed by a user named Deirdre, the program settings would be saved in this directory:

\Documents and Settings\Deirdre\Application Data\Petzold\MdiBrowser

However, for ClickOnce applications, it's recommended that program settings go in the area known as "local user application data":

\Documents and Settings\Deirdre\Local Settings\Application Data\Petzold\MdiBrowser

Although both of these areas are specific to the particular user, the regular user application data is intended for roaming—that is, when the user logs on to a different machine—while the local user application data is specific to the particular user on the particular machine.

I used the static *Environment.GetFolderPath* method to obtain the current user's Local Application Data directory, but it's also possible to use the *Application.LocalUserAppDataPath* method, which automatically uses the *CompanyName*, *ProductName*, and *ProductVersion* properties to create a directory name.

If the settings file doesn't exist, the *MdiBrowserSettings* class creates an object with default settings. The program then creates the address bar, toolbar, and menu, and it finishes up by calling the *Go* method with the user's preferred Home page. *Go* creates a new *BrowserChild* with the URL.

The override of *OnClosed* saves the new program settings. Saving settings on program termination is usually easier (and faster) than saving settings every time they change. However, there's a potential problem with this approach: Suppose you run this program and add a couple favorites. Then you run a second instance of the program. Because the first instance hasn't saved its settings, the second instance doesn't know about these newly added favorites. You terminate the first instance, and it saves all settings, including the new favorites. You then terminate the second instance, which saves the favorites that existed before the first instance ran.

One solution is to prevent multiple instances from running, possibly by creating a *Mutex* object, which is a systemwide synchronization mechanism. The first instance successfully owns the *Mutex*, but the second instance cannot. I ultimately decided that I would allow multiple instances but save the settings object after a new item was added to either the *ManualUrls* or *Favorites* list.

The MdiBrowser.ico file looks like a globe in an MDI window:

The File Menu

The File menu in MdiBrowser contains items for New, Open, Save As, three printing-related items, Properties, and Exit. Aside from New, Open, and Exit, all these items are implemented as simple method calls in *WebBrower*. The *Click* event handlers need only obtain the currently active child, which is an object of type *BrowserChild*, and access its *WebBrowser* property.

MdiBrowser.FileMenu.cs

```csharp
//-------------------------------------------------------
// MdiBrowser.FileMenu.cs (c) 2005 by Charles Petzold
// From MdiBrowser Program
//-------------------------------------------------------
using System;
using System.Drawing;
using System.Windows.Forms;

partial class MdiBrowser: Form
{
    ToolStripMenuItem itemSaveAs, itemPrint, itemPreview, itemProps;

    ToolStripMenuItem FileMenu()
    {
        ToolStripMenuItem itemFile = new ToolStripMenuItem("&File");
        itemFile.DropDownOpening += FileOnDropDownOpening;

        ToolStripMenuItem item = new ToolStripMenuItem("&New");
        item.ShortcutKeys = Keys.Control | Keys.N;
        item.Click += NewOnClick;
        itemFile.DropDownItems.Add(item);

        item = new ToolStripMenuItem("&Open...");
        item.ShortcutKeys = Keys.Control | Keys.O;
        item.Click += OpenOnClick;
        itemFile.DropDownItems.Add(item);

        itemSaveAs = new ToolStripMenuItem("Save &As...");
        itemSaveAs.Click += SaveAsOnClick;
        itemFile.DropDownItems.Add(itemSaveAs);

        itemFile.DropDownItems.Add(new ToolStripSeparator());

        item = new ToolStripMenuItem("Page Set&up...");
        item.Click += PageSetupOnClick;
        itemFile.DropDownItems.Add(item);

        itemPrint = new ToolStripMenuItem("&Print...");
        itemPrint.ShortcutKeys = Keys.Control | Keys.P;
        itemPrint.Click += PrintDialogOnClick;
        itemFile.DropDownItems.Add(itemPrint);

        itemPreview = new ToolStripMenuItem("Print Pre&view...");
        itemPreview.Click += PreviewOnClick;
        itemFile.DropDownItems.Add(itemPreview);

        itemFile.DropDownItems.Add(new ToolStripSeparator());

        itemProps = new ToolStripMenuItem("P&roperties");
        itemProps.Click += PropertiesOnClick;
        itemFile.DropDownItems.Add(itemProps);

        itemFile.DropDownItems.Add(new ToolStripSeparator());
```

```csharp
        item = new ToolStripMenuItem("E&xit");
        item.Click += CloseOnClick;
        itemFile.DropDownItems.Add(item);

        return itemFile;
}
void FileOnDropDownOpening(object objSrc, EventArgs args)
{
        BrowserChild bcActive = ActiveMdiChild as BrowserChild;

        itemSaveAs.Enabled = (bcActive != null);
        itemPrint.Enabled = (bcActive != null);
        itemPreview.Enabled = (bcActive != null);
        itemProps.Enabled = (bcActive != null);
}
void NewOnClick(object objSrc, EventArgs args)
{
        BrowserChild bcActive = ActiveMdiChild as BrowserChild;
        string strUrl;

        if (bcActive != null)
            strUrl = bcActive.WebBrowser.Url.ToString();
        else
            strUrl = settings.Home;

        Go(strUrl, false);
}
void OpenOnClick(object objSrc, EventArgs args)
{
        OpenDialog dlg = new OpenDialog(settings);

        if (dlg.ShowDialog() == DialogResult.OK)
        {
            Go(dlg.Url, true);
        }
}
void SaveAsOnClick(object objSrc, EventArgs args)
{
        BrowserChild bcActive = ActiveMdiChild as BrowserChild;

        if (bcActive != null)
            bcActive.WebBrowser.ShowSaveAsDialog();
}
void PageSetupOnClick(object objSrc, EventArgs args)
{
        BrowserChild bcActive = ActiveMdiChild as BrowserChild;

        if (bcActive != null)
            bcActive.WebBrowser.ShowPageSetupDialog();
}
void PrintDialogOnClick(object objSrc, EventArgs args)
{
        BrowserChild bcActive = ActiveMdiChild as BrowserChild;

        if (bcActive != null)
```

```
                bcActive.WebBrowser.ShowPrintDialog();
        }
        void PreviewOnClick(object objSrc, EventArgs args)
        {
            BrowserChild bcActive = ActiveMdiChild as BrowserChild;

            if (bcActive != null)
                bcActive.WebBrowser.ShowPrintPreviewDialog();
        }
        void PropertiesOnClick(object objSrc, EventArgs args)
        {
            BrowserChild bcActive = ActiveMdiChild as BrowserChild;

            if (bcActive != null)
                bcActive.WebBrowser.ShowPropertiesDialog();
        }
        void ExitOnClick(object objSrc, EventArgs args)
        {
            Close();
        }
    }
```

When you select the New item from the File menu in Internet Explorer, a new instance of the program is created with the same Web page. For *MdiBrowser*, I decided to do the equivalent, which is to create a new *BrowserChild* with the same Web page as the active child. If no child is active, the event handler creates a new *BrowserChild* and sends the child Home.

The Open option requires more work. It first invokes a small dialog box, implemented by the following class.

OpenDialog.cs

```
//-------------------------------------------
// OpenDialog.cs (c) 2005 by Charles Petzold
// From MdiBrowser Program
//-------------------------------------------
using System;
using System.Drawing;
using System.Windows.Forms;

class OpenDialog : Form
{
    ComboBox combo;
    Button btnOk;

    // Public property.
    public string Url
    {
        get { return combo.Text; }
        set { combo.Text = value; }
    }
    // Constructor.
    public OpenDialog(MdiBrowserSettings settings)
```

```
{
        // Set numerous properties.
        Text = "Open";
        AutoSize = true;
        AutoSizeMode = AutoSizeMode.GrowAndShrink;
        FormBorderStyle = FormBorderStyle.FixedDialog;
        ControlBox = false;
        MinimizeBox = false;
        MaximizeBox = false;
        ShowInTaskbar = false;
        Icon = ActiveForm.Icon;
        StartPosition = FormStartPosition.Manual;
        Location = ActiveForm.Location + SystemInformation.CaptionButtonSize +
                                    SystemInformation.FrameBorderSize;

        // Create table layout panel and controls.
        TableLayoutPanel table = new TableLayoutPanel();
        table.Parent = this;
        table.AutoSize = true;
        table.Padding = new Padding(Font.Height);
        table.RowCount = 3;
        table.ColumnCount = 4;

        Label lbl = new Label();
        lbl.Text = "Enter a URL or filename, or\r\n" +
                "Select a previously visited site from the list, or\r\n" +
                "Press Browse to select a file.";
        lbl.AutoSize = true;
        table.Controls.Add(lbl, 1, 0);
        table.SetColumnSpan(lbl, 3);

        lbl = new Label();
        lbl.Text = "Open: ";
        lbl.AutoSize = true;
        lbl.Anchor = AnchorStyles.Left;
        table.Controls.Add(lbl, 0, 1);

        combo = new ComboBox();
        combo.AutoSize = true;
        combo.Anchor = AnchorStyles.Left | AnchorStyles.Right;
        combo.TextChanged += ComboBoxOnTextChanged;
        combo.BeginUpdate();
        foreach (string str in settings.ManualUrls)
            combo.Items.Add(str);
        combo.EndUpdate();

        table.Controls.Add(combo, 1, 1);
        table.SetColumnSpan(combo, 3);

        btnOk = new Button();
        btnOk.Text = "OK";
        btnOk.AutoSize = true;
        btnOk.DialogResult = DialogResult.OK;
        btnOk.Enabled = false;
        btnOk.Margin = new Padding(Font.Height);
```

```
        table.Controls.Add(btnOk, 1, 2);
        AcceptButton = btnOk;

        Button btn = new Button();
        btn.Text = "Cancel";
        btn.AutoSize = true;
        btn.DialogResult = DialogResult.Cancel;
        btn.Margin = new Padding(Font.Height);
        table.Controls.Add(btn, 2, 2);
        CancelButton = btn;

        btn = new Button();
        btn.Text = "Browse...";
        btn.AutoSize = true;
        btn.Margin = new Padding(Font.Height);
        btn.Click += BrowseOnClick;
        table.Controls.Add(btn, 3, 2);
    }
    void ComboBoxOnTextChanged(object objSrc, EventArgs args)
    {
        ComboBox combo = objSrc as ComboBox;
        btnOk.Enabled = combo.Text != null && combo.Text.Length > 0;
    }
    void BrowseOnClick(object objSrc, EventArgs args)
    {
        OpenFileDialog dlg = new OpenFileDialog();

        if (dlg.ShowDialog() == DialogResult.OK)
        {
            Url = dlg.FileName;
        }
    }
}
```

The *ComboBox* in this control lists all the URLs in the *ManualUrls* collection in the *settings* object. An object is added to this collection in the *Go* method (in MdiBrowser.cs) when the second argument is *true*, which is the case when the user enters a URL in this dialog box. This dialog box is also capable of displaying a standard *OpenFileDialog* that lets the user pick a file to display.

The View Menu

The View menu implements three different types of commands. The first two commands let the user suppress the display of the toolbar and address bar. The *Click* handlers simply set the appropriate *Visible* property and save the value in the *settings* object. The next set of commands includes Back, Forward, Stop, Refresh, and Home, the first four of which are implemented simply by calling methods in *WebBrowser*. Finally, the View menu has a Source item that lets you view the HTML source from the *WebBrowser* control.

MdiBrowser.ViewMenu.cs

```
//---------------------------------------------------
// MdiBrowser.ViewMenu.cs (c) 2005 by Charles Petzold
// From MdiBrowser Program
//---------------------------------------------------
using System;
using System.Drawing;
using System.Windows.Forms;

partial class MdiBrowser : Form
{
    ToolStripMenuItem itemBack, itemForward, itemStop;
    ToolStripMenuItem itemRefresh, itemHome, itemSource;

    ToolStripMenuItem ViewMenu()
    {
        ToolStripMenuItem itemView = new ToolStripMenuItem("&View");
        itemView.DropDownOpening += ViewOnDropDownOpening;

        ToolStripMenuItem item = new ToolStripMenuItem("&Tool Bar");
        item.Checked = settings.ViewToolBar;
        item.CheckOnClick = true;
        item.Click += ViewToolBarOnClick;
        itemView.DropDownItems.Add(item);

        item = new ToolStripMenuItem("&Address Bar");
        item.Checked = settings.ViewAddressBar;
        item.CheckOnClick = true;
        item.Click += ViewAddressBarOnClick;
        itemView.DropDownItems.Add(item);

        itemView.DropDownItems.Add(new ToolStripSeparator());

        itemBack = new ToolStripMenuItem("&Back");
        itemBack.Click += BackOnClick;
        itemView.DropDownItems.Add(itemBack);

        itemForward = new ToolStripMenuItem("&Forward");
        itemForward.Click += ForwardOnClick;
        itemView.DropDownItems.Add(itemForward);

        itemStop = new ToolStripMenuItem("Sto&p");
        itemStop.Click += StopOnClick;
        itemView.DropDownItems.Add(itemStop);

        itemRefresh = new ToolStripMenuItem("&Refresh");
        itemRefresh.Click += RefreshOnClick;
        itemView.DropDownItems.Add(itemRefresh);

        itemHome = new ToolStripMenuItem("&Home");
        itemHome.Click += HomeOnClick;
        itemView.DropDownItems.Add(itemHome);

        itemView.DropDownItems.Add(new ToolStripSeparator());
```

```
        itemSource = new ToolStripMenuItem("Sour&ce");
        itemSource.Click += ViewSourceOnClick;
        itemView.DropDownItems.Add(itemSource);

        return itemView;
    }
    // Event handler for View menu dropping down.
    void ViewOnDropDownOpening(object objSrc, EventArgs args)
    {
        BrowserChild bc = ActiveMdiChild as BrowserChild;
        bool bActiveChild = bc != null;

        // Disable all these items if there's no active MDI child.
        itemBack.Enabled = bActiveChild;
        itemForward.Enabled = bActiveChild;
        itemStop.Enabled = bActiveChild;
        itemRefresh.Enabled = bActiveChild;
        itemHome.Enabled = bActiveChild;
        itemSource.Enabled = bActiveChild;

        // If there's an active child, enable these items based on properties.
        if (bActiveChild)
        {
            itemBack.Enabled = bc.WebBrowser.CanGoBack;
            itemForward.Enabled = bc.WebBrowser.CanGoForward;
        }
    }
    // Make toolbar and address bar visible or invisible.
    void ViewToolBarOnClick(object objSrc, EventArgs args)
    {
        ToolStripMenuItem item = objSrc as ToolStripMenuItem;
        tool.Visible = settings.ViewToolBar = item.Checked;
    }
    void ViewAddressBarOnClick(object objSrc, EventArgs args)
    {
        ToolStripMenuItem item = objSrc as ToolStripMenuItem;
        addr.Visible = settings.ViewAddressBar = item.Checked;
    }
    // Implement Back, Forward, Stop, Refresh, and Home.
    void BackOnClick(object objSrc, EventArgs args)
    {
        BrowserChild bc = ActiveMdiChild as BrowserChild;

        if (bc != null)
            bc.WebBrowser.GoBack();
    }
    void ForwardOnClick(object objSrc, EventArgs args)
    {
        BrowserChild bc = ActiveMdiChild as BrowserChild;

        if (bc != null)
            bc.WebBrowser.GoForward();
    }
    void StopOnClick(object objSrc, EventArgs args)
    {
```

```
            BrowserChild bc = ActiveMdiChild as BrowserChild;

            if (bc != null)
                bc.WebBrowser.Stop();
    }
    void RefreshOnClick(object objSrc, EventArgs args)
    {
            BrowserChild bc = ActiveMdiChild as BrowserChild;

            if (bc != null)
                bc.WebBrowser.Refresh();
    }
    void HomeOnClick(object objSrc, EventArgs args)
    {
            BrowserChild bc = ActiveMdiChild as BrowserChild;

            if (bc != null)
                bc.WebBrowser.Url = new Uri(settings.Home);
    }
    // View Source menu item.
    void ViewSourceOnClick(object objSrc, EventArgs args)
    {
            BrowserChild bc = ActiveMdiChild as BrowserChild;

            if (bc != null)
            {
                Form frm = new Form();
                frm.Text = bc.WebBrowser.DocumentTitle;

                TextBox txtbox = new TextBox();
                txtbox.Parent = frm;
                txtbox.Multiline = true;
                txtbox.WordWrap = false;
                txtbox.ScrollBars = ScrollBars.Both;
                txtbox.Dock = DockStyle.Fill;
                txtbox.Text = bc.WebBrowser.DocumentText;
                txtbox.Select(0, 0);

                frm.Show();
            }
    }
}
```

The Favorites Menu

The Favorites menu lists the *Favorites* collection from the *settings* object, of course, but it also includes an option to add the page of the currently active child window to the collection. (Unlike Internet Explorer, this item doesn't display a dialog box first, and I don't provide any way to rename the title, organize the favorites, or delete a favorite.) I also use this menu for setting the Home page to the page of the currently active child.

MdiBrowser.FavoritesMenu.cs

```csharp
//-----------------------------------------------------------
// MdiBrowser.FavoritesMenu.cs (c) 2005 by Charles Petzold
// From MdiBrowser Program
//-----------------------------------------------------------
using System;
using System.Drawing;
using System.Windows.Forms;

partial class MdiBrowser : Form
{
    ToolStripMenuItem itemAdd, itemSetHome;

    ToolStripMenuItem FavoritesMenu()
    {
        ToolStripMenuItem itemFavorites = new ToolStripMenuItem("F&avorites");
        itemFavorites.DropDownOpening += FavoritesOnDropDownOpening;

        return itemFavorites;
    }
    void FavoritesOnDropDownOpening(object objSrc, EventArgs args)
    {
        ToolStripMenuItem itemFavorites = objSrc as ToolStripMenuItem;
        BrowserChild bc = ActiveMdiChild as BrowserChild;

        // Remove everything from the drop-down menu.
        itemFavorites.DropDownItems.Clear();

        itemAdd = new ToolStripMenuItem("&Add to favorites");
        itemAdd.Enabled = (bc != null);
        itemAdd.Click += AddOnClick;
        itemFavorites.DropDownItems.Add(itemAdd);

        itemSetHome = new ToolStripMenuItem("&Make this your home");
        itemSetHome.Enabled = (bc != null);
        itemSetHome.Click += SetHomeOnClick;
        itemFavorites.DropDownItems.Add(itemSetHome);

        itemFavorites.DropDownItems.Add(new ToolStripSeparator());

        // Add favorites to the menu;
        foreach (Favorite fav in settings.Favorites)
        {
            ToolStripMenuItem item = new ToolStripMenuItem();
            item.Text = fav.Title;
            item.Tag = fav.Url;
            item.Click += FavoriteOnClick;
            itemFavorites.DropDownItems.Add(item);
        }
    }
    void AddOnClick(object objSrc, EventArgs args)
    {
        BrowserChild bc = ActiveMdiChild as BrowserChild;
```

```
        if (bc != null)
        {
            Favorite fav = new Favorite(bc.WebBrowser.DocumentTitle,
                                  bc.WebBrowser.Url.ToString());
            settings.Favorites.Add(fav);
            settings.Favorites.Sort();
            settings.Save(strAppData);
        }
    }
    void SetHomeOnClick(object objSrc, EventArgs args)
    {
        BrowserChild bc = ActiveMdiChild as BrowserChild;

        if (bc != null)
        {
            settings.Home = bc.WebBrowser.Url.ToString();
        }
    }
    void FavoriteOnClick(object objSrc, EventArgs args)
    {
        ToolStripMenuItem item = objSrc as ToolStripMenuItem;
        Go((string)item.Tag, false);
    }
}
```

The *FavoritesMenu* method is supposed to create the Favorites menu, but all it really does is create the top-level item and set a *DropDownOpening* event handler for it. That event handler re-creates the entire drop-down menu whenever it's required. Each of the favorites is given the same *Click* event handler, called *FavoriteOnClick*, that uses the *Tag* property to get the URL.

The Window Menu

The *WindowMenu* method creates the menu common in MDI applications labeled Window. Perhaps the most important statement in the *WindowMenu* method is the second one:

```
menu.MdiWindowListItem = itemWindow;
```

Setting the *MdiWindowListItem* property of the *MenuStrip* identifies this menu as the one where the child windows are to be listed, so that job involving the Window menu is now out of our hands.

The first four items on the Window menu—Cascade, Tile Horizontal, Tile Vertical, and Arrange Icons—correspond to the four members of the *MdiLayout* enumeration. I used the same event handler for all four by assigning the *Tag* property of the menu item to the appropriate enumeration value.

MdiBrowser.WindowMenu.cs

```
//-----------------------------------------------------
// MdiBrowser.WindowMenu.cs (c) 2005 by Charles Petzold
// From MdiBrowser Program
//-----------------------------------------------------
using System;
using System.Drawing;
using System.Windows.Forms;

partial class MdiBrowser : Form
{
    ToolStripMenuItem WindowMenu()
    {
        ToolStripMenuItem itemWindow = new ToolStripMenuItem("&Window");
        menu.MdiWindowListItem = itemWindow;

        ToolStripMenuItem item = new ToolStripMenuItem("&Cascade");
        item.Tag = MdiLayout.Cascade;
        item.Click += WindowArrangeOnClick;
        itemWindow.DropDownItems.Add(item);

        item = new ToolStripMenuItem("Tile &Horizontal");
        item.Tag = MdiLayout.TileHorizontal;
        item.Click += WindowArrangeOnClick;
        itemWindow.DropDownItems.Add(item);

        item = new ToolStripMenuItem("Tile &Vertical");
        item.Tag = MdiLayout.TileVertical;
        item.Click += WindowArrangeOnClick;
        itemWindow.DropDownItems.Add(item);

        item = new ToolStripMenuItem("&Arrange Icons");
        item.Tag = MdiLayout.ArrangeIcons;
        item.Click += WindowArrangeOnClick;
        itemWindow.DropDownItems.Add(item);

        itemWindow.DropDownItems.Add(new ToolStripSeparator());

        item = new ToolStripMenuItem("C&lose All Windows");
        item.Click += CloseAllOnClick;
        itemWindow.DropDownItems.Add(item);

        itemWindow.DropDownItems.Add(new ToolStripSeparator());

        return itemWindow;
    }
    // Two small Click handlers.
    void WindowArrangeOnClick(object objSrc, EventArgs args)
    {
        ToolStripMenuItem item = objSrc as ToolStripMenuItem;
        LayoutMdi((MdiLayout)item.Tag);
    }
    void CloseAllOnClick(object objSrc, EventArgs args)
    {
```

```
        while (MdiChildren.Length > 0)
            MdiChildren[0].Close();
    }
}
```

The Window menu also includes a Close All Windows item, which is handy if you want to clean up all your child windows and start afresh with a whole new family.

The Help Menu

The Help menu has two items: Help and About. For Help, the *Click* event handler simply calls the static *Help.ShowHelp* method with a file named MdiBrowser.chm. To conclude this chapter, I'll show you how to create such a file, ensure that it's in the same directory as the Mdi-Browser.exe file, and publish it to a Web site along with MdiBrowser.exe.

MdiBrowser.HelpMenu.cs
```
//----------------------------------------------------
// MdiBrowser.HelpMenu.cs (c) 2005 by Charles Petzold
// From MdiBrowser Program
//----------------------------------------------------
using System;
using System.Drawing;
using System.Windows.Forms;

partial class MdiBrowser : Form
{
    ToolStripMenuItem HelpMenu()
    {
        ToolStripMenuItem itemHelp = new ToolStripMenuItem("&Help");

        ToolStripMenuItem item = new ToolStripMenuItem("&Help");
        item.Click += HelpOnClick;
        itemHelp.DropDownItems.Add(item);

        item = new ToolStripMenuItem("&About MDI Browser...");
        item.Click += AboutOnClick;
        itemHelp.DropDownItems.Add(item);

        return itemHelp;
    }
    void HelpOnClick(object objSrc, EventArgs args)
    {
        Help.ShowHelp(this, "MdiBrowser.chm");
    }
    void AboutOnClick(object objSrc, EventArgs args)
    {
        AboutDialog2 dlg = new AboutDialog2("MdiBrowser");
        dlg.ShowDialog();
    }
}
```

I wanted the About box for MdiBrowser to display the *Version* property of the *WebBrowser* control. The MdiBrowser project includes a link to the AboutDialog.cs file (and the Book-Cover.png file) from the ControlExplorer project, and it also includes an *AboutDialog2* class that inherits from *AboutDialog*.

```
AboutDialog2.cs
//-------------------------------------------
// AboutDialog2.cs (c) 2005 by Charles Petzold
// From MdiBrowser Program
//-------------------------------------------
using System;
using System.Drawing;
using System.Windows.Forms;

class AboutDialog2 : AboutDialog
{
    public AboutDialog2(string strResource): base(strResource)
    {
        // Add a Label control.
        Label lbl = new Label();
        lbl.Parent = flow;
        lbl.Font = new Font(FontFamily.GenericSerif, 14);
        lbl.AutoSize = true;
        lbl.Anchor = AnchorStyles.None;
        lbl.Text = "Using Microsoft Internet Explorer " +
            new WebBrowser().Version.ToString();

        // Make OK button the last control.
        btnOk.SendToBack();
    }
}
```

AboutDialog2 adds a label with the *Version* property. Because the constructor in *AboutBox2* is executed after the constructor in *AboutBox*, this new label would normally appear at the bottom of the window below the OK button, but a simple call to the *SendToBack* method moves the OK button to the end of the *Controls* collection where it belongs. The wonderful, wonderful, wonderful *FlowLayoutPanel* does the rest of the magic.

The Two Tool Strips

MdiBrowser has two *ToolStrip* controls. The top one (referred to in the source code and help files as the "tool bar") has buttons for Back, Forward, Stop, Refresh, Home, and Print. The second one is referred to in the source code and help files as the "address bar."

For the buttons in the tool bar, I copied icons from the icons\WinXP directory of the Visual Studio image library (\Program Files\Microsoft Visual Studio 8\Common7\VS2005ImageLibrary.zip) to the project and flagged them as Embedded Resource. (Unfortunately, the Visual C# 2005 Express Edition doesn't contain this library.) These icons weren't always a good match to their functionality. To obtain a button for Forward, the code in the *CreateToolBar* method below has to flip the image of the Back button. For real applications, hiring graphics artists to design icons and images is probably the best solution.

Icon files usually contain several image sizes and color formats, and the ones shipped with Visual Studio include *many* different sizes. When you create an *ImageList* from icons, only one image size is copied from the *Icon* object to the list. You indicate what size you want by setting the *ImageSize* property of *ImageList*. The following code sets that property to the value returned from *SystemInformation.IconSize*, which is 32 pixels square on most systems.

MdiBrowser.ToolBar.cs

```
//----------------------------------------------------
// MdiBrowser.ToolBar.cs (c) 2005 by Charles Petzold
// From MdiBrowser Program
//----------------------------------------------------
using System;
using System.Drawing;
using System.Windows.Forms;

partial class MdiBrowser
{
    ToolStripButton btnBack, btnForward;
    ToolStripButton btnStop, btnRefresh, btnHome, btnPrint;
    BrowserChild bcLastActive;

    ToolStrip CreateToolBar(string strResource)
    {
        // ImageList for ToolStrip.
        ImageList imglst = new ImageList();
        imglst.ImageSize = SystemInformation.IconSize;  // 32x32, probably.
        imglst.Images.Add("back", new Icon(GetType(), "MdiBrowser.hotplug.ico"));
        imglst.Images.Add("stop", new Icon(GetType(), "MdiBrowser.error.ico"));
        imglst.Images.Add("rfsh", new Icon(GetType(), "MdiBrowser.idr_dll.ico"));
        imglst.Images.Add("home", new Icon(GetType(), "MdiBrowser.homenet.ico"));
        imglst.Images.Add("prnt", new Icon(GetType(), "MdiBrowser.printer.ico"));

        // Create Forward image from Back image.
        Image img = imglst.Images["back"];
        img.RotateFlip(RotateFlipType.RotateNoneFlipX);
        imglst.Images.Add("frwd", img);

        // ToolStrip with buttons.
        ToolStrip tool = new ToolStrip();
        tool.Parent = this;
        tool.Visible = settings.ViewToolBar;
        tool.ImageList = imglst;
        tool.ImageScalingSize = imglst.ImageSize;

        // The event handlers for these five buttons
        //  are located in MdiBrowser.ViewMenu.cs.
        btnBack = new ToolStripButton();
```

```
        btnBack.Text = "Back";
        btnBack.ImageKey = "back";
        btnBack.Click += BackOnClick;
        tool.Items.Add(btnBack);

        btnForward = new ToolStripButton();
        btnForward.Text = "Forward";
        btnForward.ImageKey = "frwd";
        btnForward.Click += ForwardOnClick;
        tool.Items.Add(btnForward);

        btnStop = new ToolStripButton();
        btnStop.ImageKey = "stop";
        btnStop.ToolTipText = "Stop";
        btnStop.Click += StopOnClick;
        tool.Items.Add(btnStop);

        btnRefresh = new ToolStripButton();
        btnRefresh.ImageKey = "rfsh";
        btnRefresh.ToolTipText = "Refresh";
        btnRefresh.Click += RefreshOnClick;
        tool.Items.Add(btnRefresh);

        btnHome = new ToolStripButton();
        btnHome.ImageKey = "home";
        btnHome.ToolTipText = "Home";
        btnHome.Click += HomeOnClick;
        tool.Items.Add(btnHome);

        tool.Items.Add(new ToolStripSeparator());

        btnPrint = new ToolStripButton();
        btnPrint.ImageKey = "prnt";
        btnPrint.ToolTipText = "Printer";
        btnPrint.Click += PrintOnClick;
        tool.Items.Add(btnPrint);

        return tool;
    }
    // When active MDI Child changes, alter event handlers and ToolStrip.
    protected override void OnMdiChildActivate(EventArgs args)
    {
        base.OnMdiChildActivate(args);

        if (bcLastActive != null)
        {
            bcLastActive.WebBrowser.CanGoBackChanged -= OnCanGoBackChanged;
            bcLastActive.WebBrowser.CanGoForwardChanged -= OnCanGoForwardChanged;
        }

        BrowserChild bc = ActiveMdiChild as BrowserChild;

        if (bc != null)
        {
            bc.WebBrowser.CanGoBackChanged += OnCanGoBackChanged;
```

```
            bc.WebBrowser.CanGoForwardChanged += OnCanGoForwardChanged;

        btnBack.Enabled = bc.WebBrowser.CanGoBack;
        btnForward.Enabled = bc.WebBrowser.CanGoForward;
    }
    else
    {
        btnBack.Enabled = false;
        btnForward.Enabled = false;
    }

    btnStop.Enabled = (bc != null);
    btnRefresh.Enabled = (bc != null);
    btnHome.Enabled = (bc != null);
    btnPrint.Enabled = (bc != null);

    bcLastActive = bc;
}
// Event handlers for enabling Back and Forward buttons.
void OnCanGoBackChanged(object objSrc, EventArgs args)
{
    WebBrowser wb = objSrc as WebBrowser;
    btnBack.Enabled = wb.CanGoBack;
}
void OnCanGoForwardChanged(object objSrc, EventArgs args)
{
    WebBrowser wb = objSrc as WebBrowser;
    btnForward.Enabled = wb.CanGoForward;
}
void PrintOnClick(object objSrc, EventArgs args)
{
    BrowserChild bcActive = ActiveMdiChild as BrowserChild;

    if (bcActive != null)
        bcActive.WebBrowser.Print();
}
}
```

Most of the *Click* events for these buttons are located in the MdiBrowser.ViewMenu.cs file. The Print button, however, must be handled a little differently. The Print option on the File menu invokes a print dialog box by calling the *ShowPrintDialog* method of the *WebBrowser* control. The Print button should just print without showing the dialog box. For that reason, it has its own *Click* event handler that calls the *Print* method of the *WebBrowser* control.

To properly enable and disable these buttons, the program really needs to know about the currently active child. That's why this is the file that defines a method that overrides *OnMdi-ChildActivate*. This method is called whenever the active child changes. The Back and Forward buttons should be enabled only if the *CanGoBack* and *CanGoForward* properties of the currently active child are *true*, and the other buttons are disabled if there's no active child at all. This enabling and disabling is similar to the logic in the View menu, but it occurs when the active child changes rather than when the View menu is displayed.

In addition, the *OnMdiChildActivate* method has to attach event handlers to the currently active child for the *OnCanGoBackChanged* and *OnCanGoForwardChanged* events so that the buttons can be enabled and disabled as the user is currently navigating with the child window. For each pair of event handlers that are attached, *OnMdiChildActivate* has to detach the handlers from the previously active child. Detaching event handlers occurs in programs much less frequently than attaching them, but this is one case where it's essential.

The address bar basically duplicates the functionality of the Open dialog box from the File menu and has just three controls: a label, a combo box, and a button labeled Go.

MdiBrowse.AddrBar.cs

```
//---------------------------------------------------
// MdiBrowser.AddrBar.cs (c) 2005 by Charles Petzold
// From MdiBrowser Program
//---------------------------------------------------
using System;
using System.Drawing;
using System.Windows.Forms;

partial class MdiBrowser
{
    ToolStripComboBox comboUrl;

    ToolStrip CreateAddressBar(string strResource)
    {
        // Address Bar for typing in URL.
        ToolStrip addr = new ToolStrip();
        addr.Parent = this;
        addr.GripStyle = ToolStripGripStyle.Hidden;
        addr.Visible = settings.ViewAddressBar;
        addr.SizeChanged += AddressBarOnSizeChanged;

        ToolStripLabel lbl = new ToolStripLabel("Address:");
        addr.Items.Add(lbl);

        // ComboBox for typing or selecting URL.
        comboUrl = new ToolStripComboBox();
        comboUrl.AutoSize = false;
        comboUrl.BeginUpdate();
        foreach (string str in settings.ManualUrls)
            comboUrl.Items.Add(str);
        comboUrl.EndUpdate();
        addr.Items.Add(comboUrl);

        ToolStripButton btn = new ToolStripButton();
        btn.Text = "Go";
        btn.Alignment = ToolStripItemAlignment.Right;
        btn.Click += GoOnClick;
        addr.Items.Add(btn);

        // Initialize size of Combobox.
        AddressBarOnSizeChanged(addr, EventArgs.Empty);
```

```
            return addr;
    }
    // AddressBarOnSizeChanged
    void AddressBarOnSizeChanged(object objSrc, EventArgs args)
    {
        ToolStrip tool = objSrc as ToolStrip;
        tool.Items[1].Width = tool.Width - tool.Items[0].Width
                - tool.Items[2].Width
                - 6 * tool.Items[1].Margin.Horizontal;
    }
    // Event handler for Go button on address bar.
    void GoOnClick(object objSrc, EventArgs args)
    {
        if (comboUrl.Text != null && comboUrl.Text.Length > 0)
            Go(comboUrl.Text, true);
    }
}
```

As in Internet Explorer, I wanted the combo box to extend the full width of the address bar, but I couldn't find a way to do that except by installing an event handler to be alerted when the address bar changed size and by manually recalculating the size of the combo box.

HTML Help

In a perfect world, applications would be so clear and obvious that they wouldn't need help at all. In a medium so-so OK world, application help would be designed and completed *before* the application itself had even been written. The design and coding of the application would then be driven by the ease of use and learning implied by the help file.

Alas, in the tragic world in which we find ourselves, the help file is often slapped together at the very end of a project. By relegating the subject of help to the very last section of the last chapter of this book, I am obviously not part of the solution.

The help system in common use today under Windows is called HTML Help because it is based around HTML files. (The previous WinHelp system was based on Rich Text Format files.) You use a program called the HTML Help Workshop (or a third-party substitute) to bring together a Project file with the filename extension .hhp, a Contents file with the extension .hhc, an Index file with the extension .hhk, Topic files with the extension .htm or .html, and bitmap files (.png, .gif, or .jpeg) and combine them all into a binary compressed Compiled HTML file with the extension .chm. As part of your installation process, this file is installed on the user's machine, generally in the same directory as the application's .exe file or close by. As you've seen, a Windows Forms program displays the help file using the static *ShowHelp* methods of the *Help* class.

You can obtain the HTML Help Workshop from the MSDN Web site. Go to *http://msdn.microsoft.com*, and then select Library. In the library hierarchy at the left, you're looking for the Win32 And COM Development item, then Tools, then HTML Help. There should be a section about the HTML Help SDK and, under that, a Downloads page to download HtmlHelp.exe (which installs the HTML Help Workshop program) and Help-Docs.zip, which includes a few help files in Compiled HTML format. Particularly useful files in HelpDocs.zip are htmlhelp.chm, which documents the HTML Help Workshop, and htmlref.chm, which is a handy reference to HTML tags.

Here's how I used the HTML Help Workshop to create a help file for MdiBrowser: From the File New command, I selected Project and then created a directory named Help as a subdirectory of the MdiBrowser solution directory and as a sibling of the MdiBrowser project directory. I gave the project file a name of MdiBrowser.hhp. By default, HTML Help workshop creates a compiled HTML file named MdiBrowser.chm. Using the top button in the column of buttons at the left (Change Project Options), you can set a different name and other project options.

By using repeated File New commands and selecting HTML File, I created 10 files. Each of the files gets a Title when you first create it; this Title is inserted in the HTML file. For each new file, I then selected Save File As from the File menu to save the files as shown in the following table.

Title	File Name
Welcome to MDI Browser	welcome.html
Program Overview	overview.html
The Multiple Document Interface	mdi.html
The File Menu	file.html
The View Menu	view.html
The Favorites Menu	favorites.html
The Window Menu	window.html
The Help Menu	help.html
The Tool Bar	toolbar.html
The Address Bar	addrbar.html

I then clicked the Add/Remove Topic Files button at the left, and clicked the Add button to add all 10 HTML topic files to the project. These 10 files are then listed in a section headed by [FILES] in the project options.

The next step is to create a Table of Contents by selecting the Contents tab. By default, the Table of Contents is stored in a file named Table of Contents.hhc. You create the Table of Contents by clicking buttons at the left to add headings and pages. A *page* is denoted in the Table of Contents by a little page icon and is always associated with an HTML Topic file. A heading is displayed as a folder icon, and it might or might not be associated with an HTML Topic file. It's up to you. Under a heading, there are generally nested pages and (potentially) other headings.

I first created a Heading and gave it a title of "Welcome to MDI Browser." By clicking the Add button, I was able to select the topic file with the title "Welcome to MDI Browser." I then inserted a page with a title "Program Overview" and clicked Add to pick the topic file with the same title. The next page was "The Multiple Document Interface."

Next was another heading, this one labeled "Exploring the Menu" but with no associated topic file. The HTML Help Workshop created this as a subheading under "Welcome to MDI Browser," but that's easy to fix by clicking the left arrow button. Under this heading, I created five pages for the five menu topics. I created another top-level heading labeled "Exploring the Tool Bars" and added the two remaining topics under that heading.

Clicking the Project tab again and the topmost button at the left lets you set Project Options. I assigned a title of "MDI Browser Help" and a Default File of welcome.html. Under the Compiler tab, click Compile Full-Text Search Information to enable full-text searches.

It's now possible to compile the project by selecting Compile from the File menu or clicking the Compile button. A log file indicates any possible problems. You can then view the result by picking Compiled File from the View menu or clicking the View Compiled File button (which looks like a pair of glasses). The Table of Contents should be displayed fine, but at this point, none of the topics have any content. Now, of course, the real work begins. But that's HTML, and not a proper subject for this book.

It's also possible to add an Index file, but I didn't feel that this was necessary for such a short file. In larger Help files, of course, an Index is essential.

Once you're at the point where you have a .chm file being generated, you can go back to Visual Studio and make that file part of your project. Select Add Existing Item from the Project menu, navigate to the Help directory, select the .chm file, and click Add As Link. Display the properties for the .chm file. In Copy To Output File, select Copy If Newer. That ensures that when building your project, Visual Studio copies the .chm file to the same directory as the .exe file. The program can then easily load the Help file just by specifying the file name.

Another property you'll want to change is Build Action. Set it to Content. Now go to the Publish tab of the project properties, and click the Application Files button. You'll now see the .chm file listed along with the .exe file, ready to be published to your Web site and downloaded by your users.

May your users be plentiful, your Help files illuminating, and your bugs infrequent.

Index

Charles Petzold

Charles Petzold has been writing about personal computer programming for two decades. His classic book *Programming Windows*, now in its sixth edition, has influenced a generation of programmers and is one of the best-selling programming books of all time. He is also the author of *Code: The Hidden Language of Computer Hardware and Software*, the critically acclaimed narrative on the inner life of smart machines. His Web site is *www.charlespetzold.com*.

What do you think of this book? We want to hear from you!

Do you have a few minutes to participate in a brief online survey? Microsoft is interested in hearing your feedback about this publication so that we can continually improve our books and learning resources for you.

To participate in our survey, please visit:

www.microsoft.com/learning/booksurvey

And enter this book's ISBN, 0-7356-2153-5. As a thank-you to survey participants in the United States and Canada, each month we'll randomly select five respondents to win one of five $100 gift certificates from a leading online merchant.* At the conclusion of the survey, you can enter the drawing by providing your e-mail address, which will be used for prize notification *only*.

Thanks in advance for your input. Your opinion counts!

Sincerely,

Microsoft Learning

Learn More. Go Further.